Absolute PC Security and Privacy

Absolute PC Security and Privacy

Michael Miller

SYBEX®

San Francisco London

Associate Publisher: Joel Fugazzotto

Acquisitions and Developmental Editor: Ellen Dendy

Editors: James A. Compton, Brianne Agatep

Production Editor: Mae Lum

Technical Editor: James Kelly

Graphic Illustrator: Tony Jonick

Electronic Publishing Specialist: Franz Baumhackl

Proofreaders: David Nash, Laurie O'Connell, Yariv Rabinovitch, Nancy Riddiough, Sarah Tannehill

Indexer: Nancy Guenther

Cover Designer and Illustrator: Richard Miller, Calyx Design

Library of Congress Card Number: 2002106411

ISBN: 0-7821-4127-7

This book is dedicated to my brother-in-law Dennis and my sister-in-law Stephanie, for putting up with the rest of the family.

Acknowledgments

Thanks to all the Sybex staffers and freelancers who have helped to shape and shepherd this project, including but not limited to Brianne Agatep, Franz Baumhackl, Jim Compton, Ellen Dendy, Joel Fugazzotto, Nancy Guenther, Tony Jonick, Jim Kelly, Mae Lum, and my old friend Jordan Gold.

Contents at a Glance

Contents

Introduction

I first conceived of this book when I got an e-mail from a friend—or, to be more accurate, from her e-mail program. My friend hadn't sent the message, which had a random Word document and a virus-infected file attached; the message was sent by the computer virus that was infecting her system.

It was likely, I thought, that my friend didn't know her computer had been infected; she's not the most technically literate person I know. (She's a retired music teacher, not a computer geek.) So I called her, and told her that I thought she had a virus. Her immediate reaction was panic, followed by a question: Did this mean she had to throw away her computer and buy a new one?

It didn't, I replied; then I walked her through what she needed to do to remove the virus from her system. Unfortunately, I soon discovered that the steps to recovery were harder than they needed to be, and weren't helped by the unnecessary technospeak employed by the company that supplied the chosen antivirus software.

How, I wondered, was the average computer user supposed to deal with this sort of problem on their own?

This incident was followed by a similar one, where my brother's computer became infected. He is more technically literate than my music-teacher friend, and we got the problem fixed relatively quickly. He also figured out how the virus had entered his system; it was through an e-mail attachment from a friend that he had unassumingly opened a few days prior. Why had he opened the attachment, I asked—didn't he know that's how viruses are spread? Yes, he answered, but he's in the habit of clicking everything he receives via e-mail, especially if it comes from someone he knows.

The virus incident put my brother on alert, however, and a few weeks later I received another call from him. This time he'd received an e-mail from another friend, warning him that his system was infected with some new virus, and instructing him to delete some supposedly infected files from his system. Something about the message raised his suspicions, which prompted his call to me. I quickly got online and, after a few minutes searching (fortunately, I knew where to look) I discovered that the message my brother received was a virus hoax. There was no such virus floating around, and if he deleted the files identified in the message, he'd actually do harm to his computer system.

Which caused me to think harder about the whole virus issue. All along, I'd taken it relatively lightly; after all, if you avoid opening unwanted e-mail attachments and use a good antivirus program, you're pretty much safe from infection. But it was now blindingly obvious to me that lots of people were reckless about opening file attachments, and either didn't use antivirus software or didn't keep their programs up-to-date. All of which created a dangerous environment, virus-wise, for those computer users least capable of dealing with the effects of a virus infection.

At the same time, I was dealing with a deluge of messages in my e-mail inbox. It seemed like every other message I was receiving was some sort of junk e-mail, trying to sell me cheap Viagra or subscriptions to some sexually explicit Web site. And if that wasn't enough, I kept getting virus hoaxes and chain letters from friends and family, urging me to "pass this along to everyone you know."

Ugh.

It seemed to me that computer viruses and e-mail spam are somehow related—at least in their ability to annoy. They are both, in their own way, intrusions into my private computing experience. And they are both annoyances that I want to eliminate.

This got me thinking about a book that dealt with these "computer intrusions." Not a book for computer geeks, filled with lots of technospeak and computer theory, but rather a book for the average user, filled with easy-to-follow instructions and practical advice. A book for my brother, my music-teacher friend, and anyone else plagued by viruses and spam e-mail.

After talking to the folks at Sybex, we decided to expand on this virus-and-spam idea to include other types of both annoying and dangerous computer intrusions. The book would include information about Internet-based computer attacks, and online privacy theft, and pop-up windows, and the like. And we'd give it an umbrella title that described all the various topics covered: *Absolute PC Security and Privacy*.

All of which explains how the book you currently hold in your hands came to be.

If you use a computer in your home or small business, and you're bothered by viruses and spam (or just worried about computer attacks and losing your online privacy), *Absolute PC Security and Privacy* will help you separate fact from fiction, evaluate your personal risks, and take the necessary steps to protect yourself from the most common intrusions that threaten computer users today. And, if worse comes to worst and you become a victim of some sort of Internet-based attack, you'll also learn how to recover from the attack, and get your system back up and running.

To make it easier to find specific information, this book's 31 chapters are organized into five major sections, as follows:

Part I: Computer Viruses   Learn about the many different types of computer viruses—boot record, file infector, script, macro, Trojan horses, worms, and so on—and how to protect your system against their destructive payloads.

Part II: Internet Attacks   Discover the many ways that malicious individuals can target your computer for data theft and attack, and how to guard against such online assaults.

Part III: Privacy Theft   Find out how your privacy can be compromised on the Internet, and how to defend yourself against identity theft, online predators, and other threats to your privacy.

Part IV: E-mail Spam   Discover where all those unwanted e-mail messages in your in-box come from, and how to keep them out.

Part V: Web-Based Intrusions   Find out how to avoid the many major and minor annoyances you find at too many Web sites, including pop-up advertising and inappropriate content.

In addition, any technical terms you may not be familiar with are likely to be listed in the book's glossary, following the final chapter.

Which brings up an important point: You don't have to be a computer wizard to use this book. In fact, I assume that you're a casual (Windows) PC user and aren't interested in those overly technical solutions best suited to full-time geeks. That's why I provide *practical* solutions—things you can easily do, without an undue expenditure of time or effort (or money!). And, surprisingly, you can protect yourself fairly well by doing a few simple things, which you'll learn as you read the book.

When the book presents a solution to a problem, I try to do so in as general a fashion as possible, so that it doesn't matter whether you're using Windows 95, Windows 98, Windows 2000, or Windows XP; whether you're connecting to the Internet via a dial-up or broadband connection; or whether you're a home, small business, or corporate computer user. Where specific instructions are necessary, I typically focus on the most recent versions of the applicable software. And I describe the process of selecting a series of menu options by saying "select option one ➤ option two ➤ option three"—which means pull down the first menu, select the next menu item, then select the following menu item. (It's a nice shorthand that saves you a little reading and the publisher a little space on the page.)

Throughout the book you'll find what I like to call "asides" to the main text. These include notes, time-saving tips, and warnings about pitfalls to avoid, as well as the slightly longer discussions that my publisher calls sidebars. These little asides offer interesting information that isn't always essential to the discussion at hand; we put them outside the main text for you to read them as you like.

You'll also find a lot of Web sites mentioned in the book. That's because many of the solutions to these security intrusions are available on the Internet. When I mention a Web-based solution, I include the Web site address (URL) in a special typeface, like this: `www.sybex.com`. I've made every attempt to make sure the URLs are all up-to-date; but the Web being the Web, expect some of this information (and some of these addresses) to change over time.

You don't have to read *Absolute PC Security and Privacy* front-to-back, of course; it's perfectly okay to skip to the section dealing with a particular annoyance you're encountering, and read the information of immediate interest to you. But if you stumble across a concept that you don't understand, consult the index for an earlier mention of that concept; chances are, I explained it in more detail in a previous chapter.

This gives you some idea of what to expect in this book. I hope you find the information in these pages useful, and that you come away with a more enjoyable—and more secure—computing experience.

By the way, I'd like to hear what you think of this book. Feel free to e-mail me at `security@molehillgroup.com` (and let my publisher know, too, at `www.sybex.com`). Ask questions, if you like, but know that I can't always answer all my e-mail; I do like to read your comments, however. And if you want to read more about me and my ongoing book projects, visit my Web site at `www.molehillgroup.com`. Chances are, I'm working on another new book that you might be interested in!

PART I

COMPUTER VIRUSES

CHAPTER 1

Understanding Computer Viruses

You've heard about them. You've read the news reports about the number of incidents reported, and the amount of damage they inflict. Maybe you've even experienced one firsthand. And if you haven't, count yourself fortunate.

Computer viruses are real—and they're costly.

Springing up seemingly from nowhere, spreading like wildfire, computer viruses attack computer systems large and small, damaging files and rendering computers and networks unusable. They proliferate through e-mail, Internet file downloads, and shared diskettes. And they don't play favorites; your home computer is just as likely as a Fortune 500 company's network to experience an infection.

This first section of the book is about protecting your computer from these destructive virus programs. Read this chapter to learn more about the background of computer viruses; then proceed to the following chapters to learn how to avoid and recover from specific types of virus attacks.

The Dangers of Computer Viruses

Not a month goes by without another big-time virus scare.

Tens of millions of computers are infected by computer viruses every year. In 2001, 2.3 million computers were infected by the SirCam virus, and another million computers were hit by CodeRed. Even worse, the LoveLetter virus hit an estimated 45 million computers—on a single day in 2000.

ICSA Labs (**www.icsalabs.com**), a leading provider of security research, intelligence, and certification, found that the rate of virus infection in North America in 2001 was 113 infections per 1000 computers—meaning that more than 10% of all computers they surveyed had been hit by a virus. And this rate is increasing; ICSA says that the likelihood of contracting a computer virus has doubled for each of the past five years.

Viruses hit the corporate world especially hard; a single infected computer can spread the virus among the entire corporate network. McAfee.com (**www.mcafee.com**), a company specializing in virus protection, estimates that two-third of U.S. companies are attacked by viruses each year. A third of those companies reported that viruses knocked out their servers for an average of 5.8 hours per infection, and 46% of the companies required more than 19 days to completely recover from the virus incident.

These incidents come with a heavy cost. The research firm Computer Economics (**www.computereconomics.com**) estimates that companies spent $10.7 billion to recover from virus attacks in 2001. Technology magazine *The Industry Standard* (**www.thestandard.com**) puts the cost much higher, at upwards of $266 billion. Whatever the real number, it's clear that computer viruses are costly to all concerned—in terms of both money and the time required to clean up after them.

Just look at the costs inflicted by individual viruses. For example, Computer Economics estimates that the Nimda virus alone cost companies $590 million in cleanup costs; CodeRed and LoveLetter were even more costly, running up costs of $2.6 billion apiece.

To an individual company, these costs can be staggering. ICSA Labs estimates that virus cleanup costs large companies anywhere from $100,000 to $1 million each per year.

That's real money.

Unfortunately, this problem doesn't look like it's going to go away. In fact, the problem just keeps getting worse. To date, more than 53,000 different viruses have been identified and catalogued—with another half-dozen or so appearing *every day*.

Just what is it about computer viruses that makes them so deadly—and so easily spread?

How Computer Viruses Work

As you'll see in the next section, the term *virus* was applied to this type of software very early in its history. It's an apt metaphor, because a computer virus is, in many ways, similar to the biological viruses that attack human bodies.

A biological virus isn't truly a living, independent entity; as biologists will tell you, a virus is nothing more than a fragment of DNA sheathed in a protective jacket. It reproduces by injecting its DNA into a host cell. The DNA then uses the host cell's normal mechanisms to reproduce itself.

A computer virus is like a biological virus in that it also isn't an independent entity; it must piggyback on a host (another program or document) in order to propagate.

Many viruses are hidden in the code of legitimate software programs—programs that have been "infected," that is. These viruses are called *file infector viruses*, and when the host program is launched, the code for the virus is also executed, and the virus loads itself into your computer's memory. From there, the virus code searches for other programs on your system that it can infect; if it finds one, it adds its code to the new program, which, now infected, can be used to infect other computers.

This entire process is shown in Figure 1.1.

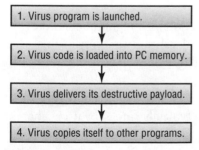

Figure 1.1 *How a virus infects your computer*

If all a virus did was copy itself to additional programs and computers, there would be little harm done, save for having all our programs get slightly larger (thanks to the virus code). Unfortunately, most viruses not only replicate themselves, they also perform other operations—many of which are wholly destructive. A virus might, for example, delete certain files on your computer. It might overwrite the boot sector of your hard disk, making the disk inaccessible. It might write messages on your screen, or cause your system to emit rude noises. It might also hijack your e-mail program and use the program to send itself to all your friends and colleagues, thus replicating itself to a large number of PCs.

Viruses that replicate themselves via e-mail or over a computer network cause the subsidiary problem of increasing the amount of Internet and network traffic. These fast-replicating viruses—called *worms*—can completely overload a company network, shutting down servers and forcing tens of thousands of users offline. While no individual machines might be damaged, this type of communications disruption can be quite costly.

As you might suspect, most viruses are designed to deliver their payload when they're first executed. However, some viruses won't attack until specifically prompted, typically on a predetermined date or day of the week. They stay on your system, hidden from sight like a sleeper agent in a spy novel, until they're awoken on a specific date; then they go about the work they were programmed to do.

In short, viruses are nasty little bits of computer code, designed to inflict as much damage as possible, and to spread to as many computers as possible—a particularly vicious combination.

The History of Computer Viruses

Where, exactly, do computer viruses come from? To answer that question, it's helpful to examine the history of computer viruses.

Technically, the concept of a computer virus was first imagined in 1949, well before computers became commonplace. In that year, computer pioneer John von Neumann wrote a paper titled "Theory and Organization of Complicated Automata." In this paper, von Neumann postulated that a computer program could be self-replicating—and thus predicted today's self-replicating virus programs.

The theories of von Neumann came to life in the 1950s, at Bell Labs. Programmers there developed a game called "Core Wars," where two players would unleash software "organisms" into the mainframe computer, and watch as the competing programs would vie for control of the machine—just as viruses do today.

In the real world, computer viruses came to the fore in the early 1980s, coincident with the rise of the very first personal computers. These early viruses were typically spread by users sharing programs and documents on floppy disks; a shared floppy was the perfect medium for spreading virus files.

The first virus "in the wild," as they say, infected Apple II floppy disk in 1981. The virus went by the name of Elk Cloner, and didn't do any real damage; all it did was display a short rhyme onscreen:

```
It will get on all your disks

It will infiltrate your chips

Yes it's Cloner!


It will stick to you like glue

It will modify ram too

Send in the Cloner!
```

At the time, Elk Cloner wasn't identified as a virus, because the phrase "computer virus" had yet to be coined. That happened in 1983, when programmer Len Adleman designed and demonstrated the first experimental virus on a VAX 11/750 computer. From Adleman's lab to the real world was but a short step.

In 1986, the Brain virus became the first documented file infector virus for MS-DOS computers. That same year, the first PC-based Trojan horse was released, disguised as the then-popular shareware program PC Write.

From there, things only went downhill, with the popularity of computer bulletin board services (BBSs) helping to spread viruses beyond what was previously physically possible. BBSs were the online precursors to the Internet; users could use their low-speed modems to dial into public and private BBSs, both to exchange messages and to download files. As any Monday-morning quarterback could predict, there were viruses hiding among the standard utilities and applications that users downloaded, thus facilitating the spread of those viruses.

To make things worse, in 1990 the first BBS specifically for virus writers was created. This virus exchange BBS, housed on a computer in Bulgaria, provided a means for virus writers to exchange virus code and learn new tricks.

Computer viruses hit the big time in 1992, when the Michelangelo virus hit. Michelangelo was one of the first viruses to spread worldwide, and garnered much media attention. Fortunately, its bark was worse than its bite, and little actual damage occurred.

NOTE *Michelangelo was more of a virus scare than a virus threat. In the days building up to Michelangelo's threatened March 6 delivery date, news stories worldwide projected that millions of computers would have their hard disks destroyed. In reality, fewer than 20,000 computers were hit, but—thanks to all the publicity—the world was forever made aware of the perils posed by computer viruses.*

The year 1996 saw the first virus designed specifically for Windows 95 and the first macro viruses for Word and Excel files. That year also saw the first virus for the Linux operating system.

By 1999, viruses had become almost mainstream. The Melissa virus, released that year, was a combination macro virus and worm that spread itself by e-mailing contacts in a user's Outlook or Outlook Express Address Book. Melissa did untold amounts of damage to computers and company networks around the world, and was followed (in 2000) by the LoveLetter worm (also known as the "Love Bug"), which shut down tens of thousands of corporate e-mail systems. Since then, viruses have continued to proliferate and mutate, with viruses being developed for personal digital assistants (PDAs), file-swapping networks, instant messaging systems, and more.

And the chaos continues.

Different Types of Viruses

Technically, a computer virus is a piece of software that surreptitiously attaches itself to other programs and then does something unexpected. There are other types of programs—such as Trojan horses and worms—that do similar damage but don't embed themselves within other program code. These programs aren't technically viruses, but they pose the same danger to computer systems everywhere. For that reason, all these programs—virus and non-virus, alike—are typically lumped together and referred to, in common parlance, as viruses. (Or, as some experts prefer, *malware*—for "malicious software.") The following chapters will examine all these different types of malicious programs, since the best defense against one is a defense against all.

That's not to say that all malicious programs work the same way, or pack the same potential punch. They don't. So it helps to know a little bit about each type of virus, to help better protect against them.

> **NOTE** *Some viruses—called hybrid viruses—include aspects of more than one virus type. An example would be a worm that can infect program files, such as the Hybris virus. This sometimes makes it difficult to precisely classify a virus—and, in fact, many viruses fall into more than one category.*

File Infector Viruses

The most "traditional" form of computer virus is the file infector virus, which hides within the code of another program. The infected program can be a business application, a utility, or even a game—just as long as it's an executable program, typically with an EXE, COM, SYS, BAT, or PIF extension.

When an infected program is launched, the virus code copies itself into your computer's memory, typically before the program code is loaded. By loading itself into memory separately from the host program, the virus can continue to run in your system's memory, even after the host program is closed down.

Before the advent of the Internet and coincident creation of macro viruses, file infector viruses accounted for probably 85% of all virus infections. Today that number is much lower, because the other types of viruses are much easier to propagate.

NOTE *Learn more about file infector viruses in Chapter 3, "Boot Sector and File Infector Viruses."*

Boot Sector Viruses

Boot sector viruses reside in the part of the disk that is read into memory and executed when your computer first boots up. (On a floppy disk, that's the *boot sector;* on a hard disk, the equivalent area is called the *Master Boot Record.*) Once loaded, the virus can then infect any other disk used by the computer; a disk-based boot sector virus can also infect a PC's hard disk.

Most boot sector viruses were spread by floppy disk, especially in the days before hard disks were common. Since removable disks are less widely used today, boot sector viruses have become much less prevalent than they were in the early 1990s.

TIP *Learn more about boot sector viruses in Chapter 3.*

Macro Viruses

Some computer viruses are created with the *macro* coding languages used with many of today's software applications. Macros are small programs that are created to do highly specific tasks within an application and are written in a pseudo-programming language designed to work with the application. The most common macro language, used in all Microsoft applications, is called Visual Basic for Applications (VBA). VBA code can be added to a Word document to create custom menus and perform automatic operations; unfortunately, VBA code can also be used to modify files and send unwanted e-mail messages, which is where the virus writers come in.

What makes macro viruses potentially more dangerous than file infector or boot sector viruses is that macros—and thus macro viruses—can be attached to document files. Older virus types had to be embedded in executable programs, which made them relatively easy to find and stop. But when any Word or Excel document you open could contain a macro virus, the world is suddenly a much more dangerous place.

The widespread, relatively nonchalant sharing of data files has contributed to the huge rise in macro virus attacks. Even users who are extra-vigilant about the programs they download often don't think twice about opening a Word or Excel document they receive from another user. Because data files are shared so freely, macro viruses are able to spread rapidly from one machine to another—and run, automatically, whenever the infected document is opened.

NOTE *Learn more about macro viruses in Chapter 4, "Macro Viruses."*

Script Viruses

Script viruses are based on common scripting languages, which are macro-like pseudo-programming languages typically used on Web sites and in some computer applications. These viruses are written into JavaScript, ActiveX, and Java applets, which often run automatically when you visit a Web page or open a Word or Excel application. With the increasing use of the Web, these script viruses are becoming more common—and more deadly.

NOTE *Learn more about these ActiveX, JavaScript, and Java viruses in Chapter 5, "Script Viruses."*

Trojan Horses

A *Trojan horse* is a program that claims to do one thing but then does something totally different. A typical Trojan horse has a filename that makes you think it's a harmless type of file; it looks innocuous enough to be safe to open. But when you run the file, it's actually a virus program that proceeds to inflict its damage on your system. It delivers its payload through deception, just like the fabled Trojan horse of yore.

Trojan horses are becoming more common, primarily through the spread of Internet-based e-mail. These e-mail Trojans spread as innocent-looking attachments to e-mail messages; when you click to open the attachment, you launch the virus.

NOTE *Learn more about Trojan horses in Chapter 6, "Trojan Horses and Worms."*

Worms

A *worm* is a program that scans a company's network, or the Internet, for another computer that has a specific security hole. It copies itself to the new machine (through the security hole), and then starts replicating itself there. Worms replicate themselves very quickly; a network infected with a worm can be brought to its knees within a matter of hours.

Worms don't even have to be delivered via conventional programs; so-called "fileless" worms are recent additions to the virus scene. While in operation, these programs exist only in system memory, making them harder to identify than conventional file-hosted worms. These worms—such as the CodeRed and CodeBlue viruses—could cause considerable havoc in the future.

NOTE *Learn more about worms in Chapter 6.*

E-Mail Viruses

An *e-mail virus* is a program that is distributed as an attachment to an e-mail message. These viruses are typically separate programs (Trojan horses, mainly) that do their damage when they're manually executed by you, the user. These viruses masquerade as pictures, Word files, and other common attachments, but are really EXE, VBS, PIF, and other types of executable files in disguise. Many e-mail viruses hijack your e-mail program and send themselves out to all the contacts in your address book.

Because of the proliferation of the Internet, e-mail is the fastest-growing medium for virus delivery today. According to Kaspersky Lab, the research arm of the company that produces Kaspersky Anti-Virus software, e-mail viruses accounted for 90% of all virus attacks in 2001.

NOTE *Learn more about e-mail viruses in Chapter 7, "E-Mail, Chat, and Instant Messaging Viruses."*

Chat and Instant Messaging Viruses

Many computer users like to chat online, either in public chat rooms or in private instant messaging (IM) conversations. Most chat and IM programs let you send files across to other users, and it's that capability that has contributed to the spread of so-called "instant" viruses.

Just as many users are in the habit of automatically opening all attachments to their incoming e-mail messages, many users are also accustomed to accepting any files sent to them when they're chatting. Unfortunately, a significant percentage of files sent via chat or IM are virus files, often Trojan horses masquerading as photographs or helpful utilities. Downloading and then opening one of these files begins the infection process.

NOTE *Learn more about these "instant" viruses in Chapter 7.*

Today's Top Viruses

With so many different types of viruses out there, what are the most widespread computer viruses today?

Unfortunately, that's a bit of a trick question. That's because most viruses have a defined and relatively short life cycle; they appear on the scene with a bang, doing considerable damage, but then—as protective methods are employed—just as quickly disappear from the radar scope. So the top viruses as I'm writing this chapter will be much different from the top viruses when you're reading it a few months from now.

(Figure 1.2 illustrates the typical virus life cycle, from creation to eradication.)

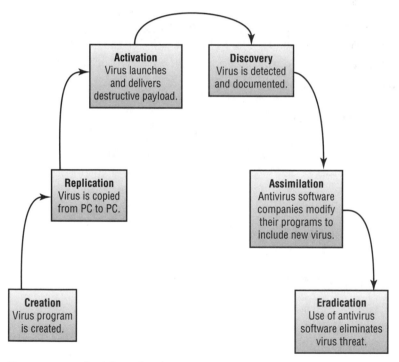

Figure 1.2 *The life cycle of a computer virus*

You can see this phenomenon for yourself by comparing two different virus "Top Ten Lists." Both lists were compiled by Kaspersky Lab. Table 1.1 details the ten most widespread viruses for the last quarter of 2001, along with the percentage of the total number of infections that each virus represents:

Table 1.1 *Top Ten Viruses for Q4 2001*

RANKING	VIRUS	PERCENTAGE OF OCCURRENCE
1	Badtrans	37.0%
2	SirCam	15.4%
3	Hybris	6.2%
4	Aliz	3.0%
5	Nimda	2.5%
6	Magistr	2.2%
7	GIP	1.8%
8	Happytime	0.5%
9	Klez	0.3%
10	Seeker	0.3%

The second list, in Table 1.2, presents the situation two months later, for the month of February 2002:

Table 1.2 *Top Ten Viruses for February 2002*

RANKING	VIRUS	PERCENTAGE OF OCCURRENCE
1	Klez	61.5%
2	Badtrans	28.5%
3	SirCam	1.5%
4	Hybris	1.4%
5	Aliz	1.2%
6	Magistr	0.7%
7	CodeRed	0.6%
8	Thus	0.4%
9	Petik	0.4%
10	Death	0.3%

NOTE *View more current virus lists from Kaspersky Lab at* www.viruslist.com.

As you can see, the big virus in September–December was Badtrans (accounting for 37% of infections), and it was still pretty big in February (28.5%). But the really big virus in February was Klez (61.5%), which accounted for just 0.3% of occurrences just two months earlier. It came out of nowhere to be a major presence—but by the time you read this book, it probably won't be around at all.

The other trend you can see in these charts is that when a virus hits, it really hits. Witness the Klez worm accounting for almost two-thirds of all virus infections in February 2002. This shows just how fast and how far a virus can spread. In fact, most major virus attacks reach their peak within a single week, or less. These viruses use the Internet to propagate across multiple computers, as fast as e-mail messages can be delivered.

It's scary how fast these viruses can spread—and how much damage they can do.

Why Viruses Exist

Computer viruses, unlike biological viruses, don't spring up out of nowhere—they're created. By people.

And the people—programmers and developers, typically—who create computer viruses know what they're doing. These code writers deliberately create programs that they know will wreak havoc on huge numbers of computer users.

The question is *why*?

It takes some degree of technical skill to create a virus. To that end, creating a computer virus is no different than creating any other computer application. Any computer programmer or developer with a minimal amount of skill can create a virus—all it takes is knowledge of a programming language, such as C, Visual Basic, or Java, or a macro language, such as VBA.

NOTE *In reality, you can create a virus even if you have very little technical knowledge, by using a "build your own virus" program—of which there are several available, via the Internet underground.*

So, by definition, a virus writer is a person with a certain amount of technical expertise. But instead of using that expertise productively, virus writers use it to generate indiscriminate mayhem among other computer users.

This havoc-wreaking is, in almost all instances, deliberate. Virus writers *intend* to be destructive. They get some sort of kick out of causing as much damage as possible, from the relative anonymity of their computer keyboards.

In addition, some developers create viruses to prove their technical prowess. Among certain developers, writing a "successful" virus provides a kind of bragging right, and demonstrates, in some warped fashion, that the writer is especially skilled.

Unfortunately, the one attribute that virus writers apparently lack is ethical sense. Virus programs can be enormously destructive, and it takes a peculiar lack of ethics to deliberately perpetrate such destruction on such a wide scale.

In the end, a virus writer is no better than a common vandal. Except for the technical expertise required, the difference between throwing a rock through a window and destroying PC files via a virus is minimal. Some people find pleasure in destruction, and in our high-tech age, such pleasure can come from writing destructive virus code.

What You Can Do About Computer Viruses

There's very little you can do, on a personal level, to discourage those high-tech vandals who create virus programs. There are plenty of laws already on the books that can be used to prosecute these criminals, and such criminal investigations—and prosecutions—have become more common in recent years. However, as with most criminal activity, the presence of laws doesn't always mean there are fewer criminals; the truth is, there's a new batch of virus writers coming online every day.

All of which means that you can't rely on anyone else to protect you from these virus-writing criminals. Ultimately, you have to protect yourself.

The next 11 chapters go into more detail about the specific types of viruses, and they offer detailed instructions about protecting yourself from those viruses. In general, however, there are some simple steps you can take to reduce your chances of becoming a virus-related statistic.

Reducing Your Chances of Infection

To make yourself less of a target for virus infection, take the following steps:

Restrict your file downloading to known or secure sources.   The surest way to catch a virus is to download an unknown file from an unknown site; try not to put yourself at risk like this unless you absolutely have to.

Don't open any e-mail attachments you weren't expecting.   The majority of viruses today arrive in your mailbox as attachments to e-mail messages; resist the temptation to open or view every file attachment you receive.

Use an up-to-date anti-virus program or service.   Antivirus programs work; they scan the files on your computer (as well as new files you download, and e-mail messages you receive) and check for any previously identified viruses. They're a good first line of defense, as long as you keep the programs up-to-date with information about the very latest viruses—and most antivirus programs make it easy to download updates.

Enable macro virus protection in all your applications.   Most current Microsoft applications include special features that keep the program from running unknown macros—and thus prevent your system from being infected by macro viruses.

Create backup copies of all your important data.   If worse comes to worst and your entire system is infected, you may need to revert to noninfected versions of your most critical files. You can't do this unless you plan ahead and back up your important data.

NOTE *Learn more about protecting your system from virus attacks in Chapter 11, "Preventing Virus Attacks."*

Diagnosing a Virus Infection

How do you know if your computer has been infected with a virus? In short, if it starts acting funny—doing anything it didn't do before—then a probable cause is some sort of computer virus. Here are some symptoms to watch for:

- Programs quit working or freeze up.
- Documents become inaccessible.
- Computer freezes up or won't start properly.
- The CAPS LOCK key quits working—or works intermittently.
- Files increase in size.
- Frequent error messages appear onscreen.
- Strange messages or pictures appear onscreen.
- Your PC emits strange sounds.
- Friends and colleagues inform you that they've received strange e-mails from you, that you don't remember sending.

NOTE *Learn more about diagnosing virus attacks in Chapter 2, "How to Catch a Virus."*

Recovering from a Virus Attack

If you're unfortunate enough to be the victim of a virus attack, your options narrow. You have to find the infected files on your computer, and then either disinfect them (by removing the virus code) or delete them—hopefully before the virus has done any permanent damage to your system.

You don't, however, have to give up and throw your computer away. Almost all viruses can be recovered from—some quite easily. All you need is a little information, and the right tools.

The right tools include one of the major antivirus programs discussed in Chapter 9, "Anti-Virus Software and Services." These programs—such as Norton AntiVirus and McAfee Virus-Scan—identify infected files and then either disinfect or delete them, as appropriate.

Quite often, running an antivirus program is all you need to do to recover from a virus infection. However, if a virus has deleted or corrupted any document or program files on your PC, you'll probably have to restore those files from backup copies—or reinstall any damaged programs from their original CD-ROMs. In a worst-case scenario, where your operating system files have been affected, you may need to reinstall your entire operating system—or even, in some instances, reformat your hard disk and rebuild your entire system from scratch.

NOTE *Learn more about recovering from a virus attack in Chapter 12, "Dealing with a Virus Attack."*

Learning More About Computer Viruses

Sometimes the best defense is a good education. To that end, there are several Internet-based resources you can use to learn more about computer viruses—how they work, and how to protect against them. Many of these sites also provide lists of the most menacing viruses, as well as alerts for newly created viruses.

Here are some of the best Web sites to visit:

- Computer Associates Virus Information Center (`www3.ca.com/virus/`)

- Computer Security Resource Center Virus Information (`csrc.ncsl.nist.gov/virus/`)

- F-Secure Security Information Center (`www.datafellows.com/virus-info/`)

- IBM Antivirus Research Project (`www.research.ibm.com/antivirus/`)

- McAfee AVERT (`www.mcafeeb2b.com/naicommon/avert/`)

- Sophos Virus Analyses (`www.sophos.com/virusinfo/analyses/`)

- Symantec Security Response (`www.symantec.com`)

- Trend Micro Virus Information Center (`www.antivirus.com/vinfo/`)

- Virus Bulletin (`www.virusbtn.com`)

- Viruslist.com (`www.viruslist.com`)

- The WildList Organization International (`www.wildlist.org`)

Summing Up

Computer viruses are malicious computer programs, designed to spread rapidly and deliver various types of destructive payloads to infected computers. Viruses have been around almost as long as computers themselves, and they account for untold billions of dollars of damage every year. While there are many different types of viruses, the best protection against them is to exhibit extreme caution when downloading files from the Internet and opening e-mail attachments—and to religiously avail yourself of one of the many antivirus software programs currently on the market.

Read on to learn more about specific types of computer viruses—and, in the next chapter, how to determine if you've been the victim of a virus attack.

CHAPTER 2

How to Catch a Virus

Everyone can agree that a computer virus is a nasty, destructive thing, and catching a virus is something to be avoided. But just *how* do you catch a virus—and how do you know when you've really caught one?

While there is general agreement about how viruses are transmitted (and a lot of facts to back that up), experts don't always agree about the specific risks involved. For example, is it safe to surf the Web? Can you catch a virus from reading an e-mail message? How likely is it that your computer will be hit by a virus? And just how large is the virus threat, anyway?

In this chapter we examine all these issues, focusing on what general behavior puts you most at risk for catching a virus.

How Viruses Spread

Before you can determine what computing behavior you want to risk, you need to know how viruses are spread from one computer to another.

While the specifics may vary, in general a virus spreads when one computer user receives a file from another computer user. That file can be delivered on a floppy disk, or downloaded from the Internet, or attached to an e-mail message—the method of distribution is almost irrelevant. It's what you do with that file when you receive it that matters.

- Just receiving the file—saving it to your hard disk—isn't risky. Your system can't be infected just by saving a file. The risk occurs when you open the file. When a program file (typically with EXE or COM extensions) is opened, the program code loads into your system's memory. If there's a virus in the code, that's when your system gets infected.

- When a document file (like a Microsoft Word document) is opened, any macros attached to the document are run. If there's a virus in the macro code, that's when your system gets infected.

So viruses spread when you receive a program or document file from another user, and then run or open that file. *That's* the activating behavior; it explains why you need to be extremely carefully when opening files sent to you—by any distribution method.

Of course, there are many ways you can receive files from other users. While all of these ways of distributing files can spread viruses, some tend to be more risky than others.

Through Infected Media

In the pre-Internet, pre-network days, the only way you could share a file with another user was to be handed the file—typically on a floppy disk. For that reason, in the early days of the personal computer era, the most common way of receiving an infected file was by infected media.

There's still a danger of receiving infected files via floppy disk, even though floppies are used much less today than they were ten years ago. You're more likely to receive files over your company's network or e-mailed to you over the Internet. Still, if you do receive a floppy from a friend or colleague, be wary and run it through a virus scanner; that little disk could contain a computer virus.

Floppy disks aren't the only storage medium that can carry computer viruses. Any medium used to store computer data can also store viruses. So you need to use caution when receiving not only floppies, but also Zip disks, recordable/rewritable CDs, or even Compact Flash and SmartMedia cards from other users.

> **NOTE** *Zip disks are removable storage media manufactured by Iomega. They function like really large floppy disks (storing either 100MB or 250MB of data), and can easily be transferred from one PC to another. Nearly all virus scanners read Zip disks. Compact Flash (CF) and SmartMedia (SM) are two formats for storing large amounts of data in rewritable electronic memory. These cards are commonly used in Palm and Pocket PC devices, but can also be found in some portable and desktop PCs. CF cards can hold anywhere from 8MB to 1GB of data; the smaller SM cards can hold from 16MB to 128MB. Although some antivirus software can work with these devices, many programs cannot; so use them with caution.*

In Files Sent Over a Network

If you work in a corporate environment, you're probably used to colleagues transferring files to you over the company network. Maybe the files are sent via e-mail; maybe the files are copied to a central directory or folder, from where you can download them to your PC. It doesn't matter; however files are sent over the network, there's a chance those files can be infected with computer viruses—and once an infected file gets on the network, it spreads *fast*.

Which argues, of course, for using your antivirus program to scan all files you receive from your colleagues, over the network.

In Files Downloaded from the Internet

Today, more files are downloaded from the Internet than are transferred via floppy disk. It's easy to go to a Web site, click a link, and have a file downloaded and saved to your computer's hard disk.

The problem is, those files you download can contain viruses.

There are many ways to download files from the Internet, and they can all spread computer viruses:

- Downloading program files from a software archive site—either with your Web browser, or with an FTP program

NOTE *FTP stands for file transfer protocol, and is an older (pre-Web) method for transferring files over the Internet. Dedicated FTP servers are used to store the files, and separate FTP programs are used to process the file transfer to your PC. (Most Web browsers can also FTP files—just enter **FTP://** instead of **HTTP://** in front of the URL.)*

- Downloading music and movie files from a media archive site
- Downloading music and movie files from other users, via peer-to-peer file-swapping services (Napster, KaZaA, Audiogalaxy, etc.)
- Downloading files from messages in Usenet newsgroups
- Downloading files from messages in other online bulletin boards

All these operations are just different ways to transfer a file from one computer to another over the Internet. They all take place while you're online, and all put you at some risk of receiving a file that contains a virus—with the risk being lower if you download from official manufacturer sites and recognized file download archives.

There is also the possibility that you could inadvertently download a virus-infected file from a Web site. Web page developers often include JavaScript and ActiveX code in their HTML pages that tries to run a script or download a file. If this happens, you'll see a dialog box asking if you want to run the script or download the file. If you answer no, you're safe; if you answer yes, you get the file downloaded to your system—and if the file includes a virus, your system gets infected. So, while it's a very different transmission method, this approach still relies on you downloading an infected file to your hard disk.

In Attachments to E-Mail Messages

Probably the most common method of infection today is via e-mail. Since more users are using e-mail to send files to one another, it only makes sense that e-mail is also used to transfer infected files.

The danger isn't in the e-mail message itself. (At least not usually; see the sidebar "Infected E-Mail Messages" for another take on this.) The danger is in any file attached to the message.

You send files via e-mail by attaching those files to a standard e-mail message. The files aren't embedded into the message; they just piggyback along for the ride. When you receive e-mail with a file attached, you have a choice—you can ignore the attachment, you can save the file to your hard disk, or you can open the file right then and there.

It's when you open the attached file that you run the risk of infection. When you run a file, you also run any embedded virus code. So when you open an e-mail attachment, you could be infecting your system with a virus.

If you're one of those users who automatically open all attached files, then your risk of being infected in this manner is high. If, on the other hand, you don't open strange or unrequested attachments, then you substantially lower your risk.

NOTE *Learn more about e-mail viruses in Chapter 7, "E-Mail, Chat, and Instant Messaging Viruses."*

Infected E-Mail Messages

It's possible—although much less common—for an e-mail message itself to contain a virus.

If your e-mail program is configured to automatically display messages in a separate preview pane, that preview will display any pictures or fancy fonts coded into the message using HTML. Since HTML code can also reference ActiveX and JavaScript code (for controls and such), and since ActiveX and JavaScript code can include virus code, it's *possible* to unknowingly launch a virus just by reading the contents of an e-mail message.

In reality, this is not a common means of infection, for a number of reasons. First, you can configure your e-mail program *not* to run ActiveX and JavaScript controls, which defeats the infection mechanism. Second, you can configure your e-mail program not to display the preview pane, which also defeats the infection mechanism. More important, this is a much more difficult way to spread a virus, from the standpoint of the virus writer. It's much, *much* easier, and much more effective, just to attach the virus file to a standard e-mail message. (Why embed the virus when you can attach it with much less effort?)

So embedding within an e-mail message is a relatively unpopular and ineffective way to spread a computer virus.

In Files Sent via Chat or Instant Messaging

A growing problem exists with files sent from user to user via Internet chat and instant messaging (IM) sessions. With both chat and IM, you participate in real-time text-based conversations with other users. It's becoming more common for users you chat with to send you files—pictures of themselves, documents they're working on, even just "something you should see." The problem is that any file someone sends you can contain a virus—especially if that user is someone you just "met" online, and don't really know.

As with all other files you download, you don't run any risk by simply downloading files that you're sent in chat and IM sessions. The risk comes after you save the file; it's when you open the file that the infection can occur.

The risk of being infected via chat or IM is similar to the risk you run with e-mail attachments. If you thoughtlessly accept and run all files sent to you when chatting, your risk of infection is high. If you're more cautious about the files you accept, you lower your risk substantially.

NOTE *Learn more about e-mail viruses in Chapter 7.*

In Document Files with Macros

It used to be that only program files could contain computer viruses. That changed in the mid-1990s, when Microsoft started including full-blown programming capability in its Office applications (Word, Excel, et al.). The programming language was a variation of Visual Basic, called Visual Basic for Applications (VBA), and was used to create macros, automate certain operations, design custom interfaces, and so on.

Unfortunately, VBA can also be used to write virus code.

So, thanks to VBA, an ambitious developer can inject a virus directly into the macro code in a Word or Excel document. When you open the document, the macro code activates, and your system gets infected.

This is a scary thought, as you probably exchange a *lot* of Word and Excel documents with your work colleagues. Theoretically, any of these documents could contain a virus infection.

Fortunately, the danger of virus-infected documents appears to have subsided, to a large degree. There are two reasons for this. First, newer versions of Microsoft Office applications have included built-in protection against rogue macro code; in most instances, documents aren't allowed to run macros without your express permission. Second, this method of infection is relatively difficult, and most virus writers have since migrated to other forms of infection that hold out a greater promise of success.

NOTE *Learn more about macro viruses in Chapter 4, "Macro Viruses."*

Through Commercial Software

You'd expect some amount of risk to be associated with blindly downloading unknown files from the Internet, but you'd think that shrink-wrapped commercial software would be pretty much guaranteed against virus infection. And you'd be right—to a point.

Mainstream software developers and distributors test their programs not only for bugs, but also for viruses. That's because a virus could possibly be inserted into the program code during development, either intentionally by a malicious programmer or unintentionally by other means. So the companies behind the programs go to great extremes to test for viruses before their products ship, and to implicitly (if not explicitly) guarantee that their products are virus-free.

So it's fair to say that almost all commercial software programs are safe from viruses. But that still leaves a slight margin for concern—because it's possible (if not exactly probable) for a virus to slip through all the detection and infect consumers' machines.

In fact, there have been a handful of documented incidences of commercial software being infected with computer viruses. While it's not something to get overly worried about, it can happen—and has happened. (For example, in Chapter 4 you'll learn about the Concept virus, which found its way onto two CD-ROMs distributed by Microsoft.)

The bottom line? Using commercial software is one of the least likely ways to contract a computer virus—but it's not 100% safe.

Which Files Can Be Infected

With all this talk about avoiding files sent to you by other users, it's important to note that not all types of files can carry computer viruses.

What types of files *can* contain viruses?

The list starts with executable files, sometimes called program files. As mentioned earlier, in Windows these files typically have **EXE** or **COM** extensions. Related, and also risky, are system files, with **SYS** extensions. All of these file types can contain virus code.

Files that automatically run executable files are also at risk. These files, sometimes called *batch files*, typically have **BAT** and **PIF** extensions. While these files probably don't contain virus code themselves, they can automatically run programs that can be infected, and as such can put your system at risk.

Visual Basic Script files are also risky, since they can function like an executable file on your system. These files have a **VBS** extension.

Document files can also be infected, thanks to macro viruses. These are the files you create in Microsoft Word and Excel and PowerPoint, with **DOC**, **DOT**, **XLS**, **XLW**, and **PPT** extensions.

Some movie files can contain virus code. In particular, WMV and AVI files pose a degree of risk in this fashion. Other types of movie files—including QT and MPEG—do *not* pose a risk of infection.

Along the same lines, digital audio files have not yet been shown to be infectable. So if you're playing MP3, WMA, LQT, WAV, or MID files, you're safe.

Image files are also virus-free. So you won't contract a virus just by looking at a JPG, GIF, TIF, or BMP file.

Table 2.1 summarizes which of these Windows file types can carry infections, and which can't.

Table 2.1 *File Types and Extensions*

EXTENSION	FILE TYPE	INFECTABLE?
ADE	Microsoft Access project	Yes
ADP	Microsoft Access project	Yes
AVI	Movie	Yes
BAS	Visual Basic module	Yes
BAT	Batch	Yes
BMP	Image	No
CMD	Windows NT command	Yes
COM	Program (MS-DOS)	Yes
DOC	Word document	Yes
DOT	Word template	Yes
EXE	Program	Yes
GIF	Image	No
INF	Setup information	Yes (makes changes to Windows Registry)
JPG (JPEG)	Image	No
JS	JavaScript	Yes
JS	JavaScript	Yes
JSE	JavaScript	Yes
LQT	Audio	No
MDB	Microsoft Access database	Yes
MDE	Microsoft Access database	Yes

Continued on next page

Table 2.1   *File Types and Extensions (Continued)*

EXTENSION	FILE TYPE	INFECTABLE?
MID (MIDI)	Audio	No
MP3	Audio	No
MPG (MPEG)	Movie	No
PIF	Batch	Yes
PNG	Image	No
PPT	PowerPoint document	Yes
QT	Movie	No
REG	Registration entry	Yes (makes changes to Windows Registry)
SCR	Screen saver	Yes
SYS	System	Yes
TIF (TIFF)	Image	No
TXT	Text	No
VB	VisualBasic	Yes
VBE	VisualBasic	Yes
VBS	Visual Basic Script	Yes
WAV	Audio	No
WMA	Audio	No
WMV	Movie	Yes
XLS	Excel document	Yes
XLW	Excel document	Yes

This information is useful only if you can see the extensions of the files you're working with. One of the more popular options in recent versions of Windows is to hide extensions for known file types. When this option is enabled, you only see the filename, not the extension. So a file named `myvirus` could be a Word document, or an MP3 song, or an executable program. Without knowing what type of file it is, you're flying blind.

WARNING *You should beware the double-dot (or double-extension) spoof, where virus writers tack a harmless-looking* .doc *or* .txt *to the end of the main filename—before the extension. If you're not viewing extensions, you'll see a file that looks like* myvirus.jpg, *while the full filename is actually* myvirus.jpg.exe. *If you don't see the* .exe, *you think you're dealing with a picture file—and are tricked into down-loading an executable program.*

Better, then, to configure Windows to show all file extensions. This way you'll know that myvirus.doc should be opened in Microsoft Word, myvirus.mp3 should be played with your favorite digital music player, and myvirus.exe is a potentially dangerous virus program.

NOTE *To learn how to show file extensions in Windows, turn to Chapter 11, "Preventing Virus Attacks."*

Are You at Risk?

Now that you know how computer viruses are spread, and which types of files can contain viruses, it's time to reevaluate the ways you use your computer. Are you doing anything that unnecessarily increases your risk of being infected by a computer virus?

The answer is probably "yes." That's because the only 100% guaranteed protection against infection is to never share files with other users, never communicate (electronically) with other users, and never connect your computer to other computers (via a network or over the Internet). The minute you plug your computer into the office network, or dial into the Internet, or accept a floppy disk from another user, you're putting your system at risk.

TIP *Changing your computer behavior is one way to reduce your risk of catching a virus; using an antivirus program is another. See Chapter 9, "Antivirus Software and Services" to learn more about these useful programs.*

Very Safe Behavior

What is the safest computing behavior you can engage in? Let's look at how you can reduce your risk of infection to practically zero.

Solo Computing

The only completely effective way to protect against catching a computer virus is to sever all contact between your PC and other computers. That means not connecting to a network, not connecting to the Internet, and never accepting floppy disks, CDs, or other media from other users. You use your computer exactly as it came out of the box, never adding any new software, never downloading any new files, and never copying any new documents. No downloading, no Web surfing, no message reading. Just you and your computer, isolated from the rest of the world.

It's like sexual abstinence; if you totally isolate yourself, you can't catch anything. Of course, you won't have any fun, either. (Computing abstinence is no more fun than sexual abstinence— although it's equally effective in protecting against infection.) Chances are, you'll find this preventive strategy a little too restrictive.

Using Only Commercial Software

You'd think commercial software would be free from viruses, and, nearly always, you'd be correct. Incidences of commercial programs being surreptitiously infected are few and far between. So while it's technically not quite as safe as computing solo, installing a new shrink-wrapped software program on your PC probably isn't going to put you at any substantial risk. In other words, it's okay to install new software on your PC—as long as it's from a major manufacturer, and you purchased it at retail, in a shrink-wrapped box. You increase your risk substantially by downloading software from the Internet, especially programs from companies (or individuals) that you've never heard of before. (See "Downloading Freeware and Shareware," later in this chapter, for additional perspective.)

Moderately Safe Behavior

If you're comfortable with using your computer to run commercial programs, and that's all, there's no need to read further. Your system will be safe from infection until the day it dies.

However, if you don't mind accepting a little risk, you can connect your computer to the Internet and partake of many of the benefits offered by online computing. These activities aren't completely risk-free, but if you watch yourself, you can have a good time without picking up any infections.

Web Surfing

Surfing the Web is a relatively passive activity. You input a Web site address, you click a few links, you surf from site to site. No big potential for harm here.

Except…

There is the possibility that a Web page can contain embedded ActiveX or JavaScript code that could launch a virus infection. You've actually seen some of this code at work if you've ever visited a Web site that automatically launched an annoying pop-up window, or tried to establish itself as your browser's home page.

So it's *possible* that you can surf to a Web page, have some malicious script launch in the background, and then find your computer infected with a virus. However, it's not *likely*, for a number of reasons.

First, before any infected file is downloaded to your computer, you'll see a dialog box asking if you want to download the file. Answer no, and the file won't download—and your system won't be infected. You're only infected if you're incautious enough to accept an unrequested download.

Second, Microsoft and other browser developers continuously update their software to plug any holes that allow rogue programs to be run in this fashion. While new holes are being discovered every day, virus writers seldom have time to exploit the holes before Microsoft issues a new browser patch. As long as you keep your browser up-to-date (which means downloading and installing all the software updates), there probably isn't much risk that you'll catch a virus by Web surfing.

Third, and probably most important, if you catch a virus from a Web page, you know who gave it to you. In an environment where virus writers operate with the utmost secrecy, it's relatively easy to track down—and prosecute—the author of a Web page. Few serious virus writers are going to attack in the open like this, which is why you don't see a lot of viruses propagated over the World Wide Web.

Reading E-Mail

As you'll read in a few pages, one of the most risky activities you can engage in is blindly opening files attached to e-mail messages. Just reading the messages, though—and *not* opening the attachments—is a relatively safe activity.

Relatively.

That's because while text-only messages are by nature completely free of any virus code, you also receive HTML messages in your e-mail. An HTML message is one that contains fancy fonts and colors and graphics; unfortunately, an HTML message (like an HTML Web page) can also contain ActiveX and JavaScript code, which can be used to launch virus-infected programs.

So it's *possible* that you can infect your system with a virus simply by reading an e-mail message. It's *unlikely*, however, because Microsoft and other developers of e-mail programs keep inserting features to protect against automatically running rogue code in this manner. (These are similar to the security features built into Web browsers.) If you're using a recent version of Outlook or Outlook Express (or any other major e-mail program), it's unlikely that your system can be infected by malicious HTML messages.

In addition, you can completely protect against these types of messages by turning off the preview pane in your e-mail program, and by not opening any HTML-formatted messages. If you can't see the message, it can't infect your system.

Chatting and Messaging

By itself, the act of exchanging text messages with other users, via Internet chat or instant messaging, is a completely safe activity. There is no way to embed virus code into a short text message, period. So go ahead and chat and message, to your heart's content; you won't catch any viruses while you're doing so.

However, you are at risk of contracting a virus if you accept any files from someone you're chatting with—or even from someone who sees that you're online and sends you a blind file. As described later in this chapter, accepting files in this fashion is a very risky behavior, and one to be avoided.

Just chatting, however, is fine—as long as you don't accept any files, from anybody.

The Dangers of Connecting

Some overly cautious users advise against any connections between your computer and the outside world. To be completely safe, they recommend that you not connect your PC to any network, or to the Internet. The thinking is that if you're not connected, there's no way a virus will find itself to your system.

This thinking is sound–to a point. That's because simply being connected to a network or to the Internet doesn't transfer infected files to your computer. The file transfer has to be triggered by another operation–downloading a file, receiving an e-mail message, accepting a file during instant messaging, and so on. And, of course, just accepting a file doesn't infect your computer; you have to open the file for the infection to occur.

So there's nothing inherently risky about the connection between your computer and other computers–at least in terms of computer viruses. Where being connected *can* cause problems is in the area of Internet-based attacks. When you're connected to the Internet (or to a network), your computer is at risk of a malicious attack by another computer; if you're not connected, you can't be attacked.

The only thing a computer attack has in common with a virus infection is that they both can seriously damage your computer system. Learn more about computer attacks in Chapter 13, "Understanding Internet-Based Attacks."

Risky Behavior

So far, so good. You can run commercial programs on your PC, surf the Web, send and receive e-mail, and even do a little chatting and instant messaging, all without putting your system at significant risk. What, then, are the behaviors that *do* put your system at risk? What activities should you avoid?

Disk Sharing

Although you probably don't do it very often, you probably shouldn't accept any floppy disks—from *anyone*. If someone hands you a floppy, *don't* insert it in your PC's floppy drive. That floppy could contain a virus-infected file, or even an extremely damaging boot sector virus.

This warning goes for any removable storage media—including ZIP disks and recordable/writable CDs. Any item that another user can copy data to can also be used to store viruses. When you insert the infected media into your PC, the infection is then transferred to your system.

File Downloading

A lot of users download a lot of files from the Internet. You can download software applications from file archives, MP3 files from digital music archives, and PC games from gaming archives. Any time you download a file, you run the risk of downloading a computer virus.

You're more at risk if you download files from lesser-known sites. The major file archives (Tucows, ZDNet, and CNET, for example) religiously check their files for infection, which makes them relatively safe. Less visible sites, especially sites run by individuals, are less diligent about checking for viruses—which makes them prime targets for virus writers looking to increase the circulation of their creations.

You also increase your risk if you don't closely monitor what you're downloading. If you have the "view file extensions" feature turned off in Windows, you won't be able to see what kind of files you're downloading. It's easy enough for an infected EXE file to masquerade as an otherwise harmless MP3 music file; if you're not sure what you're actually downloading, you could receive a big surprise when you try to open the file.

Using Freeware and Shareware

Related to the downloading behavior is the use of freeware and shareware applications—which you typically obtain by download from the Internet. Noncommercial software typically doesn't go through the same rigorous checking as commercial software, so it's not uncommon to run some free utility you downloaded from the Web and discover that the utility carries a virus and has infected your system.

In fact, some virus writers use these types of programs to spread their viruses. Create a nifty little virus, embed it in an interesting-looking utility program, and then offer that program for free through a large number of Web sites. Naive users download the program, and get infected.

Pirated versions of commercial software pose a similar risk. These illegal copies—called *warez*—are typically distributed via rogue Web sites, Usenet newsgroups, and Internet Relay Chat channels. You may think you're getting a good deal by downloading a warez version of Adobe Photoshop for free, but when you discover that it contains an embedded virus, you'll rue your lapse into illegal downloading.

File Swapping

Since the birth of Napster in the late 1990s, tens of millions of users have engaged in peer-to-peer file swapping, primarily of MP3 digital audio files. This process involves connecting your PC to the PC of another user, and copying files back and forth between the two machines.

The problem, of course, occurs when you copy files that *aren't* MP3s. Maybe it's an EXE file jigged to look like an MP3 file, or maybe it's an obvious application file that you just couldn't resist trying. In any case, it's all too easy to have a virus file swapped to your PC, especially if you're not paying attention to what is truly coming over the transom.

Document Sharing

As you read earlier in this chapter, it's not just application files that you have to watch out for. Any time you open *any* electronic document given to you by another user, you run the risk of infecting your PC with a macro virus. Macro viruses can be embedded into practically any type of business document, including Word files, Excel worksheets, and PowerPoint presentations. It doesn't matter whether you get the document on a floppy disk, attached to an e-mail message, or downloaded from a central Web or FTP server—it's possible that the document could be infected.

NOTE *One of the largest virus outbreaks in history was caused by a macro virus named Melissa that was embedded in Microsoft Word documents.*

Running E-Mail Attachments

The most popular means of transmitting a virus is via e-mail. Virus writers (and sometimes the virus programs themselves) attach innocent-looking files to e-mail messages, and then send them out to thousands of users. You receive the e-mail message, along with the attachments. If you ignore the attachments, no harm is done. But if you open the attachment—thinking that it's a picture or a Word document or a text file—you launch an executable program that contains the virus, and your system gets infected.

You can reduce your risk by not opening file attachments—even if they come from someone you know. Unfortunately, too many users open any and all attachments without thinking, and contribute to today's huge virus infection rates.

Accepting Files While Chatting and Messaging

Exchanging text messages with other users is a relatively safe activity. The activity becomes dangerous when you start receiving files from the people you talk to, or unsolicited files from other system users. Download and open one of these files, and you run the risk of infection. Ignore the file and you stay safe.

The key is to ignore requests to send you files, no matter where they come from, or what they propose to offer. Maybe it's a picture of someone you've been chatting with in a "personals" room. Maybe it's a hot new utility you can use to automate your chat session. It doesn't matter. The file might be exactly what it claims to be—or it could be a deadly virus.

It doesn't even matter if you can see the extension of the file. You know JPG files are safe to download, so you don't think twice about accepting the file `mypicture.jpg` from one of your chat buddies. But what if a malicious "buddy" actually sent you a file with a name like this?

```
mypicture.jpg                                              .exe
```

That's right, it's the old double-dot/double-extension spoof, but with a lot of spaces between the main name and the `.exe` extension. The filename is so long, in fact, that the extension doesn't show in the message window; all you see is the first part of the filename, `mypicture.jpg`. Download what you think is a picture file, and you get an infected program file instead.

The lesson here is that if you accept files when chatting or messaging, you run a very real risk of your system becoming infected.

Assessing Your Risk Potential

Given the particular way you use your computer, how likely is it that you'll catch a computer virus? Compare your computer use with the activities listed in Table 2.2 to determine how at risk you are for a virus infection.

Table 2.2 *Virus Risk Potential for Common Computer Activities*

ACTIVITY	RISK	COMMENTS
Using commercial software	Very Low	Probably the safest activity you can engage in.
Reading e-mail	Low	Risk decreases even further if you disable the preview pane in your e-mail program.
Viewing Web pages	Low	While there are viruses that load directly from Web pages (typically using Java, JavaScript, and ActiveX apps and controls), the incidence is low and they've been (to-date) relatively harmless. Plus, you can protect against these viruses by turning off the scripting controls in your Web browser.
Swapping files from P2P file-sharing services	Moderate	Risk increases when you swap non-MP3 files.

Continued on next page

Table 2.2 *Virus Risk Potential for Common Computer Activities (Continued)*

ACTIVITY	RISK	COMMENTS
Chatting and instant messaging	Low to High	Low risk if you're only chatting. High risk if you accept files from other users.
Downloading files from the Internet	Low to High	Low risk from well-known Web sites. High risk from unrecognized sites.
Opening document files	Low to High	Low risk with recent versions of Microsoft Office. Recent versions of Word and Excel include options you can use to keep macros from running automatically. High risk with older versions of Word and Excel, especially if documents have been received from unproven sources or received anonymously via e-mail.
Opening e-mail attachments	High	E-mail transmission is the most common means of infection today.
Running executable files	High	Most viruses are contained within EXE, COM, or other executable file types. Launching the program automatically infects your system—or delivers the virus' payload.

How to Know If You've Been Infected–or Not

You've been less than careful. You've willingly or unknowingly downloaded an unknown file to your computer's hard disk. And now you wonder... could your system be infected? If so, how would you know it?

Different viruses deliver different payloads. Some delete key files from your hard disk; others initiate their own bizarre behavior. If your system starts behaving differently, in any fashion, it's a good tip that it may be infected. In particular, you should watch out for the following symptoms, either singly or in groups:

- Your computer shuts down unexpectedly.

- Your computer refuses to start normally, or displays strange messages during the boot process.

- Your computer loses its CMOS settings, even with a new battery.

NOTE *The CMOS settings are those settings for your computer BIOS that are stored in nonvolatile memory. When your computer powers up, it accesses the CMOS settings to determine all the hardware connected to your PC—including your hard disk drive.*

- Running the DOS CHKDSK command reports less than 655,360 bytes available.

- Your computer exhibits erratic behavior.

- Your operating system reacts slower than normal.

- Your system continually runs out of memory.

- You can't access the hard drive when booting from the floppy drive.

- Programs take longer to load than normal.

- Programs act erratically.

- You unexpectedly run out of space on your PC's hard drive.

- Your PC's hard drive or floppy disk drive runs when you're not using it.

- Your computer makes strange sounds or beeping noises.

- Your monitor displays strange graphics or messages.

- Your system displays an unusual number of error messages.

- New files appear unexpectedly on your system.

- Old files disappear from your system.

- Files have strange names.

- File sizes keep changing (particularly program files, which typically increase in size).

- Changes appear in file or date stamps.

- Your e-mail program mails out messages to all the contacts in your address book, without your knowledge or permission.

- Word documents can only be saved as templates.

- Word file icons look like templates.

- Strange message appears when you open a Word document.

If your computer exhibits any of these symptoms, then it's *possible* that your system has been infected with a virus. Every one of these symptoms can be caused by other factors, however, so you shouldn't jump to conclusions; run an antivirus program and let it search your system for any potential viruses.

The bottom line is that not all weird computer behavior is caused by viruses. Many computer problems are caused by buggy software, incorrectly installed hardware, and good old user error. That's why you shouldn't panic if your computer goes all wiggy on you; the cause may or *may not* be a computer virus.

In particular, remember that viruses only affect software, not hardware. A computer virus cannot break your printer, or damage your monitor. If you have a problem with your printer (or scanner or mouse or whatever), chances are the problem's in the hardware itself.

Why You Shouldn't Overreact

If you've ever been hit by a computer virus, you know how damaging they can be. Still, lots of people *haven't* been hit—even users who engage in very risky behavior. And a large percentage of users who have been infected haven't recorded any lasting damage to their systems.

So how real is the virus threat?

The computer virus threat is real, as the statistics listed in Chapter 1 bear out. But the threat is sometimes overstated—and must be balanced against the benefits you receive from using your computer.

First, you should know that almost all the statistics about virus infection are compiled by companies offering antivirus software. These companies have a vested interest in selling their software—the demand for which would decrease if there wasn't an active virus threat. So it's in their best interests to, at the very least, publicize virus infections—and, at the most extreme, exaggerate the virus threat.

That's right—we're talking hype.

No one's ever done an analysis, but it's possible that the hype in the antivirus industry outpaces the actual number of active viruses. Every new virus triggers an "alert"—before the size of the threat can be accurately assessed—which is typically followed by a round of breaking stories in the technology press. If the supposed threat is sufficiently large (and who determines this?), the story might even break into the mainstream press. "Millions of Computers to Be Infected," the headlines read—which leads to an increase of traffic to the antivirus sites, and a subsequent uptick in software sales.

Call it hype, or call it scare tactics, but the antivirus industry benefits from the release of every new virus into the wild. The bigger the danger, the more necessary the protection—whether or not you're really at risk.

And, if you're an alert computer user, your risk might not be that high. If you look before you click and avoid opening unsolicited files, your risk of infection is very low indeed. The viruses might be out there, but that doesn't mean they'll find you—or that you'll let your system be infected.

Even if you get infected, the damage might not be substantial. Many computer viruses are pure pranks, or "proof of concept" viruses, in that they announce their presence but don't do any real damage. Oh, you might get a strange message on your computer screen, or even slow down your system a little, but your system probably won't end up totally baked. Or even half-baked.

That's not even getting into the topic of virus *hoaxes*. These are warnings about viruses that don't actually exist. Just because you receive e-mail from someone cautioning about some deadly new virus that's going to wipe out your hard drive a week from Thursday doesn't mean that the caution is valid. These hoax messages proliferate quickly, but seldom (if ever) serve as harbingers for actual virus attacks.

NOTE *Learn more about hoax warnings in Chapter 8, "Virus Hoaxes."*

It would be irresponsible to deny that the threat of viruses exists. It does. But the fact remains that most computer users don't get infected by most viruses. Which means you should be cautious about contracting a virus, but not paranoid about it.

You see, while you *can* engage in totally safe computing, the reduction of risk probably isn't worth the functionality you'd have to give up. As with all things in life, you have to make some compromises in order to realize any benefits—and the benefits of personal computing require you to accept some level of risk.

This concept isn't unique to computing. For example, suppose you use a credit card at a restaurant. To realize the benefit of using the charge card (not having to carry cash around, not having to pay for thirty days, etc.), you have to accept a degree of risk. You have to accept that the waiter could steal your card, or write down your card number and use it later. You have to accept that a bum or a thief could go through the restaurant's trash and obtain your card number. You have to accept that your credit card company may be using your personal information in some very disturbing ways. But nearly all of us accept those risks, because the benefits of using the charge card make for an acceptable compromise.

It's the same thing with computers and viruses. You accept some risk of infection in order to realize all the benefits of using your computer. Yes, you could receive a virus attached to an e-mail message, but it's worth the risk in order to receive e-mail from your friends and family. Yes, you could inadvertently download a virus-infected file from the Internet, but it's worth the risk in order to download all those MP3 files to play on your PC. Yes, you could open a Word file that contains a macro virus, but it's worth the risk in order to collaborate on all those reports and memos with your teammates at work.

So be cautious, but don't overdo it. Being smart is better than being paranoid—and much better than actually contracting a virus.

Summing Up

Most viruses spread when an infected program or document is opened. You run the risk of infection whenever you copy or download unknown files to your computer, by any number of methods—sharing floppy disks, downloading files from the Internet, opening e-mail attachments, and so on.

You can protect your system against virus infection by avoiding contact with other computers. That means not downloading files, or opening e-mail, or surfing the Web. More practically, you can engage in all these activities with only moderate risk by taking the appropriate precautions—chief of which is rejecting any files sent to you from untrusted sources. Even then, you only risk infection if you actually open the file.

Starting with the next chapter, we'll examine specific types of viruses—how they work, and how to deal with them. In Chapter 3 you'll learn about two of the earliest types of malicious programs—boot sector and file infector viruses.

Boot Sector and File Infector Viruses

The two earliest forms of computer viruses were those that affected the boot sector of a computer's hard (or floppy) disk and those that infected executable program files. These types of viruses were quite common fifteen years ago, and (in the case of file infectors) still very active today.

Boot sector and file infector viruses can be transmitted by a variety of methods—file downloads, e-mail attachments, and so on. These viruses can even function as Trojan horses, masquerading as other types of files, to trick you into launching them inadvertently. Once launched, both of these types of viruses can do considerable damage to the files on your system—and can even, in the case of boot sector viruses, make your hard disk totally inaccessible.

It's important to know how these basic types of viruses work, and how to defend against them. This chapter examines both types of viruses in turn, so that you'll be prepared the next time you face either one.

Understanding Boot Sector Viruses

A boot sector virus is so named because it infects the boot sector of a floppy or hard disk (or the Master Boot Record of a hard disk). The virus then launches when a PC first boots up, either hiding in system memory or delivering some sort of payload.

Boot sector viruses can be very destructive. If they damage or overwrite a hard disk's boot sector, they can prevent a computer from fully booting up. They can also destroy various data on the hard drive—up to and including the entire hard drive itself.

Fortunately, boot sector viruses, by themselves are little seen today. A pure boot sector virus is most efficiently distributed in the boot sector of an infected floppy disk; since few users boot up their PCs from the floppy drive, the opportunity for boot sector infection has decreased.

That's not to say that boot sector infection has completely disappeared. What is more likely, today, is that a hybrid virus will contain a boot sector component along with file infector, Trojan horse, or worm code. So it's still important for us to understand how boot sector viruses work—so we can recognize an infection when it occurs.

How They Work

To understand how a boot sector virus works, you have to know a little bit about how your computer boots up—and how data is stored on a floppy or hard disk.

Your PC's Boot Routine

When you turn on your computer, it goes through a complicated startup routine, shown in Figure 3.1. (This whole routine is referred to as *booting up*.) The disks and memory on your system are checked, and then the first physical sector of your boot disk is read.

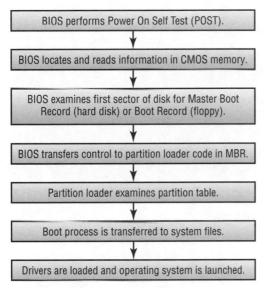

| BIOS performs Power On Self Test (POST). |
| BIOS locates and reads information in CMOS memory. |
| BIOS examines first sector of disk for Master Boot Record (hard disk) or Boot Record (floppy). |
| BIOS transfers control to partition loader code in MBR. |
| Partition loader examines partition table. |
| Boot process is transferred to system files. |
| Drivers are loaded and operating system is launched. |

Figure 3.1 *The normal boot process on a hard-drive PC*

> **NOTE** *For PCs with hard disks, the boot disk is the hard disk—disk C. You can also boot your computer from disk A (typically a floppy disk), as long as the disk is a "bootable" disk containing necessary system files.*

At this point, control is passed to your system's boot disk. If you're booting from a floppy disk or CD-ROM, the control is immediately passed to the boot sector—that part of the disk that contains the system files. If you're booting from a hard disk, control eventually goes to the boot sector, but is first passed to the Master Boot Record.

The Master Boot Record (MBR) resides at the very first location on your hard disk—in physical terms, cylinder 0, head 0, sector 1. The MBR contains a software routine that continues the boot process. This routine analyzes the Disk Partition Table (which defines how many sections your disk is partitioned into), loads the hard disk's boot sector into system memory, and then passes control to the boot sector, which then functions like the boot sector on a bootable floppy.

Infecting the Boot Sector

The way your system gets infected with a boot sector virus—the *only way* your system can get infected—is when you boot your system with an infected floppy disk in the floppy disk drive. Once the virus code is active, it can then infect your hard drive's MBR.

A boot sector virus replaces the code for your disk's load routine with its own code. This forces your system to read the virus code into system memory and then pass control to that code—not to your system's normal boot routine. (See Figure 3.2.)

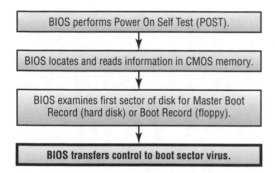

Figure 3.2 *The boot process as affected by a boot sector virus*

In the case of a floppy disk infection, the virus overwrites the code found in the disk's boot sector. In the case of a hard disk infection, a virus can infect in one of three ways:

- The virus overwrites the MBR code.

- The virus overwrites the boot sector code.

- The virus modifies the address of the boot sector found in the Disk Partition Table, to point to its own code instead of the normal boot sector code.

In most cases, the virus will move the original boot sector or MBR code to some other sector of the disk—typically the first available sector. This means that a boot sector infection can generally be undone by copying the original boot sector or MBR code back to its original location—or by restoring that sector of the hard disk by using the FDISK /MBR command.

WARNING *The* FDISK /MBR *command, executed from the DOS prompt, essentially reformats the MBR—with a brand-new copy of the boot routine. It also deletes all the data on your hard drive, so make sure you back up your data before you run this command.*

Once the virus code is in place, the virus remains memory resident and controls your computer—and also copies itself onto any floppy disks used while the virus is loaded into memory.

It's these infected disks that spread the virus, infecting all subsequent machines that boot from the disks.

NOTE *Since all boot sector viruses overwrite either the MBR or boot sector, it's virtually impossible for two such viruses to coexist on the same system. The second boot sector virus will overwrite the first, often resulting in a freeze of your entire computer system.*

Many boot sector viruses can also cause the loss or destruction of data on your hard drive. Some, such as the famed Michelangelo virus, do this immediately on infection. Others work with companion viruses to deliver a destructive payload at a later time. All will infect and cause damage to subsequent floppy disks you use on your system.

Common Boot Sector Viruses

While boot sector viruses are relatively uncommon today, at one time they were among the most feared of all computer viruses. Of course, some boot sector viruses were more common than others; here's a short list of the most frequently seen viruses of this type.

Frankenstein   Frankenstein is an encrypting memory-resident boot sector virus. It infects hard drive Master Boot Records and floppy disk boot sectors. As part of its payload, it deletes disk sectors on the infected disk.

KILROY-B   Also known as LUCIFER.BOOT, this virus overwrites the boot sector of the infected hard drive, on execution.

Matthew   The Matthew virus infects floppy boot sectors and hard disk Master Boot Records. It does not have a destructive payload; on infection, it displays random characters onscreen prior to the boot process.

Michelangelo   This virus, also known as Stoned.Michelangelo, Stoned.Daniela, and Daniela, gained worldwide attention in 1992, when it was feared that millions of computers would fall prey to its destructive payload. It infects floppy disk boot sectors and hard disk partition tables; the infection occurs when a PC is booted from a floppy disk infected with the virus. Once the virus is loaded into memory, it stays there—and then, on March 6th of each year, deletes all the files on the infected system. Although the risk of infection was high at the time, the actual infections were counted in the thousands, not the millions.

PARITY   This relatively new virus infects the boot sectors of floppy disks and the partition tables of hard disks. Fortunately, it does not have a destructive payload; it displays, at random, the message PARITY CHECK, and forces a reboot of the infected system.

Stoned   The Stoned virus, also known as New Zealand, Stoned.NearDark, and NearDark, infects PCs when the system is booted from an infected floppy disk. It infects floppy boot sectors and hard disk partition tables.

Current Risk

Since the mid-1990s the risk of becoming infected with a discrete boot sector virus has been small. Not that there haven't been new boot sector viruses; there have, most noticeably the PARITY virus, developed in 2001. But it's become increasingly difficult to catch a boot sector virus, as the use of bootable floppy disks (the most common means of transmitting a boot sector virus) has significantly declined. (About the only reason you'd boot from a floppy today is if you had a failure of your hard disk.)

Detecting a Boot Sector Virus

If your system has been infected by a boot sector virus, you will generally see obvious changes to the boot procedure. The typical boot sector virus will slow up the boot routine, often displaying unusual messages on the computer screen.

An antivirus program can find boot sector viruses by scanning the boot sector or MBR code. Most viruses contain an identifying text string that wouldn't otherwise be present in the boot sector or MBR. For example, the Stoned virus contains the following text string:

```
Your PC is now Stoned!
```

Further evidence of infection is any change in the size of the MBR. The standard MBR occupies less than half a sector on the hard disk, and most viruses are noticeably larger than that. The presence of a larger-than-normal MBR indicates that the original code has been replaced by virus code.

How to Remove a Boot Sector Virus

If your system happens to fall prey to a boot sector virus, there is good news: Boot sector viruses (in general) are easily identified and easily removed.

Today's antivirus programs can easily remove most boot sector viruses. The procedure is as follows:

1. Turn off your computer.

2. Boot your computer from an uninfected, write-protected, bootable floppy disk.

3. Use a floppy-based version of your antivirus program to scan and clean the files on your hard disk.

4. Remove the floppy and reboot your machine as normal, from the hard disk.

You should then use the full version of your antivirus program to scan and clean all your floppy disks; if your hard disk was infected with a boot sector virus, chances are all the floppies you've used are also infected.

How to Protect Against a Boot Sector Infection

The easiest way to protect against a boot sector infection is to not share floppy disks with other computer users. If you must share a floppy, use your antivirus software to scan the floppy before you use it.

Understanding File Infector Viruses

Throughout the short and storied history of computer viruses, file infector viruses have been among the most common—and most destructive—types of malicious files. A file infector virus (sometimes called a *program virus*, or just a *file virus*) works by embedding its code into the code of a program file; when that program is subsequently opened, the virus loads itself into memory to deliver its payload.

File infector viruses have been around ("in the wild," as the experts say) since the 1987 discovery of the Jerusalem virus at Hebrew University in Israel. Today, the majority of viruses include file infecting code, delivered through a variety of methods—e-mail, Trojan horses, file sharing, and so on.

How They Work

It's simple to remember how file infector viruses work. They infect files.

How they infect files differs from virus to virus. In fact, there are seven different ways that file infector viruses can infect individual files:

Parasitic Viruses   Parasitic viruses are those that change the contents of the infected files, but in a way that allows those files to remain completely or partly usable. These viruses do this by appending themselves to the very beginning (top) or end (bottom) of a file, or inserting themselves somewhere in the middle. In most instances, the original code is moved up or down to make room for the virus code, with the unfortunate side effect (in some cases) of losing any program code that doesn't fit within the original file parameters. In the cases where virus code is inserted into the middle of the file, the insertion is made into a "cavity"—a currently unused area of the file. Parasitic viruses, however, typically retain a large enough portion of the original program code to enable the program to work more or less as normal.

Overwriting Viruses   An overwriting virus does just what the name implies—it overwrites the original program code with its own code. This destroys the original code, of course, which causes the program file to stop working properly.

Entry-Point Obscuring Viruses   A particularly subtle way of infecting a file is to insert not the virus code itself, but instead code that launches separate virus code. These viruses—called Entry-Point Obscuring (EPO) viruses—have no distinct entry point in the host file and thus don't load themselves into memory when the host file is run. The instruction to run the virus code is typically executed under specific program conditions, thus enabling the virus to "sleep" inside a file for an extended period of time.

Companion Viruses   A companion virus doesn't alter the infected file; instead, it creates a clone of the host file, which is then run instead of the original file. This was fairly common in the DOS operating system, which would run a `COM` file instead of a similarly named `EXE` file. The virus might create a clone of `xcopy.exe`, for example, named `xcopy.com`; when the user entered the `xcopy` command, assuming to run the `xcopy.exe` file, the infected `xcopy.com` file would run instead. Companion viruses can also work by renaming the target file and assigning the original file name to the infected clone, or by altering the DOS path to find the infected file before the original file.

Worms   A worm is a special type of companion virus that is not connected to any pre-existing file. Instead, a worm copies its code to a completely new file, in the hope that the user will accidentally execute the new file. To that end, worm files typically have semi-familiar names that invite an action, such as `install.exe` or `run.bat`. Worms can also insert the command to run the infected file into `BAT` files, or into the Windows Startup folder.

NOTE *This type of worm, more technically called a* file worm, *is distinct from the category of* network worms, *which use network and Internet protocols to proliferate. To learn more about worms, turn to Chapter 6, "Trojan Horses and Worms."*

Link Viruses   A link virus, like a companion virus, does not change the physical contents of a host file. Instead, when the host file is run, the operating system is forced to execute the virus code. The virus does this by modifying the first cluster of the host file to point to a different cluster, which actually contains the virus code. Thus, when the host program is launched, the virus is launched simultaneously—as if it were included in the host file itself.

OBJ, LIB, and Source Code Viruses   A less common family of file infector viruses spreads via a modification of the object modules, compiler libraries, and source code of host files. Essentially, the virus adds its source code to the source code of the host program and is executed when the host program is run.

Once the virus has infected a file, it lies dormant until the file is run. Then the following process occurs:

1. The virus code is loaded into your system memory—before the program code is loaded.

2. The virus, now in system memory, looks for other files it can infect in the current folder/directory and (often) in the root directory. It then injects itself into these files.

3. The virus delivers whatever payload it has been programmed to deliver.

4. The virus returns control to the host program, which finishes loading and opens onscreen.

Figure 3.3 illustrates this process.

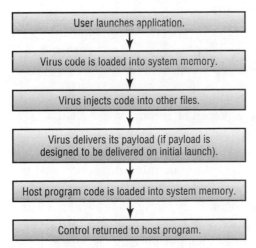

Figure 3.3 *How a file infector virus works*

Adaptable Viruses

A file infector virus can be described as either *static* or *polymorphic*. A static virus is one that never changes; the virus code, as originally written, stays intact throughout any number of infections. A polymorphic virus, on the other hand, is capable of changing itself as it travels from one system to another. The virus changes in some discernable fashion with each infection, which makes it more difficult to detect.

In addition, many newer viruses combine file infection with boot sector infection. These *multipartite viruses* are multiple-threat infectors, capable of attacking a system from a number of different angles.

Both polymorphic and multipartite viruses have become more common in recent years. Compared to older, more stable viruses, these viruses are able to spread further and faster, and cause more damage to infected systems.

Common File Infector Viruses

File infectors are among the most common forms of computer viruses. Any time you receive an executable file (EXE, COM, etc.) from another user (or from the Internet), it's possible that that file carries a file infector virus.

Because of this, there are a large number of potentially destructive file infector viruses circulating in the wild. The most common of these viruses are listed here.

CASPER   CASPER is an encrypting file infector virus from the early 1990s. It infects COM files, including `command.com`. On April 1, when an infected file is executed, CASPER overwrites the first track of the drive where the infected file is stored. When the drive is subsequently accessed, `Sector not found` errors occur.

Chernobyl   This virus, also known as W95/CIH, is named after the nuclear plant accident of the same name—and is programmed to trigger on the same day of the month as the Chernobyl accident. On the 26th of each month, the Chernobyl virus attempts to overwrite the host computer's flash BIOS, which will then prevent the computer from booting. At the same time, the virus overwrites the entire hard disk with garbage files. (Some variations of this virus trigger only once a year, on April 26—the anniversary of the Chernobyl nuclear accident.) The Chernobyl virus was extremely destructive in late 1998 and on into 1999, but has since been fairly effectively defended against by all major antivirus programs.

CRUNCHER   CRUNCHER infects COM files—although not `command.com`. It compresses the files that it infects; as a result, all infected files are decreased in size.

Die-Hard 2   This virus, alias DH2, is a symbiotic, memory-resident file infector. It's very stealthy and infects both COM and EXE files. Infected files increase in size by 4000 bytes, while system memory decreases by 4000 bytes.

Fun Love   The Fun Love virus infects all EXE, SCR, and OCX files in both Windows 9x and Windows NT. It searches for shared network folders with write access and then infects the files within; it can also infect files in the Program folder (and subfolders) on the host machine. One unique feature of this virus is that it infected several file downloads (called Hotfixes) on Microsoft's technical support Web site; users downloading these Hotfixes found their systems infected. (Fortunately, this particular problem has since been caught and dealt with.)

Jerusalem   Jerusalem is a notorious virus from the late 1980s, still active today, whose bark was worse than its bite. There have been many variants of this virus over the years, under many pseudonyms. The virus infects COM, EXE, SYS, BIN, PIF, and OVL files—and can reinfect the same file multiple times. A half hour after the first infection, the infected system will slow down by a factor of ten. It typically executes on a Friday the 13th, and then deletes any program you try to run.

Junkie   Junkie (also known as Junkie-Boot) is a multipartite virus, which infects COM and EXE files, corrupts COM files, and infects the boot sector on floppy disks and the MBR on hard disks.

Magistr   This is a memory-resident polymorphic virus. It incorporates complex anti-debugging routines that make it difficult to analyze. Magistr is part virus and part worm, in that it infects the local system as well as all files with EXE and SCR extensions. Five minutes after the virus is launched, it attempts to send infected files to other users via Outlook and Outlook Express, using contact names in the user's Address Book. Being polymorphic, the virus can use a variety of subject headers, message bodies, and attachments for its mailings; it randomly picks text strings from DOC and TXT files on the host computer to create the subject and message text. The virus' payload trashes the user's primary hard disk controller, overwrites CMOS memory, and erases all flash memory (BIOS); variations of this virus can also delete or overwrite key Windows system files. Because it is self-distributing and is able to change over time, this is one of the more dangerous file infector viruses in the wild today.

Natas   Natas (Satan spelled backward) is a polymorphic multipartite virus that goes after COM, EXE, and OVL files, as well as boot sectors and MBRs. It can cause widespread destruction of hard disk information.

Nimda   Nimda (Admin spelled backward) is a combination virus and Internet worm that is capable of rapid transmission. It typically arrives via e-mail, as a file attachment. The Nimda virus creates a new `load.exe` file and overwrites the existing `riched20.dll` file in the Windows System folder. It then makes an entry in the `system.ini` file to load both these files on system startup. It spreads the infection by creating new files in the Windows Temp directory, and by attaching itself to the `explorer.exe` file. This virus can also use various network resources to spread across a company network and infect network servers. It compromises network security by sharing local drives to the network. After its initial flurry of destructive activity in 2001, this virus continues to mutate and plague computer users worldwide.

OneHalf   This is a polymorphic, multipartite virus. It affects COM and EXE files, as well as boot sectors and MBRs. With each boot, it corrupts the hard disk two cylinders at a time, starting with the end of the first disk partition. When one half of the drive has been corrupted, the following message is displayed:

```
Dis is one half. Press any key to continue…
```

Plagiarist   Also known as 2014, this is a multipartite virus that attacks both COM files and boot sectors. Infected files increase in size by 2014 bytes, hence its alias.

SIMILE   This entry-point obscuring virus is nondestructive. The virus searches for and infects EXE files on the target system; it inserts into the host files random instructions that eventually transfer control to the virus code. The virus can be detected by the resulting increase in the size of the infected file.

Vienna   The Vienna virus, along with its many variants, infects COM files; each time an infected file is executed, the virus attempts to infect one more file in the same folder. Interestingly, this virus was written by a high school student in Vienna, Austria, as an experiment, back in 1988.

Current Risk

While the risk of being infected by any given file infector virus is low, the overall risk of file infection is moderate to high, depending on your computing activities. If you don't download program files from the Internet, don't open e-mail attachments, and don't accept program files from other computer users, you lower your risk of infection. If you engage in any or all of these activities, you increase your risk.

Detecting a File Infector Virus

The easiest way to detect a file infector virus is through file size. Since these viruses insert themselves into the code of the host file, comparing the current size of the host file against a historical file size will alert you to any potential infection. You typically do this by comparing the current version of the file against a version made during an earlier backup operation. If an executable file suddenly increases in size—even by just a few bits—something had to cause the change in file size, and that something was probably a file infector virus.

Antivirus programs also have other ways to identify file infector viruses. Some of these programs search the source code looking for telltale text strings contained within the more common viruses. Other programs monitor access to executable files; EXE and COM files typically are read-only, so any writing done to any of these programs is suspicious behavior.

How to Remove a File Infector Virus

If an executable file is infected by a well-written file infector virus, it's fairly easy to separate the virus code from the original program code. When the virus code is extracted, the original file is restored to a pristine state. A poorly written virus, however, can damage the host file during infection, making it harder to restore the file to its original condition.

The procedure to remove a file infector virus is as follows:

1. Turn off your computer.

2. Boot your computer from an uninfected, write-protected, bootable floppy disk.

3. Use a floppy-based version of your antivirus program to scan and clean the files on your hard disk.

4. Remove the floppy and reboot your machine as normal, from the hard disk.

To be safe, you can perform a second scan with the full version of your antivirus program after you've rebooted from your hard disk.

How to Protect Against a File Infector Attack

You can protect against file infector viruses by not downloading or transferring executable files to your computer—and not running any of these files you may have previously downloaded. File infector viruses don't activate until the host program is run, so as long as you don't open any infected programs, your system is relatively safe from infection.

It also helps to run a regular scan of your system with an antivirus software program. In particular, the antivirus program should search for known file infector viruses, and compare the size of your program files to the size of the program's backup copies.

Summing Up

While boot sector viruses are relatively uncommon these days, file infector viruses are still very much alive, and still very dangerous. You should know that these viruses can infect *any* EXE, COM, or other program file, and thus deliver their payloads whenever the infected programs are run.

The best protection against file infector viruses is to not add unknown or untrusted programs to your computer system. Boot sector viruses can be avoided by simply not using floppy disks given to you by other computer users.

In Chapter 4 you'll learn about another type of computer virus—the increasingly common macro virus.

Macro Viruses

Macro viruses are different from boot sector and file infector viruses in that they infect document files rather than program files. While a boot sector or file infector virus is activated by launching an infected executable program, a macro virus is launched when you open an infected document.

Most macro viruses tend to be embedded in Microsoft Word documents. Because most computer users create several new Word documents every day, and because Word documents are often shared (and collaborated on) between users, you can see how serious is the threat posed by this type of virus.

Compared to other types of viruses, the macro virus is a relatively new phenomenon. The first known macro virus, the Concept virus, was discovered in 1995—and infected millions of Microsoft Word documents. Concept's spread was helped when it was embedded in documents contained on two legitimate Microsoft CD-ROMs, the *Microsoft Windows 95 Software Compatibility Test,* and the *Microsoft Office 95 and Windows 95 Business Guide,* as well as a document found on ServerWare's *Snap-On Tools for Windows NT CD.* All three CDs were quickly withdrawn from the market, but the damage was done—and the age of the macro virus was upon us.

How Macro Viruses Work

A macro virus uses an application's built-in macro programming language to distribute itself. Applications, such as Microsoft Word, let users create macros to automate certain program operations; the macros are created with a built-in programming language. Virus writers exploit this capability by using the macro programming language to create macros that function as viruses. When executed, a macro virus can inflict damage on the host document, on the host application, and on other files and applications on your computer system.

Unlike file infector viruses, macro viruses don't infect program files. Instead, they infect document files, such as Word DOC files or Excel XLS files. Because documents can be shared across computer platforms, macro viruses can infect both Windows and Macintosh computers.

Most macro viruses work by exploiting an application's *auto-execute* macros. These are macros that load and run automatically when a document is opened, or when another program event occurs, without any prompting or action by the user. Once the macro is running, if there is malicious code within the macro, it can delete text, delete files, rename files, copy itself to other documents and templates, and cause untold other damage. Most macro viruses also copy themselves to the application's default template (in Microsoft Word, that's the Normal template, with the filename `normal.dot`), so that they run whenever you open *any* document within that application. And since the default template is used whenever you create a new document with that application, all subsequent documents you create will be infected.

Figure 4.1 shows how a typical macro virus is loaded and executed. The process starts when you launch an application and open an infected document. When the document is opened, it is loaded into memory, and the macros contained within the document are also loaded. If a macro is written to run automatically, the virus macro loads into your system memory and then delivers its payload.

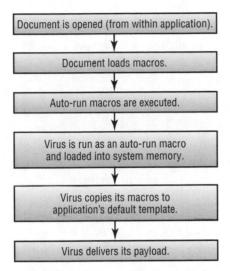

Figure 4.1 *How a macro virus infects your system*

Obviously, the macro virus spreads when you share an infected document with other users. Whoever opens the infected document will have their computer infected, and all new documents created on that computer will also be infected. When that user shares a document with yet another user, the infection spreads again.

Which Types of Documents Can Be Infected?

Virtually any document or document template that contains macros can theoretically be infected with a macro virus. In practice, Microsoft Office applications have been the recipients of most macro virus attacks, with Microsoft Word a particular target.

That said, macro viruses have been discovered that target documents in the following applications:

- Microsoft Word (DOC and DOT files)
- Microsoft Excel (XLS and XLW files)

- Microsoft Access (ADE, ADP, MDB, and MDE files)
- Microsoft PowerPoint (PPT files)
- CorelDRAW and Corel Photo-Paint (CSC Corel SCRIPT files)
- Lotus Ami Pro (SAM files)

NOTE *The number of non-Microsoft macro viruses can practically be counted on one hand, simply because of Microsoft's increasing domination of the applications market.*

Common Macro Viruses

Since the introduction of macro viruses in the mid-1990s, a profusion of these viruses has inundated computer users worldwide. These are some of the most common macro viruses:

Atom   Also known as Atomic, this Word macro virus is similar to the Concept virus.

Colors   The Colors virus (also known as Rainbow or WordMacro.Colors) infects Microsoft Word files and attempts to alter the underlying Windows color settings. It infects the Normal template and is capable of turning on Word's auto-exec macros feature—even if you've manually turned it off. The virus loads the following macros, which can be viewed in the Tools ➤ Macro ➤ Macros dialog box: AutoClose, AutoExec, AutoOpen, FileExit, FileNew, FileSave, FileSaveAs, and ToolsMacro.

Concept   The Concept virus was the very first Word macro virus, and the most widespread. First spotted in 1995, Concept goes by a variety of names, including Prank, WW6Macro, WinWord.Concept, Word Basic Macro Virus (WBMV), and Word Macro 9508. Concept works by copying itself into the Normal template and then replicating itself in new document files, which it saves as DOT templates. It's easy to spot a Concept infection; when you open the infected document, Word displays a message box with the simple message, 1. The virus loads the following macros, which can be viewed in the Macros dialog box: AAAZFS, AAAZAO, AutoOpen, and PayLoad. In response to this virus, Microsoft implemented a variety of anti-virus features in Microsoft Word, which reduced the risk of infection.

DMV   The Demonstration Macro Virus (DMV) is a test virus, first written in 1994 (*before* the release of the Concept virus). There are versions of DMV that infect both Word and Excel files, but neither version does any harm to infected systems.

FormatC   When this Word macro virus is executed, it attempts to open a DOS session and format your system's C drive. FormatC loads but a single macro, AutoOpen.

Gala   This macro virus, also known as CSC/CSV-A, infects Corel SCRIPT files, used in Corel's graphics applications (CorelDRAW and Corel Photo-Paint). The main impact of a Gala infection is that infected scripts stop executing properly, or they generate runtime error messages. On June 6th the payload is launched, displaying a message box titled `GaLaDRieL ViRUS bY zAxOn/DDi`, along with a selection of poetry (in the Elven language) from *Lord of the Rings*.

Hot   The Hot virus infects Word documents. It sleeps for up to 14 days, and then deletes the contents of the currently opened document. The virus loads the following macros: AutoOpen, DrawBringInFrOut, InsertPBreak, and ToolsRepaginat. However, after Word is infected, these macros are copied to the Normal template and renamed to StartOfDoc, AutoOpen, Insert-PageBreak, and FileSave.

Melissa   Perhaps the most widespread macro virus, Melissa was destructive enough to bring down several large international corporations for several days in March of 1999. Melissa is coded into a Microsoft Word document; when the document is opened, Melissa opens Micro-soft Outlook and sends e-mail copies of itself to the first fifty names it finds in the user's Address Book. The subject of the e-mail is typically `Important Message From <name>`, with the user's name inserted—although some variants of this virus send messages with blank subject lines. The text of the message is as follows:

```
Here is that document you asked for … don't show anyone else :-)
```

An infected DOC file is attached to the e-mail; the initial file was named `list.doc`, but variations to this have appeared over time. Melissa infects the user's `normal.dot` file, and if the minute of the hour matches the day of the month (for example, 3:31 on March 31st), inserts the following message into the current Word document:

```
Twenty-two points, plus triple-word-score, plus fifty points for using
all my letters. Game's over. I'm outta here.
```

Melissa's destructive power was not in its payload, however, but rather in the huge amount of e-mail traffic it generated—enough to equate to a denial of service attack on some servers. In this aspect, Melissa was a very effective *worm*.

NOTE *A worm is a very specific type of malicious file. Learn more about worms in Chapter 6, "Trojan Horses and Worms."*

Nuclear   Also known as Winword.Nuclear, Wordmacro-Nuclear, and Wordmacro-Alert, this virus infects both DOC and DOT files, as well as certain COM and EXE files. This is because Nuclear is both a macro virus and a file infector virus. It loads the following macros, which can be viewed in Word's Macros dialog box: InsertPayload, Payload, DropSurviv, AutoOpen, AutoExec, FileExit, FilePrint, FilePrintDefault, and FileSaveAs. Fortunately, Nuclear is a relatively innocuous virus; its primary payload is to insert the following line at the end of every twelfth printed document:

```
And finally I would like to say: STOP ALL FRENCH NUCLEAR TESTING IN THE
PACIFIC!
```

The virus also attempts to delete key system files on April 5th of each year, but does so ineffectively.

PPoint.Attach   Also known as PowerPoint.Attach, this virus attacks PPT-format Power-Point presentation files. It's a nondestructive virus, whose main goal appears to be simply to infect other PPT files.

Current Risk

For a period of time in the mid- to late-1990s, macro viruses were the dominant virus threat, especially to corporate computer users. However, as macro virus protection was added to anti-virus software programs—and within Microsoft Office applications—the threat substantially diminished.

Today, macro viruses still represent a threat—especially in Microsoft Word documents—but a relatively low one. It's more likely that you'll be hit by a file infector virus delivered via e-mail than by an infected Word document shared with a business colleague.

Still, if you share a lot of documents with other users, you could be at risk. The risk is unnecessarily increased because most users aren't in the habit of scanning document files. (For some reason, Word documents seem safer than program files to most users—even though both can carry potentially destructive virus code.) If you have a similar nonchalant attitude toward the document-based infections, your risk level is higher.

Detecting a Macro Virus

The presence of a macro virus is typically revealed by unusual behavior of the host application. For example, if Word is acting somehow unusual, it's possible that your system has been infected by a Word macro virus.

In particular, look for the following signs of infection:

- You can't convert a Word document to another format.

- Word DOC files have been changed to the DOT template format.

- The normal document icon looks like a template icon.

- You can't save a Word document to another folder or disk with the Save As command.

- You're prompted to enter a password for a file that you know isn't password protected.

- When you open a document, an unexpected dialog box appears.

- The properties of a given document (shown when you select File ➤ Properties) are unexpectedly altered.

- Unexpected files appear in the Word or Excel Startup folder.

- Excel workbooks contain unexpected, redundant, or hidden sheets.

One way to search for macro viruses is to open the application's macro feature; if you have an infected document, you'll see a bunch of unfamiliar macros in the macro list. In Word, you do this by selecting Tools ➤ Macro ➤ Macros. When the Macros dialog box appears (shown in Figure 4.2), the macro virus should appear on the list of macros.

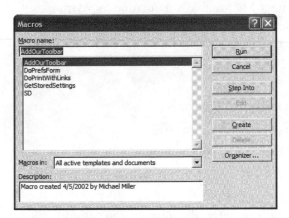

Figure 4.2 *Searching for macro viruses in Microsoft Word*

The only problem with this method, of course, is that you don't know how the macro virus is named. It's a sure bet that the virus writer didn't name the virus Macro Virus. (Some macro names you might look for include AAAZAO, AAAZFS, and PayLoad—all of which contain virus code.)

In addition, some macro viruses actually disable the Macro menu item within the host program. If you find that you can't access the list of macros for a given document, that's a good sign that that document is infected.

Poorly written macro viruses—or some viruses written for an older or newer version of your program—might not run "properly" on your system. If your system displays one or more error messages relating to macros not running (or something to do with WordBasic or VBA) when you load a document, that's an indication that the document contains a macro virus—which, fortunately, is not running on your system.

Another sign of macro virus infection concerns the default program settings in Word, Excel, and other Office applications. Many macro viruses change some of the default settings, which are typically found in the program's Options dialog box. If you find your default settings suddenly changed, your system could be infected.

How to Remove a Macro Virus

The easiest way to both detect and remove macro viruses is to use one of the major antivirus programs, as discussed in Chapter 9. Virtually all of these programs include scanning and disinfecting for macro viruses, especially for viruses that infect Microsoft Word documents. With these programs, removing a macro virus is as easy as clicking a button.

If you're ambitious, you can attempt to remove a macro virus by removing each of the virus macros from an infected document or document template. In Microsoft Word XP (also called Word 2002), you'd follow these steps:

1. Select Tools ➤ Macro ➤ Macros to open the Macros dialog box.

2. Select the macro(s) to delete from the Macro Name list.

3. Click Delete.

WARNING *If you think you've just opened an infected document, you should use this procedure to delete the suspect macros before you close the document or exit the program. Since many macro viruses auto-execute when you close the file or exit the program, you'll do more damage by exiting than by keeping the program open.*

The problem with deleting macros manually is that, unless you're dealing with a well-known, well-documented virus, you might not catch all the macros you need to delete. Also, your system may have already been infected by the virus, which means that your program will probably be reinfected the next time you use it.

A much better approach is to use the antivirus software. These programs can catch virtually *all* infected macros, as well as any subsidiary infections caused by the virus.

Most antivirus programs also attempt to clean any infected documents on your system. You can perform a manual clean by copying the entire text of the infected document into a newly created document. If you do this, copy all the text *except* the final paragraph mark.

How to Protect Against a Macro Virus Infection

Macro viruses can be spread in any way that document files are distributed. That means that you can receive an infected document via e-mail, shared floppy disk, shared network folder, or from a Web or FTP site on the Internet. You should therefore be cautious when receiving and opening document files from unknown sources.

The best protection against macro viruses is a combination of safe computing (don't accept unrequested documents), antivirus software, and use of the application's built-in macro protection features. For example, you can configure Microsoft Word to alert you any time it loads a document containing macros; you then have the choice of running the macros or loading the document without the macros (the safest option). You enable this protection (in Word XP) by following these steps:

1. Select Tools ➤ Macro ➤ Security.

2. When the Security dialog box appears (shown in Figure 4.3), select either Low (which runs all macros—an inherently unsafe option), Medium (which prompts you before running macros—a good compromise setting, or High (which disables all macros except those from trusted sources—the most secure option).

3. Click OK.

TIP *Other Microsoft programs have similar settings for macro security. If your version of Microsoft Word doesn't include this level of macro security, you should upgrade to a newer version ASAP. For versions prior to Word 7.0a, you can download the Microsoft Virus Protection Tool (ScanProt) to add a minimal level of macro virus protection to your system.*

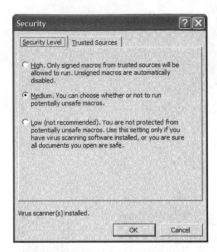

Figure 4.3 *Enabling macro security in Microsoft Word XP*

Summing Up

Macro viruses work by attaching destructive macros to document files; the infection occurs when the infected document is opened within the associated application.

Most macro viruses target Microsoft Word files. You can lower the risk of infection by configuring Word *not* to automatically run macros when a document is loaded. In addition, most antivirus programs do a good job of protecting from—and cleaning up after—macro viruses.

Because of the rigorous defensive measures taken in recent years, the risk of infection from macro viruses is relatively low—provided you employ safe computing tactics.

In the next chapter you'll learn about a type of virus that is closely related to the macro virus—the script virus.

CHAPTER 5

Script Viruses

As you learned in Chapter 4, "Macro Viruses," a macro virus uses an application's macro programming language to infect individual document files. In most applications—particularly those in the Microsoft Office suite—the macro programming language is actually a kind of scripting language. That means that the code is actually a script, where each line executes a specific command.

There are many different scripting languages, used to create everything from Web pages to auto-run routines in the Windows operating system. These scripting languages are typically easier to learn than traditional programming languages, so it should come as no surprise that virus writers have adopted these languages for their malicious endeavors.

Viruses created with these scripting languages—called *script viruses*—can be quite destructive. They can also spread very quickly, as the script code can be inserted into Web pages, attached to e-mail messages, or even embedded in e-mail messages. Some of today's most common viruses are script viruses, and they're a threat you need to recognize.

How Script Viruses Work

Script viruses are so named because they're written in one of several script programming languages. A script language differs from a traditional programming language (such as C or Visual Basic) in that it is typically less complex and more plain English-like in its approach. In a script language, the code is called a script, and each line of the script contains a simple instruction. The instructions are executed one line at a time, from top to bottom.

Several of these script languages—including Visual Basic Script (VBS), JavaScript (JS), and ActiveX—make use of Microsoft's Windows Scripting Host to activate themselves on Windows computers, which allows viruses in these scripts to infect other files. The viruses are launched whenever the user runs the appropriate script file.

NOTE *Macro viruses are a type of script virus—because a macro language is actually a script language. We discussed macro viruses separately (in Chapter 4) because their method of distribution (via document files) is distinct from the way other script viruses are distributed.*

Other types of script viruses activate whenever the coded document is opened or viewed. For example, HTML viruses automatically execute the moment an infected HTML page is viewed with a Web browser, or when HTML e-mail is viewed from within an e-mail program. VBS and JavaScript viruses load when the VBS or JS file is executed.

Script viruses can be propagated through infected documents (in which case they fall into the macro virus category, as described in Chapter 4), infected Web pages, e-mail messages, files attached to e-mail messages, and Internet Relay Chat (IRC) sessions.

Probably the biggest factor in the rise of script viruses over the past few years is that, like macro viruses, they're relatively easy to write (particularly for those who use the "virus kits" discussed in the "Build Your Own Script Virus" sidebar). Using VBS or JavaScript is a lot easier than writing code in C or regular Visual Basic; this has enabled nonprogrammers to become closet virus writers. In addition, these script languages make it easy to change existing scripts. Practically any Tom, Dick, or Mary can change a few lines of script code and produce a new virus variant.

How easy is it to write a virus script? First, you don't need a fancy development environment to create script code; the script itself is just plain text. For example, a VBS file is nothing more than a text file with a **VBS** extension. That means you can write your script using any text editor, even Windows Notepad.

In addition, scripts are easily constructed. All scripts are built from single-line commands; once you know the commands and the syntax, it's easy to string together a series of instructions to accomplish the desired task.

For example, the following four lines of VBS code ask for user input, then use that input to display a pop-up window with a message about the user's age:

```
Set WshShell = WScript.CreateObject("WScript.Shell")

currentage = InputBox("Enter your current age:")

newage = currentage + 10

WshShell.Popup "In ten years you will be " & newage & "."
```

When you're finished writing your code, save the file with a **VBS** extension, and—if you've used the commands and syntax correctly—you have an executable script.

This script is executed anytime the VBS file is run. No application has to be opened; all you have to do is click the file in My Computer, or open the file if it's attached to an e-mail message. The Windows Scripting Host (built into the Windows operating system) then runs the code, line by line, executing each individual command in turn.

Virus Creation Kits Pave the Way for Aspiring Vandals

One of the factors leading to the upsurge in script viruses is the underground availability of software that can be used to generate new viruses quickly and easily. With one of these virus creation "utility sets," an aspiring vandal can create their own customized VBS virus, without an extensive knowledge of script programming.

The most infamous of these virus-creation programs is the VBS Worm Generator 2, which was used to create the VBS/SST (AnnaKournikova) virus discussed later in the chapter. The Worm Generator can create quite complex VBS viruses and worms. Worms created with the kit can directly access a user's Internet connection and automatically morph into new variants as they propagate.

Continued on next page

Virus Creation Kits Pave the Way for Aspiring Vandals *(Continued)*

Another popular virus-creation utility is the VBS Love Generator, which is used to create customized variants of the popular LoveLetter virus.

So where do people go to find these generators? Sad to say, but there are dozens of underground Web sites, Usenet newsgroups, and IRC channels that specialize in this sort of destructive software. The locations of these sites and channels are constantly changing, but any potential virus writer can find them if he looks hard.

Different Types of Script Viruses

In the antivirus field, script viruses are further classified by the scripting languages used to create them. Reflecting the different types of scripting languages used in the personal computing and Internet environments, there are a number of types of script viruses that can be found in the wild. The most popular type of script virus is the Visual Basic Script (VBS) virus; other types of viruses are much less common.

The most common types of script viruses include the following:

Visual Basic Script   VBS is a script-based version of the popular Visual Basic programming language. VBS code is used to automatically execute batch commands in the Windows operating environment, much as batch files automatically executed commands in the DOS environment.

Windows Script   The Windows Scripting Host (WSH), found in all versions of Windows from Windows 98 on, was designed to let you automate tasks on your computer, much the same way batch files worked in the old DOS operating system. WSH enables Windows to run files created with a variety of scripting languages, including VBS, ActiveX script, and JavaScript. These scripts—as well as scripts with the WSH extension—can control various Windows features, including folders, files, dial-up networking, and the Windows Registry.

ActiveX   ActiveX is a Microsoft technology that enables Web pages to download and run embedded programs on the fly. ActiveX controls can include buttons, counters, marquees, and other "active" parts of a page. Any embedded ActiveX controls run when the Web page is loaded into the Web browser. ActiveX controls are created using the ActiveX scripting language, and can be programmed to create, change, and delete files—automatically, without user intervention. Because of this destructive capability, and their ability to run in the background undetected, ActiveX viruses are particularly dangerous.

NOTE *Microsoft has attempted to mitigate the effect of ActiveX viruses by incorporating the mechanism for encrypted security certificates in the Internet Explorer browser. "Authorized" ActiveX controls are assigned an official security certificate, and Internet Explorer can be configured to ignore those controls that aren't officially signed in this manner. Theoretically, ActiveX viruses would not be signed and thus would not execute.*

Java   Java is a cross-platform development environment, developed and championed by Sun Microsystems. The Java programming language is designed to create full-blown applications, as well as applets, that can be embedded into HTML Web pages. Java is designed to be platform-independent, which means that any virus created in Java can infect Windows, Macintosh, and Linux computers alike. By default, Java will not allow a program to write to a user's filesystem, without explicit permission. This means that any Java virus attempting to infect other files would (theoretically) first generate a warning message; unless you explicitly allow this procedure to continue, the virus won't be able to spread. Because of this built-in limitation to the Java environment, the few Java viruses that have been reported to date have been mostly harmless. The exceptions come when the virus infects machines running some obscure Web browsers (Internet Explorer and Netscape are both safe), and when the Java interpreter on a PC is somehow incorrectly installed or configured—that is, when disk write access is enabled.

JavaScript   JavaScript is the scripting language version of Java, designed to be incorporated into standard HTML code when creating Web pages. In the way it works, JavaScript has more in common with ActiveX than it does with the Java language; JavaScript scripts can be run via the Windows Scripting Host and embedded in Web pages and HTML e-mail messages.

HTML   Hypertext markup language (HTML) is the code used to create Web pages. HTML code itself cannot contain virus code, but an HTML page *can* include embedded VBS, JavaScript, and ActiveX scripts—all of which can contain self-launching virus code. Because of this, most so-called HTML viruses are actually VBS, JavaScript, or ActiveX viruses.

MIME   MIME viruses exploit a little-known "hole" in Internet Explorer that enables an e-mail attachment to be opened automatically when a Web page is visited. Recent versions of Internet Explorer have patched this hole, but users with older versions are still vulnerable.

NOTE *To learn more about MIME exploits and e-mail transmission of viruses, see Chapter 7, "E-Mail, Chat, and Instant Messaging Viruses."*

PHP   Hypertext Preprocessor scripting language (PHP) is a server-side scripting language used to generate dynamic Web pages. PHP scripts can be used to launch various system operations when launched by a visiting Web browser.

Windows Help   Windows Help (HLP) files can contain not only text, but also hypertext links and scripts. Instructions coded into one of these scripts can be used to trigger various system operations; when an infected Help file is surreptitiously placed on your machine and subsequently opened, the scripts are executed, and the virus payload delivered.

INF   Windows INF files contain information that is used during the installation of new software, or when upgrading currently installed programs. INF files are opened when the associated installation program is launched. All INF files utilize a special script language, which is what the virus uses to call its malicious code.

REG   REG files are used to automatically add new entries to the Windows Registry. (The Registry is the database that holds all configuration information for the Windows operating system and applications.) A virus contained within a REG file can add inappropriate entries to the Registry, which can affect the operation of the host PC.

Common Script Viruses

There are many, many different script viruses to be found in the wild. Here's a brief list of the most common types of viruses you might be unfortunate enough to come across.

666test   This worm, written in VBS, spreads via e-mail and IRC. When executed, it displays a message that starts with the line

```
Does your name add up to 666? Enter your name
```

If you press Enter without entering a name (or simply click Cancel), the worm proceeds to its next stage, where it tries to e-mail itself to other current IRC users and to contacts in your address book.

777   This is a very dangerous parasitic virus, written in Windows Script language. When the script is launched, the virus searches for and infects other VBS files in both the current folder and the Windows folder, along with selected subfolders. It inserts its code at the top of the infected file, so that that the file's original contents aren't damaged. On the second of each month, from 9:00 to 10:00 A.M., the virus searches for all DOC and TXT files on the C and D drives and overwrites them with a character-based picture of a man giving the finger, along with the message

```
Greetings from CTRL-ALT-DEL /CB + AVM - http://www.codebreakers.org -
```

NOTE *The Codebreakers Web site no longer exists.*

Babylonia   Babylonia is a virus hiding within an infected Windows Help file named `Serialz.hlp`; the file is typically spread via e-mail attachment and IRC. The Help file appears to be a list of serial numbers for infected software, but instead contains virus code. The code installs its files on your hard disk, rewrites specific Windows Registry entries, and attempts to download a file named `Virus.txt` from the Internet. During the month of January, the virus modifies your `autoexec.bat` file and sends a message to the virus writer's e-mail address, so that the number of infections can be tracked.

BeanHive   BeanHive is a Java virus capable of hiding itself in other infected files. The code itself is very short—just 40 lines that, when loaded into memory, connects to a remote Web server, downloads the *main* virus code (saved in the `BeanHive.class` file) and then runs that code as a Java subroutine. This subroutine calls six additional CLASS files, also downloaded from the remote Web server. These files are used to spread the infection to other files.

BubbleBoy   BubbleBoy is an *embedded* script virus spread via e-mail; this means that the virus is coded into the e-mail message itself and can be launched by simply opening or viewing an infected message. (You don't have to open an attachment to get infected.) Technically, BubbleBoy is a worm, written in VBS, which is coded into an HTML e-mail message. (Read more about BubbleBoy in Chapter 6, "Trojan Horses and Worms" and Chapter 7.)

Exploit-MIME.gen   This virus exploits the MIME header vulnerability in older versions of Microsoft's Internet Explorer. (If you have IE version 6 or higher—or if you've installed the appropriate software patch, as discussed in Chapter 11, "Preventing Virus Attacks"—you're safe.) The virus launches when an infected e-mail message is read, or when an infected Web page causes the infected e-mail message to open and display.

FreeLink   This VBS virus is actually a worm that spreads via e-mail and IRC. On execution, the worm creates a new file named `rundll.vbs` in the Windows System folder and then modifies the Windows Registry so that this script is executed every time Windows starts up. The worm then displays the following message:

```
This will add a shortcut to free XXX links on your desktop. Do you want
to continue?
```

If you answer yes, the virus creates a shortcut on your desktop with the URL to an adult Web site—the virus copies itself to all the network drives accessible from your computer. The virus also spreads via Microsoft Outlook, sending messages to address book contacts with the virus attached (as the file `links.vbs`). In most cases, the subject of the e-mail is

Check this, and the message text is Have fun with these links. The virus also searches for installed copies of the mIRC and Pirch IRC client programs, and then creates a script file to automatically send the links.vbs file to other IRC users in your current channel.

Hard   The Hard worm is written in VBS and spreads via Outlook Express (*not* Microsoft Outlook). Messages are e-mailed to contacts in your Outlook Express address book, with the infected file www.symantec.com.vbs attached. The subject of this message is typically FW: Symantec Anti-Virus Warning, and the message contains text purporting to warn the reader about a new worm spreading across the Internet. When the attached file is opened, it creates and displays a fake Symantec Web page about the non-existing VBS.American-HistoryX-II@mm virus. It then creates several files that it later uses to spread itself to other users. In addition, on November 24th of each year, the virus displays the following message on your computer screen:

> Some shocking news/Don't look surprised!/It is only a warning about
> your stupidity/Take care!

HLP.Demo   This script infects Windows Help (HLP) files. When an infected HLP file is opened, the Windows Help system processes the virus script and executes all functions written there. These functions scan the Windows kernel and obtain the addresses of necessary Windows functions; the virus then looks for all Windows Help files in the current folder, and infects them all. Since this is a "demonstration" virus, it delivers no destructive payload; instead, it displays a series of message boxes warning of its presence.

HTML.Internal   HTML.Internal is the first known virus to infect HTML files; it searches for and infects all HTML files on the local drive. The virus spreads slowly, as it has no efficient way to replicate itself to other computers. It is also compatible only with Internet Explorer, and then only when the infected Web page is hosted on a Microsoft Internet Information Server (IIS). (So if you're using the Netscape browser, you're safe; the virus is also rendered ineffective by any other Web server software.) When executed, the virus appends a short message to the HTML code, typically without destroying the existing code. An infected page will display the following title in the Web browser's title bar: HTML.Prepend /1nternal.

KakWorm   The KakWorm (also known as JS/Kak, or just plain Kak) is written in Java-Script. It uses Outlook Express (not Microsoft Outlook) to propagate, embedding its code into the body of the message itself; it does not attach a file to the message. Because you never see the code, the virus launches invisibly when you open the infected e-mail message. It does nothing until the first day of each month, at 5:00 p.m., when the virus displays the following message:

> Kagou-Anti-Kro$oft says not today !

Then it forces Windows to reboot. The virus spreads by sending similar infected e-mail messages (using Outlook Express) to all contacts in the address book.

WARNING *The KakWorm is a particularly difficult virus to protect against, as few antivirus programs scan for JavaScript code embedded in HTML e-mail messages.*

Links   This VBS worm sends itself as an attached file to all the contacts in your Microsoft Outlook Address book. It also uses the mIRC and Pirch programs to send itself to users when they enter your current Internet chat channel.

LoveLetter   This virus, also known as I Love You and Lovebug, is probably the most famous (or infamous) VBS worm. First discovered in May 2000, it had mutated into more than 80 different variants just a year later. It e-mails itself to the first 300 contacts in your Microsoft Outlook address book, and also spreads itself to Internet chat channels via the mIRC client. The subject of the message it sends is typically `ILOVEYOU`, and the message typically contains the text

    Kindly check the attached LOVELETTER coming from me.

Attached to the message is a file named `Love-letter-for-you.txt.vbs`, or a variant related to the variant subject line. The infection occurs when this file, often mistaken for a TXT file, is opened. On launch, the worm overwrites files on both local and network drives, including those with the following extensions: `AVI`, `BAT`, `COM`, `CPP`, `CSS`, `DOC`, `GIF`, `HTA`, `HTM`, `HTML`, `INI`, `JPEG`, `JPG`, `JS`, `JSE`, `MP2`, `MP3`, `MPEG`, `MPG`, `QT`, `PSD`, `SCT`, `SWD`, `TXT`, `VBE`, `VBS`, `WAV`, `WRI`, `WSH`, and `XLS`. The contents of these files are replaced with the worm's source code; for example, it might take the file `myfile.mp3`, and create a new file named `myfile.mp3.vbs`, containing the LoveLetter virus code. Some variations of this worm attempt to download a password-stealing Trojan horse program from the Web.

NOTE *Read more about LoveLetter in Chapter 6.*

Lucky   Lucky is a simple VBS virus that, when executed, overwrites all files in the current folder. It also displays the following message:

    You Have Been infected by The Vbs.Shakira Virus.

Monopoly   Monopoly is a Melissa-like worm, spread through e-mail attachments. It differs from Melissa (discussed in Chapter 4) in that it's written in VBS, not Word's built-in macro language. The virus arrives via an e-mail message with the file `monopoly.vbs` attached. When the file is opened, it displays a picture of a monopoly board with Bill Gates' face superimposed, accompanied by the following message:

    Bill Gates is guilty of monopoly. Here is the proof.

The worm spreads by sending copies of itself to all contacts in your Outlook Address book; the message typically has the subject `Bill Gates joke`. Then the virus sends a separate message to five distinct e-mail addresses (`monopoly@mixmail.com`, `monpooly@telebot.com`, `mooponly@ciudad.com.ar`, `mloponoy@usa.net`, and `yloponom@gnwmail.com`). This message includes a list of names and address from your Outlook and ICQ address books, as well as specific information about your system, culled from the Windows Registry (user name, organization, computer name, DVD region, country, area code, language, Windows version, and Internet Explorer start page).

NewWorld   NewWorld is a virus written in the PHP scripting language. It is spread when you visit a Web page and execute an infected script; it cannot be spread further, from your machine.

NoWarn   The NoWarn family of viruses searches for and infects HTML files on your local drive. Written in VBS, NoWarn adds its code to the top of an HTML file, without destroying the existing code.

Pando   Pando is a VBS virus that searches for and overwrites all VBS files in the current folder.

Pirus   Pirus is a virus that infects PHP script programs. When the virus is executed, it searches for and infects all PHP and HTM files in the current folder. The virus adds a command to the end of the infected file that calls the separate virus code; when the infected file is opened, the virus code is then called and subsequently executed. All infected files call the same virus file.

Pluma   This virus infects Windows Help files. When an infected Help file is opened, the Windows Help system processes the virus script and executes all instructions coded into the script. One of these instructions searches for and infects all other HLP files on your hard disk; another displays a Spanish-language message.

Rabbit   Rabbit was one of the first viruses written in VBS. It searches for VBS and JS files in the current folder and then overwrites them. It also infects all files in the Web browser cache and copies them to the user's desktop; the desktop then fills up with icons for the infected files.

Regbomb   This virus, contained within a REG file, adds a key to the Windows Registry that formats drive C (thus deleting all data) whenever the My Computer icon is double-clicked. The REG file is sent under various guises, as part of a Trojan attack.

Script.Inf   This virus, also known as Vxer, infects Windows INF files. When you run an installation program that calls an infected INF file, the virus code embedded in the INF file is executed and creates the `vxer.txt` file, copies the host file to that file, and then appends several new commands to the end of your system's `autoexec.bat` file. When you reboot your computer, these commands search for the first INF file in the `Windows\Inf\` folder, and overwrite that file with virus code that was stored in the `vxer.txt` file.

NOTE *The Script.Inf virus should not be confused with the Script.ini worm, which is spread via Internet Relay Chat. (The* `script.ini` *file is the mIRC program's default script file; see Chapter 7 for more information.)*

Strange Brew   This is the first known Java virus. It infects Java class files (with the `CLASS` extension) when Java's access to disk files is enabled. It does not pose a threat if you're using a major Web browser (Internet Explorer or Netscape) with the Java interpreter properly configured to block disk write access. (This is the default setting.) You can also be infected if you run the CLASS file directly, instead of through the normal means (as an applet within your Web browser).

VBS/SST   Also known as VBSWG or the AnnaKournikova virus, this is a VBS worm that spreads via e-mail. The e-mail arrives with the subject line `Here you have, :o)`, with the message text `Hi: Check This!`. Attached to the message is a file that appears to be a JPG of tennis star Anna Kournikova, but actually is a VBS file with the filename `AnnaKournikova .jpg.vbs`. When run, it attempts to mail itself to other contacts in your address book.

Win95.SK   Win95.SK is a virus that, among other malicious activities, infects Windows Help (HLP) files. When running, this virus will destroy all your hard disk files whenever you try to run an antivirus utility.

WinREG   This virus is coded within a REG file, and when executed, inserts the following key into the Windows Registry:

```
HKEY_LOCAL_MACHINE\Software\Microsoft\Windows\CurrentVersion\Run "virus
command" "
```

This key causes Windows to run the file named `virus command`, which happens to be a DOS batch file that searches for and infects REG files in the Windows System directory.

Current Risk

If you use the Internet to send and receive e-mail and to browse Web pages, then you run a moderate risk of being infected by a script virus. That's because the majority of script viruses are distributed via e-mail, as described in Chapter 7. It's fairly easy to use VBS or JavaScript to create a script virus, and fairly easy to distribute that virus over Web pages or through e-mail messages.

It's also fairly easy—and, these days, necessary—to activate protection against rogue scripts. You can reduce your risk by disabling the ability to automatically run ActiveX controls and JavaScript applets in both your Web browser and e-mail program.

Fortunately, the risk of infection from script viruses is decreasing from its peak in mid-2000. This is due, in part, to the efforts of large corporations to stop company-wide infections from script viruses. A company can employ a filtering script at its gateway to the Internet, and stop all script viruses from entering the company's network. Since most viruses do the most damage when they hit a large concentration of computers on a company network, these script filters really take the teeth out of the script virus threat.

Detecting a Script Virus

Script viruses are detected in much the same way you detect a file infector virus. In general, you look for unusual behavior from your PC—slowed operation, unusual onscreen messages, e-mail sent without your knowledge, and so on. Specific viruses can also be identified by specific behavior, or signatures left behind on your hard disk; most antivirus programs look for these signatures when scanning your system for infection.

How to Remove a Script Virus

Removing a script virus is similar to removing a file infector virus. You use an antivirus program to find the infected files, and then either remove the virus code from the files or delete the files from your hard disk. Because of the way scripts are constructed, removing the script code is actually easier than removing traditional virus code from an infected file.

How to Protect Against a Script Virus Infection

The basic steps you take to protect against a traditional virus infection also apply when defending yourself against script viruses. Use an antivirus program religiously (and keep it regularly updated), don't open files sent as e-mail attachments, and don't accept unexpected files when chatting or instant messaging. In addition, there are specific steps you can take to keep script viruses from running on your computer.

Configure Your Browser and E-Mail Programs

To be safe, you should configure your Web browser and e-mail program not to automatically run ActiveX controls and JavaScript applets. How you do this depends on the program you're using.

Configuring for Security in Internet Explorer 6

In Internet Explorer 6 and later versions, you should do the following:

1. Select Tools ➤ Internet Options.

2. When the Internet Options dialog box appears, select the Security tab (shown in Figure 5.1).

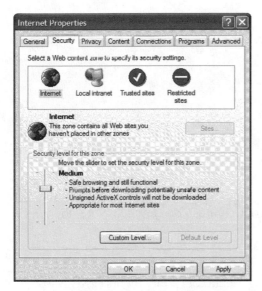

Figure 5.1 *Configuring Internet Explorer to guard against script viruses*

3. Select the Internet option and click the Default Level button.

4. Make sure the slider is set to at least the Medium setting.

5. Click OK.

Configuring for Security in Outlook Express 6

In Outlook Express 6, you make a similar configuration by following these steps:

1. Select Tools ➤ Internet Options.

2. When the Options dialog box appears, select the Security tab (shown in Figure 5.2).

Figure 5.2 *Configuring Outlook Express to guard against script viruses*

3. In the Virus Protection section, check the Restricted Sites Zone and Do Not Allow Attachments To Be Saved or Opened options.

4. Click OK.

This will prevent Outlook Express from downloading executable attachments (EXE, VBS, and other similar files) and from displaying ActiveX controls in HTML e-mail.

Security in Microsoft Outlook

Microsoft Outlook, unfortunately, does not have a similar configuration option. Instead, you should make sure that you've updated your version of Outlook with the latest security patch (see Chapter 11), which should block the downloading of potentially infected files and messages. (The latest version of Microsoft Outlook, included with Microsoft Office XP, includes this protection built in.)

Disable Windows Scripting Host

One of the things that make script viruses—in particular, VBS, JavaScript, and Windows Script viruses—so dangerous is that they run automatically in the Windows environment, thanks to the built-in Windows Scripting Host (WSH) function. However, you can turn off WSH, which will disable the running of these scripts. With WSH turned off, script viruses such as LoveLetter and Melissa simply won't run on your system.

WARNING *Turning off Windows Scripting Host may also cause some applications not to run properly. (Note, however, that WSH is not widely used, so this probably won't be an issue.) If you find that program functionality is affected after disabling WSH, however, you should reinstall WSH from the Add/Remove Programs utility.*

WSH is automatically installed on all versions of Windows starting with Windows 98; in addition, it can be manually installed on systems running Windows 95. There are several ways to disable WSH, depending on the version of Windows you're using.

NOTE *To determine if WSH is enabled on your system, select Start ➤ All Programs ➤ Accessories ➤ Command Prompt. When the Command Prompt window appears, type* `wscript` *and press Enter. If WSH is enabled, a Windows Script Host Settings dialog box will appear.*

Of course, removing WSH is a rather extreme option, and you really don't know how it will affect the operation of other applications on your system. Fortunately, the other, less extreme, measures you can take are equally effective in stopping script viruses.

TIP *Symantec offers a free utility that lets you dynamically disable/enable WSH. You can download* `Noscript.exe` *from the Symantec Web site, at* `www.symantec.com`.

Disabling Scripting in Windows 95

If you're running Windows 95, follow these instructions:

1. Double-click the My Computer icon on your desktop.

2. When My Computer opens, select View ➤ Options.

3. When the Options dialog box appears, select the File Types tab.

4. Select VBScript Script File (VBS) from the Registered File Types list, and click Remove.

5. Click OK.

NOTE *If VBScript Script File isn't listed, then you don't have WSH installed on your system.*

Disabling Scripting in Windows 98

If you're running Windows 98, follow these instructions:

1. Select Start ➤ Settings ➤ Control Panel.

2. When Control Panel opens, double-click Add/Remove Programs.

3. When the Add/Remove Programs utility opens, select the Windows Setup tab and double-click Accessories.

4. When the Accessories dialog box opens, find Windows Scripting Host in the Components list and deselect it.

5. Click OK, and then click OK again.

Disabling Scripting in Windows NT 4

If you're running Windows NT 4, follow these instructions:

1. Double-click the My Computer icon on your desktop.

2. When My Computer opens, select View ➤ Options.

3. When the Options dialog box appears, select the File Types tab.

4. Select VBScript Script File (VBS) from the Registered File Types list, and click Remove.

5. Click OK.

WARNING *To change these settings in Windows NT, you must be logged on as the administrator.*

Disabling Scripting in Windows Me, Windows 2000, and Windows XP

If you're running Windows Me, Windows 2000, or Windows XP, follow these steps:

1. Double-click the My Computer icon on your desktop.

2. When My Computer opens, select Tools ➤ Folder Options.

3. When the Folder Options dialog box opens, select the File Types tab (shown in Figure 5.3).

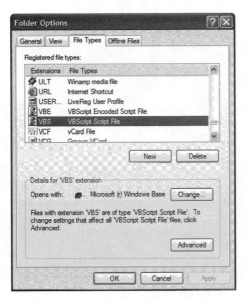

Figure 5.3 *Disabling Windows Scripting Host in Windows XP*

4. Select VBScript Script File (VBS) from the Registered File Types list and click Delete.

5. Click OK.

WARNING *To change these settings in Windows 2000 or Windows XP Professional, you must be logged on as the administrator.*

Summing Up

Script viruses are easy to create, but they are also easy to guard against.

Because script viruses are written in relatively easy-to-use script languages—such as VBS and JavaScript—they're easier to code than more traditional viruses. Many script viruses will also run automatically in the Windows environment, and can be embedded into Web pages and HTML e-mail.

Standard virus protection methods also protect your system against script virus infection. In addition, you can configure your Web browser and e-mail program not to automatically run the most common types of embedded scripts. As a more extreme alternative, you can disable Windows Scripting Host on your PC, which will keep all VBS and JavaScript scripts from running.

In the next chapter you'll learn about two very common virus variations—the Trojan horse and the worm.

CHAPTER 6

Trojan Horses and Worms

Two of today's most malicious types of code aren't technically viruses. Trojan horses and worms are two different types of *malware* (malicious software) that can attack your system and deliver destructive payloads—even though (in the case of Trojans) they don't replicate themselves or (in the case of worms) they don't infect existing files on your hard drive.

Both Trojans and worms do, however, cause significant damage to millions of computers every year. Trojans fool you into thinking they're something they're not, and then—after you've downloaded them to your system—proceed to deliver their payloads. Worms infect your system without your knowing it as they wriggle their way across the Internet, congesting online traffic (and possibly delivering destructive payloads) on their way.

This chapter discusses both Trojans and worms and describes how they are different from true computer viruses. You'll also learn about the most infamous of these nonviral infectors, and—most important—how to protect yourself from attack.

Understanding Trojan Horses

Put simply, a Trojan horse is a malicious program that masquerades as a benign application or file. Because you think the file is something it's not, you explicitly enable the file to be copied to your computer system. Once downloaded, it delivers its payload and reveals its true nature.

Trojans differ from viruses in that they don't replicate themselves. They can, however, be every bit as destructive as the worst file infector viruses.

How Trojan Horses Work

A Trojan enters your life pretending to be something that it's not. For example, you may receive an e-mail with an attachment purporting to be an image file of some sort. When you open the supposed image file, destructive code is executed that does harm to your system.

Trojans can masquerade as virtually any type of file—applications, documents, images, screen savers, games; you name it. There are even particularly devious Trojans that pretend to be antivirus utilities, but instead introduce virus code to your system.

The key to a successful Trojan horse is deception. Something about the file, or its method of distribution, has to convince you that the file is not only safe to open, but *should* be opened. It's like a con game: you're conned into running the Trojan file; once you do that, the destruction occurs.

Just what can trick you into running an unknown computer file—when you really should know better? Here are some of the tricks that have been used by Trojan writers:

Attach the file to an e-mail from a trusted sender.   If you know who's sending you a file, you're more likely to open it, no questions asked. The problem is, many Trojan horses can hijack a user's e-mail program (and its address book), sending the malicious code to friends and colleagues without the original user knowing that a malicious file has been sent in his or her name.

Make the file so interesting that you can't resist opening it.   The LoveLetter worm is embedded in a file that purports to include a love letter from an anonymous admirer. (Who doesn't want to be loved?) The Naked Wife virus purports to be a nude picture of a neighbor's wife. (Who doesn't want to see their neighbors in the nude?) The MyLife virus purports to be a humorous cartoon or screensaver of former President Bill Clinton. (Who doesn't want to have a laugh at our former commander-in-chief?) If the attached file looks interesting enough, many users will open it—even though they should know better.

NOTE *This type of deception is sometimes referred to as social engineering—the ability to trick a user into performing an operation or providing information that the user wouldn't normally perform or provide. You'll learn more about social engineering and other security threats in Chapter 14, "Different Types of Attacks."*

Hide the real file type.   Trojans are typically distributed via executable files, with EXE, COM, VBS, PIF, and (sometimes) SCR extensions. By using the double-dot or double-extension trick, the real extension is appended to a file that has a fake "normal" extension, such as JPG or GIF or TXT. Users who've chosen not to show file extensions in Windows see only the `thisfile.jpg` part of the filename (for example), not knowing that the entire filename is `thisfile.jpg.exe`.

Hide the real filename (Part II).   Some Trojans even fool users who choose to display file extensions, by adding a lot of spaces between the first (fake) extension and the second (real) extension, like this:

`thisfile.jpg                                        .exe`

When the user views the filename, all those spaces push the real extension off the side of the screen, so they only see the first extension—and think that the file is safe to open.

Because Trojans, behind the masquerade, are executable programs, they load into memory and deliver their payload when opened. Their payload can be innocuous (displaying a mocking message) or destructive (deleting files from your hard disk). They can also include worm-like characteristics, proceeding to e-mail themselves to other users—typically contacts in your address book.

So-called "backdoor" Trojans, discussed next, deliver a particularly nasty payload—they open a backdoor on your computer that enables attackers to remotely access and control your machine, any time you're connected to the Internet. Once the backdoor is created (thanks to the Trojan), *any* attacker can find and co-opt your system.

The First Trojan Horse

The term "Trojan horse" comes from that epic work of fiction, Homer's *Iliad*. In this story, the Greeks, led by the noble Achilles, had laid siege to the city of Troy, in an attempt to rescue the kidnapped Helen. (She had "the face that launched a thousand ships"–those Greek ships that sailed to her rescue.) The siege, now in its tenth year, had been wholly unsuccessful; Achilles needed a new plan in order to rescue his beloved Helen.

Under Achilles' orders, the Greeks built a giant wooden horse–with a hollow belly. The Greeks then convinced the Trojans that they were giving up and sailing for home, with the giant horse left behind as a peace offering. Unbeknownst to the Trojans, however, the hollow belly of the horse contained a handful of armed Greek soldiers.

The trick worked. The Trojans pulled the giant horse inside the well-fortified walls of the city, and proceeded to celebrate their victory. That night, under cover of darkness (and with the Trojan troops either drunk or asleep), the Greeks climbed out of the horse, killed the Trojan sentries that were still guarding the city, and then opened the city gates–enabling their fellow soldiers to storm and capture the city.

Trojan horse files are so named because, like that Trojan horse of old, they purport to be a "gift" to the user, but actually conceal a destructive purpose. Let the fall of Troy be a warning; don't let today's Trojan horses infiltrate and lay waste to *your* computer system!

Backdoor Trojans

A *backdoor* program is a network administration utility that enables an individual PC on a network to be remotely controlled by another computer—typically a computer operated by the network administrator. These utilities are common in the corporate world, where network administrators use them to configure PCs across the network, and to remotely troubleshoot malfunctioning machines.

In the virus world, a *backdoor Trojan* is a backdoor program that is surreptitiously installed on an individual computer. With the backdoor Trojan installed, the unsuspecting user can find his or her PC hijacked by another user—an attacker operating via remote control across the Internet.

NOTE *Backdoor Trojans are also called remote access Trojans and remote access trapdoors—both of which go by the RAT acronym.*

To attack your system, that other user has to know your PC's IP address. Some backdoor Trojans announce your system's availability by posting your IP address in an IRC channel. Even if your IP address doesn't get posted publicly, attackers can use port-scanner programs to search the Internet for PCs that have an open backdoor. Once the attacker finds your PC, it's a simple matter of using remote-control software to co-opt your system for whatever purposes the attacker has in mind.

Backdoor Trojans, such as Back Orifice and NetBus, are among the most potentially destructive malicious programs you can encounter. Ceding control of your computer to another user is a surefire recipe for disaster; it's hard to imagine any good coming from the situation. Indeed, most attackers use the backdoor programs to wreak havoc on the controlled machines, running applications and deleting files at will. Among the applications favored by backdoor attackers are so-called "keystroke loggers," which capture everything you type with your keyboard—including user names, passwords, and credit card numbers. The impact is mind-boggling.

NOTE *Learn more about backdoor attacks in Chapter 13, "Understanding Internet-Based Attacks."*

Common Trojan Horses

In recent years, some of the most destructive malicious infections have come from Trojan horses. File Trojans such as Badtrans and LoveLetter con their way onto your system via deceptive e-mail messages and attachments, while backdoor Trojans such as Back Orifice and NetBus enable attackers to take control of your system for their own nefarious purposes. Whatever the Trojan, they're all bad news, and they're all difficult to completely defend against.

NOTE *Many of these malicious programs tamper with the Windows Registry. You can view entries in the Registry by selecting Start ➤ Run and running the* regedit *program. While you can use this program to examine the Registry, you shouldn't attempt to edit the Registry on your own, unless you're technically capable and aware of the impact of any changes you may make.*

BackDoor-Sub7   This backdoor Trojan, also known as BackDoor, BackDoor-J, SubSeven, and Badman, typically disguises itself as a JPG image file. When opened, the virus installs two files into your hard disk's Windows folder; these files (named msrexe.exe, systempatch .exe, run.exe, windos.exe, or mueexe.exe) enable other users to access and operate your system via remote control. An infected system typically displays unexpected or unusual dialog boxes, and exhibits random keystroke entry.

Back Orifice   Back Orifice is a particularly insidious backdoor program that spreads via Trojan techniques. Once implanted on your system, it runs in the background and enables attackers to operate your computer via remote control. Attackers can steal your passwords, delete your files, format your hard disk, or perform practically any operation they want—all without your knowledge or consent. Back Orifice is typically spread via e-mail or IRC, and you can detect it by examining the following Windows Registry key: `HKEY_LOCAL_MACHINE\SOFTWARE\Microsoft\Windows\CurrentVersion\RunServices`. If Back Orifice is present, a service named `.exe` (that's all—nothing before the dot) will be displayed. You can also search your hard disk for files named `wind11.dll` or `boserve.exe`; the presence of either file indicates that Back Orifice is installed on your system. Fortunately, this Trojan can be detected and deleted by most antivirus programs, although it can potentially do a lot of damage if left undetected.

NOTE *Back Orifice is sometimes euphemistically referred to as a "network-administration utility," which misstates its true purpose. Its name is derived from Microsoft's Back Office network administration application.*

Badtrans   Badtrans is a destructive worm that spreads via Trojan techniques. It preys on users' curiosity, in that the message line is uninformative (reading simply `Re:`) and the message text is typically `Take a look at the attachment`. The filename for the attachment varies, but is typically innocuous; it uses a random combination of filename, fake extension, and real (hidden) extension, using the variables shown in Table 6.1. For example, the attached file might be named `new_napster_site.mp3.pif` (appearing as `new_napster_site.mp3`), or `hamster.zip.scr` (appearing as `hamster.zip`); you can think of the table as a "one from column A, one from column B, one from column C" menu. Badtrans' payload is discussed in the "Common Worms" section, later in this chapter.

Table 6.1 *Variables Used to Name File Attachments by the Badtrans Worm*

FILENAME	EXTENSION (FAKE)	EXTENSION (REAL, HIDDEN)
card	\<none\>	pif
docs	doc	scr
fun	mp3	
hamster	txt	
humor	zip	
images		
info		

Continued on next page

Table 6.1 *Variables Used to Name File Attachments by the Badtrans Worm (Continued)*

FILENAME	EXTENSION (FAKE)	EXTENSION (REAL, HIDDEN)
me_nude		
new_napster_site		
news_doc		
pics		
readme		
s3msong		
searchURL		
setup		
sorry_about_yesterday		
stuff		
you_are_fat!		

LoveLetter LoveLetter is a particularly widespread worm that propagates via Trojan techniques. The con (in the original version of the worm) is that you've received a love letter from a secret admirer; the attached file uses the double-extension trick to disguise a VBS file as a TXT file, like this: `Love-letter-for-you.txt.vbs`. Subsequent variants have changed the con to make it seem as if the attachment contains important information of some sort, an "official" virus fix, and other seemingly benign messages. Variant subject lines for LoveLetter include the following:

```
Clinton and Lewinski phone messages
Cure for CANCER!?!?!?!
Dangerous Virus Warning
Event Information
Free Cellular Phone
FREE SEXSITE PASSWORDS
FREE SURF
fwd: Joke
Hello Kitty
I Can't Believe This!!!
```

```
Important information
IMPORTANT: Official virus and bug fix
Important! Read carefully!!
Joke of the Day
Links!!!
LOOK!
Mothers Day Order Confirmation
New Variation on LOVEBUG Update Anti-Virus!!
Party Time
Recent Virus Attacks-Fix
Rock the Vote
Security alert!!!
Staff memo
Thank You For Flying With Arab Airlines
Variant Test
Virus ALERT!!!
Virus Warnings!!!
Where are you?
Wish you were Here!
You have a secret admirer!
You May Win $1,000,000! 1 Click Away
You must read this!
```

Naturally, the name of the attached file mutates to match the variant subject line. Love-Letter's payload is discussed in the "Common Worms" section later in this chapter.

Naked Wife   This Trojan worm, also known as W32/Naked@MM and HLLW.JibJab@mm, is spread via Microsoft Outlook and preys on the user's curiosity. It delivers a message to all the contacts in your Outlook address book, with the subject FW: Naked Wife and the message

```
My Wife never looks like that :), Best Regards
```

The attached file, which some users assume is a naked picture of a friend's wife, is named **NakedWife.exe**. After the mass e-mails are sent, the worm displays the following message on your PC:

```
You're now F****d! (c) 2001 by BGK (Bill Gates Killer)
```

The worm also displays a Flash window that states `JibJab loading`, and then deletes a variety of system files from your hard disk, including DLL, INI, EXE, BMP, and COM files.

NetBus   NetBus is a backdoor Trojan, similar to—but predating—Back Orifice. It gives attackers unauthorized remote access to your computer, which means they can run applications, delete files, steal passwords, and so on. NetBus is typically spread via e-mail and IRC, and it can be detected by examining the following Windows Registry key: `HKEY_LOCAL_MACHINE\SOFTWARE\Microsoft\Windows\CurrentVersion\Run`. If NetBus is present, this key will be associated with a NetBus file. (NetBus' presence can also be confirmed by the presence of two new files on your system: `sysedit.exe` and `keyhook.dll`.)

NOTE *Other common Trojans include KILLMBR.G, Magistr, and Nimda, discussed in Chapter 3, "Boot Sector and File Infector Viruses"; Melissa, discussed in Chapter 4, "Macro Viruses"; and FreeLink, Hard, Monopoly, and VBS/SST (AnnaKournikova), discussed in Chapter 5, "Script Viruses."*

Current Risk

The risk of infection by a Trojan horse is moderate to high, especially if you're incautious when reading e-mail, chatting and messaging, and downloading files from the Web.

Trojans prey on the naive carelessness of the average computer user; they depend on you to automatically open file attachments, unquestioningly accept transferred files during chat sessions, and blindly run files you download from unfamiliar Web sites. If you're the kind of user who clicks before you think, you run a *very* high risk of Trojan infection.

If, on the other hand, you apply normal caution—that is, if you *don't* open e-mail attachments, *don't* accept files during chat sessions, and *don't* download and run files from unsafe Web sites—then your risk falls into the moderate (or even low) category. Trojans are more about trickery than technology, and the more you can defend yourself against these high-tech cons, the safer you'll be.

Detecting a Trojan Infection

The signs of a Trojan infection depend on the type of Trojan. File Trojans, such as Badtrans and LoveLetter, can be detected by the damage they leave behind, typically in the form of deleted files. The major antivirus software programs can also detect most file Trojans.

Looking for a backdoor Trojan is a bit more involved. In essence, you have to determine if your computer is "listening" for instructions from another computer—which you can do via a DOS-based utility called Netstat, included as part of the Windows operating system.

To use Netstat to search for the presence of a backdoor Trojan, follow these steps on a Windows XP system:

1. Close all currently running applications and reboot your computer.

2. When your computer restarts, do *not* establish a dial-up Internet connection. (It's okay to allow your PC to connect to your network, or to the Internet via a broadband connection.)

3. Open a DOS window by selecting Start ➤ All Programs ➤ Accessories ➤ Command Prompt. (Alternately, select Start ➤ Run and enter **Run** in the Open field.)

4. When the DOS window appears, type the following and press Enter: **netstat -an >>c:\netstat.txt**.

5. Close the DOS window and select Start ➤ All Programs ➤ Accessories ➤ Notepad to open the Notepad application.

6. Open the **netstat.txt** file, located in the **c:** folder.

Your **netstat.txt** file should look similar to the one in Figure 6.1. To search for evidence of a backdoor Trojan, look for those active connections that are in a "listening" state. If a backdoor Trojan is present, your system will be listening for one of the addresses found in Table 6.2. Fortunately, none of the addresses in the table appear in my Netstat listing.

```
netstat - Notepad
File  Edit  Format  View  Help

Active Connections

  Proto  Local Address          Foreign Address        State
  TCP    0.0.0.0:135            0.0.0.0:0              LISTENING
  TCP    0.0.0.0:2869           0.0.0.0:0              LISTENING
  TCP    0.0.0.0:3031           0.0.0.0:0              LISTENING
  TCP    0.0.0.0:5000           0.0.0.0:0              LISTENING
  TCP    24.208.200.7:139       0.0.0.0:0              LISTENING
  TCP    127.0.0.1:3001         0.0.0.0:0              LISTENING
  TCP    127.0.0.1:3023         0.0.0.0:0              LISTENING
  TCP    192.168.0.1:139        0.0.0.0:0              LISTENING
  TCP    192.168.0.1:4861       0.0.0.0:0              LISTENING
  UDP    0.0.0.0:135            *:*
  UDP    0.0.0.0:445            *:*
  UDP    0.0.0.0:3024           *:*
  UDP    0.0.0.0:3040           *:*
  UDP    0.0.0.0:3041           *:*
  UDP    24.208.200.7:138       *:*
  UDP    24.208.200.7:1900      *:*
  UDP    127.0.0.1:4903         *:*
  UDP    192.168.0.1:123        *:*
  UDP    192.168.0.1:2234       *:*
```

Figure 6.1 *The contents of a typical* **netstat.txt** *file*

Table 6.2 *Netstat Addresses for Common Backdoor Trojans*

TROJAN	LOCAL ADDRESSES
Back Orifice	31337 or 31338
Deep Throat	2140 or 3150
Devil	65000
Evil FTP	23456
GateCrasher	6969
GirlFriend	21544
Hackers Paradise	456
ICKiller	7789
ICQTrojan	4590
Masters Paradise	3129, 40421, 40422, 40423, or 40426
NetBus	12345 or 12346
NetBus 2 Pro	20034
Phineas Phucker	2801
Remote Grab	7000
Remote Windows Shutdown	53001
Sockets de Troie	5000, 5001, or 50505
Whack-a-mole	12361 or 12362

For example, if you're infected with the Back Orifice Trojan, you'll see the following entry in the Local Address column: **0.0.0.0:31337**. If you're infected with NetBus, you'll see this entry: **0.0.0.0:2140**. Presence of these particular addresses is a good tip-off that the backdoor Trojan is installed and active on your system.

NOTE *Most systems will show several Local Address entries in the* netstat.txt *file; this is normal, unless the addresses are those listed in Table 6.1. (For example, if you're running a Web server on your PC, Netstat will show that port 80 is active.)*

How to Remove a Trojan Horse

Trojan removal techniques resemble the removal techniques for file infector viruses. In most cases, your antivirus program should be able to both detect the Trojan and remove it from your system. Depending on the Trojan, you might be able to disinfect the infected files; if not, you should either isolate the infected files in their own folder, or delete them completely from your system.

If the damage from a Trojan is significant, you may be forced to wipe your entire system with a clean installation of the operating system and all applications. This is an arduous procedure, but on rare occasions the only way to completely eradicate the Trojan code from your system.

NOTE *Learn more about clean installations in Chapter 12, "Dealing with a Virus Attack."*

How to Protect Against Trojan Horses

Protecting yourself against Trojan horses is a simple matter of engaging in safe computing behavior. Here's what you need to do—without exception:

- *Never* open unrequested attachments to e-mail files—even from people you know and trust.

- *Never* open **attac**hments to e-mail files from people you don't know.

- *Never* accept files transferred to you during Internet chat or instant messaging sessions.

TIP *If you use the mIRC program to participate in Internet relay chat, disable the "auto DCC get" feature. This will prevent the program from automatically accepting files sent to you by other users.*

- *Never* download files from "unofficial" sites; restrict your downloading to major archives (Tucows, ZDNet, CNET, etc.) and official company sites.

- *Always* have your antivirus program up and running, to scan all new files that arrive on your system.

- *Always* configure your operating system to display file extensions—and examine those extensions carefully for any file you download or copy to your system.

TIP *In Windows XP, you enable file extensions by selecting Start ➤ Control Panel ➤ Folder Options. When the Folder Options dialog box appears, select the View tab and uncheck the Hide Extensions for Known File Types option.*

When it comes to backdoor Trojans, you should engage in all the traditional activities to protect against the original infection, but you should also employ a firewall program to defend against unwanted remote access. (Firewall programs block Internet-based attacks on your computer and are discussed in Chapter 17, "Choosing a Firewall.")

In addition, many security experts believe that standard antivirus programs are not effective enough against a backdoor Trojan infection. There are also specific utilities designed to scan for and protect against backdoor Trojans; these programs include:

- BOClean (`www.nsclean.com/boclean.html`)
- PestPatrol (`www.safersite.com`)
- Tauscan (`www.tauscan.com`)
- The Cleaner (`www.moosoft.com`)
- Trojan Defense Suite (`tds.diamondcs.com.au`)
- TrojanHunter (`www.mischel.dhs.org/trojanhunter.jsp`)

Trojans, Viruses, and Worms

The terms *Trojan horse*, *worm*, and *virus* are all used to describe malicious files—pieces of code that do intentional damage to computer systems. As you've seen, however, there are subtle differences between the three types of malware. Here's a quick recap:

- A Trojan horse, unlike worms and viruses, does not replicate (make copies of) itself—although it can deliver a destructive payload to the host computer, or enable unauthorized remote access to the host system. Instead of virus-like replication, a Trojan disguises its true purpose and "tricks" its way onto a host system.

- A computer virus inserts itself into computer files, much as a biological virus invades living cells. The virus not only damages the host, but also attempts to infect other computer systems.

- A worm is self-replicating like a virus, but it typically doesn't alter the host files, residing instead in system memory. Unlike viruses, worms can spread automatically over a network or the Internet with no user intervention, using the (normally invisible) file-sending and receiving facilities of the host operating system. Worms are often noticed only when their replication clogs up system or network resources.

Some malicious files fall into more than one of the above categories. For example, both viruses and worms can use Trojan techniques to replicate across systems. A virus can also use worm-like techniques to replicate across the Internet, and a worm can deliver virus-like payloads.

Continued on next page

Trojans, Viruses, and Worms *(Continued)*

A good example of this "cross-categorization" is LoveLetter. You first read about LoveLetter in Chapter 5, where it was described as a script virus. Earlier in this chapter you also saw it described as a Trojan horse—and later in this chapter you'll see it described as a worm. Which is it?

The answer is *all three!* LoveLetter is the perfect example of a malicious program that is a virus, Trojan, and worm, all rolled into one. It's a Trojan because it tricks you into thinking it's a text file, not an executable. It's a virus because it infects files on your hard disk. It's a worm because it propagates over the Internet, via automatic e-mail and IRC messaging. Because it's a triple-threat, LoveLetter is a particularly dangerous piece of malware—no matter what you call it!

To most users, then, it doesn't matter whether you have a Trojan, virus, or worm—the end result is pretty much the same. It matters to antivirus researchers, however, since they're the ones developing "antidotes" to each specific type of infection. So in this book we make note of the specific category for each type of malicious file, while recognizing that some malware fits within more than one of these categories.

Understanding Worms

A worm is a computer program that copies itself from one machine to another, typically without explicit user action. It typically spreads via e-mail messages, Internet chat channels, and instant messaging. Worms can deliver destructive payloads, or they may just clog up networks (and the Internet) with all their self-propagating activity.

How Worms Work

Unlike viruses, worms don't rely on human beings (much) for their distribution. Instead, they use the file-sending mechanisms built into many of today's applications to automatically send themselves (typically via the Internet) to other computers.

The most common method of worm propagation is via e-mail. A worm can hijack your e-mail program, harvest e-mail addresses from your address book (or from recently viewed Web pages stored in your browser cache), and then e-mail itself to those addresses. Your personal involvement in this process is nil.

Other worms spread via a similar process using Internet relay chat programs, such as mIRC and Pirch. These programs enable users in chat channels to send files to each other; a worm can hijack your IRC program and, totally unknown to you, send itself to everyone chatting in the currently open channel.

It's also possible for a worm to propagate via instant messaging. Such a worm would harvest the names of your instant messaging "buddies," and—if they're online—send itself to them via the instant messaging protocol.

The most insidious worms, however, are so-called *network worms*, which exploit known security holes in Web servers and browsers, infecting the host system in a completely invisible manner. These worms infect a network system, then use that computer as a base of operations to infect other servers and networks. You never know they're there, and you're not aware of what they're doing. That makes them extremely difficult to track down.

Where Worms Come From

The term "worm" comes from John Brunner's 1972 science fiction novel *The Shockwave Rider*. This novel described the fall of an Orwellian society brought about by a "tapeworm" program that crawled its way through computer networks.

The first real-world computer worm was created in 1982 in the Xerox Palo Alto Research Center (PARC). Researchers John Shoch and Jon Hupp were trying to automate the installation of performance-measuring software on more than 100 computers at Xerox PARC; they devised a program that could send and install itself across the network, automatically. They called this program a worm, after the tapeworm program in Brunner's novel.

The disturbing part of this story is that Shoch and Hupp's program developed a bug, and the bad code automatically spread across the entire network. The defective program ended up crashing all 100 computers, foreshadowing the type of malicious code attacks we see today.

Common Worms

The number of worms in the wild is growing every day. Here is just a sampling of the types of worms you may encounter at some point or another.

Badtrans   As described earlier in this chapter, Badtrans is an extremely dangerous massmailing worm that has infected a large number of systems since its discovery in April of 2001. It sends itself by replying to unread e-mail messages in Microsoft Outlook folders. The subject of the message is a simple `Re:`, while the message may contain the text `Take a look at the attachment`. When launched, the worm displays a message box titled `Install error`, with the following message: `File data corrupt; probably due to a bad data transmission or bad disk access`. It then installs a remote-access (backdoor) Trojan on your system, which attempts to mail your system IP address to the virus' author. (Actually, there are more than a dozen different e-mail addresses that Badtrans attempts to mail to.) If this information is successfully transmitted, the attacker can connect to your PC via the Internet and steal personal information stored on your hard disk—passwords, user names, and so on. In addition, the Trojan also contains a key-logger program, which can capture other information (credit card numbers, bank account numbers, etc.) as it's typed on your keyboard.

BubbleBoy   BubbleBoy (which you first encountered in Chapter 5) is a VBS script worm that propagates via e-mail. It uses a known security hole in Internet Explorer and Microsoft Outlook to deliver a script file when an infected e-mail message is viewed; you don't need to open an attachment to infect your system. The script file, `Update.hta`, is placed in your system's Startup folder, so that it's executed the next time—and each subsequent time—you start your computer. This script file uses Outlook to send the worm-infested HTML e-mail to all the contacts in your Outlook address book. The subject of the e-mail is `BubbleBoy is back!`, and the message includes the following text:

```
The BubbleBoy incident, pictures and sounds
http://www.towns.com/tom/bblboy.htm.
```

CodeRed   The CodeRed worm exploits a known vulnerability (known as a *hole*) in Web servers running Microsoft Internet Information Server (IIS) software. The worm starts its attack by attempting to connect to TCP port 80 on a randomly chosen host system. If the connection is accepted (only on an IIS server that hasn't received the appropriate security update), all Web pages on the server are rewritten with the following message:

```
HELLO! Welcome to http://www.worm.com! Hacked by Chinese!
```

(Subsequent variants of the virus may display other messages.) The worm delivers two additional time-based payloads: connection to other servers to propagate the worm (days 1–19), and launch of a denial-of-service attack on a specific IP address (days 20–27). Since CodeRed is entirely memory resident, the current instance of the worm can be purged by rebooting the infected system; however, unless defensive measures are taken, further infection is likely.

Hybris   Hybris is a mass-mailing worm that arrives as an e-mail with the subject `Snowhite and the Seven Dwarfs - The REAL story!` One of several files is typically attached; the filenames include `sexy virgin.scr`, `joke.exe`, `midgets.scr`, or `dwarf4you.exe`. The worm attempts to mail itself to any user you send valid e-mail to; you'll send a message, which will typically be followed by a separate Hybris message. The virus' payload varies, but it typically slows down the operation of your PC, displays a spiral graphic or large black circle on your screen, or blocks Web access to major antivirus sites.

Klez   As mentioned in Chapter 1, "Understanding Computer Viruses," the Klez worm rapidly rose to the top of the "most popular" virus lists in early 2002. Since then, Klez has stayed at the top of the lists as a crafty series of permutations have forced even the best antivirus programs into a game of catch-up. (As I write this in May 2002, I'm receiving three or four Klez-infected messages *daily*.) Klez propagates via hijacked e-mail, sending itself to e-mail addresses found in your address book or on recently visited Web pages stored in your Web browser's cache. The worm also uses these addresses to spoof the From: field in infected messages, which causes a whole new set of problems; for example, someone receiving an infected message may see your name in the From: field and think it came from you, just because you happened to be in that user's address book—your computer doesn't actually have to be infected for your address to be used in this fashion. (As a result, *you* might be contacted by outside users telling you your PC is infected, when it actually isn't.)

Klez also exploits the MIME header problem found in older (and unpatched) versions of Internet Explorer to run automatically when an infected message is viewed, and then removes most popular antivirus programs from memory. The worm itself is found in an attached BAT, EXE, PIF, or SCR file, with a randomly generated name; the subject of the message is also randomly generated. The infected message is often accompanied by a second, "clean" file, scrounged from the PC of the previous victim, which can distribute confidential information without the sender's knowledge. The Klez worm not only infects executables on the infected machine, it also drops a *second* virus (the Elkern file-infecting virus) to wreak even more havoc. As you can see, Klez uses everything except the kitchen sink, which has made it the most pervasive computer virus in history.

LoveLetter   As described earlier in this chapter (and in Chapter 5), LoveLetter is combination file infector virus, e-mail worm, and IRC worm. Also known as I Love You and Lovebug, this malicious file typically sends itself in a message with the subject `ILOVEYOU` and a file attachment named `Love-letter-for-you.txt.vbs`. When opened, this file sends itself to the first 300 entries in your Microsoft Outlook address book, spreads to Internet chat channels via mIRC, destroys dozens of different types of files on your hard disk, and changes your Internet Explorer start page. Since its creation in 2000, more than 80 LoveLetter variants have been discovered. These variants use a variety of related and unrelated subject lines and attachment names, making this a very difficult worm to track and defend against.

MyLife   This is a mass-mailing worm, written in Visual Basic, that purports to display a humorous drawing of former President Clinton. It uses Microsoft Outlook to send itself to all contacts in the Outlook address book, as well as users on the MSN Messenger contact list. The worm's e-mail typically has the following subject: `bill caricature`. The message text promises that the attachment contains a "bill caricature," and purports to be already scanned for viruses; the phrases `No Viruses Found` and `MCAFEE.COM` typically appear somewhere in the message text. Attached to the message is the file `cari.scr`, which, when opened, displays a cartoon of President Clinton (holding his saxophone). The worm then copies itself to the Windows System folder, and then fires up Outlook to continue its propagation. At 8:00 A.M. the next morning, it deletes all files from drives C, D, E, and F.

Nimda   Nimda was briefly discussed in the Chapter 3 survey of file infector viruses. It's a very robust worm that uses multiple methods of distribution. It spreads via mass mailings, network share propagation, MIME headers, and other methods. The virus also attempts to create network shares and utilize the system backdoor created by the CodeRed worm. When it sends itself via e-mail, Nimda is difficult to detect; the subject line varies, the message text is blank, and the attachment name also varies (although the most common variant sends a `readme.exe` file). Some Nimda variants contain an executable attachment type that launches when the message is viewed in the Microsoft Outlook or Outlook Express preview pane; no user interaction required. (E-mail messages are sent to all contacts in the Windows address book, as well as e-mail addresses harvested from previously viewed Web pages—although some variants "sleep" for up to ten days before sending any messages.) When the virus infects Web pages (ASP, HTM, and HTML documents, as well as any files named `index`, `main`, and `default`), it appends JavaScript code that causes any computer viewing the infected page to open a new browser window that contains the infectious e-mail message. Thus simply viewing the infected Web page can infect a computer.

SirCam   This mass-mailing worm attempts to send itself, along with selected documents on your hard drive, to all contacts in the Windows address book and to all e-mail addresses in recently visited Web pages (stored in your Web browser's temporary cache). The subject of the e-mail message is chosen at random, and typically includes the name of the attached file. The message text is short and simple:

> `Hi! How are you? I send you this file in order to have your advice.`

Or, alternately,

> `I hope you can help me with this file that I send.`

or

> `I hope you like the file that I sendo you.`

or

> `This is the file with the information that you ask for.`

The file attached to the message has a double extension; the filename itself varies, but it's typically a GIF, JPG, JPEG, MPEG, MOV, MPG, PDF, PNG, PS, or ZIP file from your hard drive with the added BAT, COM, EXE, LNK, or PIF extension. So an attached file might look like this: myfile.jpg.pif. When the file is opened, it attempts to send itself again, and (depending on the variation) might try to delete files from your hard disk, or fill up hard disk space by adding multiple text entries to a SirCam recycle bin file.

NOTE *As you can see from the preceding message text, it's common to find wild misspellings and awkward English in these types of virus and worm messages. In some cases, the misspellings are a deliberate attempt to sound disarmingly naive (a form of social engineering); in others, they're indicative of the non-American nationalities of many virus writers.*

NOTE *Other common worms include Magistr and Nimda, discussed in Chapter 3; Melissa, discussed in Chapter 4; and 666test, FreeLink, Hard, KakWorm, Monopoly, and VBS/SST (AnnaKournikova), discussed in Chapter 5.*

Current Risk

The current risk of being the victim of an Internet worm is high. Badtrans, Nimda, SirCam, and other common worms are definitely in the wild, propagating like rabbits. For some users, not a day goes by that they don't receive some sort of worm via e-mail.

Put simply, the worm is the fastest-growing type of malicious code today. As this book goes to press in mid-2002, more than half the malicious programs on the current "top ten" lists are worms. There are a lot of worms out there, and each one has many variants—which makes them a major threat to all computer users, no matter how careful.

Detecting a Worm

Many worms don't inflict noticeable damage to your system, so you might not know that you've been infected. However, you can typically deduce an infection from the after-effects:

- Your system exhibits unexplained hard disk activity.

- Your system connects to or accesses the Internet of its own volition, without any interaction on your part.

- If you're running a Web server, the server shows a heavy load of external connections to port 80 on other systems.

- Your system appears to be short on available memory, even if no other programs are running.

- Friends, family, or colleagues notify you that they received an odd e-mail message from you, that you're *sure* you didn't send.

For those worms that *do* deliver a destructive payload, you'll know you're infected when the damage is done. This damage is typically in the form of deleted files, although some worms can go so far as to completely wipe out your hard disk, or render it unusable.

How to Remove a Worm

Some worms reside exclusively in memory; these worms are removed whenever you turn off your computer system. (However, if you've been infected once, you're likely to be infected again—which means simply rebooting your machine won't eliminate the risk.)

Other worms reside in new files that the worm installs to your hard disk. If you can find these files, you can delete them—and rid your system of the infection. (You may also need to find and remove specific keys in the Windows Registry, placed there by the worm code.)

> **WARNING** *If a worm file is in use by your system—that is, if the worm has current control of your computer—you may not be able to delete that file. If this is your situation, you'll need to reboot your system from a bootable floppy disk, and then delete the worm file from the DOS prompt. When you reboot your system normally (from the hard disk) after doing that, the worm file will no longer be present to infect your system.*

Given all this, the easiest way to remove a worm is with an antivirus software program. In addition, some antivirus software developers provide worm-specific fixes—programs (typically available for free download) created with the single goal of removing a particular type of worm from your computer system. If you suspect that your system has been infected by a worm, visit the Web site for the antivirus program you use, and search for a fix for the worm you think you have.

How to Protect Against Worms

Most antivirus software programs do a good job of protecting against known worms. However, because script-based worms can mutate quickly, it's essential that you update your antivirus program with new virus definitions on a regular basis—once a week, at the minimum. If you let your virus definitions get out of date, your antivirus program won't recognize the latest worm mutations—leaving your system open for infection.

It's also important that you update your Web browser and e-mail program with the latest security patches. When new worms discover ways to exploit security holes in these programs, your system is at a high risk of infection. However, you can minimize the risk by downloading and installing security patches (provided by the software developer—which means Microsoft, for most users) that fix the underlying holes.

Naturally, you can also protect yourself by not opening unsolicited e-mail attachments, and not accepting files sent to you during IRC and instant messaging sessions. You should also set the security levels on your Web browser and e-mail program high enough to stop the loading of unauthorized ActiveX controls. Chapter 11, "Preventing Virus Attacks," shows how to do this in Internet Explorer and Outlook.

Protection against a worm attack requires the cooperation of network administrators to detect and halt suspicious traffic—although antivirus programs can also be of help in this task. Network administrators can help to stop worms by filtering e-mail attachments at the gateway— the corporate network's connection to the Internet. When you're working at home or in a small business without a corporate firewall, the preventive steps outlined above and in Chapter 11 are particularly important.

Still, worms are difficult to catch—and almost impossible to kill. As long as a single copy of a worm exists in the wild, that worm is capable of propagating. To completely eradicate a worm would entail finding and deleting every existing copy of the code—which is virtually impossible. It's analogous to eradicating a biological virus; as long as a single sample exists, the virus can still potentially spread.

Summing Up

Trojan horses and worms are not technically computer viruses. Trojans infect a system by deceptive means, but don't replicate once they've been downloaded. (They can, however, deliver destructive payloads.) Worms replicate automatically, typically via e-mail, IRC, or instant message—but without explicit user action; they typically don't alter files on the host computer.

Both Trojans and worms are extremely widespread, and can cause widespread damage. Particularly dangerous are the backdoor Trojans that enable other users to access and operate your system via remote control. Like other types of Trojans and worms, most backdoor Trojans can be detected by antivirus software.

In the next chapter, we examine three popular ways of propagating Trojans, worms, and viruses—e-mail, Internet chat, and instant messaging.

CHAPTER 7

E-mail, Chat, and Instant Messaging Viruses

In the early days of personal computing, most viruses were spread by the sharing of infected floppy disks. Today, the primary means of propagation are more high-tech—most viruses are spread via e-mail, Internet Relay Chat (IRC), and instant messaging (IM).

This chapter discusses all three means of Internet-based virus distribution. While there are lots of specifics to absorb, keep one key point in mind: *don't open unrequested files!* It doesn't matter whether the file comes as an attachment to an e-mail message, or is sent to you by a chat or IM buddy. Most viruses today are spread via files sent over the Internet; any time you open a file you receive online, you're putting your system at extreme risk of infection.

Understanding E-mail Viruses

E-mail is the most-used Internet application; most of us send and receive dozens of e-mail messages every day.

Because of the near-ubiquity of e-mail, it is the medium of choice for anyone wishing to distribute malicious code. The simple fact is that the vast majority of viruses and worms today are spread via e-mail; if you want to reduce your chance of infection, you need to understand how to protect yourself from e-mail-based attacks.

The Myth of the E-mail Virus

Technically, there is no such beast as an e-mail virus. That's because there is no way for a virus to infect a plain text e-mail message. In spite of anything you've heard, there is absolutely no way you can infect your system by simply reading a plain text e-mail.

You *can*, however, infect your system by reading an HTML e-mail. HTML e-mail messages are just like HTML Web pages—and can contain embedded ActiveX controls and JavaScript applets, both of which can launch malicious code. (More on this in the next section of this chapter.) But these viruses, while they are spread via e-mail, are technically script viruses—*not* e-mail viruses. (That's why they were covered in Chapter 5.)

You can also infect your system by opening a file attached to a plain text e-mail. But you can't blame the e-mail message for the virus; the virus is in the attachment, and you have to deliberately open the attachment to become infected.

How E-mail Spreads Viruses

If there is no such thing as an e-mail virus, how is e-mail used to infect so many computers? There are three primary ways to use e-mail to spread viruses and worms: via attachments (typically using Trojan techniques, discussed in Chapter 6), by exploiting security holes (typically via so-called MIME exploits), and with embedded code in HTML messages.

Attachments

The most common way of spreading malicious code via e-mail is to attach the infected file to an e-mail message. When a user receives the message, no infection occurs unless the attached file is opened. When the file is opened, however, the virus executes and delivers its payload—which typically involves hijacking your e-mail program to mail additional copies of itself to other users.

If you don't open the attachment, your system remains clean. An attacker, then, needs to somehow trick you into opening the attached file. There are many ways to do this, all of which fall under the heading of a Trojan horse attack and were discussed in the last chapter. The virus may send the message from a "friendly" source—by hijacking a friend or colleague's e-mail program, and sending the message under their name. The virus may use the double-extension trick to make you think that an EXE or PIF file is actually a TXT or JPG file. The virus may entice you by promising something interesting or useful when you open the file—a picture of a naked young female tennis star, or even an antivirus utility.

In any case, the virus is totally harmless unless and until you open the attached file. If you simply delete the message (and its attachment), no harm is done to your system.

MIME Exploits

When a file is attached to an e-mail message, it uses an Internet standard called Multipurpose Internet Mail Extensions, or MIME. This specifies how binary files are encoded, so that any e-mail program can correctly interpret the file type.

A well-known flaw in older versions of Microsoft's Internet Explorer enables files of certain MIME types to be opened automatically. A virus writer can exploit this flaw by creating an HTML e-mail with an executable attachment, disguising the attachment as one of the problem MIME types. When the HTML e-mail is displayed, the attached file opens automatically—and then executes the embedded virus code.

> **NOTE** *Internet Explorer is used to render HTML e-mails in both Microsoft Outlook and Outlook Express.*

This type of attack—called a *MIME exploit*—requires the attacker to modify the MIME header information in the attached file. Internet Explorer reads the fake MIME header, identifies the attachment as one that should be opened automatically, and then does so.

Microsoft has since fixed this flaw, essentially correcting the table of MIME types used within Internet Explorer. If you're running Internet Explorer version 5 or 5.5, you can download the patch from the Microsoft Web site. Later versions of IE have the fix built-in.

NOTE *Chapter 11, "Preventing Virus Attacks," shows how to download the Microsoft patches to Internet Explorer.*

Embedded Code

Even more insidious than viruses that exploit Microsoft's MIME header vulnerability are those that embed JavaScript code in HTML e-mail messages. The JavaScript code runs automatically when the message is viewed; no attachment has to be opened by the user. This enables virus code to be launched without any human intervention.

Fortunately, embedded-code viruses are very rare, probably because they're so difficult to implement. (It's much easier just to attach a virus file to an e-mail message.)

Plain Text vs. HTML E-mail

In the early days of the Internet, all e-mail was plain text—there was no boldfacing or color or embedded URLs. That remains true today; by default, many e-mail programs create plain text messages. And, when it comes to viruses, plain text is good; you can't embed a virus in plain text.

To refresh your memory, here's an example of a plain-text e-mail message:

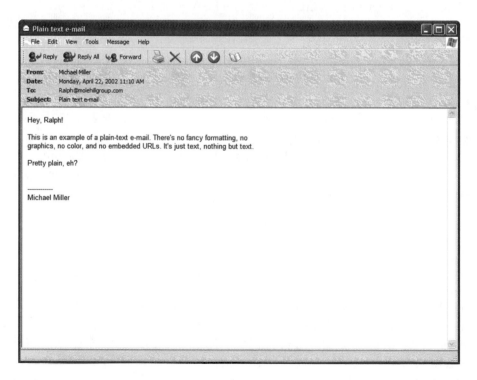

Continued on next page

Plain Text vs. HTML E-mail *(Continued)*

Newer e-mail programs let you send not only plain-text messages, but also messages that incorporate HTML code. These messages look more like Web pages and can include boldface and italic text, color, graphics, and embedded Web page links. Here's what an HTML e-mail message can look like:

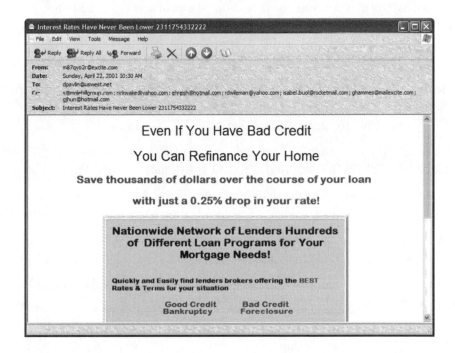

(As you can see, HTML e-mail is ideal for sending out spam advertisements, as you'll learn about in Chapter 27, "Understanding Spam.")

The problem with HTML e-mail, from a virus standpoint, is that—like any HTML page—it can include embedded script viruses. For that reason, plain-text e-mail is the safer format.

Common Viruses Spread via E-mail

There are many types of viruses and worms that use e-mail as their primary means of propagation. The following malicious programs, discussed in more detail earlier in this book, are commonly spread via e-mail.

666test   A worm spread via traditional e-mail messages. You must manually open the attached VBS file to enable the infection.

Babylonia   A virus spread via traditional e-mail messages. A Windows Help file is attached to an e-mail message; when the Help file is opened, the infection occurs.

Badtrans   A Trojan worm spread via traditional e-mail messages. You must manually open the attached file (a PIF or SCR disguised as a DOC, MP3, TXT, or ZIP file) to enable the infection. (Note: Some variants of this virus exploit the Microsoft fake MIME header vulnerability to open the attached file automatically.)

BubbleBoy   A self-executing worm spread via HTML e-mail messages. It exploits the Microsoft fake MIME header vulnerability to force an e-mail program to automatically open the file attached to an e-mail message.

FreeLink   A Trojan worm spread via traditional e-mail messages. You must manually open the attached file (a VBS file disguised as free links to adult Web sites) to enable the infection.

Hard   A Trojan worm spread via traditional e-mail messages. You must manually open the attached file (a VBS file disguised as a warning about a new virus) to enable the infection.

Hybris   A Trojan worm spread via traditional e-mail messages. You must manually open the attached EXE or SCR file to enable the infection.

KakWorm   A self-executing worm spread via JavaScript code embedded in HTML e-mail messages. The virus launches automatically when the infected e-mail message is displayed.

Klez   A self-executing worm that exploits the Microsoft fake MIME header vulnerability to open the attached file automatically.

Links   A worm spread via traditional e-mail messages. You must manually open the attached file to enable the infection.

LoveLetter   A Trojan worm spread via traditional e-mail messages. You must manually open the attached file (a VBS file disguised as a text file) to enable the infection.

Melissa   A Trojan worm spread via traditional e-mail messages. You must manually open the attached Word document to enable the infection.

Monopoly   A Trojan worm spread via traditional e-mail messages. You must manually open the attached file (a VBS file disguised as proof of Bill Gates' monopolistic tendencies) to enable the infection.

MyLife   A Trojan worm spread via traditional e-mail messages. You must manually open the attached file (a SCR file disguised as a caricature of former President Bill Clinton) to enable the infection.

Naked Wife   A Trojan worm spread via traditional e-mail messages. You must manually open the attached file (an EXE file disguised as a naked picture of someone's wife) to enable the infection.

Nimda   A worm that uses multiple methods of propagation. Some versions of this worm spread via traditional e-mail; you must manually open the attached EXE file to enable the infection. Other variants exploit the Microsoft fake MIME header vulnerability to open the attached file automatically.

SirCam   A Trojan worm spread via traditional e-mail messages. You must manually open the attached file to enable the infection.

VBS/SST   Also known as AnnaKournikova; a Trojan worm spread via traditional e-mail messages. You must manually open the attached file (a VBS file disguised as a JPG of tennis star Anna Kournikova) to enable the infection.

Current Risk

Since e-mail is the primary means of virus distribution today, your risk of receiving malicious code via e-mail is high. Your chance of actual infection, however, varies according to the degree of preventive measures you employ.

If you never open any e-mail attachments and disable the preview pane in your e-mail program, your risk of infection is low to nil. If you enable the preview pane but don't open attachments, your risk is slightly higher, but still low. If, however, you unthinkingly open any and all files attached to the e-mail messages you receive, your risk of infection is high.

How to Protect Against Infection via E-mail

The most effective protection against e-mail-based infection is quite simple: *don't open file attachments*—even if they come from known sources. This warning is especially true if the file was unrequested, and if it has an EXE, COM, PIF, SCR, VBS, or other executable extension.

This means you need to carefully examine every attached file you receive. You should enable the display of file extensions in Windows, and then look at the extension of each file you receive. Don't be fooled by the old double-extension trick; `myfile.txt.exe` is an executable file, *not* a text file. Also, make sure that the entire filename is visible; multiple spaces in the filename can push the real extension off the side of the screen.

If you want to be doubly safe, turn off the preview pane in your e-mail program. Since there are some viruses that can launch on viewing (no attachments need to be opened), not viewing—or even *previewing*—messages is the safest possible route to take. (It's also extremely inconvenient, but that's a risk-versus-rewards analysis you need to make for yourself.)

Of course, you should also employ one of the major antivirus programs. Most antivirus programs can be configured to scan all incoming e-mail messages for viruses and worms. These programs will examine any HTML code in the message body, as well as all attachments. If an infected message or attachment is detected, you'll be prompted how to dispose of the infection. (In some cases, an infected message can be salvaged; in others, the message is deleted before it's downloaded to your inbox.)

In addition, most e-mail programs have some degree of built-in antivirus protection. We'll look at the antivirus features of the three most popular e-mail programs (Microsoft Outlook, Outlook Express, and Eudora), as well as measures that corporations can take to protect network users from e-mail-borne infection.

Virus Protection in Microsoft Outlook

Surprisingly, Microsoft Outlook—the e-mail client used in most major corporations—doesn't have the most robust antivirus features. The primary means of protection is the use of Web content zones to prevent downloading of certain types of HTML e-mail.

You configure Outlook's security settings by following these steps:

1. Select Tools ➤ Options.

2. When the Options dialog box appears, select the Security tab (shown in Figure 7.1).

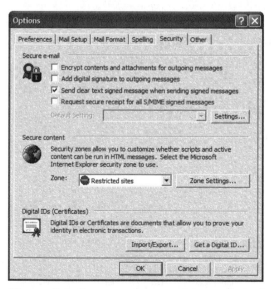

Figure 7.1 *Security options in Microsoft Outlook*

3. In the Secure Content section, pull down the Zone list and select Restricted Sites.

4. Click OK.

This setting does the following:

- Disables the downloading of all ActiveX controls

- Disables the automatic downloading of all files

- Disables all scripting

- Disables the scripting of all Java applets

You can selectively enable any of these options (and more) by clicking the Zone Settings button in the Options dialog box, and then clicking Custom Level; this displays the Security Settings dialog box, shown in Figure 7.2. From here, you can check the options you want to enable, and uncheck those you want to disable.

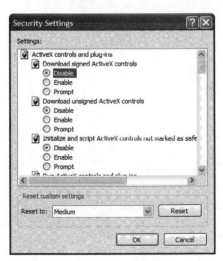

Figure 7.2 *Changing security settings for Microsoft Outlook*

For extra safety, you can also disable Outlook's Preview pane. To do this, pull down the View menu and deselect the Preview Pane option. With the Preview pane hidden, all you'll see are message headers; any self-executing viruses you receive will not be able to run.

Virus Protection in Outlook Express

The Windows XP version of Outlook Express actually has more security features than its "big brother" program, Microsoft Outlook. You access these features by following these steps:

1. Select Tools ➤ Options.

2. When the Options dialog box appears, select the Security tab (shown in Figure 7.3).

Figure 7.3 *Configuring security options in Outlook Express*

3. To enable the highest level of protection when viewing HTML messages, check the Restricted Sites Zone option.

4. To prevent auto-replicating worms from hijacking your e-mail program, check the Warn Me When Other Applications Try To Send Mail As Me option.

5. To block the receipt of executable files attached to e-mail messages, check the Do Not Allow Attachments To Be Saved Or Opened That Could Potentially Be A Virus option.

6. Click OK.

You can also configure Outlook Express to hide the Preview pane. Follow these steps:

1. Select View ➤ Layout.

2. When the Layout dialog box appears (shown in Figure 7.4), uncheck the Show Preview Pane option.

3. Click OK.

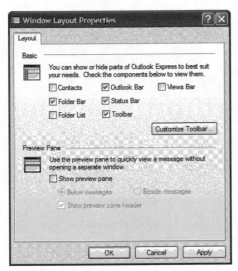

Figure 7.4 *Disabling the Preview pane in Outlook Express*

Virus Protection in Eudora

If you want to reduce your risk of infection via e-mail, consider switching programs. Most e-mail-borne viruses target users of Microsoft Outlook and Outlook Express—because so many people use these programs. Few, if any viruses, target less-used programs, such as Eudora. You can reduce your chances of being infected simply by moving out of the attackers' crosshairs.

In addition to not being actively targeted by virus writers, Eudora has several antivirus measures built into the latest version of the program. One of the most effective is the warning messages (such as the one in Figure 7.5) that pop up when you try to open file attachments with the EXE, COM, BAT, LNK, and VBS extensions. This makes you think twice before you open a potentially virus-infected file.

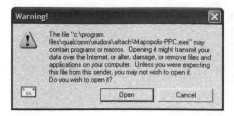

Figure 7.5 *Eudora warns you that you might be opening a virus file.*

You can further protect yourself by disabling Eudora's preview pane and the automatic open-ing of messages. Just follow these steps:

1. Select Tools ➤ Options.

2. When the Options dialog box appears, select Viewing Mail (shown in Figure 7.6).

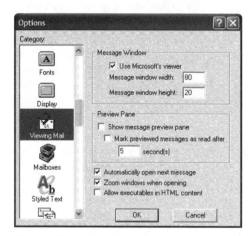

Figure 7.6 *Disabling the Preview pane and automatic message opening in Eudora*

3. Uncheck the following options: Show Message Preview Pane, Automatically Open Next Message, and Allow Executables in HTML Content.

4. Click OK.

Protecting Corporate Networks

Corporate networks can protect against e-mail infection by installing an e-mail gateway to pro-vide a barrier between the Internet and the company's internal e-mail servers. These gateways can be configured to automatically scan all attachments (even the contents of zipped files) and block selected file types, such as EXE, VBS, and other executable files.

WARNING *The only problem with e-mail filters is that they're not perfect—they sometimes block valid e-mail along with any potential viruses. (A similar problem exists with spam-blocking software and services, as discussed in Chapter 28, "Dealing With Spam.")*

The more popular network e-mail gateways include the following:

- Interscan VirusWall (`www.datatel-systems.com/virus.htm`)
- MailMonitor (`www.nwtechusa.com/mailmonitor.html`)
- MailScanner (`www.sng.ecs.soton.ac.uk/mailscanner/`)
- MAILsweeper for SMTP (`www.mimesweeper.com/products/mailsweepersmtp/`)
- Symantec AntiVirus Enterprise Edition (`enterprisesecurity.symantec.com/products/`)
- WebShield SMTP (`www.mcafeeb2b.com/products/webshield-smtp/`)

There are also third-party services that enable companies to outsource the virus scanning process. These services include Activis (`www.activis.com`), MessageLabs (`www.messagelabs.com`), and The Electric Mail Company (`www.electricmail.com`).

Understanding IRC Viruses

Internet Relay Chat (IRC) is a separate Internet network that enables users to "chat" with each other via real-time text messages. You use IRC programs ("clients") such as mIRC and Pirch to connect to a network of chat servers; group conversations take place in public chat channels.

One feature of IRC is the ability to engage in private conversations, via a type of one-on-one connection. This feature also enables users to transfer files back and forth; it's this last feature that enables the spreading of viruses and worms.

NOTE *The IRC protocol that enables file transmission and one-on-one chats is called the Direct Client-to-Client protocol, or DCC. DCC in itself isn't dangerous, although enabling the automatic acceptance of all sent files (via the Auto-DCC-Get feature) is dangerous; you should never blindly accept all files sent by other users.*

How IRC Viruses Work

There are two related methods for spreading viruses across IRC networks. The first is simply sending a file from one user to another, typically via Trojan techniques. In this approach, a user sends you a file, typically under the guise of it being a useful utility, picture, game, or other harmless file. You can choose to reject or accept the file; when you accept the file, you download the virus code to your hard disk. You're still safe, however, until you open the file. That's when the virus code launches.

The second method of IRC-based infection uses something called an IRC script. An IRC script is like any type of computer script; it's a type of batch file that contains a series of simple instructions, executed line-by-line. Script files are used to automatically send worm files to all members of a given chat channel. The worm file, when accepted by a user, substitutes itself for a similarly named file on the user's computer and then begins its own worm attack.

The files that contain the worm are typically named either `script.ini` or `mirc.ini`. Both of these files are script files that automatically execute a series of commands.

The most common type of infection occurs when the worm places its own `script.ini` file in the parent mIRC folder. All script files located in this folder are automatically executed, so the worm goes to work as soon as it's installed.

Installation can occur automatically if you've enabled an mIRC feature called Auto-DCC-Get. When enabled, Auto-DCC-Get tells mIRC to automatically accept all files that are sent from other users. Obviously, this is *not* a feature that you want to enable, as it allows virus and worm files to be copied to your hard disk without your notice or approval.

Fortunately, some IRC worms exist simply to spread; unfortunately, others contain a destructive payload. IRC is especially capable of spreading the kinds of backdoor Trojans discussed in Chapter 6. These programs, such as Back Orifice and NetBus, enable other users to take control of your computer and operate it via remote control—thus enabling the attacker to destroy files and access your personal data, including passwords and credit card numbers.

Common IRC Viruses

If you're an active IRC user, you should be on the lookout for any or all of the following IRC-borne viruses and worms:

Acoragil   Along with Simpsalapim, discussed later in this section, Acoragil was one of the first two IRC worms. When a user with an infected system enters the word **acoragil** during a chat session, all other infected users are automatically expelled from the chat channel. Other "code words" (such as **hi**, **cya**, and **the**) are used to trigger the sending of system files to specific IRC users. This worm is spread via the `/dcc send` command, which sends infected scripts to all users in the current chat channel.

Back Orifice   As you learned in Chapter 6, Back Orifice is a powerful backdoor Trojan, distributed via both e-mail and IRC. In IRC channels, the Back Orifice files are typically sent to users disguised as some other file.

Bat   This Trojan worm distributes itself as a BAT file masquerading as a JPG file. Once executed, it creates a bogus `script.ini` file and sends itself to other IRC user. It also attempts to create a backdoor that attackers can use to access your system via remote control.

Dmsetup   Also known as Dmsetup.Viagra, this worm uses mIRC to propagate across the IRC network. It is typically distributed as an EXE file (sometimes disguised as a JPG file), under a variety of filenames. When run, Dmsetup opens a DOS window and prompts the user to `Press any key`. When a key is pressed, colorful ovals are displayed until another key is pressed. Then the worm displays the message

```
START UP ERROR: Can not find vital data! Attempting safe close down
(This may take several minutes)
```

After a few moments, a second message is displayed:

```
100% Done! Safe recovery successful!
```

The worm copies both the `script.ini` and `mirc.ini` files to the new file `bakupwrks.ini`. It also adds a line to the `autoexec.bat` file to launch the worm whenever the host computer is turned on. When active, it changes the mIRC title bar to read `your mirc is buggy`.

Flood   This IRC Trojan is used to initiate denial-of-service attacks on other users. You can tell that this file is present when your system manually prompts you to locate the file `c:\windows\system\mirc.hlp`.

NOTE *Learn more about denial-of-service attacks in Chapter 14, "Different Types of Attacks."*

Fono   This memory-resident virus spreads via IRC and infects Windows files. The virus writes itself to the end of the `mirc.ini` file; these instructions disable mIRC security settings and enable the virus to create new `script.ini` and `inca.exe` files, both of which are used to send the virus to other IRC users.

Goner   This worm, also known as Gone and Pentagone, infects both IRC and ICQ users. Goner propagates via a screensaver file named `gone.scr`. It uses the mIRC program to install a backdoor Trojan named `remote32.ini`, which can be used to initiate denial-of-service attacks on IRC channels.

Links   This Trojan worm sends itself to all the members of your current chat channel. It also propagates as an attachment to e-mail messages.

Millennium   This worm spreads via bogus `script.ini` files, and then sends itself to other IRC users. When executed, Millennium installs a variant of the Back Door Trojan, which can be used to remote control your system.

NetBus   NetBus is a backdoor Trojan, similar to Back Orifice. It is distributed on IRC channels disguised as some other type of file.

pIRCH.Events   This is a worm specific to the Pirch IRC program. It sends itself to every user who joins an infected chat channel. Infected systems exhibit changes to standard text and commands; for example, entering **query** reports infected systems to a "caller" program, and entering **exit** kicks the infected user from the channel. Other keywords are used to trigger more destructive events, such as deleting all data on the infected system's hard disk.

Script.ini   This worm sends a bogus `script.ini` file to other users who join the chat channel that you're currently in. The `script.ini` file is an mIRC script filled with commands that allow other users to watch your IRC conversations, control your IRC session, and even disrupt your session.

Sheep   Also known as Dolly or Dolly_The_Sheep, this is a worm that automatically sends itself to other users in your IRC chat channel.

Simpsalapim   This worm is similar to the Acoragil worm. When an infected user enters the code-word **simpsalapim** during a chat session, all other infected users are automatically expelled from the current chat channel. In addition, if you enter the code-word **ananas**, your operator rights are hijacked and granted to the attacker. The worm uses the IRC `/dcc send` command to send the infected script to all users in the current chat channel.

Stages   Also known as Life Stages, this VBS worm appears as a file named `LIFE_STAGES.TXT.SHS`. (This worm is also distributed via e-mail, typically with the subject `Funny`, `Jokes`, or `Life Stages`.) Opening this file causes Windows Notepad to open and display a text file full of jokes about the male and female stages of life. While users are distracted by this file, another script is executing in the background. This particular worm spreads via both mIRC and Pirch programs, as well as via the ICQ instant messaging network.

Winhelper   This malicious program creates or modifies the `mirc.ini` and `win.ini` files on infected systems.

Current Risk

Your risk of contracting an IRC virus is low *if* you don't accept files sent to you by other users. If you accept an unknown file—and especially if you enable the Auto-DCC-Get feature—your risk of receiving an infected file is high.

Detecting an IRC Virus

IRC viruses and worms are typically detected by their aftermath. For example, if other users message you to tell you that they've been receiving unsolicited files from you, then it's a good bet that your system is infected.

In addition, most antivirus programs can detect the most common IRC malware. You can use your antivirus program to scan for existing infections, as well as to scan all files you receive during the course of an IRC session.

How to Remove an IRC Virus

Most IRC viruses and worms can be removed by antivirus software. In addition, those IRC worms that utilize the **script.ini** file can be removed by deleting that file.

If you know you've been infected with the Script.ini worm, you can disable (but not remove) the worm by entering the **/events off** command. This will keep the worm from sending itself to other users during your current session. To fully delete this particular worm, you have to exit mIRC and then search for the **script.ini** file on your hard drive (typically in the mIRC program folder). When you find the file, *delete it*.

Help for IRC Viruses—Online

The IRC community provides a raft of resources for detecting, removing, and protecting your system from IRC-borne viruses. These resources include:

- The **#virushelp** IRC channel
- The **#vigilantes** IRC channel
- The **#hackfix** IRC channel
- The #VirusHelp Web page (**www.fruitloop.net/virushelp/**)
- The #Virusfix Web page (**www.geocities.com/TimesSquare/Alley/2794/**)
- The Hackfix Web page (**split.netset.com/hackfix/**)
- The IRC Security page at the IRC Help Web site (**www.irchelp.org/irchelp/security/**)

How to Protect Against IRC Viruses

The best protection against viruses and worms sent via IRC is to decline any files sent you by other users. The safest way to ensure this behavior is to configure your IRC program not to accept any files sent.

In mIRC, you configure the program by following these steps:

1. Select DCC ➤ Options.

2. When the Options dialog box appears, select DCC in the Category list (shown in Figure 7.7).

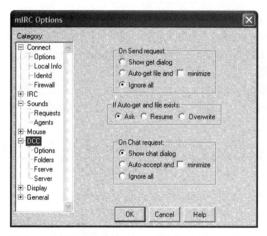

Figure 7.7 *Configuring mIRC not to automatically accept sent files*

3. In the On Send Request section, check the Ignore All option.

4. In the If Auto-Get And File Exists section, check the Ask option.

5. Click OK.

This disables the Auto-DCC-Get feature and makes it impossible for any virus or worm files to be copied to your system. You will, however, need to manually enable file reception if you *want* to receive a file—one from a known source, presumably.

Social Engineering and Chat Attacks

Most virus and worm attacks that take place on IRC and instant messaging networks (and via e-mail) do so by exploiting gullible users. They trick users into explicitly accepting malicious files by techniques that experts call *social engineering*.

Social engineering is a fancy name for deceit. For the virus to spread, the attacker has to convince you to do something you know you shouldn't do—download and open an unknown file.

The most common forms of social engineering prey on human weakness. For example, the attacker might disguise an infected file as an antivirus utility, or a digital music file, or even a piece of pornography. People are trusting and curious creatures, and find the promise of these files tempting. They should know better, but they open the files anyway.

Social engineering can also be used to gather user name and password information from unsuspecting users. Have you ever been messaged by someone purporting to be an employee of your Internet service provider? (This is a common tactic on America Online.) They tell you that there's some problem with your account, and you need to give them your username and password—or in extreme cases, your credit card number. If you fall for this trick, you've just provided the means for an attacker to log onto the Internet under your name—to send and receive e-mails, and to access all variety of Web sites, disguised as you.

Here's a variation on that approach, used to spread worms across the IRC network. You're contacted by another user, or by someone who purports to be a channel manager, who sends you the following message:

```
You are infected with a virus that lets hackers get into ur machine and
read ur files, etc. I suggest you to download <url> and clean ur
infected machine. Otherwise you will be banned from the IRC network.
```

If you go to that URL, you'll be prompted to download a file—a file that just happens to contain an IRC worm, virus, or backdoor Trojan.

The lesson here is that there are people on the Internet who are intent on causing mischief, and they're very inventive in how they go about it. Not that you should be paranoid about it, but you shouldn't automatically trust everyone you encounter online. Some of these people *are* out to get you. (You'll learn more about social engineering in Chapter 14.)

Understanding Instant Messaging Viruses

IRC viruses have been in the wild for some time, now, but they haven't received a lot of attention. That's because relatively few Internet users use IRC. Instead, most online chatters—90 million of them, by the end of 2001—use one of several popular instant messaging (IM) programs. These programs enable one-on-one messaging between users, and are a lot easier to use than the sometimes-obtuse IRC clients.

> **NOTE** *The most popular instant messaging programs/networks are AOL Instant Messenger (AIM), MSN Messenger and Windows Messenger (sharing the same network), ICQ, and Yahoo! Messenger.*

It was only a matter of time, then, before viruses entered the world of instant messaging. Though still relatively rare, IM viruses are here, and they're ready to spread.

How Instant Messaging Spreads Viruses

Instant messaging is used to distribute viruses and worms much the same way e-mail is used for the same purpose. Malicious files are attached to instant messages and sent across the IM network to other users. Users have to explicitly accept the infected file, and then deliberately run the file, for the virus to infect their systems. At present, there is no known method for a virus or worm to automatically execute without this user interaction.

IM viruses are typically specific to a single IM network. So if a virus is designed to work on the MSN Messenger network, it won't be found on the AIM or ICQ networks. This network-specificity may play a part in the relatively slow growth of IM viruses to date.

Common Instant Messaging Viruses

Fortunately, there aren't a lot of IM viruses out in the wild—yet. Here's a short list of those IM viruses that have been discovered to date.

Choke   This worm infects MSN Messenger users. It sends messages (sometimes from the alias `george.w.bush@whitehouse.gov`) to users, floods their screens with smiley-face icons, and attempts to get them to accept a file named `choke.exe`, `ShootPresidentBUSH.exe`, `Hotmail.exe`, or `<yourfirstname>.exe`. The message accompanying the file is

    President bush shooter is game that allows you to shoot Bush balzz hahaha

If you accept and run the file, the worm displays a message box (titled `Choke`) which displays the message

    This program needs Flash 6.5 to Run!

Clicking OK in the message box displays additional messages and sends the worm to other Messenger users.

Goner   This worm, also known as Gone and Pentagone, infects ICQ users. (It also spreads via IRC and Trojan e-mail.) Goner propagates via a screensaver file named `gone.scr`. When run, the worm displays an "about" message box, and then generates the following error message:

```
Error While Analyze DirectX!
```

The worm looks for folders on your hard disk associated with antivirus, firewall, and other security programs, and attempts to delete them. It also places a backdoor Trojan named `remote32.ini` on your system, which contains commands to initiate denial-of-service attacks on other users.

Hello   The Hello virus (also called W32/Hello) infects MSN Messenger users. The virus arrives as a file named `Hello.exe`. If you download and run this file, it sends copies of itself (accompanying the message `I have a file for u. its real funny`) to all the members of your Messenger contact list.

Reeezak   The Reeezak worm, also known as Maldal and Zacker, infects MSN Messenger users. (It also spreads via Trojan e-mail.) It purports to be a Macromedia Flash holiday greeting, masquerading as the file `christmas.exe`. When executed, the worm sends itself to all your contacts, disables your antivirus software, and disables selected keys on your keyboard.

Stages   As discussed in the "Common IRC Viruses" section, this worm (AKA Life Stages) infects both IRC and ICQ networks. It is propagated via a file attachment named `LIFE_STAGES.TXT.SHS`.

Current Risk

Currently, the risk of virus infection over an instant messaging network is minimal—but growing. If you're a frequent IM user, you should familiarize yourself with existing IM viruses, and keep up-to-date on IM-related virus news.

Detecting an Instant Messaging Virus

IM viruses are typically visible only by their exploits. For example, if other users message you and question why you're sending them files, you probably have an infection (especially if this behavior comes shortly after you've accepted a file from another user).

How to Remove an Instant Messaging Virus

Removing an IM virus or worm is just like removing any virus or worm. Use your antivirus program to locate and disinfect (if possible) all infected files, or manually delete those infected files that have been placed on your system.

How to Protect Against Instant Messaging Viruses

Most antivirus programs will scan the files you download via your instant messaging software. The best defense, however, is simply not to accept any unrequested files sent to you via instant messaging. If you don't download and open a file, it can't infect your system. It's that simple.

Fortunately, most IM networks include their own security systems. AOL, for example, goes to great extremes to secure its AIM network, as well as its proprietary e-mail system. ("Both systems have security measures built into them," confirmed an AOL spokesperson in a recent interview.)

Summing Up

E-mail, IRC, and instant messaging are all used to spread computer viruses and worms. E-mail is the most popular means of propagation, typically via a file attached to a deceptive message. If you open the attached file, you execute the malicious code.

Likewise, instant messaging programs can be used to send infected files to other users. On the IRC network, script files can be employed to automatically infect other users of a chat channel with viruses and worms.

The best protection against malicious software spread via these methods is not to accept or open any files you receive. If you don't download and run the file, you can't be infected.

In the next chapter I'll talk about those viruses that aren't really viruses—the wide, wide world of virus hoaxes.

CHAPTER 8

Virus Hoaxes

Computer users are a helpful bunch. It's not uncommon to open your e-mail and find a message from a friend or colleague, warning you about some newly discovered computer virus that threatens to wreak havoc on computer users worldwide. You read the message, note the precautions you're supposed to take, and take a minute to thank the sender for passing on this warning.

The only problem is, the virus you were warned about doesn't really exist.

Almost as big as the problem caused by real computer viruses is the problem of virus hoaxes—fake warnings that needlessly clog network bandwidth, unnecessarily frighten millions of users, and grab unwarranted headlines around the world. Even worse, some of these hoaxes advise you that you've *already* been infected, and that you should delete certain files on your hard drive. Follow that advice, and you do real damage to your own system—and have no one but yourself to blame.

How a Virus Hoax Works

A virus hoax is a simple thing. It's a phony warning, typically delivered via e-mail, about a non-existent computer virus. The sender of the warning—actually, the *resender*—is typically earnest in intent; he or she was sent the same warning, believed it, and wanted to warn you (and others) about the pending danger.

It's the original author of the warning who's the prankster here. And the way these things work, that person is so far removed that they can't be traced.

Virus hoaxes are like chain letters—they spread far and fast, against all common sense. It's much too easy to click the Forward button in your e-mail program and send the phony message to an additional set of users; that's how these messages proliferate.

> **NOTE** *Virus hoaxes are closely related to other Internet-based hoaxes, chain letters, and urban legends—which, these days, are often spread via e-mail. To learn more, turn to Chapter 29, "Dealing with Other Unwanted E-mails."*

The hoax is perpetrated when an unsuspecting user receives the fake warning, in an e-mail message. Instead of deleting the message, the recipient believes the warning and—trying to be helpful—forwards the message to friends, family, and colleagues. Some or all of these recipients also believe the message, and forward it along to additional users—who forward it to even more people. Before long, the hoax has spread to literally millions of computer users, all around the world.

For a virus hoax to be propagated, it must convince you of its authenticity. To that end, most successful hoaxes have two things in common: technical-sounding language, and some sort of credibility-by-association. The more technical the language, the more a message impresses many nontechnical readers. (If it's really technical-sounding, it must be true!) The same goes for the source of the message; you might not believe a hoax if it came from the janitor at your local super-market, but if it's from someone with a big title who works at an official-sounding company or organization, the message suddenly becomes more reliable. (It doesn't matter whether the individual, title, or organization is real or not—it just needs to *sound* real.)

So if you believe the warning is real, you pass it along. *That's* how hoaxes are spread.

Fortunately, most virus hoaxes are only warnings—they don't deliver any actual damage to your computer system. Some recent hoaxes, however, don't warn of a possible infection—they claim that your system is *already* infected, and that you have to take steps to remove the virus. These steps typically involve searching for and removing specific files from your hard disk. Naturally, these are real files—Windows system files, typically—that shouldn't be deleted. If you follow the instructions in the hoax message, you run the risk of damaging your operating system, and affecting the operation of your computer.

WARNING *Some virus hoaxes actually have a real virus component. In most cases, this occurs when an individual takes an existing hoax and attaches a virus-infected file to the hoax message—masquerading as a TXT file or a utility to remove the hoax virus. When you open the attached file, your system actually becomes infected.*

The Real Cost of Virus Hoaxes

The most obvious result of a virus hoax is unnecessary panic. Panic not only leads to physical stress; it sometimes causes users to do stupid things, like deleting perfectly good (and eminently useful) files from their hard disks.

"I have a virus!" they say, after reading a hoax e-mail. "I have to delete these files to remove the virus!"

And so they do.

The files that users most often remove as a result of virus hoaxes are files that shouldn't be deleted—Windows system files, typically. When these files are deleted, the user's computer doesn't work right anymore. It's almost as if they've been hit with a virus, but without actually being infected.

Recovery from accidental file deletion can be easy, or it can be extremely difficult.

It's easy if you haven't emptied the Windows Recycle Bin; you can "undelete" a recently deleted file by following these steps:

1. Double-click the Recycle Bin icon.

2. When the Recycle Bin window opens, select the file(s) you want to undelete.

3. Select Restore the Selected Items from the Recycle Bin Tasks pane. (Alternately, you can right-click the selected items and select Restore from the pop-up menu.)

If the files you deleted no longer exist in the Recycle Bin—maybe you've emptied the Bin, or it's been so long that the files have been permanently deleted—then you have a bit more work ahead of you. In essence, what you have to do now is restore the deleted files from your Windows installation CD. In many cases, the only way to do this is to reinstall Windows on your system. This isn't necessarily a difficult thing to do, but it is extremely time-consuming.

Even if you experience no actual damage from a virus hoax, society's costs of dealing with the hoax add up—fast. Just reading and then deleting the hoax e-mail takes time, and time is money. Let's say that it takes 60 seconds to read the hoax message and then click the Delete button. Let's also say that this same hoax message eventually was mailed to 10 million people. Then let's assume that your time (everyone's time, actually) is worth $20 an hour.

When you do the math, the costs add up as follows:

10,000,000 (people) × 1/60 hour × $20/hour = $3.33 million

That's a huge cost—just to ignore a hoax.

NOTE *You might question the 10 million number. It's a guess, of course, but it's reasonable once you consider how fast these types of messages can spread. If you receive a message and then forward it to 10 people, each of whom forwards it to another 10 people, who forward it to another 10 people, and so on, it only takes seven generations to hit the 10 million mark.*

Common Virus Hoaxes

The first online virus hoax was sighted in 1988, before Internet use became widespread. This particular hoax circulated over commercial bulletin board systems (BBSs), under the e-mail subject line `Really Nasty Virus`, and announced a virus that could reconfigure the user's modem settings and infect the host computer's hard disk.

The virus hoaxes circulating today aren't all that different from that pioneering hoax. Most hoaxes warn against some new computer virus ("the worst ever!") and urge you to forward the warning message to all your e-mail contacts. The details may vary, but the general thrust of each hoax is surprisingly similar.

Judge for yourself; here's a short list of some of the most widespread virus hoaxes:

Blue Mountain Cards   This hoax dates back to 1999. It warns that e-mail greeting cards from Blue Mountain Arts contain a virus, and should not be viewed on your computer. There is no truth to this warning, of course; e-mail greeting cards from all major Web sites are demonstrably safe to view.

Good Times   Dating from December of 1994 (and still circulating today), Good Times was probably the first virus hoax to hit the Internet on a widespread basis. The original version of the hoax message warned about a virus on America Online, named Good Times, that would erase your hard drive. (Subsequent versions of the hoax claim that "no program needs to be exchanged for a new computer to be infected.") In the almost eight years since the Good Times hoax's inception, there have been no verified sightings of any virus with this name—even though the hoax itself continues to mutate and propagate.

Help   This hoax, which arrives in a message from "Dept. IS," purports to inform you about a virus named Help. According to the hoax message, if you receive an e-mail with `Help` as the subject, you should neither open or pass your mouse over the message, because the virus will automatically activate and erase your hard disk and BIOS. You're instructed to wait 48 hours after the virus has arrived to delete it. Naturally, there is no such virus—nor any virus that can't be deleted for two days.

It Takes Guts to Say "Jesus"   This hoax warns you that your computer will die if you read an e-mail with the subject `It takes guts to say "Jesus"`. It's probable that this hoax is a response to a common chain letter circulating with the `It takes guts to say "Jesus"` subject line; if you think the chain letter contains a virus, you'll be less likely to open it and pass it on.

MusicPanel (MP3)   This hoax circulates as a bogus "press release" warning of an "imbedded hybrid virus" named MusicPanel. This virus supposedly is spread by downloading unauthorized songs from Napster, Gnutella, and other file-swapping networks; on July 4th, anyone who has downloaded any of 500 popular songs "will find their illicit music unusable and their computers frozen due to the timed release of this bomb." Not to worry; there is no such virus, and your downloaded MP3 files won't suddenly become unlistenable on Independence Day.

New Pictures of Family   This virus hoax comes in a message warning against opening an e-mail attachment named `NEW PICTURES OF FAMILY` or `FAMILY PICTURES`. The virus will purportedly delete all DLL files from your computer, keeping it from booting up. As with all other hoaxes, there is no virus by this name or description.

New Ice Age   This hoax virus warning opens with a plea to

`PLEASE SEND THIS TO EVERYONE YOU KNOW AND TELL EVERYONE YOU KNOW!!!`

The warning supposedly comes from an outfit by the name of "Digital Technologies Programming Software Development Laboratories," and concerns a virus named The New Ice Age (NIA) that was stolen from their labs by "an unknown group of terrorists." This NIA virus can purportedly attach itself to any file or e-mail, "infect your computer's hard drive and backup," and "render your computer powerless in a matter of minutes." You're invited to click a link to a Web site (`www.dtpmucis.com/tnia/`) to obtain more information; the site actually exists, but it's a phony—just like the warning. There is no NIA virus, which makes this nothing more than an elaborate deception.

Pretty Park   This hoax has a grain of truth to it. To start with, there is a virus named Pretty Park, which can delete data on your hard disk, open a backdoor to system attackers, and e-mail itself to all the contacts in your Address Book. The Pretty Park message circulating on the Internet, however, overstates the dangers of the Pretty Park virus, and includes other prank information. The message starts with a warning not to open the `Pretty Park` file, because it "will erase your whole 'C' drive." (This isn't true; Pretty Park doesn't delete entire drives.) You're then exhorted to forward the warning message to "everyone in your address book." A variation on this message adds a second warning about another virus that comes through e-mail with the subject `An Internet Flower For You`, and removes all DLL files from your computer. This second warning is a pure hoax; there is no such e-mail virus in circulation.

Sulfnbk.exe   This is a rather insidious hoax that urges you to delete a legitimate Windows system file. The file, `sulfnbk.exe`, is used by Windows to restore long filenames to files with truncated names; it's a very real file that poses no threat at all to your system. The hoax message (under the subject `NEW VIRUS`) tells you that it's likely your system has been infected by a new "non detectable" virus "that is made to destroy yr computer on the 25th." There follows four numbered steps that show you how to locate and delete the `sulfnbk.exe` file. If you delete the file, you remove a key functionality from the Windows system, and will need to restore the file or reinstall the entire Windows operating system.

WARNING   *A variation of the Sulfnbk.exe hoax sends a second e-mail with a "replacement"* `sulfnbk.exe` *file. This file contains the Magistr virus, and should not be saved or opened.*

Very Bad   This hoax arrives in a message with the subject `A Very Bad Virus`. The hoax message describes a virus classified by "West Dakota Research Corp. (WDRC)" and "The Department of Decease Control" as "the most destructive ever!" According to the message, this virus (named A Very Bad Virus) adds a hidden file to your computer that "has the ability to move itself every 30 seconds, making it impossible to locate and delete." The virus supposedly adds random comments to your e-mail message; the hoax message itself appears to be infested with many such rude comments. The virus is supposedly nicknamed Turret's Virus, after "Turret's Syndrome" (actually Tourette's Syndrome); recipients are urged to forward the warning message to everyone in their address book. Thanks to all the misspellings in the warning message, this hoax is easily spotted.

WOBBLER   This virus hoax (also known as the California hoax) has been circulating since 1997, making it the most-circulated virus hoax in history. Based on the earlier Good Times hoax, this hoax arrives in a message warning you that if you receive an e-mail with a file named `California`, not to open it. This file purportedly contains the WOBBLER virus, which is "a very dangerous virus, much worse than 'Melissa' in that there is NO remedy for it at this time." The virus supposedly erases all documents on your hard drive. Naturally, there is no such WOBBLER virus, and no files named `California` circulating over the Internet.

WARNING *Some individuals have modified the WOBBLER warning message to include a file attachment named* `Wobbler.txt.jse` *or* `Wobbler.txt.vbe`; *don't open this attachment, as it is likely to contain some type of malicious code.*

WTC Survivor Virus   This hoax, first circulated about a month after the terrorist attacks on the World Trade Center, warns against opening a file named `WTC Survivor`. The file is supposedly a virus that will erase your C drive by removing all DLL files from your computer. Obviously, there is no virus by this name.

When a Real Virus is More Like a Hoax

When it comes to computer viruses, the bark is often worse than the bite.

In a large number of instances, the press has reacted to the announcement of a newly discovered virus with a burst of coverage. Think about it—how many stories have you read about a new virus that is set to infect "millions" of computers and wreak untold amounts of damage on corporations and individuals worldwide? And how many times have you seen a follow-up story that presents the *real* impact of the virus—which is typically much lower than anticipated?

It's the "pending catastrophe" stories that make the news; the realistic assessments of the aftermath don't get covered at all.

Which, of course, helps to paint an unduly alarmist picture. That's because most viruses *don't* infect millions of computers, and don't wreak untold amounts of damage. Most virus infections get stopped (by the major antivirus companies) before they do much harm—and what harm they actually do is typically minor in nature.

Why, then, is there such over-the-top reporting of computer viruses? Maybe because it's a good story—technology gone bad, and on a destructive rampage. Maybe it's because the general populace fears things it doesn't understand—and viruses definitely fall into that category. Maybe it's because the virus warning happened to fall on a slow news day. Or maybe it's because the big antivirus companies benefit from this artificial hysteria by selling more copies of their software.

Continued on next page

When a Real Virus is More Like a Hoax *(Continued)*

Whatever the cause, big media reporting on computer viruses typically overstates both the threat and the potential damage. And seldom do the reporters follow up on the initial warning with a realistic assessment of the number of infections and the resultant amount of damage.

For example, the Naked Wife worm received a lot of media attention when it was discovered in 2001. News organizations around the world speculated that this worm would spread from its Brazilian birthplace around the world. In reality, the threat fizzled out within a matter of days, with MessageLabs finding only *63 infections* across three continents. *That* number didn't make the news!

Another example of overblown coverage dates back to 1992, when the Michelangelo virus was set to disable computers worldwide. Numerous "experts" estimated that Michelangelo would affect five million computers when it delivered its payload on March 6; Reuters predicted that one out of four PCs in the U.S. would be hit. The reality, however, is that fewer than 20,000 computers were damaged. There was little or no follow-up in the press.

(Note, however, that Michelangelo rears its head every year at the beginning of March; news stories continue to warn of the potential dangers on the virus' March 6 launch date.)

The Vmyths.com Web site (`www.vmyths.com`) is particularly vocal about the media's overblown coverage of computer viruses. The site likens such alarmist coverage to virus hoaxes; the news stories hurt more people than they help, by causing undue panic. While that might be a bit of an overstatement, the point is well taken; sometimes the fear of a virus is worse than the virus itself.

How to Tell a Hoax from the Real Thing

It would be a mistake to ignore all virus warnings that hit your inbox; some might actually be legitimate. That said, you have to guard against the huge number of prank warnings circulating across the Internet today. To that end, consider these signs that you're the victim of a virus hoax:

- The message came from the friend of a friend—*not* a genuine computer security expert or antivirus company.

- The message urged you to forward it to everyone you know.

- The message didn't include a direct link to more information on the Web. (Or if it did, the link was to a bogus page—or just a general link to the home page of one of the major antivirus Web sites.)

- The message urged you to take immediate action by deleting specific files from your hard disk.

An even better way to ferret out hoax messages is to visit one of several Web sites that post news of the latest virus hoaxes. (Symantec has a particularly good list, at `www.symantec.com/avcenter/hoax.html`.) If your particular message appears on the hoax list, no threat exists, and you can ignore the warning.

Hoax Resources

To keep up-to-date on the most recent virus hoaxes, check out the following Web sites:

- Don't Spread That Hoax! (`www.nonprofit.net/hoax/`)
- F-Secure Hoax Warning (`www.datafellows.com/virus-info/hoax/`)
- Hoaxbusters Internet Hoax Information (`hoaxbusters.ciac.org/HBHoaxInfo.html`)
- HoaxKill (`www.hoaxkill.com`)
- Snopes.com Urban Legends Reference Pages (`www.snopes2.com/ulindex.asp`)
- Symantec Security Response Hoaxes (`www.symantec.com/avcenter/hoax.html`)
- Virus Hoaxes and Netlore (`www.hoaxinfo.com`)
- Vmyths.com (`www.vmyths.com`)

How to Stop Virus Hoaxes

There's a simple way to stop the spread of virus hoaxes:

Don't forward them!

When you receive a hoax message, don't forward it, and don't send a nasty message to the person who sent it to you. Just hit the Delete button, and be done with it.

Summing Up

Virus hoaxes are warnings about nonexistent computer viruses. At their most innocuous, these hoaxes unnecessarily scare naive computer users and eat up valuable time and bandwidth. At their worst, they trick users into deleting real files from their computers.

You can typically spot a virus hoax by its exhortations for you to forward the message to as many other users as possible—and by its lack of credible, verifiable information. If you suspect that you've been sent a hoax message, check it against one of the many lists of virus hoaxes on the Internet.

Phony viruses behind us, the next chapter returns to the world of real virus attacks—and tells you how to prevent such attacks on your computer system.

CHAPTER 9

Antivirus Software and Services

If you're serious about protecting your computer against virus and worm attacks, it's essential that you install and use an antivirus software program. Antivirus programs vigilantly guard your system from any viruses that might arrive via file download or e-mail attachment, scan all the files on your system for hint of infection, and either clean or delete any files found to be infected.

If you don't yet have an antivirus program installed on your PC, you can use the information in this chapter to determine which program you want to buy. If you *do* have an antivirus program already installed, you may want to peruse this information to see how your program stacks up against the competition. And if you're using one of the Big Two antivirus programs—McAfee VirusScan or Norton AntiVirus—you can follow the step-by-step instructions presented here to get the most out of your program.

This chapter also provides a look at a new alternative (or supplement) to keeping antivirus software updated on your own computer—connecting to online antivirus services for immediate scanning.

So read on to learn more about McAfee, Norton, and dozens of other antivirus programs—as well as those Web-based antivirus services.

What to Look For

While most antivirus software is similar in features and functionality, there are some very important differences between programs. This means that you probably want to do a little feature comparison when you shop, and not spring for the first (or the cheapest) program you encounter.

What should you look for when you're evaluating antivirus programs? Here's a short list of features and functions:

Signature Scanning   This feature is pretty much a given. What is signature scanning? As you'll learn in the next chapter, each virus contains a unique sequence of binary code that can be used to identify it—its *code signature*. You want your antivirus program to scan against the code signatures of known viruses, and virtually all programs do just that. If you can compare, the more virus signatures in the product's virus definition database, the better.

Heuristic Scanning   Heuristic scanning is a way to scan for new and unknown viruses that don't yet appear in the program's virus definition database. Instead of looking for specific known sequences of code, it looks for virus-like behavior, such as attempting to change the Windows Registry. Most major antivirus programs incorporate some sort of heuristic scanning, to help catch new viruses before they become well known.

NOTE *Learn more about signature and heuristic scanning in Chapter 10, "Identifying New Threats."*

Manual Scanning   Once a week or so, it's a good idea to scan all the folders and files on your computer system. Almost all antivirus programs let you initiate these scans manually, as well as schedule regular whole-system scans. (Some programs also let you specify individual folders and files to scan.)

Real-Time Scanning   "Dynamic system monitoring" means that your antivirus program is always on, working in the background to catch any infected files that may be copied or downloaded to your system. Real-time scanners should check all new files as they arrive, whether they arrive from floppy disk, e-mail attachments, IRC or instant messaging, or P2P file-swapping services, or Web site download.

E-mail Scanning   Since most viruses and worms arrive as e-mail attachments, you want your antivirus program to dynamically scan all files attached to e-mail messages.

Download Scanning   Dynamic scanning should also check every file that is copied or downloaded to your system, *before* that file hits your hard disk.

Script Scanning   Your antivirus program should scan for script viruses, whether written in ActiveX, JavaScript, or whatever. This should be part of the real-time scanning feature.

Macro Scanning   A good antivirus program not only scans executable and script files, it also scans document files (from Word, Excel, and so on) for macro viruses. In some programs, this may be part of the script scanning function.

Initial Price   Naturally, you want to consider the initial purchase price of the program—although most commercial programs will be in the same price range.

Update Subscription Cost   Another cost to consider is the cost of updating the virus definition database. Many programs offer free updates for a given time period, typically a year. After the free period, you may have to pay to receive additional updates—unless you upgrade to the latest version of the program.

You should also consider how well each program does its job—in terms of how effective the program is in detecting various types of viruses. Fortunately for all of us, most of these products get good performance marks.

For example, a recent test of twenty different antivirus programs by the Business-Information-Workgroup of the University of Magdeburg and GEGA IT-Solutions GbR, (`www.av-test.org`) found that all the programs tested caught at least 98% of all viruses, with more than half achieving a 100% success rate. A similar test from *Virus Bulletin* (`www.virusbtn.com/100/vb100sum .html`) found that more than a third of all products tested achieved a 100% detection rating.

You can also look to see if a particular program has been certified by ICSA Labs. This independent organization awards its Antivirus Product Cleaning Certification to all products that correctly identify and remove all known viruses. Among the products carrying this certification are Command AntiVirus, McAfee VirusScan, Norton AntiVirus, Panda Antivirus Platinum, and PC-cillin.

TIP *See* www.icsalabs.com *for more information on ICSA certification.*

Commercial Antivirus Software

Most users are best served by one of the commercial antivirus software programs currently on the market. These programs can be purchased from any retailer who sells computer software or (in most cases) directly from the manufacturer's Web site. (When you purchase online, you typically have the option of receiving a shrink-wrapped version via the mail, or downloading the software right then and there; this last option is feasible if you have a fast enough Internet connection.)

Table 9.1 compares the leading commercial antivirus programs. Unless otherwise noted, all programs are Windows-compatible. (More details on each program are provided following the table.)

Table 9.1 *Commercial Antivirus Programs*

PROGRAM	APPROX. PRICE	MANUAL DISK & FILE SCANNING	DYNAMIC REAL-TIME PROTECTION	E-MAIL SCANNING
AVG Professional Edition	$40	Yes	Yes	Yes
Command AntiVirus	$60	Yes	Yes (separate application)	Yes (separate application)
eTrust EZ Antivirus	$20 (one-year subscription)	Yes	Yes	No
F-Prot Antivirus	$25	Yes	Yes	No
F-Secure Antivirus	$70	Yes	Yes	No
Kaspersky Anti-Virus	$50	Yes	Yes	Yes
McAfee VirusScan	$40	Yes	Yes	Yes
NOD32 Antivirus System	$40	Yes	Yes	Yes
Norton AntiVirus	$50	Yes	Yes	Yes
Panda Antivirus Platinum	$30	Yes	Yes	Yes
PC-cillin	$40	Yes	Yes	Yes
Vexira Antivirus	$50	Yes	Yes	Yes

hard disk. It can also (via its Safe & Sound feature) back up selected files and directories, to safeguard your most critical files. Unlike some other programs (such as Norton AntiVirus), VirusScan is also capable of scanning the contents of compressed (ZIP) files.

Another unique feature is VirusScan's ability to block access to specific IP addresses and URLs on the Web, as well as protect against rogue ActiveX and Java code. This lets you use VirusScan as a Web content filter, to protect family members from inappropriate Web content. VirusScan also includes a personal firewall, to protect your system from nonvirus attacks over the Internet.

NOTE *McAfee VirusScan is available from Network Associates (*www.mcafee-at-home.com*) for approximately $40.*

NOD32 Antivirus System

NOD32 Antivirus System is a full-featured antivirus program. In additional to normal file scans, it can also scan all incoming e-mail messages, as well as the contents of ZIP-format and other compressed files. NOD32 incorporates both signature and heuristic scanning, and can catch additional viruses, script viruses, macro viruses, worms, and Trojans.

NOTE *NOD32 is available from Eset (*www.nod32.com*) for approximately $40.*

Norton AntiVirus

Norton AntiVirus is the current best-selling consumer antivirus program, and it ranks consistently among the best performing products in this category. The latest version of this program (Norton AntiVirus 2002) features a streamlined interface and simplified operation that performs all of its work in the background, with little or no user interaction necessary.

This program performs whole-disk scans, e-mail scanning, and scans for script-based viruses. It scans *outgoing* e-mail attachments, to protect against an e-mail worm hijacking your system and sending itself to all your contacts.

When you're online, Norton's LiveUpdate feature checks for new virus definitions every four The update subscription runs about $10 per year.

NOTE *Norton AntiVirus is available from Symantec (*www.symantec.com*) for approximately $50.*

TIP *Don't put undue emphasis on the approximate price of these programs. The price listed is the manufacturer's suggested retail price; actual selling price is almost always lower—and, in fact, many of these programs have "street prices" in the $20-$30 range.*

Despite the large number of available programs, the consumer market for antivirus products is dominated by two programs: McAfee VirusScan and Norton AntiVirus. Both products receive rave reviews from the critics, although Norton typically ranks slightly higher than the McAfee product. For example, the June 2001 issue of *PC Magazine* named Norton AntiVirus as the best product in the category; CNET's online comparison of virus scanners awarded Norton AntiVirus its Editor's Choice designation.

Of these two programs, the big difference comes in ease-of-use. McAfee is a little more complicated than Norton, making it more suited to experienced or advanced users. Less experienced and casual computer users will probably be more comfortable with Norton's easier-to-use interface, although both products do a superb job of scanning and cleaning viruses from your system.

The following sections will examine the major commercial antivirus programs, from AVG to Vexira. More detailed information about using the Big Two products is presented at the end of this chapter.

NOTE *In addition to these consumer products, there are many products tailored to the large corporate market. These enterprise antivirus products include Norman Virus Control (*www.norman.com*) and Sophos (*www.sophos.com*). Both McAfee and Symantec (Norton) also offer enterprise versions of their top-selling consumer antivirus programs; see their Web sites for more information.*

AVG Professional Edition

AVG Professional Edition offers two different interfaces, Basic and Advanced, for different levels of users. The product uses both signature and heuristic scanning, as well as a separate e-mail scanner for both incoming and outgoing messages. Virus definition updates are free for the life of the product.

This product is available for all versions of Microsoft Windows—9x, Me, NT, 2000, and XP. AVG Professional Edition is ICSA certified.

NOTE *AVG Professional Edition is available from Grisoft, Inc. (*www.grisoft.com*) for approximately $40.*

Command AntiVirus

The base version of Command AntiVirus is a bare-bones scanner. It's fast and accurate, but it lacks some of the features found in more popular programs—such as real-time monitoring and the automatic updating of its virus definition database. (Real-time file, script, and e-mail scanning are performed by a sister application, Dynamic Virus Protection, that must be purchased and run separately.)

On the plus side, its bare-bones nature enables it to present a very simple, intuitive interface. All options are straightforward, and less experienced users won't be confused by unnecessary technical gobbledy-gook. The program also includes both signature and heuristic scanning, so it does a good job of catching both known and unknown virus types.

NOTE *Command AntiVirus is available from Command Software Systems (*www
.commandsoftware.com*) for approximately $60.*

eTrust EZ Antivirus

EZ Antivirus is a bare-bones scanner, priced slightly lower than competing products. (The low price—about $20—is actually a one-year *subscription* to the product; after that, the annual renewal fee is about $10.) It lacks many features found in other, higher-priced programs, such as e-mail attachment scanning and automatic definition updating.

The EZ Antivirus program does offer scanning for all types of viruses, including macro viruses, worms, and Trojans. It includes both signature and heuristic scanners, and is available for all versions of Windows, including Windows XP. The program is ICSA certified.

NOTE *EZ AntiVirus is available from eTrust (*www1.my-etrust.com/products/
Antivirus/*) for approximately $20 (one-year subscription).*

F-Prot Antivirus

F-Prot Antivirus contains one of the most powerful scan engines on the market, incorporating both signature and heuristic scanning. Interestingly, the F-Prot scanning engine is licensed to several other antivirus companies for use in their products; you can find the F-Prot engine in F-Secure AntiVirus and Command AntiVirus products.

F-Prot is available for both Windows and Linux operating systems. Virus definition updates can be scheduled automatically.

NOTE *F-Prot is available from Frisk Software International (*www.f-prot.com*) for approximately $25.*

F-Secure Antivirus

F-Secure Antivirus is a product aimed at the corporate market. It can be installed automatic over a network, by the network administrator. Versions are available for all major operating tems, including Windows, Macintosh, Linux, Solaris, NetWare, OS/2, and MS-DOS.

F-Secure's program uses multiple scanning engines—including scanners from F-Prot and Orion—to detect and clean viruses on your system. This enables the program to det plex polymorphic viruses that may be missed by a single scanner. The product also inclu built-in firewall to detect non-virus Internet attacks.

NOTE *F-Secure Antivirus is available from F-Secure Corp. (*www.f-secure
products/antivirus/*) for approximately $70.*

Kaspersky Anti-Virus

Kaspersky Lab produces several different versions of its Kaspersky Anti-Virus softy versions for Windows, Linux, and the Palm OS. The Kaspersky product is very ful on-demand scanning, background scanning, and e-mail scanning for all popular e including Outlook, Outlook Express, Exchange, Eudora, Pegasus Mail, and Ne

The program uses a combination of signature scanning, integrity scanning scanning to scan for traditional viruses, script viruses, macro viruses, and wor compressed and archive files. Its virus definition database is updated daily.

NOTE *Kaspersky Anti-Virus Personal is available from Kaspersky .com) for approximately $50.*

McAfee VirusScan

McAfee VirusScan is one of the Big Two antivirus programs. It does pre ton AntiVirus does, but with its own unique approach and interface.

VirusScan offers the expected manual and real-time scanning optic load, files attached to e-mail messages (in a variety of e-mail program

Panda Antivirus Platinum

Panda Antivirus Platinum is a powerful virus scanning program, which includes a unique voice feature that literally talks you through the disinfection process if it finds a virus. It also offers a lot of configuration settings to play around with, if you like more complete control over the virus-scanning process.

This plethora of options might overwhelm less-technical users; Panda is definitely not the easiest-to-use antivirus program on the market. If you can figure out how to use it, Panda is a very effective program. It also updates its virus definitions on a daily basis, ensuring that the program is consistently up-to-date.

NOTE *Panda Antivirus Platinum is available from Panda Software* (`www.panda-security.com`) *for approximately $30.*

PC-cillin

PC-cillin is a simple yet effective antivirus program. It can scan your entire hard disk (or selected folders), document files and macros, e-mail attachments, and all manner of script files. Its interface is perhaps the easiest of all the commercial programs, making it a good choice for inexperienced users.

The PC-cillin package goes beyond virus scanning to include a personal firewall, Web browser content filtering, and security features for your PDA. It works with all versions of Windows, including Windows XP.

NOTE *PC-cillin is available from Trend Micro* (`www.antivirus.com/pc-cillin/`) *for approximately $40.*

Vexira Antivirus

Vexira Antivirus is an antivirus program designed for corporate, small-network, or individual desktops. It's a full-featured program, complete with on-demand, real-time, and e-mail scanning.

Updates to Vexira's virus definition database are performed weekly. The program protects against traditional viruses, worms, and Trojans as well as malicious ActiveX and Java code. It also scans all manner of compressed files, including ZIP files.

NOTE *Vexira Antivirus is available from Central Command* (`www.vexira.com`) *for approximately $50.*

Shareware and Freeware Antivirus Programs

These commercial programs aren't the only antivirus programs available today. There are also a number of shareware and freeware programs, available for downloading from the Internet, that perform basic virus-protection operations. These programs typically don't offer the same level of ongoing support as do commercial programs; they do have the advantage of a lower initial price—or, in some instances, of being available free of charge.

NOTE *Shareware is software that is initially available at no charge, often in a limited version; you receive full functionality when you pay to register the product. Freeware is software that is available totally free of charge.*

The following are some of the more popular shareware and freeware antivirus programs:

- Achilles'Shield and MailDefense (`www.indefense.com`)
- ADinf (`www.adinf.com`)
- avast! (`www.securenet.org/avast_info.html`)
- BoDetect (`www.cbsoftsolutions.com/Products/products.htm`)
- Dr.Web (`www.drweb-online.de/index_e.htm`)
- Integrity Master (`www.stiller.com`)
- InVircible (`invircible.co.il`)
- Jammer (`www.agnitum.com/products/jammer/`)
- MailWasher (`www.mailwasher.net`)
- Net-Commando (`www.deltadesignuk.com/IRDC/nc2000.htm`)
- Perforin (`www.vdsarg.com/perforin/perforin.htm`)
- Protector Plus (`www.pspl.com`)
- Quick Heal (`www.quickheal.com`)
- RAV AntiVirus Desktop (`www.rav.ro`)
- RegRun Security Suite (`www.greatis.com/regrun3.htm`)
- Spy Cop (`www.computer-monitoring.com/antispy.htm`)
- Spytech NetArmor (`www.spytech-web.com/netarmor.shtml`)

- Tauscan (`www.agnitum.com/products/tauscan/`)

- Trojan Defense Suite (`tds.diamondcs.com.au`)

- Trojan Remover (`members.aol.com/simplysup/tremover/`)

- V-Buster AntiVirus (`www.v-buster.com`)

- WormGuard (`wormguard.diamondcs.com.au`)

Online Antivirus Services

In addition to these various software products, there are a handful of antivirus *services* available over the Internet. These services work like software programs, but they don't require you to install discrete software on your system. Instead, the antivirus functions (scanning only, typically) are initiated from the host Web site; your computer has to be online for the service to work.

The chief advantage of these online services is their immediacy. If you think your system has been infected, you can visit one of these sites and receive an immediate checkup. You don't have to go purchase the software, install the software, configure the software, or whatever. Just go online, click a few buttons, and get a scan.

Another advantage of *some* of these services is that they're free. (McAfee charges for their VirusScan Online service.) Of course, you get what you pay for; these online services are typically scan-only, and they don't perform a lot of file-cleansing operations. For that, you need to invest in a full-featured antivirus software package.

The bigger disadvantage of these services is that they offer on-demand scanning only—they don't stay active in the background, checking files you download or copy to your hard disk. For dynamic real-time protection, you need antivirus software, not an online service.

Still, if you think you have a virus infection and don't have antivirus software installed on your system—or if your virus definitions are outdated—being able to get an immediate online scan is a good thing. If you find you actually do have an infection, you can then purchase a full-fledged antivirus package, disinfect your system, and be prepared for any future attacks.

Command on Demand

This is a Web-based version of the Command AntiVirus program. It both scans and cleans any infected files—including traditional viruses, macro viruses, and Trojans. The program is also capable of scanning compressed files and files on CD-ROM.

NOTE *Command on Demand is available from Command Software Systems* (www
.commandondemand.com); *pricing is about $4 for a single scan, or about $20 for a
full-year subscription.*

HouseCall

Trend Micro's HouseCall is a free online virus scanner. It both scans for and cleans viruses and
Trojans from your system. HouseCall was introduced in May 1997. According to Trend Micro,
more than 170,000 people use HouseCall each month.

NOTE *HouseCall is available at no charge from Trend Micro* (housecall
.antivirus.com).

McAfee VirusScan Online

McAfee VirusScan Online is probably the most robust online antivirus service. It's based on the
best-selling VirusScan retail product and offers both signature and heuristic scanning. If you
have an always-on broadband connection, VirusScan Online can also function as a background
scanner, with 24/7 protection provided by a worldwide network of more than 8000 servers.

Thanks to this full feature set, VirusScan Online is possibly the only online virus scanning
service that can replace dedicated desktop software.

NOTE *VirusScan Online is available from Network Associates* (www.mcafee.com) *for
an annual subscription fee of approximately $30.*

Symantec Security Check

Security Check is a free service that scans for computer viruses on your system. It's a scan-only
service, however; it doesn't actually clean your system if you have an infection. (For that, Symantec suggests you purchase a copy of Norton AntiVirus.) It does, however, scan for both viruses
and other Internet security risks.

NOTE *Security Check is available at no charge from Symantec* (www.symantec.com/
securitycheck/).

Resolving Problems with Antivirus Software

Even though antivirus software exists to solve a problem, that doesn't mean that the antivirus programs are without their own problems. In particular, some antivirus software can interfere with some essential system operations—such as defragmenting your hard disk, or installing new software.

Since antivirus programs monitor all file activity on your hard disk, they can get in the way of any hard disk maintenance you may undertake. In particular, antivirus programs have been known to significantly slow down disk defragmenting. Because of this, it's a good idea to disable your antivirus before attempting this type of system maintenance.

More problematic is the fact that some antivirus programs interfere with the act of installing some new software programs. The antivirus program can read the essential acts of copying EXE files and modifying the Windows Registry as hostile operations and block the installation of the new software. If this happens to you (and you're sure that the software you're installing is safe), turn off your antivirus program before installing the new software.

Using an Antivirus Program

If your system already has an antivirus program installed, chances are it's either Norton AntiVirus or McAfee VirusScan. The balance of this chapter shows you how to use each of these programs, for both manual and automatic virus scanning.

Using Norton AntiVirus

Norton AntiVirus is, by most accounts, the number-one antivirus program on today's market. It's also one of the easiest-to-use programs; the 2002 version of this program doesn't require a lot of user interaction to do its job.

There are three main screens in the Norton AntiVirus window. The Status screen, shown in Figure 9.1, is the default screen. It tells you what program features are activated, and when your virus definitions were last updated.

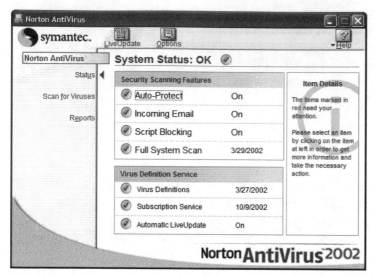

Figure 9.1 *The Norton AntiVirus Status screen*

Running a Full-System Scan

Norton AntiVirus enables you to scan your complete system, individual drives, individual folders, or individual files. To initiate a scan, follow these steps:

1. Select the Scan for Viruses option.

2. When the Scan for Viruses screen appears (shown in Figure 9.2), select what you want to scan—your computer, all removable drives, all floppy disks, drives, folders, or files. (If you select drives, folders, or files, you'll then be prompted to select specific items.)

3. Click Scan.

Norton now starts the scan, and displays a Scan Progress window. When the scan is complete, a Scan Summary screen is displayed, as shown in Figure 9.3. If Norton finds an infected file, the program prompts you for what action to take. Read the section, "Dealing with an Infected File," to learn how to proceed.

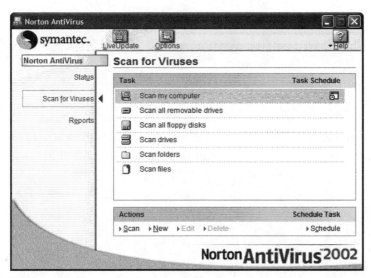

Figure 9.2 *Scanning for viruses with Norton AntiVirus*

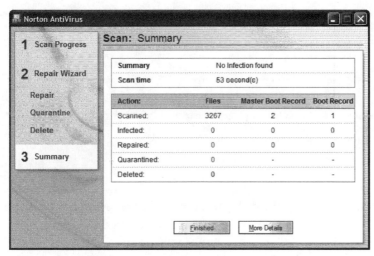

Figure 9.3 *The results of a Norton AntiVirus system scan*

Scheduling Scans

You can configure Norton AntiVirus to perform system scans according to a prearranged schedule. Just follow these steps:

1. Select the Scan For Viruses option.

2. Select Scan My Computer and click Schedule (at the bottom of the window).

3. When the Scan My Computer dialog box appears (shown in Figure 9.4), pull down the Schedule Task list and select how often you want to scan—Daily, Weekly, Monthly, Once, At System Startup, At Login, or When Idle.

Figure 9.4 *Scheduling your scans*

4. After you make your selection, the rest of the dialog box changes to reflect appropriate timing options (start time, day of the week, and so on). Make the desired selections and click OK.

Configuring for Real-Time Protection

Before you use Norton AntiVirus, you need to configure the program so that it's constantly scanning your system for real-time infection. Norton comes with its Auto-Protect feature enabled by default, but there are still many options you can set to personalize the scanning for your particular system.

Follow these steps:

1. Click the Options button (at the top of the Norton window).

2. When the Norton AntiVirus Options window appears, select Auto-Protect from the System panel (on the left side of the window).

3. The Auto-Protect screen, shown in Figure 9.5, has numerous options that determine how the background scanning operates. I recommend you choose the following settings: Enable Auto-Protect, Start Auto-Protect When Windows Starts Up, Show The Auto-Protect Icon In The Tray, Automatically Repair The Infected File, and Comprehensive File Scanning.

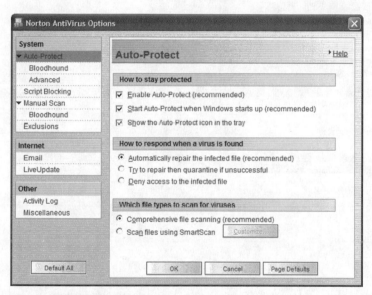

Figure 9.5 *Configuring Norton's Auto-Protect background scanning*

4. To enable heuristic scanning (what Norton calls its Bloodhound feature), select Bloodhound from the System panel, and make sure that Default Level of Protection is selected.

5. To enable blocking of malicious script code, select Script Blocking from the System panel; then choose Enable Script Blocking and either Ask Me What To Do (recommended) or Stop All Suspicious Activities And Do Not Prompt Me (if you want to avoid all decision-making).

6. To enable e-mail scanning, select Email from the Internet panel (shown in Figure 9.6). I recommend you choose the following options: Scan Incoming Email, Scan Outgoing Email, Automatically Repair The Infected File, Protect Against Timeouts, Display Tray Icon, and Display Progress Indicator When Sending Email.

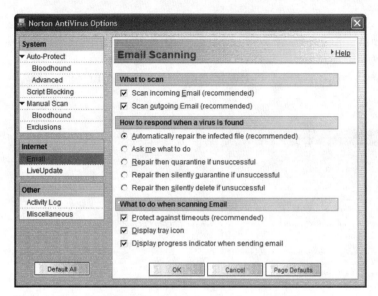

Figure 9.6 *Enabling Norton's e-mail scanning*

7. Click OK when done configuring.

Dealing with an Infected File

When Norton AntiVirus identifies an infected file, how it proceeds depends on the options you've selected.

If you've selected Automatically Repair The Infected File (as described in the previous section), Norton attempts to disinfect the file. If the file can be successfully cleaned, great; if not, it then attempts to quarantine the file in a special folder. If, for some reason, the file can't be quarantined, access to the file is permanently blocked.

If you chose the Ask Me What To Do option (available with e-mail and manual scanning—*not* with Auto-Protect), Norton displays a message when it finds an infected file, with three options to choose from.

Repair   Attempts to remove the virus code from the infected file.

Quarantine   Moves the file to a quarantine folder, where it can be further analyzed—but not activated.

Delete   Completely deletes the infected file from your system.

In most cases, you want to select the Repair option; this potentially lets you salvage the original file by removing the virus code.

However, Norton AntiVirus can't repair all infected files. If the file can't be repaired, you'll be prompted to take further action—either Quarantine or Delete.

When you quarantine a file, you move it to a special folder on your hard drive. This preserves the file, but blocks active access to it. This way, if a cure for the infection is found at a later date, you still have the file around to clean. This option is also good if you have a new or unknown virus; you then have the option of sending the infected file to the Symantec Security Response experts for further analysis.

However, if you're like most users, you're just as well off deleting the infected file. That's because you probably won't ever bother with that file again—so why let it take up valuable disk space? Just select the Delete option and be done with it.

Analyzing—and Repairing—Quarantined Files

When a file is held in quarantine, it's because you think there may be some future use for the file. One such use, if the virus is an unknown one, is to send the file to the Symantec Security Response team so they can analyze it and add it to their virus definition database.

To send a new or unknown virus file to Symantec for further analysis, follow these steps:

1. Select the Reports option.

2. When the Reports screen appears, click the View Reports button next to the Quarantined Items option. This displays a list of all files you have quarantined.

3. In the left panel, select Quarantined Items.

4. In the right panel, select the file(s) you want to send to Symantec.

5. Click the Submit Item button at the top of the window.

6. When the Scan And Deliver Wizard appears, answer the questions and follow the onscreen instructions to submit the file.

Continued on next page

Analyzing–and Repairing–Quarantined Files *(Continued)*

Note that not all quarantined files should be submitted for analysis. The wizard will inform you if this is a known file, in which case you shouldn't submit it; you should only submit files that Symantec doesn't yet know about.

If the file is known, however, you might want to try repairing the file again. It's possible that Symantec knows more about the virus now than it did when the file was first quarantined, so a second attempt at repair might be successful.

To effect a second repair, select the file from the Quarantined Items list and click the Repair Item button.

Updating Virus Definitions

The last thing you need to know about Norton AntiVirus is how to update its virus definition database. You can perform what Norton calls a LiveUpdate manually, or schedule updates to occur regularly.

To perform a manual update, just click the LiveUpdate button, at the top of the Norton AntiVirus window. You'll be presented with the LiveUpdate Wizard, which walks you through the process of selecting which items need to be updated. Just follow the onscreen instructions, make sure you're connected to the Internet, and the update will proceed as directed.

To schedule regularly occurring updates, follow these steps:

1. Click the Options button at the top of the Norton AntiVirus window.

2. When the Options window appears, select LiveUpdate from the Internet panel.

3. Check the Enable LiveUpdate option, and then select Apply Updates Without Interrupting Me.

4. Click OK.

LiveUpdate will now go online and check for new updates every four hours.

TIP *You should only enable the scheduled LiveUpdate if you have an always-on Internet connection, via a corporate network, DSL, or cable modem. It's not a feasible option if you have to manually dial up your Internet service provider. If you have a dial-up connection, use the LiveUpdate Wizard to perform manual updates.*

Using McAfee VirusScan

McAfee VirusScan is the number-two antivirus program, second only to Norton AntiVirus. It's a very powerful program, capable of stopping just about any type of virus that might try to infect your system. It even scans all incoming e-mail messages, to protect against virus-infected attachments.

As you can see in Figure 9.7, the main VirusScan window tells you when you last scanned your system, when you last updated your virus definitions, and the status of the program's background settings. From these screens you can perform an on-demand virus scan, or adjust the program's configuration.

Figure 9.7 *The main VirusScan window*

> **TIP** *Many new computers come with a trial version of McAfee VirusScan preinstalled. This trial version typically works for a limited period of time, after which you need to purchase the full version to continue to receive new and updated virus definitions. If you have the trial version and haven't updated virus definitions for awhile, don't assume that you're getting full protection; you need to spend a little money to ensure the program's continuing effectiveness.*

Running a Full-System Scan

Scanning your system for viruses with VirusScan is as simple as clicking a few buttons and links. Just follow these steps:

1. From the main VirusScan window, click the Scan For Viruses Now button.

2. When the Select A Location To Scan window appears, select what you want to scan. You can opt to scan your entire computer, a specific drive, or a specific folder (or subfolder) on that drive.

3. Click the Scan button to start the scan.

The program now begins the scan and displays the VirusScan Progress window. When the scan is complete, you see the VirusScan Summary window, shown in Figure 9.8. This window shows how many files were scanned, found to be infected, cleaned, quarantined, and deleted.

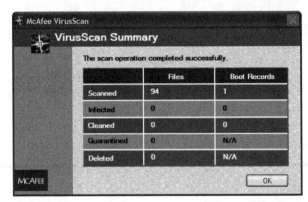

Figure 9.8 *The results of a VirusScan scan*

When VirusScan finds an infected file, it prompts you for what action to take. Read the section "Dealing with an Infected File," to learn how to proceed.

TIP *By default, VirusScan uses only its signature scanner—not the heuristic scanner. To enable heuristic scanning, click the Scan For Viruses Now button; then click the Scan Settings button. When the Scan Settings dialog box appears, select the Detection tab and click the Advanced button; when the Advanced Scan Settings dialog box appears, check the Enable Heuristics Scanning option, and then check the Enable Macro and Program File Heuristics Scanning Option. Click OK when done.*

Scheduling Scans

If you'd like to automate your full-system scans, you can configure VirusScan to schedule your scans in advance. Just follow these steps:

1. From the main VirusScan window, click the Pick A Task button.

2. When the Pick A Task window appears, click Change My VirusScan Settings.

3. When the Pick The Type Of Settings To Change window appears, click View And Edit Scheduled Scans.

4. When the Manage A Scheduled Task window appears, select the Scan My Computer item and then click the Edit button.

5. When the Task Properties dialog box appears, select the Schedule tab, shown in Figure 9.9.

Figure 9.9 *Setting a VirusScan schedule*

6. Check the Enable box, and then select how often you want to run the scan: Once, At Startup, Hourly, Daily, Weekly, or Monthly.

7. Enter a start time in the Start At box, and make sure all the days are checked.

8. Click OK.

VirusScan will now run an automatic scan of your system on the schedule you specified.

Configuring for Real-Time Protection

While on-demand scans are useful, it's even better if VirusScan is working in the background, checking all new files introduced to your system. To configure VirusScan for real-time scanning, follow these steps:

1. From the main VirusScan window, click the Pick A Task button.

2. When the Pick A Task window appears, click Change My VirusScan Settings.

3. When the Pick The Type Of Settings To Change window appears, click Configure VShield Background Scanning.

4. When the Select Your Background Scanning Settings window appears (shown in Figure 9.10), check the desired settings.

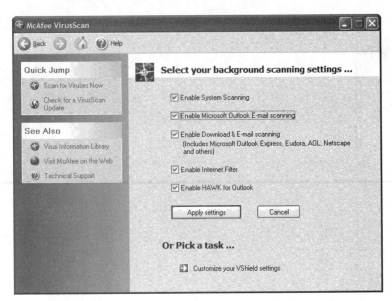

Figure 9.10 *Configuring VirusScan's VShield background scanning*

5. Click the Apply Settings button.

Here are the background scanning options you can enable:

Enable System Scanning   Activates the VShield background scanner—you have to select this option to use any of the real-time scanning options.

Enable Microsoft Outlook E-mail Scanning   Scans messages and message attachments received via Microsoft Outlook.

WARNING *The Enable Microsoft Outlook E-mail Scanning option works only with Microsoft Outlook, not with Outlook Express; if you're using Outlook Express, you'll want to check the next option, Enable Download & E-mail Scanning.*

Enable Download & E-mail Scanning   Scans messages and message attachments received via Outlook Express, Eudora, Netscape Mail, and AOL Mail; also scans other files you download from the Internet.

Enable Internet Filter   Blocks potentially harmful ActiveX and Java classes from activating when you visit pages with your Web browser.

Enable HAWK for Outlook   The Hostility Activity Watch Kernel monitors your outgoing e-mail to prevent viruses from spreading themselves via Outlook.

Most users should select the Enable System Scanning, Enable Download & E-mail Scanning, and Enable HAWK for Outlook options. If you're using Microsoft Outlook (the Microsoft Office application), you should also select Enable Microsoft Outlook E-mail Scanning. In most instances, you don't need to enable the Internet Filter, as it duplicates options available from within Internet Explorer.

Dealing with an Infected File

When VirusScan finds an infected file, it displays a dialog box informing you of the infection, and then prompts you for which action to take. You'll see the following choices:

Clean   Attempts to remove the virus code from the infected file.

Delete   Completely deletes the infected file from your system.

Add To Quarantine   Moves the file to a quarantine folder, where it can be further analyzed—but not activated.

In most cases, you should select the Clean option; this potentially lets you salvage the original file by removing the virus code.

However, VirusScan can't clean all infected files. If the file can't be disinfected, you'll be prompted to take further action. In this instance, the best options are Add To Quarantine and Delete.

When you quarantine a file, you move it to a special folder on your hard drive. This preserves the file, but blocks active access to it. This way, if a cure for the infection is found at a later date, you still have the file around to clean. This option is also good if you have a new or unknown virus; you then have the option of sending the infected file to McAfee for further analysis.

TIP *To send an infected file to McAfee for analysis, e-mail the file to* virus_research@nai.com.

It's unlikely, however, that you'll ever do anything with the infected file. For that reason, the Delete option is probably more practical. If you think the infected file is a lost cause, this is the option to choose.

Automatically Dealing with Infections

By default, VirusScan asks for your input when an infected file is found. If you prefer not to be bothered in this manner, you can reconfigure the program to deal with infected files automatically, without additional input. Just follow these steps:

1. From the main VirusScan window, click the Scan For Viruses Now button.
2. When the next window appears, click Scan Settings.
3. When the Scan Settings dialog box appears, select the Action tab.
4. Pull down the When A Virus is Found list, and make a selection.
5. Click OK.

What action options are available? Here are your choices:

Prompt User For Action   The default setting; requires your input for each infected file.

Quarantine   Automatically quarantines infected files.

Clean Infected Files Automatically   Automatically tries to disinfect the file; if the file can't be cleaned, it's quarantined.

Delete Infected Files Automatically   Automatically deletes all infected files.

Continue Scanning   Records any infected viruses so you can deal with them at your convenience—a good option if you like to scan when you're away from your computer.

Continued on next page

Automatically Dealing with Infections *(Continued)*

If you're a user who doesn't want to be bothered when an infection is found—or isn't sure what action to take in which circumstances—then choose the Clean Infected Files Automatically option. With this configuration, VirusScan will do as much disinfecting as it can, automatically, and then isolate (quarantine) those files it can't clean.

On the other hand, if you like to be involved when problems arise, keep the default Prompt User For Action setting. Of course, you'll end up choosing the Clean File action most of the time, but at least you'll feel like you're an important part of the process.

Updating Virus Definitions

As with all antivirus programs, you need to periodically update VirusScan's virus definition database. You can do this manually, or schedule the updates to happen on a regular basis.

To manually download new definitions, all you have to do is click the Check For A VirusScan Update option on the main VirusScan window. If you're connected to the Internet, VirusScan will go online, look for new or updated definitions, and prompt you to download the updates.

To set a schedule for downloading these updates, follow these steps:

1. From the main VirusScan window, click the Pick A Task button.

2. When the Pick A Task window appears, click Change My VirusScan Settings.

3. When the Pick The Type Of Settings To Change window appears, click Configure Instant Updater.

4. When the window shown in Figure 9.11 appears, click Configure Automatic Updates.

5. When the Choose An Automatic Update Method window appears, select the Auto Update option, and then click Apply.

TIP *You should only enable the automatic update feature if you have a relatively fast always-on Internet connection, via a corporate network, DSL, or cable modem. It's not a feasible option if you have to manually dial up your Internet service provider. If you have a dial-up connection, use the Check For A VirusScan Update option to perform manual updates.*

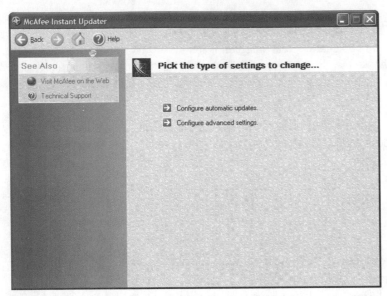

Figure 9.11 Configuring VirusScan for automatic virus definition updates

VirusScan will now connect to the Internet on a regular basis, and then automatically download and install new and updated virus definitions—with no interaction necessary on your part.

Summing Up

One of the best ways to protect your system against virus infection is by installing and using an antivirus program. There are dozens of these programs on the market, all of which offer similar features and performance.

The two most popular antivirus programs are Norton AntiVirus and McAfee VirusScan. You can configure both programs to perform manual and prescheduled full-system scans, as well as to monitor your system for real-time virus infection. Both programs guard against all types of infection, including viruses transmitted via file downloading and e-mail attachment; both programs also guard against script and macro viruses.

In the next chapter, we go beyond the viruses of today and examine how these antivirus programs look for viruses they don't yet know about.

CHAPTER 10

Identifying New Threats

The antivirus programs discussed in the last chapter all do a good job of identifying virus infections—those they know about, that is. But what happens if a new virus pops up? How do new viruses get identified, and how do you protect your system against these previously unknown threats?

First things first. The number of virus infections is increasing; according to ICSA Labs, the rate of infection in North American corporations increased 13% from 2000 to 2001. This means that there is a constant stream of new viruses that must be identified and defended against—several new viruses each week, to be exact.

In addition, these new viruses are becoming increasingly more dangerous and harder to identify. Each new virus builds on the "success" of previous viruses, as attackers learn from each other.

How do we keep up with the deluge?

Signature Scanning

To understand how new viruses show up on the antivirus companies' radar screens, you first need to know how antivirus programs scan for previously identified viruses.

The primary method of detection used by virtually all of today's antivirus programs is called *signature scanning*. As you can see in Figure 10.1, this method compares a scanned file with the characteristic signature (individual bytes of program code) of a known virus stored in the antivirus program's virus definition database. If the scanned file matches a known signature (contains the same code pattern), the program marks the file as infected and takes appropriate action.

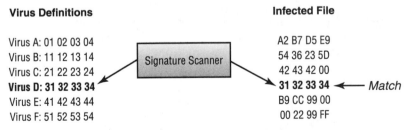

Figure 10.1 *How signature scanning identifies known viruses*

NOTE *Signature scanning is sometimes called* pattern matching, *since the software tries to match the patterns it finds in a file with the patterns of known viruses in its definition database. Most major virus definition databases hold signatures for a half million or more known viruses.*

Finding New Viruses

Antivirus companies have several ways to search for new viruses in the wild and then add the newly discovered virus signatures to their definition databases. Among the most popular methods are the following:

User Reporting   If you stumble across a previously unknown virus on your computer (that is, if your virus scanner identifies virus-like behavior that doesn't match any known virus), you're encouraged to submit a sample of that virus to your antivirus company. Company researchers will analyze the virus, to determine just what it is that you found. If it's really a new virus, they'll decode its signature and add it to their virus definition database—so that future attacks can be prevented.

Research Analysis   The researchers at the antivirus companies are constantly analyzing new virus samples, looking not only for new viruses but also for new infection techniques. Fortunately, this research is used for good, not evil, as what they discover in the lab can be added to their product's virus definition database.

Web Searching   Some antivirus companies take the proactive approach and go actively looking for new viruses. In most cases this search takes the form of a Web crawl, with "spider" software sent across the Web, looking for specific signatures or behaviors. For example, Symantec's Bloodhound system is essentially a Java-based Web crawler that looks for virus-like behavior on the Internet. When it finds something suspicious, it sends it back to the Symantec AntiVirus Research Center (SARC), to be analyzed—and possibly added to the company's virus definition database.

The Problem with Signature Scanning

The big problem with signature scanning is that it's only as good as the data in the database. What happens when there's a new virus in the wild, with a signature that doesn't yet appear in the virus definition database?

Once an antivirus company knows about a new virus, it updates its virus definition database. But it may take days—or weeks—to realize that a new virus is making the rounds. And it may take more days—or weeks, or even *months*—before users download the updated virus definitions.

Which means that signature scanning is good at catching viruses *after the fact*. It's practically useless in catching a virus when it's new.

During the period between the creation of the virus and the updating of your antivirus program, your computer is at risk of catching the new virus—simply because your copy of the antivirus software doesn't yet know about the new virus. If your antivirus company identified the virus quickly, and you update your virus definitions frequently, you won't be at risk for long.

However, if your antivirus company is slow on the ball, or if you *don't* update your virus definitions on a regular basis, you're at major risk of being hit by the new infection.

This is a particular problem now that most viruses are spread via the Internet. Thanks to light-speed online communications, a new virus can be released into the wild and potentially spread to millions of computers within a matter of hours—long before the antivirus companies are able to update their virus definitions.

Compounding the problem is that, by default, most users only update their virus definitions once a week. In fact, many users don't update nearly that frequently, and a large number of users don't update their programs *at all*.

So, as you can see, relying on signature scanning is problematic.

Fortunately, there are other ways to sniff out viruses—especially new ones, before they become famous.

NOTE *It's important to note that no single method of identifying viruses is 100% foolproof. That's why many antivirus programs include multiple types of scanning, to let as few viruses as possible fall between the cracks.*

Integrity Checking

An established alternative to signature scanning is *integrity checking*. This older technique is relatively simple, in that it looks for any changes to the size of individual files.

An integrity checker starts by scanning all the program files on your hard disk, and registering the size of each file in a database. Each subsequent time you run the checker, it compares the current size of each file against its original size, as shown in Figure 10.2. If a file has changed in size, that's a good sign that it has somehow been infected with virus code. The integrity checker then alerts you to the possibility of having an infected file.

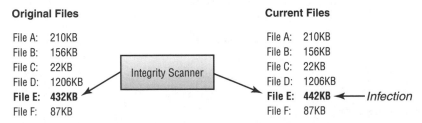

Figure 10.2 *How integrity checking identifies viruses*

Integrity checkers are good for those files that are supposed to stay constant, like executable files. But they're relatively useless for those files, such as documents, that are frequently modified.

In other words, you can use an integrity checker to guard against file infector viruses, but not against macro or script viruses.

Heuristic Scanning

Probably the most often-used alternative to signature scanning is *heuristic scanning*. Heuristic scanning doesn't look for viruses, it looks for virus-like *behavior*. In other words, a heuristic scanner doesn't rely on specific virus signatures; instead, it looks for general code sequences that are typically found only in viruses—not in legitimate software programs.

> **NOTE** *The word "heuristic" comes from the Greek for "to find." In the context of antivirus techniques, it refers to the ability to find specific behavior.*

For example, legitimate software programs typically don't modify the Windows Registry. If a heuristic scanner finds a piece of code in a program that attempts to modify the Registry, that program is flagged as a possible virus.

This way, new viruses whose signatures haven't yet been registered can be identified. Heuristic scanning software identifies files that have a virus-like profile, and then takes appropriate action—long before traditional signature scanners can do their thing. (And, yes, this type of "virus profiling" is similar to "traveler profiling" to target potential terrorists on airline flights—you look for telltale characteristics of malicious intent, rather than waiting for a deliberate act to take place.)

Most major antivirus programs today incorporate some form of heuristic scanning, in addition to the main signature scanner. When the heuristic scanner finds a suspicious file, it typically generates a message, rather than automatically taking action. Depending on what the scanner finds, this message may advise you to delete the file, quarantine the file and wait for further instructions, or send the program code to the antivirus company for analysis.

Different Types of Heuristic Scanning

There are different ways to implement heuristic scanning—different approaches, embraced by different companies, that produce slightly different results.

Content Filtering

Content filtering is the most traditional of all heuristic scanning methods. A content filter compares the underlying code of all incoming programs to a built-in rule base. It doesn't look so much for a specific virus signature for specific types of code that are typically used only by virus programs, as shown in Figure 10.3.

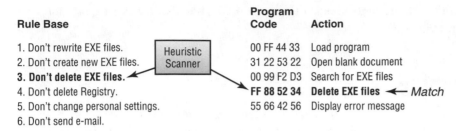

Figure 10.3 *How content filtering identifies viruses*

In this example, the content filtering software has in its rule base the fact that normal programs don't delete EXE files. So when the software examines an incoming program and finds code to delete EXE files, it records a match to the rule base—and flags the program as a potential virus.

It's important to note that a content filter doesn't identify a program as a specific virus. That can only be done via signature scanning, where specific code from a known virus is used to identify additional copies of that virus. With content filtering, no code from specific viruses is used; the software looks only at the likely ways that a virus writer might code a suspicious activity.

NOTE *Another benefit to content filtering is that, unlike signature scanning, it can read compressed files.*

There are several standalone content-filtering products available, targeted at the corporate e-mail market. (A company would install these programs at their e-mail gateway, to scan all incoming e-mail attachments.) The two leading products are Antigen (`www.sybari.com`) and MIMEsweeper (`www.mimesweeper.com`).

Sandboxing

Sandboxing is an interesting approach to virus scanning, in that it allows the code of an incoming program to run inside a virtual "sandbox." This is something like the way a bomb squad tests a suspicious package to see whether it's a real explosive; they isolate the program and "set it off." This way, if it contains malicious code, that code is launched within a protective environment, where it can't harm or infect the rest of your system.

As you can see in Figure 10.4, when a suspect program is launched within the "sandbox" (actually, a simulation of the computer's operating environment, or a virtual computer), the sandboxing software looks for specific activities—attempts to delete files, modify operating system settings, edit the Registry, and so on. If any of these activities are spotted, the software alerts you that the file potentially contains a virus.

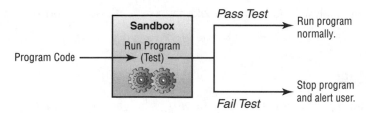

Figure 10.4 *How sandboxing identifies viruses*

There are two major suppliers of sandboxing technology, Pelican Security (`www.pelican-security.com`) and Finjan Software (`www.finjan.com`). Both companies offer products that work both on corporate networks and on individual PCs.

Behavior Analysis

Unlike other heuristic methods, behavior analysis doesn't look at program code. Instead, it looks at the program's *behavior*—or, more precisely, your system's overall performance. Based on how your system reacts to a specific program, the behavior analysis software can determine whether a virus or hacker attack is in progress.

Behavior analysis software runs in the background, tracking everything your system does. As you can see in Figure 10.5, it monitors every system command and Registry operation, and it reacts to any deviation from standard operating procedure. It can also isolate the problem, keeping your system up and running while it halts the running of the malicious code.

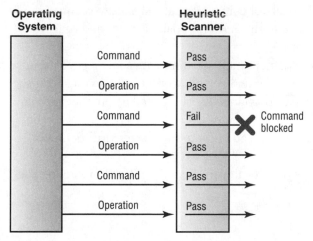

Figure 10.5 *How behavior analysis identifies viruses*

The primary proponent of behavior analysis is Okena (`www.okena.com`), with their Storm-Watch software.

Advantages and Disadvantages

The chief advantage of heuristic scanning is that it can catch new viruses before they've been added to a virus definition database. This means that heuristic scanning is vital for identifying new viruses and worms before they go widespread; in fact, this early warning system can often stop a new virus in its tracks, keeping it from becoming a bigger threat.

The primary disadvantage of heuristic scanning is that it's kind of a hit-or-miss affair. It produces a lot of false alarms—tagging harmless programs as viruses, based on inexact profiling. It also misses a lot of viruses—malicious code that happens not to fit the heuristic profiles.

So even though experts claim that heuristic scanning has a 70%–80% detection rate for new and unknown viruses, it's far from perfect. That means that it's best not to rely exclusively on heuristic scanning, but rather to use heuristic scanning in conjunction with the more traditional signature scanning.

Summing Up

Most major antivirus programs look for viruses using signature scanning technology, searching for individual pieces of code that are identified with specific viruses. These virus signatures are contained in large virus definition databases, which are updated when new viruses are discovered and analyzed. The problem with this approach, of course, is that a signature scanner cannot catch new viruses that haven't yet been added to the definition database, leaving your system vulnerable to attack by new and unknown viruses.

Because of this, most antivirus companies augment their software with some form of heuristic scanning. This type of scanning looks for general virus-like behavior rather than for specific viruses. Thanks to this program profiling, suspicious programs can be isolated before they've been identified by the antivirus industry at large. Then, once rendered harmless, a new virus can be sent to the antivirus company for further analysis—and addition to the master virus definition database.

In the next chapter we get past all the theory and deal with the nitty-gritty of protecting your system from virus attack.

CHAPTER 11

Preventing Virus Attacks

By now you should be convinced that the computer virus threat is real, and that your PC is at risk of contracting a potentially destructive infection. What can you do to reduce your risk and prevent future attacks?

Fortunately, there's a lot you can do to protect your system. And if you follow all the experts' advice, you can successfully defend against practically all known types of viruses.

But what if it isn't practical to follow *all* the experts' advice? The fact is, you can spend a lot of time and effort (and money!) trying to protect your computer from malicious attack. Maybe you don't want to go to all that trouble, or you're not diligent enough to be on constant lookout for signs of potential virus infection.

That's where this chapter comes in. I've sorted all the virus-preventive measures into three groups—those that are relatively easy to implement, those that take a bit more effort on your part, and those that are probably more trouble than they're worth. (Unless you're extremely obsessive about this sort of thing, of course.) Pick actions that best fit your computing style and level of risk, and you'll be that much safer than you were previously.

Easy Measures

Some computer users are obsessive about virus protection. They install multiple antivirus programs, subscribe to virus alert newsletters, and shy away from virtually all contact with other computer users. (See "Extreme Measures," later in this chapter, if this fits your personal profile.)

Most users, however, don't have the time or the inclination to put that much effort into protecting themselves from computer viruses. It's not that they're not concerned—they are, especially if they've been hit by a virus attack in the past—it's just that they don't want their defensive actions to get in the way of their daily computing activities.

The good news is that some simple modifications to the way you use your computer can stop the vast majority of malicious infections. A little effort on your part will have major impact on the security of your system.

The following measures don't require anything more on your part than a bit of diligence. You don't have to buy or install any software, or reconfigure your operating system and applications. All you have to do is be alert for possible dangers—which isn't that hard to do.

Don't Open Unrequested E-mail Attachments

This is the big one; this simple change in behavior will have the most impact on your virus risk. The behavioral change is easy, as it involves *not* doing something. In this case, the thing you don't do is automatically open any file you receive attached to an e-mail message. It doesn't matter what type of file the attachment appears to be, or who it came from. Just ignore it. Don't save it to your hard disk, and don't open it.

Consider this a zero-tolerance policy. Even if a file appears to be a harmless JPG image, it could be a Trojan horse virus in disguise. Even if it appears to come from someone you know, it could be a worm that hijacks the host's e-mail program and sends itself to everyone in that person's address book, without their knowledge. If you don't open any attachment, you won't risk infection. Period.

Now, all rules have exceptions. For example, if you specifically request a file from a friend or co-worker, and that file arrives exactly as expected, it's probably safe to open that file.

In any case, if you take this simple step and ignore all unrequested e-mail attachments, you reduce your risk of virus infection by a significant amount.

Don't Accept Files When Chatting or Instant Messaging

E-mail isn't the only way to receive potentially infected files. Users can also employ Internet Relay Chat and instant messaging to send files back and forth—which means that viruses can also be transmitted in this fashion.

The rule, then, is to decline any unrequested files sent to you when you're chatting or instant messaging. When that little message box pops up and asks you if you want to accept a file from a certain user, just say no—whether you know that user or not. You might think that person is sending you a personal picture; in reality, that file you download and open could contain a virus or a worm, and deliver a destructive payload.

WARNING *Some IRC programs can be configured to automatically receive files from other users, without your express consent. See Chapter 7, "E-mail, Chat, and Instant Messaging Viruses," to learn how to disable this feature.*

Don't Share Floppy Disks

You're starting to see a trend here. Don't accept files sent via e-mail. Don't accept files sent via IRC. Don't accept files sent via instant messaging.

And don't accept files given to you on floppy disk.

The logic is simple. Any file you receive can potentially carry a computer virus. It doesn't matter what that file looks like (its filename and extension) or who gave it to you; the bottom line is that you don't know where that file came from. If you run that file on your system—either from floppy or after you've saved it to your hard disk—any malicious code it contains can infect and potentially trash your system.

So if someone hands you a floppy and says "check this out," politely decline.

This advice applies to any form of removable storage media, by the way, not just floppies. An infected file is an infected file, whether it's stored on a floppy disk, Zip disk, or recordable/rewritable CD or DVD. It's not the medium that's important, it's what's stored there that could damage your system.

> **WARNING** *Floppy disks are doubly dangerous in that they can contain boot sector viruses, as discussed in Chapter 3, "Boot Sector and File Infector Viruses." If you use an infected floppy to boot your computer, you can infect your system without actually downloading or running an infected program.*

Display–and Check–File Extensions

The previous items were all about what *not* to do. This item requires a bit more effort on your part, because it gets down to the real cause of the problem.

Certain types of files can carry virus infections. Certain types of files can't. If you know, for example, that a certain file really truly is a JPG image file, you know that it's safe to open, because JPG files can't be infected.

To discriminate between different types of files, of course, you have to know two things— what type of file it is you're looking at, and what types of files are capable of carrying infections.

Let's start with the first point. Recent versions of the Microsoft Windows operating system do a good job of hiding file type information from you. That's because, since Windows 95, the operating system's default configuration turns off the display of file extensions. So when you look at a list of files in My Computer or My Documents, all you see is the main part of the filename, *not* the extension. You'll see something like `my picture file`, but not know whether it's `my picture file.jpg`, `my picture file.gif`, `my picture file.doc`, or `my picture file.exe`.

Yes, Windows will display an application icon beside the filename, but this can be easily changed. It's much better if you can see the file extension for yourself.

How you reconfigure Windows to display file extensions differs slightly by version, although the same logic applies. If you're using Windows XP, for example, you follow these steps:

1. Select Start ➤ Control Panel.

2. From Control Panel, select Folder Options.

3. When the Folder Options dialog box appears, select the View tab.

4. In the Advanced Settings list, uncheck the Hide Extensions for Known File Types option.

5. Click OK.

Once you have all your file extensions displayed, you need to know which file types are safe to open, and which can carry infections. This was covered back in Chapter 2, "How to Catch a

Virus," in Table 2.1. To refresh your memory, the following file types are *bad*, in that they can carry an infection:

BAT	SCR
COM	SYS
DOC	VB
DOT	VBE
EXE	VBS
INF	XLS
JS	XLW
REG	

WARNING *You should also avoid ZIP files, as they can contain compressed files of any type—including executable files.*

The following file types are safe, in that they can't be infected:

BMP	QT
GIF	TIF
JPG	TXT
MP3	WAV
MPEG	WMA

So if you're tempted to open an e-mail attachment, make sure file extensions are displayed, and then see if the file is on your safe list.

However...

One of the more common Trojan activities is to disguise a bad file type as a safe file type. There are many ways to do this, but the most common is the double-dot, or double-extension, exploit. This is accomplished by adding a `.jpg` or `.txt` to the first part of the filename, before the real extension. You end up with a name like `thisfile.jpg.exe`, which, if you're not fully alert, might appear to be a safe file.

This exploit is further exacerbated by the inclusion of spaces after the "middle" extension, like this:

```
thisfile.jpg                .exe
```

In some programs, the last part of the filename—the *real* extension—gets pushed off the screen, so you don't see it and think you're opening a safe file.

Which is why it's safer to avoid opening any files you receive, period.

Don't Use Illegal Software

This last piece of advice is good advice, period—viruses or no. Illegally copied software is bad business, as the creators of the software don't receive any revenues for those illegitimate copies. If the creators don't get paid, they won't have any incentive to create anything new—which will eventually cause the flow of new and innovative software to dry up.

Illegal software can be bad for you when it's infected with malicious code. This isn't something you have to worry about when you purchase a shrink-wrapped program off the shelf; all major software manufacturers submit their software to rigid pre-release virus checks. But software you download from an underground Web site, or receive from a Usenet newsgroup, isn't checked for infection. In fact, many malefactors deliberately infect pirated software and then post it online, knowing that this is an effective way to distribute their malicious code.

The bottom line is that if you download pirated software, you'll eventually get your just rewards. Stick to shrink-wrapped programs—or programs downloaded from legitimate Web sites—to avoid this type of malicious infection.

What About Antivirus Software?

You may wonder why I didn't include the use of antivirus software in the "Easy Measures" section. The answer is simple—it isn't an easy measure.

I personally believe that using antivirus software is an essential action, and include it as one of the items in "The Least You Need to Do," later in this chapter. But is it one of the easiest things to do? No, it doesn't pass that test.

You can think of the "Easy Measures" section as "Virus Protection for Lazy People." Most of the actions in this category involve *not* doing something—not opening e-mail attachments, not accepting files over IRC or instant messaging, not using illegal software. Using antivirus software is more deliberate, and it requires a bit more effort and technical expertise—not to mention the expenditure of some cash.

In addition, while you *should* use an antivirus program, you really don't have to. (I know, this will sound like heresy to some users—but bear with me.) The single most effective thing you can do to reduce your risk of virus infection is to refuse any files sent to you (via e-mail, IRC, or instant messaging) without your explicit request. The amount of protection you receive from an antivirus program is incremental to the effect of this simple behavioral change.

So if you want to reduce your risk with the least effort, skip the antivirus program and do everything recommended in the "Easy Measures" section. If you want a higher level of protection, then read on to "Moderate Measures"—and install that antivirus program!

Moderate Measures

The "Easy Measures" just presented involve only a slight adjustment of your computer use to be a little more cautious about the files that you download and run on your PC. While these measures provide for a substantial degree of defense against malicious infection, they won't catch every virus or worm that comes your way.

To increase your level of protection, you have to put more effort into defensive measures. That means getting into your software and doing a little reconfiguring, and installing and using an antivirus program. (If you're really serious, it also means preparing for the worst by backing up your crucial data files—and being aware of the latest viruses bouncing around the Internet.)

So this next batch of preventive measures requires a bit more effort on your part, and maybe even a slight expenditure of funds. The result will be an even lower risk of virus infection for your system, and greater peace of mind for you.

Install (and Use) an Antivirus Program

This is the big next step. Antivirus programs protect against infection, and clean up your system if you've been infected. If you want to be as safe as possible in today's environment, a good antivirus program is as essential as word processing or e-mail applications.

When you install an antivirus program, you should configure it to run automatically, in the background, whenever your computer is turned on. Running in this fashion, the program will scan any file you try to copy to your hard disk, any floppy disks you insert in your PC's floppy drive, and any files attached to e-mail messages. If a virus is found, the file's download will be blocked, and you'll be alerted to the problem.

There are many different antivirus programs you can choose from, as you remember from Chapter 9, "Antivirus Software and Services." That chapter presented detailed information about several of these programs, but if you have to make a quick choice, it's safe to choose one of the two best-selling programs: McAfee VirusScan (www.mcafee-at-home.com) and Norton AntiVirus (www.symantec.com). You won't be disappointed with either of these two programs; they both do a good job of scanning and disinfecting files on your system.

Keep Your Antivirus Program Updated

Purchasing an antivirus program isn't a one-time thing. That's because any program you use has to be kept updated with information on new viruses as they're discovered.

Every antivirus program includes a built-in database of virus descriptions (sometimes called "definitions"). You need to configure your program to periodically go online and download the latest virus definitions. (Downloading once a week is a good idea; wait much longer than that, and you're likely to miss the definition for any "hot" virus circulating that week.)

Most antivirus software companies provide some number of definition updates free of charge; after that, they charge you for new updates, typically on a subscription basis. That's why purchasing these programs isn't a one-time thing; you have to keep paying to keep the programs up-to-date. (But it's necessary—and worth it.)

WARNING *The biggest mistake users of antivirus programs make is not updating their virus definitions. If you don't update the definitions, the program won't be able to protect against new and improved computer viruses.*

Perform a Weekly Virus Scan

Once your antivirus program is installed, you have to use it. One of the most useful things you can do is to have the program scan all the files on your hard disk, looking for infected files. This type of all-system scan will find any bad files that got through the first line of defense, and alert you to the problem.

If an infected file is found, most antivirus programs go through several stages of action. The first action attempted is disinfection; the program tries to remove the virus code from the infected file. If the file can't be disinfected, you're typically presented with two options—you can opt to "quarantine" the file, keeping it on your hard disk but inaccessible, or you can choose to delete the file, permanently.

TIP *The only reason you might want to quarantine rather than delete a file is if the file contains information that can't be duplicated and you have hope that some future development will enable you to disinfect the file and save its information. Otherwise, an unusable quarantined file is useless; you might as well delete it and be done with it.*

Scan All E-mail Attachments

Naturally, you want to configure your antivirus program to scan all incoming e-mail messages for infected attachments. If you have your antivirus software scanning your attachments, it becomes safer to open those attachments that pass muster. If an attachment is found to contain a virus, your antivirus program will block the download of the file and alert you of the infected message. The infected file never makes it to your hard disk, and your system remains safe.

Scan All Files You Download

Your antivirus program will also scan all files you try to copy or download to your hard disk—whether that file comes from the Internet or from a floppy disk. If an infected file is found, it won't be copied; you can then feel reasonably secure about running any programs or opening any files that make it past the antivirus scanner.

Don't Download Files from Suspect Web Sites

Of course, you save yourself a lot of problems if you simply don't download files that could possibly be infected with malicious code. The best way to do this is to restrict your file downloads to legitimate, big-name Web sites—and to avoid downloads from underground sites, private sites, and sites that you've never heard of before.

What sites are typically safe for downloading? Here's a short list:

- Official manufacturer sites—for both hardware and software (this includes Microsoft's Web site, where you can find downloadable driver files for many different programs).

- Major file archives, such as CNET's Download.com (`download.cnet.com`), FileMine (`www.filemine.com`), Jumbo (`www.jumbo.com`), Shareware Place (`www.sharewareplace.com`), Tucows (`www.tucows.com`), ZDNet Downloads (`www.zdnet.com/downloads/`).

The files on these sites are actively scanned for virus infection, and they are typically safe to download.

Downloading files from less reputable sites—or from individual users via a P2P file-swapping network—is more risky.

WARNING *Theoretically, downloading an MP3 file via a file-swapping service should be safe, since MP3 files can't contain viruses. However, the old double-dot/double-extension scam can be used to trick you into downloading an infected file that you think is an MP3 file. Plus, some tricksters have been known to change an infected file's extension to MP3, fooling you into running an infected file by mistake. For these reasons, you're probably better off avoiding these public file-swapping services, and opting instead for one of the commercial music services, such as EMusic (`www.emusic.com`), pressplay (`www.pressplay.com`), or RealOne (`www.realone.com`).*

Back Up Your Files

This next item requires a bit of work on your part, but it's sound disaster preparation.

Because a computer virus can delete files from your hard disk—or, in the worst cases, make your hard disk completely inaccessible—it makes sense to keep backup copies of your most important files. Then, if a virus does delete files from your hard disk, you can recover from the disaster by restoring your work from the backup copies.

It's no secret that backing up isn't a popular activity; despite the good reasons to perform regular backups, the vast majority of users just don't do it. That's because backing up your files is tedious, technically challenging (for some users), and time-consuming.

That doesn't mean that you shouldn't make backup copies of your document files, however. If you have a Zip drive or recordable/rewritable CD, along with the proper backup software, it isn't *too* difficult to make daily or weekly backups of your most critical files to a Zip disk or CD-R/RW. (I don't advise doing your backup to floppy disks—you'd need too many blank disks to copy even the minimal amount of data you have stored on your hard disk.)

Most versions of Windows come with a built-in Backup utility. You can typically launch this utility by selecting Start ➤ All Programs ➤ Accessories ➤ System Tools ➤ Backup. The instructions for operating Backup are relatively straightforward; you select the files you want to back up, and the location you want to back them up to, and then start the process. Restoring files from your backup copy is equally easy; start the program and choose Restore instead of Backup, then follow a similar set of instructions.

You may want to go with a backup program that's even more automated than the Windows Backup utility. Among the more popular third-party backup programs are:

- Backup Exec (`www.veritas.com/products/`)
- Backup Plus (`www.backupplus.net`)
- NTI Backup NOW! (`www.ntibackupnow.com`)
- Retrospect Backup (`www.retrospect.com`)

Update Your Web Browser

One of the more popular ways to attack your computer system is through flaws in your Web browser. Because Internet Explorer is the most-used browser, it's also the browser of choice for virus writers. Known security holes in Internet Explorer can provide a convenient backdoor for many different malicious programs.

Give Microsoft credit, however; as soon as a security hole (such as the famous MIME header flaw, discussed in Chapter 7) is discovered, the company just as quickly issues a patch to stop up the hole. Of course, unless you download and install the update patch, your browser remains vulnerable.

Which means, of course, that you need to (1) stay on top of any and all security patches available for your Web browser, and (2) make a conscious effort to download and install said patches.

Assuming that you're using Internet Explorer, the place to go for browser updates is `www.microsoft.com/windows/ie/downloads/critical/`. This page keeps you informed of new patches, and includes links for downloading all available patches. You're probably safe in checking this page once a month, and making the appropriate updates.

Even better than updating your old browser is upgrading to a newer version. If you're running anything prior to Internet Explorer 6, go to `www.microsoft.com/windows/ie/` and download the latest version of IE. This new version should contain fixes for all previously discovered security flaws—as well as improved antivirus and security features.

WARNING *Just because you download a new browser doesn't mean that it won't have its own security holes. You still need to watch for new updates for your new browser, and download those patches as necessary.*

Update Your E-mail Program

Everything that was said about updating your browser also applies to your e-mail program—especially if you're using one of the two Microsoft programs (Microsoft Outlook or Outlook Express). Attackers are constantly targeting these programs to exploit newly discovered security holes; as Microsoft patches these holes, you need to update your program to keep up with the patches.

The place to check for Microsoft Outlook updates is `office.microsoft.com/Downloads/`. Outlook Express updates are listed on the Internet Explorer update page, at `www.microsoft.com/windows/ie/downloads/critical/`.

Update *All* Your Programs

For that matter, you should ensure that all the programs you use are updated regularly—especially Microsoft's application programs, such as Word and Excel. Applications that use macros are most at risk for security breaches, and later versions of these programs typically include protection for unauthorized macro use—in other words, protection against macro viruses. You should regularly check the software manufacturer's Web sites for any important security updates, and seriously consider upgrading to the latest and greatest version of the program—especially if the new version includes more robust antivirus and security features.

Turn Off Macros in Word and Excel

While we're on the subject, you can decrease your risk of infection by disabling the automatic running of macros in your applications—especially in Word and Excel. The latest versions of both of these programs enable you to run macros selectively, based on whether the macros come from a trusted source, or whether you explicitly okay their running. Activating this macro protection feature protects you against macro viruses that run automatically when you open an infected document.

To enable the macro protection in either Microsoft Word XP or Microsoft Excel XP, follow these steps:

1. Select Tools ➤ Macro ➤ Security.

2. When the Security dialog box appears, select either the Medium or High settings. (Medium prompts you before running macros; High disables all macros except those from trusted sources.)

3. Click OK.

Turn Off Scripts in Internet Explorer and Outlook/Outlook Express

As you learned in Chapter 5, "Script Viruses," some Web pages can contain automated elements, created with ActiveX controls and JavaScript scripts. These controls and scripts can also be used to automatically spread malicious code, without any intervention required on your part.

To increase your safety, you can configure the latest version of Internet Explorer to turn off the automatic running of these scripts. Just follow these steps:

1. Select Tools ➤ Internet Options.

2. When the Internet Options dialog box appears, select the Security tab.

3. Select the Internet option and click the Default Level button.

4. Make sure the slider is set to at least the Medium setting.

5. Click OK.

HTML e-mail can contain similar ActiveX and JavaScript code, so you should also configure your e-mail program to disable the automatic running of these scripts. While this procedure differs from program to program, the steps are similar to those found in Outlook Express 6:

1. Select Tools ➤ Internet Options.

2. When the Options dialog box appears, select the Security tab.

3. In the Virus Protection section, check the Restricted Sites Zone option.

4. Click OK.

Stay Alert to Virus-Related News

The final bit of advice that can help reduce your risk of virus attack is to stay aware of the latest virus-related news. In particular, you want to be alert to any new viruses that might be coming your way, so you can take the appropriate steps to protect your system from infection.

While it's easy to become obsessed with this type of information (see the next section), it's also easy to stay marginally aware of developing situations. The best way to do this is to add one of the major technology news sites to your daily Web browsing. CNET News.com (`www.news.com`) is good for this, as are ZDNet News (`www.zdnet.com/zdnn`) and TechTV's Web site (`www.techtv.com`). While these sites don't focus exclusively on viruses, they do carry stories whenever there's a major new virus attack—so you can be alerted to the pending danger.

Extreme Measures

This final batch of antivirus measures is somewhat extreme. These measures require a *lot* of effort on your part—and, frankly, some of them verge on the paranoid. Still, if you're obsessed with the entire topic of computer viruses and you want *ultimate* protection, following these steps will provide it.

Subscribe to Virus Alerts and Bulletins

You remember that "moderate" advice about keeping aware of virus-related news? If you're really into it, you can take the next step and subscribe to one of several antivirus/security bulletins. These bulletins are sent to you via e-mail, either on a regular basis or as breaking news requires.

The most popular of these antivirus bulletins include:

- F-Secure Computer Virus News (`www.datafellows.com/v-descs/`)

- Sophos Virus Info Email Notification (`www.sophos.com/virusinfo/notifications/`)

- Symantec Security Response Newsletter (`www.symantec.com/avcenter/newsletter.html`)

- Virus Alerts Mailing List (`www.viruslist.com/eng/maillist.html`)

- *Virus Bulletin* (`www.virusbtn.com`)

In addition, it pays to frequently visit the major antivirus information Web sites. Most of these sites have breaking news pages, where you can find all the latest virus alerts.

The best of these sites include:

- Computer Associates Virus Information Center (`www3.ca.com/virus/`)

- McAfee AVERT (`www.mcafeeb2b.com/naicommon/avert/`)

- Safer-Hex (`www.safer-hex.com`)

- Symantec Security Response (`www.symantec.com/avcenter/`)

- VirusList.com (`www.viruslist.com`)

Use Multiple Antivirus Programs

If one antivirus program is good, two must be better, right? Actually, some extremely cautious users swear by the simultaneous use of two or more programs. That's because different programs often check for different things. True, most programs work from similar databases of virus definitions, but beyond that, the differences emerge.

Most antivirus programs not only protect against known viruses, but also attempt to diagnose new and unknown viruses based on how they're written or how they behave. Most use some sort of heuristic diagnostic, although every company has their own formula—and thus performs with lesser or greater (or just plain different) effectiveness.

For this reason, it may pay to install multiple antivirus programs on your system. You can configure your main program to scan via the virus definition database, but then use the heuristic scanners on all the programs to look for different signs of infection.

WARNING *If you do use multiple antivirus programs, you should know that not all programs work well together. You may want to configure one program for real-time scanning, but then turn that program off to run a manual scan with the second program.*

NOTE *Learn more about how antivirus programs search for new and unknown viruses in Chapter 10, "Identifying New Threats."*

Perform a *Daily* Virus Scan

Scanning once a week isn't enough for some users. Even though it's time-consuming, you get a finer level of protection when you scan more frequently. Once a day is good; every few hours is recommended if you're extremely paranoid.

Block E-mail Receipt of Executable Files

If you can't trust yourself not to open e-mail attachments, and you don't trust your antivirus programs to catch all infected files, why not just stop the problem at the source—and configure your e-mail program not to download any executable programs, period? It's easy to do with newer versions of some e-mail programs. For example, in Outlook Express 6, you follow these steps:

1. Select Tools ➤ Options.

2. When the Options dialog box appears, select the Security tab.

3. Check the Do Not Allow Attachments To Be Saved Or Opened That Could Potentially Be a Virus option.

4. Click OK.

Express' big brother, Microsoft Outlook, doesn't include this explicit option—because it blocks all executable attachments, automatically. (You can't turn this feature off.) The chief competing program, Eudora, doesn't block executable downloads—it just warns you every time you try to open one.

Stop Using DOC Files in Word

After all this, if you're still worried about possible virus infection, it's time for more extreme measures.

For example, if you want to eliminate the possibility of macro virus infection in Microsoft Word documents, you can always quit using Word's default DOC file format. Since the DOC format enables the use of macro code, if you instead save your files in the RTF (Rich Text Format) format, there won't be any macros to worry about. (RTF files don't support macro capability.)

Since RTF files are fully compatible with all recent versions of Word, you'll still be able to exchange files with other users—you just won't be able to use any useful macros that are attached to the original DOC files.

Stop Using XLS Files in Excel

Along the same lines, you can eliminate the risk of macro virus infection in Microsoft Excel worksheets by abandoning Excel's default XLS file format. Use the alternate CSV format instead (which doesn't include macro support), and you won't have to worry about receiving any unwanted macro code.

Switch to Earlier (or Alternate) Versions of Your Applications

For that matter, you can abandon the current versions of your applications and revert to older versions that didn't include macro capability.

For example, PowerPoint didn't include macro capability until version 8. So if you switch back to PowerPoint 7 (or earlier), you won't have to worry about macro viruses in your presentations.

It's harder to go back to older versions of Word and Excel, since they both had macro capability early on. You can, however, switch allegiances and go with alternate programs—WordPerfect for Word, or 1-2-3 for Excel—that, while they include their own macro languages, will shield you from the more common Microsoft-specific macro viruses in the wild today.

Switch from Outlook/Outlook Express to Eudora

While we're on the topic of switching applications, one somewhat popular switch is from Microsoft Outlook/Outlook Express to Eudora. The reasoning is simple. Since virus writers specifically target the weaknesses in Microsoft's products (because Microsoft holds the lion's share of the market), they're *not* targeting Eudora. So while Microsoft users have to worry about downloading this week's security patch, Eudora users are immune from the Microsoft-specific attacks.

It's not that Eudora is a more secure program, it's just that it's less of a target.

Use a Viewer Program to View Your Files

At those times when all you're doing is looking at a document, you don't have to risk macro infection by opening the document from within an application. Instead, you can use a document viewer program to view the document's contents (and, often, its formatting) without actually launching any embedded macros.

Official viewer programs for Microsoft applications can be found at `www.microsoft.com /office/000/viewers.asp`. There are also a handful of third-party viewer programs, including Drag And View (`www.canyonsw.com/dnv.htm`) and MegaView (`www.xequte.com/megaview/`). While none of these programs let you edit a document, they also don't run any macros—or macro viruses.

Turn Off Windows Scripting Host

You can eliminate the risk of any script-borne infection by turning off the Windows Scripting Host function. WSH is what enables the running of VisualBasic and JavaScript scripts; disabling WSH removes some of the operating system's functionality, but it also protects you against all script viruses.

To disable WSH, see the instructions for your operating system in Chapter 5.

Don't Use IRC or Instant Messaging

Since some viruses arrive via IRC or instant messaging, you can completely eliminate this means of infection by not using either IRC or instant messaging. For some users this may be extreme, but it's effective.

Don't Use File-Swapping Services

Along the same lines, since it's possible to receive a Trojan MP3 or infected executable file when swapping files on Audiogalaxy, Morpheus, and other file-swapping services, you can achieve complete protection by not using any of these services. You simply can't trust other users *not* to send you infected files.

Don't Download *Any* Files from the Internet

For that matter, why download *any* files from the Internet? Even the best sites aren't perfect, and let some infected files through to users. Why risk it? When it comes to downloading files, just say no!

Don't Connect to the Internet

The next logical step, of course, is to sever your connection to the Internet. Since almost all viruses today come from some sort of online activity, if you don't connect, you significantly decrease your risk of infection. If you consider the Internet kind of the wild, wild west of the computing world, you can stay safe by not going west at all.

Don't Connect to the Network

The ultimate in protection is to avoid *all* contact with other computer users. That means no sharing floppy disks, no Internet, and no connecting to other PCs over a network. Your boss at work might not like it, but you'll have the one computer that isn't hit the next time a virus infection spreads through the company network.

The Least You Need to Do

Okay. Now you know all you *can* do to protect your system from a virus attack—including some extremely obsessive measures that most users will have the good sense not to employ. What, then, is the least you need to do—the most essential measures you need to implement?

Consider the following items a checklist for commonsense virus protection:

☑ Don't open any files attached to e-mail messages that you didn't specifically request.

☑ Don't accept any files sent to you while you're using IRC or instant messaging services.

☑ Don't accept or use floppy disks from other computer users.

☑ Configure Windows to display file extensions, and beware of any files you receive that have the following extensions: BAT, COM, DOC, DOT, EXE, INF, JS, REG, SCR, SYS, VB, VBE, VBS, XLS, XLW, and ZIP.

☑ Don't download files of any kind from any Web site that isn't an official software site or a major software archive.

☑ Install and use a major antivirus program—and update the program on a weekly basis.

☑ Configure your antivirus program to scan all files you download and all e-mail attachments you receive—and to perform a weekly full-system scan.

☑ Keep your Web browser and e-mail program updated with the latest security patches; check for new patches once a month.

☑ Configure your Microsoft Office applications not to automatically run macros.

Do all these things, and chances are you'll block 99% of the virus infections currently floating around the Internet.

Summing Up

The most impact you can have in reducing your risk of virus infection is to not download or run any files you receive via e-mail, chat, or instant messaging. You should also configure Windows to display all file extensions, and train yourself to avoid downloading any file types that are known to be infectable.

To further reduce your risk of infection, you should install and consistently use a good antivirus program, such as McAfee VirusScan or Norton AntiVirus. You should keep your antivirus program up-to-date by regularly downloading the latest virus definitions; you should also keep your Web browser and e-mail program up-to-date by downloading and installing the latest security patches.

While there are other measures you can take—some of them quite extreme—curtailing your downloading and using antivirus software will stop the vast majority of potential virus infections.

In the next chapter we examine what happens if you don't have a good defense—how you recover from a destructive virus attack.

CHAPTER 12

Dealing with a Virus Attack

When you realize your computer has been infected with some sort of virus, the most common initial reaction is panic, often followed by despair. While this type of reaction is understandable, it's important to know that catching a virus isn't the end of the world. Most virus attacks can be successfully recovered from, with just a little effort on your part. You don't, as a friend of mine once thought, have to throw away your PC and buy a new one; with today's antivirus tools, you can extricate the virus from your system and recover most infected files, with relative ease.

The ease and degree of recovery depends, of course, on the amount of disaster preparation you've done ahead of time. The more prepared you are, the less affected you'll be by most virus attacks.

Disaster Preparation

Before you ever receive your first virus infection, you need to make some plans. In particular, you have to plan for what you'll do *if* you get infected in the future.

Preparing for a virus infection is remarkably similar to preparing for any type of computer disaster, like a hard disk crash or total system failure. You want to have the proper tools on hand to get your system up and running again, and you want to have backups of any important data you could lose during the disaster.

In short, you want to follow the steps in the following Disaster Preparation Checklist:

- ☑ Install antivirus software on your system, and keep the installation CD and instruction booklet handy.

- ☑ Use your antivirus software to create an emergency disk.

- ☑ Use Windows to create a bootable startup floppy disk (or, if you're running Windows XP— which doesn't use a startup floppy—keep the Windows XP installation CD handy).

- ☑ Keep your Windows installation CD handy.

- ☑ Keep the installation CDs for all your programs handy.

- ☑ Make a regular backup of your key document files, and keep the backup copies handy.

- ☑ If you're running Windows Me or Windows XP, create a regular System Restore Point (described later in this chapter).

NOTE *Most antivirus programs enable the creation of an emergency disk, which can be used to disinfect your system in the event of a catastrophic virus infection. Refer to your program's manual or help system for specific instructions on how to create this disk.*

With these tools at your fingertips, you'll be ready to perform all the emergency operations necessary if and when your system falls victim to a virus attack.

Immediate Response

If you think your system has been infected by a virus (see Chapter 2, "How to Catch a Virus"), the first thing to do is ***DON'T PANIC!***

Let's go through those steps again:

1. Don't panic.

2. There is no step two.

That's right, the first action to take, if you think you've been infected, is no action at all. Don't pound the keyboard, don't delete any files, don't double-click any icons, don't click OK or close any pop-up windows, don't run any new software, don't reboot your PC, don't *turn off* your PC. And don't pull your hair out!

Just sit back, take a deep breath, and calm yourself down.

Then, after you're nice and calm, you can figure out what to do next—which mainly depends on what symptoms your system is exhibiting.

What to Do If Your System is Still Running

If your computer is still up and running—albeit slowly, or exhibiting some unusual behavior—you're in good shape. Excellent shape, actually.

In this situation, all you have to do is scan your system to see if it really is infected, and then (if the news is bad), remove the infection.

It's as simple as that.

Just follow these general steps:

1. Use your antivirus software to run a manual scan of your system.

TIP *If you don't have antivirus software installed, go online and visit one of the Web sites mentioned in Chapter 9, "Antivirus Software and Services," to run a Web-based scan of your system.*

2. If infected files are found, make note of the type of infection; then try to clean or disinfect those files.

3. If an infected file can't be cleaned, delete the file.

4. Go online to your antivirus software's Web site, and search for information about the type of virus identified during the scan; follow any additional instructions given on the Web site for completing the removal of that specific virus. (For example, you may be instructed to delete or edit certain entries in the Windows Registry.)

5. If you were forced to delete any document files, restore those files from a backup copy.

6. Reboot your system.

That's it, really. Most virus infections—those that don't crash your system, that is—can be simply and easily dealt with by your antivirus software. Just run the software and follow all instructions; then look for additional information online.

TIP *In some instances, there may be a specific "fix file" available from your antivirus software's Web site. These programs are specifically designed to remove a particular virus from your system, and supplement the normal virus-removal operation of your antivirus software.*

What to Do If Your System Isn't Running

If a virus causes your computer to lock up or not start, then you have bigger problems. You'll need to get your system up and running again, and then go through the necessary virus-removal techniques. You'll also need to restore any files damaged during the infection—and you'll probably have some damaged files.

TIP *At this point, if you're not comfortable with troubleshooting technical problems, you may want to call in a friend or colleague who likes to tinker with PCs in this manner. Alternately, you can bundle up your computer and take it to your local computer reseller or repair shop. (The big chains like CompUSA are always a good choice, if you have one nearby.)*

Here are the general steps you'll need to take:

1. Turn off your computer.

2. Insert your antivirus emergency disk into your computer's drive A.

3. Turn on your computer.

4. If your computer starts, follow the instructions in your antivirus software manual to run an emergency scan operation. (With some antivirus software, this emergency scan will start automatically when you boot from the emergency disk.)

5. If your computer doesn't start with the antivirus emergency disk, turn off your computer, insert the Windows startup disk in drive A, and restart your computer. When your computer finishes booting, remove the Windows startup disk, replace it with the antivirus emergency disk, and proceed with the emergency scan operation.

TIP *Windows XP doesn't use a startup floppy. Instead, you insert the Windows XP installation CD in your computer's CD-ROM drive and restart the computer this way. The computer will boot from the installation CD, and you can continue from there.*

6. The emergency scan operation will attempt to clean any infected files it finds. If it can't clean a file, it will deny further access to the bad file.

7. When the emergency scan operation is finished, note any messages or information displayed onscreen, then remove the emergency disk from drive A and turn off your computer.

8. Make sure that drive A is empty, and restart your computer.

9. When your system finishes booting, launch the normal version of your antivirus software and run a full system scan.

10. If additional infected files are found, make note of the type of infection, and then try to clean or disinfect those files; if an infected file can't be cleaned, delete the file.

11. Go online to your antivirus software's Web site, and search for information about the type of virus identified during the two scans; follow any additional instructions given on the Web site for completing the removal of that specific virus.

12. If you were forced to delete any document files, restore those files from a backup copy.

The only possible kink in this procedure is if you can't restart your system normally after performing the emergency scan. This can happen if the emergency scan doesn't detect the infection, if the scan can't repair the infected files, or if key system files are irreparably damaged by the infection. If this happens, you have several possible courses of action, in ascending order of magnitude:

WARNING *These options, except for the first one, are fairly drastic and should only be attempted by experienced computer users—and then only if you're sure your problem can't be fixed any other way.*

- Use someone else's computer to access your antivirus software's Web site and search for an alternative solution, if available.

- Restart your system from the Windows startup disk or CD, and use Windows System Restore (on Windows Me and Windows XP) to restore your system to a previous Restore Point. (See "Using Windows System Restore," later in this chapter, for detailed instructions.)

- Restart your system from the Windows startup disk or CD, and reinstall the entire Windows operating system.

- Restart your system from the Windows startup disk or CD, reformat your hard drive, reinstall the entire Windows operating system, reinstall all your software applications, and then restore all your document files from backup copies.

WARNING *Reformatting your hard drive will completely delete everything on the drive—including all your software programs and document files. (It will also delete any virus files—which is the point of the exercise.)*

It goes without saying that by the time you get to the last option, you've reached the point of last resort. It's probably worth consulting a more experienced user or technical support person before you reach this point—there may be other, less extreme, options available that you haven't yet thought of.

Cleaning Your System

Cleaning a virus from your system is normally as easy as running a system scan with your antivirus software, and choosing the "clean" option when an infected file is found. This type of file cleaning, however, doesn't always work—and there are sometimes other options available.

General File Cleaning

When you run a virus scan, your antivirus software looks for any and all infected files on your hard drive. When an infected file is found, you're typically presented with three options:

- Clean/disinfect/repair
- Quarantine
- Delete

Just what do these options actually mean—and which should you choose?

Clean/Disinfect/Repair

The option to clean (or disinfect or repair—they're all different names for the same action) an infected file looks straightforward. When you select this option, your antivirus software attempts to remove the virus code from the infected file. If the virus is "neat" about what it does, the infected code is easily identifiable, thus easily removed. All the antivirus program has to do is cut the virus code out of the infected file and then save the altered file under its original file-name. If all goes well, the cleaned file is identical to the original, uninfected file, and everything works fine.

Problems arise if the virus code *isn't* neat but is instead jumbled in with the file's original code. This makes it difficult, if not impossible, to isolate and surgically extract the virus code without damaging the original file.

Other problems arise if the insertion of the virus code caused some of the file's original code to get chopped off. This can happen if the original file is supposed to be a certain size, and the virus code pushes the original code past the cut-off point. If any of the original code is lost, the "cleaned" file won't function properly.

NOTE *Read more about how virus code is inserted into a program file in Chapter 3, "Boot Sector and File Infector Viruses."*

Still, if you have the choice, you should first try to clean (or "disinfect") an infected file. If the file can't be successfully cleaned, then you turn to one of the remaining options.

Quarantine

The word "quarantine" is confusing to many users, even though it certainly sounds like it has something to do with viruses. When you select the quarantine option, you choose to isolate the infected file so that it can't be accessed by you or your computer system. The antivirus software does this by moving the file to a special folder, to which normal access is blocked. The file is thus isolated, so it can't do further harm to your system.

Why should you choose to quarantine a file, rather than simply delete it? If attempting to clean the file didn't work and you think it has been infected by a relatively new virus, there are two possible benefits to choosing this option:

- Current cleaning techniques might not work with a new virus, but as the antivirus community learns more about the virus, more effective techniques may be developed. So if the infected file contains important information, you might decide to keep it "on ice" until your antivirus software is updated and the file can be better cleaned.

- You might also want to send a copy of the file to your antivirus software company for more thorough analysis. This is a good idea if you've been infected by a new virus, or a new strain of an existing virus. The antivirus software company can use the infected file to update its virus definition database, and thus help protect other users from the virus infecting your system.

If you have no intention of sending the infected file to the antivirus software company, and doubt the file can ever be cleaned, then skip this option and just delete the darned thing.

Delete

When you choose to delete an infected file, you remove it from your hard disk—simple as that. When a file is deleted, it can do no further harm, and it won't take up any valuable disk space.

Plus, deleting an infected file has a satisfying finality to it that might be the only pleasure you get out of this entire exercise.

Cleaning Specific Viruses

Some of the more "popular" viruses have inspired antivirus software companies (and others) to create virus-specific fixes. These fixes typically come in the form of a small software program that you download to your system and then run. The fix program then searches for and cleans any files infected by the particular virus, as well as makes any additional changes to your system—removing the virus' settings from the Windows Registry, for example.

These fix programs are great if you don't have any other antivirus software installed on your system, and if you know you've been infected with a particular virus. In most cases, however, your regular antivirus program does exactly the same job as the fix program—so running the program would be a duplication of effort.

Restoring Your System

Just cleaning a virus from your system might not be enough. If a virus damaged files to the extent that they had to be quarantined or deleted, you need to somehow restore those no-longer-usable files to your hard disk.

This task is made easier if you had the foresight to create backup copies of your data files. It's also easier if you're running Windows Me or Windows XP—which both include a nifty system restore feature.

Before you try to restore any files, however, you need to know *what* files to restore. This is an easy task, if you take the time to write down the names of any files that your antivirus software has to quarantine or delete. (Your antivirus program should display the name of each infected file it finds; get out your pencil and paper, and write down the names as they appear onscreen.)

Once you know which files you need to restore, then you have to figure out what restoration methods to use:

- If the unusable files are document files—Word DOC or DOT documents, Excel XLS or XLW worksheets, or even JPG and GIF graphics—you'll probably need to restore these files from the backup copies you (hopefully) made.

- If they are application files (typically EXE files for a particular software program), then you'll probably need to reinstall that entire piece of software.

- If they are Windows system files (with a variety of extensions, including COM, DLL, DRV, EXE, and SYS), then you'll need to do one of the following: use Windows System Restore to revert to a previously saved version, reinstall that particular file from your Windows installation CD, or reinstall the entire Windows operating system from your Windows installation CD. Obviously, you should start with the easiest method first.

Restoring Backup Files

If you had the prescience to make a backup of your key data files (as described in Chapter 11, "Preventing Virus Attacks"), you can use the Windows Backup utility to restore the backup copies to your hard disk. (In Windows XP, you launch Backup by selecting Start ➤ All Programs ➤ Accessories ➤ System Tools ➤ Backup.)

Each version of Windows has its own version of Backup. The version in Windows XP starts with the Backup Or Restore Wizard (shown in Figure 12.1), which makes it very easy to do what you need to do—identify the files you want to restore, and then restore them. It's not a difficult procedure, assuming you actually have backed up the files that you need to restore. (Remember, you want to choose the *restore* option—*not* the backup option!)

Older versions of Windows require you to select the Restore option manually, and then select which files to restore (and from where). Even without a wizard, it's a relatively easy process.

WARNING *Depending on when you made your backup, the backup copies you restore could be older than the files that were deleted—but that's still better than having no backup at all.*

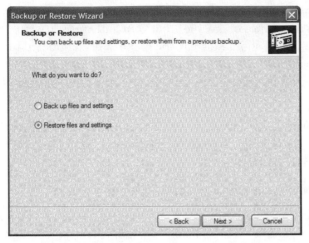

Figure 12.1 Use Windows XP's Backup Or Restore Wizard to restore files to your hard disk.

Using Windows System Restore

In most cases, you make backup copies of your document files—*not* of every file on your system. That's because, when you count all the operating system and program files, there are just too many files to bother with. (And, besides, these files aren't constantly changing, as your document files are.)

If you use Windows Me or Windows XP, you have access to a handy utility called Windows System Restore. This utility automatically restores key system files to the state they were in before your problems, virus or otherwise, cropped up.

The way it works is that System Restore creates a "mirror" of key system files and settings (called a *restore point*) every ten hours, whenever you install a new piece of software, or whenever you manually indicate. When something goes wrong on your system (a virus eats some important system files, for example, or resets essential settings), you can revert to a restore point from before the problem occurred, and very quickly put your system back in working order.

> **WARNING** *Make sure that you close all open programs before starting the System Restore process.*

To use System Restore to return your system to a previous state, follow these steps:

1. Select Start ➤ More Programs ➤ Accessories ➤ System Tools ➤ System Restore.

2. When the System Restore window opens, choose the Restore My Computer To An Earlier Time option, and click Next.

3. When the Select A Restore Point screen (Figure 12.2) appears, you'll see a calendar showing the current month. Any date highlighted in bold contains a restore point. Select a restore point, and click the Next button.

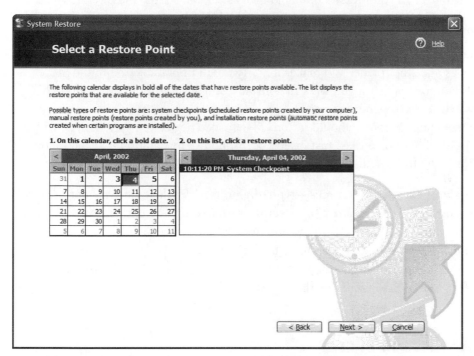

Figure 12.2 *Restore system files and settings with Windows System Restore.*

4. When the confirmation screen appears, click Next.

System Restore now goes to work, restoring your system files and settings to the way they were at the selected point in time. Note that this is a somewhat slow process, which could take a half hour or more to complete.

Reinstalling System Files

Unfortunately, System Restore doesn't restore *every* system file on your hard disk. And, of course, if you're using an older version of Windows, you don't have the System Restore utility to work with. This means that you still may need to install some Windows system files manually—if you can.

Some older versions of Windows let you browse the installation CD and search for individual files. If you can find the file you want, you can copy it from the installation CD to your hard drive. Other versions of Windows let you browse the installation CD, but they store all the system files (pre-installation) in a compressed format known as *cabinet (CAB)* files. While you *can* extract single files from CAB files, you have to know which CAB file contains the file you want, and then use a CAB-extraction utility to pull out the individual file—which isn't a job for casual or inexperienced computer users.

Windows XP goes one step further and makes it pretty much impossible to browse the installation CD. Which means that if you want to reinstall a single system file in Windows XP, you have to reinstall the entire operating system.

Fortunately, reinstalling Windows should restore all damaged or deleted system files, without harming any application or data files. Just insert your Windows installation CD and follow the instructions to effect a full installation.

WARNING *In some extreme instances—typically caused by destructive boot sector viruses—you may be forced to start from scratch and reformat your hard disk. If this happens to you, you'll lose all programs and data currently stored on the hard disk, and you'll have to reinstall Windows and all the other programs you use. The instructions for this operation are beyond the scope of this book; consult with a technical expert before you undergo this irreversible procedure.*

Reinstalling Application Files

If a virus has damaged the files of a particular application, you probably won't be able to run that application at all—until you've replaced the damaged or deleted files. With most applications, that means reinstalling the complete program, from scratch. Get out your original application installation CD and follow the specific installation and setup instructions.

Some programs may require you to delete the existing version of the program before you try installing it again. To do this, go to the Windows Control Panel and choose the Add or Remove Programs option. When the Add or Remove Programs window appears, select the program you want to delete, and then click Remove. Once the uninstallation is complete, you can install a fresh version of the program from the original installation CD.

Summing Up

If your computer is hit by a virus attack, there's no need to panic. Instead, you have to get your program up and running, and then remove the virus from your system. When your system is functional and clean, you can then work on restoring any files that were damaged or deleted during the infection and removal processes.

In most instances, the cleaning procedure can be accomplished by running a full-system scan with your antivirus software. If your system is damaged to the point where it can't start, you'll need to reboot your system using the emergency disk created by your antivirus software, or with the Windows startup disk (or CD) created by Windows. You can then run an emergency scan to remove the virus from your system, then reboot under more normal conditions.

In any case, you need to keep several items handy as part of your disaster preparation plans. You'll need the following: antivirus software, antivirus emergency disk, Windows startup disk, Windows installation CD, backup copies of your data files, and the original installation CDs for all the programs installed on your hard disk. With these tools handy, you should be able to recover from all but the most destructive virus attacks.

This ends our coverage of computer viruses. The next section of this book moves on to another type of computer attack—the type perpetrated by hackers, crackers and other individuals who want to take over your system. So turn the page and start reading Chapter 13, "Understanding Internet-Based Attacks."

PART II

INTERNET ATTACKS

Understanding Internet-Based Attacks

Having your system infected by a computer virus isn't the only way your computer can be attacked.

Malicious individuals can attack your computer directly, accessing your system via some sort of backdoor and then stealing important data, deleting files and folders, or using your computer to initiate additional attacks on other computers, networks, or Web sites. Particularly malevolent attackers can even flood your system with data requests and e-mails, overloading your system until it crashes or goes offline.

A detective analyzing a crime looks for three things—means, motive, and opportunity. When it comes to those attacks that we classify as *computer crime*, the means comes from the easy-to-use hacker and cracker tools freely available on the Internet; the motive comes from the desire of the attacker to do specific harm, prove his computer skills, or achieve some financial gain; and the opportunity comes from the lack of security prevention found on most individual computers and computer networks today.

This chapter looks at the broad topic of Internet-based attacks—what they are, why they happen, and what you can do to stop them. Remember, even though the attacker has means and motive, if you remove the opportunity—if you increase your system's security—you can stop most attacks before they occur.

The Dangers of Internet Attacks

In one 48-hour period in February 2000, seven of the largest Internet sites fell victim to devastating attacks.

It started at 10:20 A.M. on February 7, when Yahoo! was flooded with data requests from thousands of different computers. The flood of requests pushed the portal's system to overload and knocked it offline. Yahoo! stayed offline for three hours, until the attack subsided and the Web site could be brought back online.

The next day, at 10:30 A.M., Internet retailer Buy.com experienced a similar attack, which knocked it offline for several hours. At 3:20 P.M., another attack hit eBay, which went down for 90 minutes; CNN.com was hit at 4:00 P.M. and Amazon.com at 5:00 P.M., knocking both sites offline. The attacks continued into the morning of February 9, with E*Trade attacked at 5:00 A.M. and ZDNet at 6:45 A.M.

This wave of malicious incidents, presumably from the same perpetrator, showed how vulnerable the Internet is to attack. If Yahoo! and Amazon.com can be hit so hard that they have to shut down, what about all the other sites on the Web—and all of us users who are connected?

According to security provider Riptech (`www.riptech.com`), the number of Internet-based attacks increased 79% from mid-2001 to the end of the year. These attacks ranged from the relatively benign (tech-savvy vandals defacing corporate Web pages) to the highly destructive (knocking entire sites offline, or stealing databases of credit card numbers and passwords).

NOTE *Interestingly, the Riptech data contradicts monthly reports by the Federal Computer Incident Response Center (FedCIRC, at* www.fedcirc.gov)*, which shows Internet-based attacks falling off by roughly a third after the September 11th terrorist attacks on the World Trade Center and the Pentagon. The U.S. Space Command Computer Network Operations Center (*www.spacecom.mil)*, which tracks computer attacks for the U.S. Department of Defense, confirms that cracker attacks fell off immediately following September 11, but picked up again about a month later.*

Your risk of attack depends a lot on who you are and what you do. Obviously, large companies are more at risk than individuals (39% of all attacks are targeted at specific companies), with different types of companies facing different risks.

For example, Riptech says that companies in the high-tech, financial services, media/entertainment, and power and energy fields show the highest number of attacks per company—more than 700 attacks per company, on average, over the last six months of 2001. Even within this group, there are wide differences, with power and energy companies being assaulted twice as often as other types of companies.

Size matters, too. Companies with 500 or more employees had at least 50% more attacks than companies with fewer than 500 employees. Public companies suffer approximately twice as many attacks as private and nonprofit companies.

NOTE *The number of Internet-based attacks reported by businesses and individuals probably represents just the tip of the iceberg. According to CSI's 2002 Computer Crime and Security Survey, 90% of the survey respondents had detected computer security breaches in the past year, but only 34% had reported those attacks to authorities. That's because there's little incentive to report an attack; there's typically little the authorities can do, and the resulting negative publicity can harm the company's bottom line.*

It goes without saying that these attacks can be costly. Respondents to the *2002 Computer Crime and Security Survey* (www.gocsi.com), conducted by the Computer Security Institute (CSI) in conjunction with the FBI, reported an average cost of $204,181 per attack. This cost comes from the theft of proprietary information and in straightforward financial losses (lost business, financial fraud, and so on).

Unfortunately, this risk of attack is only likely to increase—in both the number and destructive capability of attacks. The world is getting less safe—and that includes the cyberworld that envelops computers and computer networks.

Internet Attacks and Terrorism

In the post-September 11th world, the likelihood of terrorist attacks on individual computers or networks, or on the Internet as a whole, is now a distinct possibility.

Bruce J. Gebhardt, CSI's Executive Assistant Director (and former Special Agent-in-Charge of the FBI's San Francisco Office) detailed the threat in the CSI survey:

"The United States' increasing dependency on information technology to manage and operate our nation's critical infrastructures provides a prime target to would-be cyberterrorists."

How likely is it that cyberterrorists will target your personal computer or small network? Not very. But it is possible that these online criminals will target larger systems on which you depend—large ISPs, major e-mail services, even the Internet backbone itself. A major attack that shut down the Internet's most popular sites could disrupt communications commerce across the civilized world, making the February 2000 attacks look like child's play.

And this isn't just speculation. Growing tensions between the U.S. and China in 2001 led to a spate of minor-league attacks from crackers of both countries, the Chinese crackers attacking U.S. firms around May Day, and amateur U.S. crackers responding in kind shortly after. While none of these attacks caused major disruption, these incidents demonstrate that Internet attacks can be used for political, as well as personal, gain.

Why Crackers Attack

One reason for the recent increase in Internet attacks is that it's becoming easier to conduct an attack. There are now more than 30,000 hacking/cracking-oriented sites on the Web (most of them underground), and untold number of "click and crack" programs and scripts that attackers can use to initiate an attack; when it comes to executing an online attack, detailed technical expertise isn't particularly necessary.

A person who initiates one of these attacks—a *cracker*, in technical parlance—is typically a male, aged somewhere between 13 and 28. Crackers are smart, they learn fast, and they're easily bored with work or schoolwork. Many of them are social misfits, to a degree, and prefer computers over other forms of activities and entertainment. Not surprisingly, most older crackers are employed in computer-related professions.

As to *why* a cracker does what he does, there are many possible reasons. He could be a disgruntled employee (or former employee), trying to get back at the company that "did him wrong." He could be a prankster, cracking into systems for the fun of it. He could be doing it for profit, using cracking as a form of industrial espionage against competitors. In this day and age, he could even be a terrorist, trying to cause chaos in the online community.

Interestingly, a cracker could also be attacking systems for the sheer challenge of it. Figuring out how to crack into a protected system is a definite intellectual challenge; making it past all the security can prove to the cracker (and to his friends) how talented he really is. It ends up being an ego thing; these crackers like to brag about their exploits, leaving their names (actually, their "tagging names") all over the compromised systems.

Other crackers have a more criminal intent. They're after credit card numbers and other data of real value. Or, on a higher level, they may not be above extorting a company to pay for the return of stolen data or for relief from an onslaught of attacks. These crackers are the ones that do the most damage, and—unfortunately—are good enough to be seldom caught.

Hackers and Crackers

A lot of folks use the term "hacker" generically, to refer to any person who initiates attacks against computer systems. However, that's actually a misuse of the term.

Technically, a hacker is a person who enjoys exploring the details of computer systems and programming code. A hacker might "hack" his way into a protected computer system, only to look around and expand his knowledge. In other words, hackers don't deliberately cause mischief (although damage can inadvertently result from a sloppy hack).

A person who *maliciously* breaks into a computer system is more accurately called a *cracker*. Hackers don't cause damage; crackers do.

Believe it or not, there is very little overlap between the hacker and cracker communities. Most hackers condemn the activities of crackers. So don't get confused by the terminology; hackers are (mostly) good guys, while it's crackers who cause most of the damage.

One final term, just in case it comes up: A cracker who cracks a phone or communications network (to make free long-distance calls, for example) is called a *phreaker*, and communications cracking is called *phreaking*.

Is Your Child a Cracker?

Most crackers are kids. Your kid has a computer. Your kid spends a lot of time online, alone in his room, with the door closed.

Is your child a cracker?

Just because a kid spends a lot of time with his computer doesn't mean that he's up to anything remotely malicious. Still, there are some warning signs that might indicate that your child has cracker tendencies:

- Spending more time online than with their friends in the real world. (This goes without saying.)

- Quickly switching screens (or closing windows) on the computer when you enter the room. (They could be looking at something they don't want you to see.)

- Lots of short (one- or two-minute) phone calls to suspicious long-distance numbers. (Check your monthly phone bill; this could indicate that your child is participating in illegal telephone conferences, or dialing into underground bulletin board systems.)

- Surreptitious use of prepaid calling cards. (See above.)

- Reading hacker/cracker-related magazines, such as *2600* or *Blacklisted*.

- Unexpected and extravagant purchases. (Where did the money come from—illegal online activities?)

- Phone calls asking for your child by his online username. (Other hackers and crackers won't know his real name, only his "handle.")

- Calls or notices from your Internet service provider about account or policy violations. (This occurs when someone complains that your computer was used for some abusive or malicious activity.)

What should you do if you suspect your child is engaging in malicious online activities?

One of the most effective reactions is to move the computer from his room to a more public area, like the family room. (It's tough to hack or crack when the whole family's watching.) This is a much better approach than installing software to limit access to specific Web sites or content; content-blocker software is effective enough for younger children but can easily be defeated by technically proficient teenagers.

You can also limit your child's computer use to certain hours during the day. In particular, rule out late-night usage, as this is when most hackers and crackers gather online. Computing in the afternoon is a much safer bet.

Even better, take a positive approach and try to steer your child's talent (and it *is* a talent, even when it's misused) to more productive purposes. Maybe he can volunteer at the local library or community center, or even offer his services to a local business. If your child is talented enough to hack or crack into secure computer systems, he has a real skill—one that should be used for good, not for evil. It's your job to channel that talent, not to suppress it—or to let it get out of hand.

How to Initiate a Computer Attack

How difficult is it to execute a computer attack over the Internet?

Unfortunately, it isn't that difficult at all—if you know what you're doing, if you have the right tools (in the form of cracker software), and if you've identified a computer system with inadequate security.

Steps to an Attack

Let's say you wanted to initiate an attack on some computer system somewhere. Just how would you go about it?

Believe it or not, there are plenty of Web sites that provide very explicit instructions for this type of malicious activity. But without getting into those kinds of specifics, we can go through the basic steps of an attack, as illustrated in Figure 13.1:

1. Choose a target.

2. Footprint the target—identify IP addresses, domain name servers, phone numbers, key personnel, and other information that might be useful in infiltrating the system.

3. Scan and map the target network, to identify systems and devices.

4. Identify vulnerable services and systems resources.

5. Choose a part of the network—typically an individual computer—with a particular vulnerability.

6. Exploit the vulnerability, by whatever method appropriate.

7. Take control of the system and perform desired activities.

In short, you target a network or Web site, find its weakness, exploit that weakness to gain entrance, and then do your dirty work. With the right tools—cracker software, available at the aforementioned underground Web sites—this isn't difficult to do.

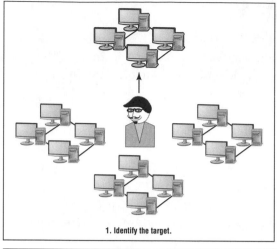

1. Identify the target.

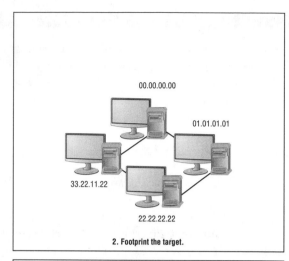

2. Footprint the target.

3. Scan and map the target.

4. Identify vulnerable resources.

5. Choose a PC that's vulnerable.

6. Exploit vulnerability.

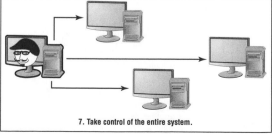

7. Take control of the entire system.

Figure 13.1 How to attack a computer network

Examining a Real-World Attack

Let's look at how this works in the real world—by examining the method behind the February 2000 attack on the seven big Web sites.

This attack started some time before February 7th. That's because the attacker had to "recruit" thousands of slave computers (called *zombies*) to do his dirty work. The attacker used a software program called a *port scanner* to troll the Internet for computers he could hijack. These computers, ideally, had a fair bit of computing power, as well as persistent (always-on) high-speed connections to the Internet.

In practice, that meant a lot of university-based computers connected via T1 and T3 lines, as well as some home computers connected via cable and DSL. In this particular instance, the attacker chose computers using the Linux, Unix, and Macintosh operating systems. (His backdoor software didn't work on Windows machines—although lots of newer backdoor software does.)

Once the zombie machines were identified, the attacker sent them each a backdoor Trojan program. Not all the systems accepted the software, but many did. With the backdoor program installed on each machine, the attacker could then control them remotely—at his convenience.

It's likely that all this prep work took place weeks before the initial February 7th attack. In the meantime, the zombie computers all operated normally, with the backdoor software "sleeping" in the background, ready to take control when ordered to do so.

On the morning of February 7th, the attacker went to work. He sent instructions to each of the zombie computers, probably via some sort of batch file. (It's unlikely he sent individual instructions to thousands of different computers, manually.) These instructions commanded each zombie computer to send a series of data requests (called *pings*) to the Yahoo! site, the first victim on the attacker's hit list. Each computer sent hundreds or thousands of pings, one after another, as rapidly as they were capable. These pings, coming simultaneously from so many different machines, were more than the Yahoo! servers could handle. The result was a slowdown, and then a shutdown, of the Yahoo! Web site, until the attack subsided.

NOTE *It goes without saying that all the attacker's instructions were suitably encrypted, so they couldn't be traced back to his personal machine. It's also likely that the instructions were filtered through multiple layers of machines, to further mask where the instructions originated.*

It's worth noting that the amount of activity coming from the zombie computers probably couldn't continue for long without being noticed. That sort of constant repetitive pinging would likely slow down the rest of the hijacked system, and jam up the system's Internet connection. As the zombie activity was identified (typically by the zombie's network administrator), it could then be shut down. That's why attacks like these typically diminish over a matter of hours, as zombie after zombie is taken out of the loop.

This type of attack, which has as its goal the shutdown of the victim's system, is called a *denial-of-service* attack. It's just one of many different types of Internet-based attacks, as you'll see next.

Different Types of Attack

If an attacker wants to execute an attack on a particular computer system, just what sort of things can he do? If you think of a computer attack as something like a home invasion, you can see that the attacker has his choice of malicious activities. He can rob the victim, vandalize the property, destroy the property, or co-opt the property for his own nefarious use.

> **NOTE** *If you want to learn more about the specific methods of attack—including the notorious denial-of-service attack—turn to Chapter 14, "Different Types of Attacks."*

Robbery

Robbery is often a prime attack activity. In a computer attack, the robbery takes the form of *data theft*, where the attacker steals valuable data stored on your system—usernames, passwords, credit card numbers, back account numbers, and the like. With these numbers in hand, the attacker can then access all your accounts (including your ISP account, bank accounts, and stock trading account) and perform additional thefts. He can also log onto your ISP and use your account to perform additional malicious activities—like sending thousands of spam e-mails, leaving insulting messages on message boards and in chat rooms, and harassing other users—all using your name.

> **NOTE** *Learn more about this type of identify theft in Chapter 20, "Protecting Your Privacy."*

Vandalism

An attacker doesn't have to steal something to do damage. Once he's inside your system, he can do all sorts of damage by deleting and altering valuable files—including the files that make up the pages of your Web site.

Like real-world vandalism, computer vandalism can take many forms. We'll look at the three primary forms of computer vandalism: data destruction, data diddling, and Web site defacement.

Data Destruction

Data destruction is fairly straightforward. The attacker gains access to your system and starts deleting things. He deletes data files, program files, even the system files necessary to keep your computer up and running. The damage comes from the missing files, which often can't easily be replaced.

(Obviously, fastidious data backups can minimize the impact of data destruction—even though your system or network might need to be taken offline until the restore procedure can be completed.)

Data Diddling

Data diddling is more insidious than data destruction. This type of vandalism occurs when the attacker enters your system and makes changes to selected files. He doesn't delete the files—merely edits and corrupts the data in some fashion.

Imagine an attacker entering your company's employee database and making subtle changes to the employee salary field. When the next payday arrives, your employees notice that their paychecks aren't right—they're paid either a lot less or a lot more than they should be. It could take weeks, if not months, to straighten out the problem—all because the vandal diddled with your data.

Or how about an attacker targeting your customer database, so that your next customer mailing includes a variety of rude comments to your valued customers? Or maybe it's the financial files that get diddled—throwing off your next financial statements. Or maybe the product photos in your marketing database have been replaced with nude pictures of Pamela Anderson.

You get the idea. Data diddling can do tremendous damage, and it isn't quickly—or easily—noticed. It might take some time for you to discover all the diddled data, and even then it's likely to be the results you notice, after the damage has been done.

Web Site Defacement

One of the most visible forms of computer vandalism is Web site defacement. This is when an attacker invades your Web site and replaces existing Web pages with new pages.

An attacker might completely replace your page with a new, typically offensive, page. He might change key information on your page, to confuse or insult visitors. He might change the links on your page to point to different, possibly offensive, pages. He may even insert hostile Java applets or ActiveX controls into the page.

It's likely that you'll first notice a Web site defacement when a visitor e-mails you about the changes. Actually, the visitor will probably be *complaining* about the changes—likely offended by the new content. To deal with the problem, you'll need to take your Web site offline, and then reconstruct all the pages. (From a backup copy, hopefully.)

Assault

You might want to call this one "pummeling into submission." These are attacks—like the February 2000 denial-of-service attack—designed to crash your system, typically by inundating it with pings and e-mails and other forms of electronic requests. As your system receives more and more of these requests, it begins to slow down, and then finally crawl to a halt.

According to CSI's 2002 *Computer Crime and Security Survey*, 40% of responding firms reported at least one denial-of-service attack in the previous twelve months. (This compares to 85% who reported one or more computer virus attacks.) These attacks are surprisingly easy to organize, and (if done properly) almost impossible to track. The attacker remains anonymous, while the target of the attack is left to pick up the pieces and try to bring the network or Web site back online.

Hijacking

The final form of attack might not do any damage to your system, but likely results in damage to someone else's network or Web site.

In a hijacking attack, the attacker surreptitiously installs backdoor software on your PC, so that he can operate it via remote control. With your PC under his control, the attacker then uses it to initiate a larger attack on another system.

For example, the February 2000 denial-of-service attacks used hijacked computers (called *zombies*) to send the pings that inundated Yahoo!, eBay, and the other sites. By co-opting thousands of unsuspecting computers, the attacker was able to amplify the attack—and provide a safety layer between himself and the targeted Web sites.

What You Can Do About Internet-Based Attacks

Computer attacks happen—that much you know. But what can you do to minimize your chances of being an attack victim?

Recognizing Your Vulnerabilities

Far too many individuals and companies (small and large) consider themselves essentially immune from an Internet-based attack. This kind of naive thinking leads to sloppy security and an increased risk of being caught unaware by a surprise attack.

Why do so many people ignore the risks of attack? It's a form of complacency resulting from faulty thinking, like the following:

Crackers only target large, high-profile companies, not small companies or individuals. If you think you're safe because you're a small target, think again. Small or not, you're still a potential target—particularly in this age of always-on broadband connections. Even if it's just you and your home PC, your computer can still be useful to a cracker putting together a denial-of-service attack on a bigger system. And you have all sorts of valuable personal information—passwords, credit card numbers, and the like—stored on your hard disk, that *someone* might find interesting. It doesn't matter how small you are, or how large you are, if you're out there, you're fair game.

It takes too much time and effort to pull off a large attack. Internet-based attacks are getting easier to perpetrate. A determined cracker can find all the tools he needs by browsing a few underground Web sites or IRC channels. "Script kiddies," who can't write their own code but *can* run existing cracker software, are legion. (And there's plenty of that software available; just check out Hackers.com—at **www.hackers.com**—to get your eyes opened.) Cracking isn't hard, and it doesn't take that much effort—just a bit of determination and a malicious intent.

The odds of being attacked are too small to worry about. (It could never happen to me.) The odds *are* small—but the danger is real. You only have to be hit once to feel the pain. (And your odds increase the longer you're connected to the Internet; anyone with a cable or DSL connection has particular reason to be concerned.)

All that said, if you're a typical home PC user, you shouldn't get paranoid about these types of Internet-based attacks. The simple fact is that home users are much less likely than businesses to be the direct or indirect targets of a computer attack. Crackers typically pick big targets—and the PC sitting in your den most likely isn't that important, or visible.

In a recent interview for Wired News, Paul McNabb, deputy director of the Center for Advanced Research in Information Security, put the matter in perspective:

"Except for a virus delivered by e-mail, most home users are unlikely to be affected by the security holes that have been plaguing the corporate world. Very few hackers have much interest in attacking home computers."

That doesn't mean you *can't* be attacked, or that you *won't* be attacked. It merely means that there are bigger targets around—which reduces your risk of attack.

Reducing Your Chances of Attack

Even if you are a small target, that doesn't mean you shouldn't take precautions. There are a few things you can do to reduce your risk of attack—and to minimize the impact if an attack does occur.

- Install and activate a firewall program, to create a buffer between your PC and the Internet.

NOTE *Firewall programs restrict the flow of data from your PC to the Internet, and vice versa. Learn more about firewalls in Chapter 18, "Choosing a Firewall."*

- Deactivate file sharing on your PC, so attackers won't be able to access your personal files.

- Activate password protection to access your PC—and use a long password (seven digits or more) with a combination of letters, numbers, and special characters (!, @, #, $, etc.).

- Make regular backup copies of your important data—just in case.

NOTE *Learn more about preventing Internet attacks in Chapter 15, "Protecting Your System from Attack."*

Recognizing an Attack

What are the signs that your computer is under attack, or being used to attack another computer? Here are some behaviors to look out for:

- An unusual amount of hard disk activity—especially when the system isn't being used.

- An unusual amount of modem use—especially when you're not browsing the Web or using e-mail.

- An unusual number of e-mail messages appearing in your inbox.

- If you connect via a dial-up connection, your system automatically dialing into the Internet, without your prompting.

- If you're running a small network, an unusual amount of network or Internet traffic.

- If you run a Web site, an unusual amount of Web site traffic.

- Changed or missing Web pages on your Web site.

- Missing or edited files on your hard disk.

NOTE *Most of these behaviors can also have benign causes, such as background operating system activity, or automatic online updating of your software.*

Stopping—and Recovering from—an Attack

The first thing to do if you're attacked is to stop the attack. Disconnect your system or network from the Internet, which should break off the attack. (If you lease Web space from a Web hosting service, you may want to give them a call and alert them to your attack—they may be able to block the attack from their end.)

Once you're offline, run a round of system diagnostics. You should also run a virus scan, particularly looking for backdoor Trojan programs (like Back Orifice, discussed in Chapter 6, "Trojan Horses and Worms").

You should then look for any missing or changed files on your system. If you're running a Web site, look for any changes to your Web pages. Replace any missing or vandalized files, make any necessary system repairs, and then prepare to go back online.

Once you're back online, you may find that you're still being attacked. (This is likely if you're the victim of a denial-of-service attack.) If you have the proper software (discussed in Chapter 18), you can block access to your site from specific domains—which should enable you to identify and block the heaviest attackers. If this is beyond your capabilities, go back offline and telephone your ISP or Web site hosting service to alert them of the attack. They'll take things from there.

Reporting an Attack

It goes without saying that you should report any attack on your system. You should notify your ISP and your Web site hosting service (if you use one). You should also, if you can, backtrace the source of the attack and report it to the hacker's ISP.

NOTE *There is specific backtracing software for this purpose; some consumer-level firewall software (such as the BlackICE and Sygate product lines) will also perform this task. In Chapter 18 you'll see how to backtrace an attack, using Sygate Personal Firewall.*

If you run a small network and you had a large attack, consider reporting it to the proper authorities—the National Infrastructure Protection Center (NIPC, at `www.nipc.gov/incident/incident.htm`) is a good place to start.

Whoever you report it to, make sure you can provide enough information to make the report worthwhile. Indicate the time of the attack, the details of the attack (what was attacked, and how), and any other data you might have. Naturally, you should know your domain name and IP address, and other key information about your system—anything that can help the authorities track down the perpetrators.

WARNING *If your system is attacked, it's your responsibility to fend off the attack and report it to the proper authorities. Don't expect your ISP or Web site hosting service to do this for you.*

Learning More About Internet-Based Attacks

One of the best ways to prepare for and prevent online attacks is to get smarter about the topic. Fortunately, there are numerous Web sites devoted to Internet-based attacks; some of the best of these online security resources include:

- AntiOnline.com (`www.antionline.com`)
- CERT Coordination Center (`www.cert.org`)
- Computer Security Institute (`www.gocsi.com`)
- Computer Security Resource Center (`csrc.nist.gov`)
- Info Security News (`www.infosecnews.com`)
- *Information Security* magazine (`www.infosecuritymag.com`)
- InfoSysSec (`www.infosyssec.com`)
- Microsoft Security (`www.microsoft.com/security/`)
- National Infrastructure Protection Center (`www.nipc.gov`)
- Security News Portal (`www.securitynewsportal.com`)
- SecurityFocus (`www.securityfocus.com`)
- Stay Safe Online (`www.staysafeonline.info`)

Summing Up

Malicious computer users can use various methods to attack Web sites, corporate and small networks, and individual computers connected to the Internet. These attacks can take the form of data theft, vandalism, denial-of-service (via system overload), and system hijacking. In this last type of attack, the attacker uses backdoor software to remotely control your system, and then use it in a further attack on another system—thus isolating himself from possible identification.

The people who attack computers in this manner are called crackers. They're typically young males with a surfeit of computer skills—although a number of "click and crack" programs exist that make it easy for even nontechnical users to crack into unsecured systems.

If you're the victim of an Internet attack, the first thing you should do is sever your system's connection to the Internet. Then you can repair any damage resulting from the attack, and remove rogue software (including backdoor Trojans) from your system. Once the attack has subsided, you can go back online—and report the attack to the proper authorities.

In the next chapter you'll learn more about the mechanics of computer attacks—the different methods attackers use to infiltrate unsuspecting systems.

CHAPTER 14

Different Types
of Attacks

I t's an unfortunate fact of online life that there are many different ways for a determined cracker to attack your computer—or your company's network, or your Web site. Attacks can be very low-tech (impersonating a company employee in a phone call) or extremely high tech (redirecting a Web site's address to another server). And, depending on the motives of the attackers, they can do tremendous damage.

This chapter presents the most common types of Internet-based attacks. Some of these attacks are more geared toward networks and Web sites, rather than individual computers. But all have been used, and will likely continue to be used, to attack all types of computers all around the globe.

Prepare to be shocked.

Social Engineering Attacks

A social engineering attack is like an old-fashioned con game. The attacker uses human nature to fool the victim into allowing improper access or revealing private information.

Social engineering attacks can come in a number of guises. For example, you may receive an e-mail from some official-sounding source, asking you to verify your Internet password via return mail. When you do so, you send your password to the attacker, who can now access your account at will. (A variation of this approach requests that you change your password to a specific word, for some technical-sounding reason; when you do so, the attacker can use the new password—which he supplied—to access your account.)

Instant messaging and Internet Relay Chat (IRC) are two other popular media for social engineering attacks. You may get a message from a stranger, supposedly sending you naked pictures or MP3 files or something else of interest or value; when you download the file, it contains a backdoor Trojan (or something worse). Or you may get the official-sounding message from a user with a fancy, authoritative title, asking you to change passwords or supply credit card information. If you go along with the con, you provide personal information to the attacker.

Of course, social engineering attacks don't have to be technical in nature. Smooth-talking conmen have always been able to talk their way into just about any situation they want. Take the example of the would-be attacker who phones your company's switchboard or IT department, impersonating a real-life employee and asking for information such as the network's private dial-in phone number, or that user's password. ("I forgot my password—can you believe it?") Once he has the required information, the attacker can gain access to the company's network—and do his dirty work.

It's surprising how often this sort of con actually works.

Human beings being... well, *human*, it's virtually impossible to protect against social engineering attacks. You can educate your family and colleagues until you're blue in the face, but some people will always be gullible enough to provide information that they shouldn't. All you can do is look out for yourself, and do your best to resist these types of official-sounding cons—and, as always, refuse any files send over chat or instant messaging and never, *never*, send private information unless you're sure you're talking to an honest-to-goodness official authorized representative of the company at hand.

> **WARNING** *Valuable information can also be stolen by more traditional methods. For instance, many attackers retrieve passwords and other information by "dumpster diving," and looking for scraps of paper used to write down important numbers and then thrown in the trash. In addition, many employees write their passwords on Post-It notes and leave them affixed to their computer screens; a data thief in the parking lot with a pair of binoculars (or an attacker posing as part of the cleaning crew) can obtain a wealth of information, thanks to these sloppy security habits.*

Impersonation Attacks

While a social engineering attack is about fooling people, an *impersonation attack* is about fooling computers. This type of attack occurs when an attacker steals the access rights of an authorized user. The attacker can then configure his computer to impersonate the other, authorized computer, and gain access to otherwise-closed systems.

An impersonation attack works because all the security apparatus thinks that it's dealing with the original computer. It's like stealing someone's ID, but on a more technical level; by all accounts, you *are* that person, and your actions are never questioned.

A typical impersonation attack starts when a cracker uses some sort of "sniffer" software to eavesdrop on an individual connecting to an ISP, or company network. This software records the data flowing back and forth, which includes the user's username and password. This information at hand, the attacker can then log onto the ISP or network using the stolen username and password, and then do anything and go anywhere permitted by the original user's access level.

Once the damage has been done, the attacker can log off, with absolutely no fear of ever being caught. Even if the damage can be traced, it will be traced back to the impersonated user, who (unknowingly) had his or her password stolen—*not* to the attacker himself.

Impersonation attacks are difficult to protect against. Perhaps the best defense is to require all users to change passwords frequently (once a week or so). This way the risk for an impersonation attack is always limited in duration, until the impersonated password is officially changed.

Sniffers and Scanners

When you're connected to a network (or to the Internet via a network—including the type of network used in cable modem connections), your presence can be detected by a "sniffer" program. Sniffers listen to network traffic and then examine what exactly comes across the network. These programs can not only watch network traffic, but can also grab unencrypted communications—including usernames and passwords sent in plain text format. (Sending information to a non-secure Web site opens you up for sniffer theft; using a secure Web site will thwart most sniffers.)

Your online presence can also be detected with port scanning software. A port scanner is a robot program that examines computers connected to the Internet, looking for what services each computer is running. When an unprotected port is detected, that information is sent back to the attacker—who then knows which computers are vulnerable to attack, and can target his attacks accordingly.

Most firewall software will detect port scans and alert you of unusual activity. There are also several dedicated software programs, such as Genius (`www.indiesoft.com`) and Nuke Nabber (`www.rogerdidit.com/nonuke.html`), that detect all port scans of your system and alert you.

Transitive Trust Attacks

This type of attack exploits the inherent trust in a host-to-host or network-to-network relationship. This type of trust typically enables computers outside the current network to access the network as though they were part of the network—without the typical passwords and protocols necessary for remote access. By breaking into this trusted relationship, the attacker can then access the network without a password.

For example, a network administrator can create a database of "trusted" host computers (typically other servers in a big company), so that users from those computers can log in without giving a password. If an attacker can edit that list of trusted computers to include his own computer, then he can gain access to the network without even needing a password.

Another way this works is via an administrator account—the type of account provided to network administrators, which enables them access to configuration and control operations that normal users typically can't access. If an attacker can compromise one of these administrator accounts, he is automatically "trusted" by the system to perform all manner of file operations.

Transitive trust attacks can be limited in scope if internal firewalls are put into place between different parts of the network, or installed on individual PCs. This way an attacker gaining privileged access to the network would be thwarted when they attempted to exploit those privileges.

WARNING *Wireless networks are particularly vulnerable to impersonation attacks, as roaming computers typically connect without a lot (if any) manual user interaction.*

Exploits

An *exploit* is an attack that takes advantage of a bug or hole in a piece of software or operating system.

And, unfortunately, there are many such holes.

In the current world of bloated, poorly programmed, and inadequately tested software, bugs and holes are the norm. Most software and operating systems today—including the latest Microsoft OS, Windows XP—have security added as an afterthought, if at all. With hackers and crackers diligently looking for holes big enough to break in through, it's no surprise that attacks-via-exploits are increasingly common.

TIP *Keep abreast of known exploits by browsing the AntiCode Archives or visiting the AntiOnline InfoSec Mailing List forums, both at* www.antionline.com.

This type of attack exploits a known software weakness. Once inside the system (thanks to the security hole), the attacker can then wreak whatever havoc he desires.

You learned about a well-publicized MIME exploit in Chapter 7, "E-mail, Chat, and Instant Messaging Viruses." A security hole in Internet Explorer (later patched) enabled files of certain MIME types to be opened automatically; an attacker could exploit this hole by recoding the header of a virus file to look like one of the "auto open" MIME types.

Naturally, for an exploit to occur, there first has to be an identified security hole. But once the hole exists, it's there for any inspired cracker to exploit.

The best defense against computer exploits is to keep all your software updated with the latest security patches. In most cases, a manufacturer reacts to the discovery of a security hole with an immediate security patch. If you're aware of newly discovered holes, and up to date on your patching, you'll reduce your risk of being the victim of an exploit attack.

NOTE *Many exploits utilize a programming bug called a buffer overflow. When the data buffer of an affected program is overloaded with data (thanks to the attacker), the original program code is forced out and the buffer is rewritten with malicious code. This essentially (if temporarily) reprograms the program, enabling the attacker to execute his own malicious code.*

Infrastructure Attacks

An infrastructure-based attack exploits weaknesses in a technical protocol or particular infrastructure. It's like an exploit, except more widespread—it isn't limited to a particular piece of software, it's system-wide. And, with few exceptions, the security holes exploited in infrastructure attacks are not easily fixed; the weaknesses are inherent in the infrastructure.

There are many types of infrastructure attacks, most of which allow an attacker (with the proper tools) to gain access to your computer or network. What the attacker does with that access, of course, is up to him.

NOTE *The following are relatively technical topics, mostly relating to larger corporate networks. Home and small network users typically aren't at high risk from these types of infrastructure attacks.*

DNS Spoofing

DNS spoofing takes place when an attacker hijacks the name (actually, the DNS name corresponding to your IP address) of your computer or Web server. The attacker maps your computer's DNS name (`mycomputer.com`) to his own computer's IP address; any user referencing `mycomputer.com` is automatically routed to the attacker's computer, instead.

By using DNS spoofing, an attacker can also gain access to other servers and networks, via a transitive trust attack. If Network A grants trusted access to Server B, and an attacker spoofs Server B (by mapping Server B to Computer C), then Computer C can access Network A at will.

FTP Bouncing

FTP bouncing is a form of session hijacking, which you'll read more about in a few pages. In this instance an unwitting FTP server is used to send e-mail to other computers, thus hiding the source of any e-mail-based attack.

FTP bouncing begins when an attacker finds an FTP server that has a writable upload area. The attacker uploads an e-mail message to the server, and then uses another script or program to send the e-mail from the FTP server to the target recipient(s). When the recipient receives the message, it appears to come from the FTP server—*not* from the attacker's normal e-mail address.

FTP bouncing can be used to send a flood of spam to multiple recipients, or multiple messages to the same recipient (thus clogging the recipient's inbox with what is called an *e-mail bomb*).

Anyone running an FTP server must carefully manage the server traffic to prevent this type of hijacking—or eliminate all write privileges for anonymous users. When you're the ultimate recipient of the e-mail, there's not much you can do except delete the unsolicited—and unwanted—messages.

NOTE *Learn more about e-mail spam in Chapter 27, "Understanding Spam."*

ICMP Bombing

The Internet Control Message Protocol (ICMP) is used by Internet routers to notify a host computer when a specified destination is unreachable. An attacker can effectively knock a computer off the Internet by "bombing" it with bogus ICMP messages. (This effect is similar to that of a denial-of-service attack, discussed later in this chapter.)

The best defense against an ICMP bombing is a strong firewall, configured to block all ICMP messages.

Source Routing

This is a sophisticated attack that uses ICMP bombing and DNS spoofing as interim steps in the larger attack. It takes advantage of an infrastructure quirk that requires source-routed traffic over the Internet to return via the same route from which it came.

This type of attack starts with an ICMP attack on a trusted host on the target network. This knocks the host off the Internet, and enables the attacker's computer to take that computer's place—by setting its address to that of the bombed computer. The host computer for the network that is the ultimate target of the attack now views all communications from the attacking computer as coming from the trusted host, coming over the expected source route. This enables the attacking computer to gain access to the target network, and do whatever.

A strong firewall is a good defense against this type of attack. Heavy-duty network firewalls will block source-routed data and trigger alarms during a possible attack.

Racing Authentication

This is a fun little attack, where the attacker's goal is to "fill in the blank" faster than the victim he's trying to impersonate.

In this type of attack the attacker begins to log into the target network at the same time as another user. The attacker uses the other user's username, and waits until the user has entered all but the last digit of his or her password. Then, before the user can enter the final digit, the attacker enters a single character, guessing at the proper response. If the attacker guesses correctly—and types fast enough—he enters the target network, while the slower-typing user gets locked out.

If the password is numeric-only, the attacker has a 1-in-10 chance of guessing correctly. (Not bad odds.) If the password is alphanumeric, however, the odds of guessing correctly diminish—which reinforces the security value of a password that combines letters, numbers, and special characters.

TCP Sequence Guessing

This type of attack enables a flow of attack data to infiltrate the target network. The technique hinges on the fact that connections over the Internet are numbered, in a semi-random, increasing-number sequence. The attacker intercepts the current connection to the target computer, and (using the appropriate software) guesses the number of the next possible sequence. If the attacker guesses correctly, a new connection to the target computer is established, and malicious data or instructions can then be transmitted.

As with most infrastructure attacks, a TCP sequence attack can be thwarted by a correctly configured network firewall—which should identify any attempts to guess at a connection sequence.

TCP Splicing

TCP splicing is the cracker equivalent to splicing into a coaxial cable to steal a cable television signal. The attacker positions himself somewhere on a network path between two computers and waits for a legitimate connection to be established between the two. Once the connection is established, the attacker splices into the connection, effectively hijacking the data stream and "becoming" one of the users. Once connected in this fashion, the attacker can do anything the original user could do.

This type of attack, however, is limited by the effective use of application-level passwords on the target computer. Even though the attacker can imitate the original user, he won't know all of that user's passwords—and thus won't be able to access password-protected programs and data.

Wireless Vulnerabilities

Wireless computer networks present a unique set of infrastructure-related security concerns. With more and more companies and households installing networks based on the WiFi wireless protocol (which transmits data via radio waves), the risk of wireless intrusion is rising.

While WiFi has its own built-in encryption system (called Wired Equivalent Privacy, or WEP) to protect against intrusion, this feature is not automatically activated during a basic installation. (According to an informal survey by security firm I-Sec at `www.i-sec.biz`, two-thirds of all WiFi networks don't have WEP turned on.) Without this encryption, it's relatively easy for someone to crack into the network, no wires necessary.

Some potential attackers hunt for wireless networks to crack via "war-driving" expeditions. Essentially, this involves driving around major business districts using a laptop PC (fitted with a wireless network card) and some sort of makeshift antenna. (Old coffee cans and empty Pringles tubes are said to perform especially well.) Once an insecure wireless network has been identified, the cracker uses his standard box of tools to break into the network, and do whatever damage he wants.

This WiFi vulnerability isn't an issue just for crackers. If one of your neighbors has a wireless network, without WEP enabled, you may inadvertently access their network from your WiFi-equipped PC. Yes, there's a distance limitation (that's why crackers use an additional antenna, to boost the signals), but if you're in the neighborhood, any unsecured wireless network is fair game.

Denial-of-Service Attacks

A denial-of-service (DoS) attack floods a computer or network with data or messages, essentially overwhelming the system and preventing it from being used. This is perhaps the most destructive type of Internet-based attack, as it can completely shut down a target computer or Web site—for several hours, or even days.

Denial-of-service is probably the most common form of Internet attack today. According to CSI's 2002 *Computer Crime and Security Survey*, 40% of responding firms reported at least one denial-of-service attack in the previous twelve months. (This compares to 85% who reported one or more computer virus attack.)

There are many ways to initiate a denial-of-service attack, including:

- Use ICMP bombing (discussed earlier) to throw the router off the Internet.

- Use e-mail bombing to overwhelm the target's e-mail server.

- Flood the target computer with garbage data packets to overwhelm its Internet bandwidth.

- Repeatedly ping the target computer to overwhelm its Internet bandwidth, as in an ICMP attack.

Most DoS attackers utilize multiple remote-controlled computers (*zombies*, discussed next) to better flood the target computer. A large-scale denial-of-service attack—technically called a *distributed denial-of-service* attack—can utilize thousands of zombie computers, all simultaneously flooding the target with junk data.

There is little one can do to protect against DoS attacks. Once an attack begins, however, it can be shut down by blocking the attacking computers' access.

NOTE *Don't confuse a DoS attack with the old DOS (actually, MS-DOS) operating system. DoS attacks can come from any type of computer running any type of operating system—including, but certainly not limited to, DOS.*

Session Hijacking

This type of attack doesn't affect the target computer, but rather uses it to perpetrate a further attack on another computer. Session hijacking occurs when an attacker gains remote control of your computer. Instead of inflicting damage on your machine, the attacker uses it to participate in a denial-of-service attack or to execute some other form of Internet-based attack. Since the attack comes from a hijacked computer, it can't be traced back to the original attacker; your machine is nothing more than a zombie, doing its master's bidding.

Most session hijacking is enabled by the installation of backdoor Trojan software (such as the infamous Back Orifice program) on the zombie machine. You can avoid session hijacking by taking the normal precautions against Trojan infection, as discussed in Chapter 6, "Trojan Horses and Worms."

WARNING *Session hijacking is often accompanied by the use of keylogger software. These programs secretly log all the keystrokes entered on your machine, and then send that information back (via the Internet) to the attacker—who can use the information to steal any passwords or personal information you type with your keyboard. Learn more about keyloggers in Chapter 20, "Protecting Your Privacy."*

Data-Driven Attacks

A data-driven attack is a virus or Trojan attack. You receive a file—via e-mail, IRC, or instant messaging—and then download and run the file. Once launched, the file performs some sort of malicious action.

In a network environment, the most common data-driven attack is the backdoor Trojan. In a backdoor Trojan attack, the attacker somehow convinces you to download and run a program that opens a backdoor to your computer system. This backdoor enables the attacker to remotely access and control your computer—and, if you're on a network, to remotely access the entire network via your hijacked PC.

As you learned in Chapter 11, "Preventing Virus Attacks," the best defense against a data-driven attack is to avoid receiving and running unrequested files, and to use an anti-virus program. Installing a firewall will also help mitigate the effects of a backdoor Trojan, by blocking remote-control access by the attacker.

Future Attacks

All of these different types of computer attacks are what we know about today. But what kinds of attacks can expect to find tomorrow?

First, we should expect to see more of the same. Software and protocols will remain buggy and insecure, and crackers will devise new ways of exploiting these weaknesses. In addition, users will continue to exhibit their human foibles, enabling slick attackers to gain unauthorized access and information via social engineering schemes.

Beyond that, however, it's almost impossible to predict what new types of attacks we'll see in the future. All you can do is remain diligent, keep abreast of new security initiatives, install all the proper security patches, and keep your eyes and ears open. There will always be crackers testing the limits of the system, and there will always be technicians plugging newly discovered security holes.

Somehow, we'll muddle through.

Summing Up

There are many different types of Internet-based attacks. The simplest attacks utilize some form of social engineering, where an individual is somehow conned into revealing important information. That information is then used either for its own inherent value (credit card info, etc.), or to gain further access for additional attacks.

Many attacks use some form of impersonation or spoofing; the attacker can pretend to be another user (by stealing a username and password), or another computer (by redirecting a DNS address). Other attacks require the hijacking of one or more computers, which are then used to perform further attacks on other computers.

The most destructive attacks are those that bomb a target computer with e-mail messages or data requests. These denial-of-service attacks so overwhelm the target computer that it's forced to shut down until the attack subsides.

Some of these attacks can be defended against, by normal diligence and the use of firewall software. Other types of attacks (including denial-of-service attacks) can't be prevented, although they can be shut down once they begin.

In the next chapter you'll learn how to protect *your* system from these types of attacks.

CHAPTER 15

Protecting Your System from Attack

By now, you should be sufficiently alerted to the potential danger posed by Internet-based attacks on your computer or small network. How can you protect against these types of attack—and what can you do to reduce your risk of being attacked?

Your risk, of course, depends on how you use your computer, and how you connect to the Internet. Reducing your risk is a matter of taking some very sensible precautions and installing some protective software.

Read on to learn how at risk you are—and how you can reduce that risk.

Evaluating Your Risk

If you're a typical home computer user, you can rest easy. The simple fact is that individual users have a relatively low risk of Internet-based attack. That risk is lower if you connect to the Internet via a dial-up connection, and even lower if you're the sole user. Your risk increases if you have an always-on Internet connection, and if your spouse and kids (and household visitors) also use your computer.

Even if you have a small network, you're less at risk than large companies with big corporate networks. However, if you run your own Web site, your risk increases; it doesn't matter how big the site is—it's out there, and it's visible, and it's a target.

The following questions should be taken into account to determine how at-risk your system is to outside attack.

Who Uses Your Computer?

The more people who use your computer, the higher your risk of attack.

Children (including teenagers) are typically less diligent with security precautions than adults are. So if you have younger computer users in your household, your risk is higher.

For that matter, you're presumably more diligent than your spouse. (You're the one reading this book, right?) Unless your spouse is employed in the IT profession or happens to be a security expert, your risk increases whenever he or she is online.

Your risk is also higher if you have guests or friends who frequently use your computer—even if they're just checking e-mail while they're away from home. (Guests on your computer also put you at risk for *internal* attacks; make sure your data is password-protected before you allow your guests to log on.)

How Do You Connect to the Internet?

If you connect to the Internet via a dial-up connection, your security risk is rather low. If you have an always-on broadband connection, however, your risk increases considerably.

That's because the longer you're online, the more likely it is you'll be noticed. When you're connected 24/7, that's just more hours when a would-be attacker can use sniffer or scanner software to discover your presence.

There is a particular security problem with cable modem connections. Your connection is actually one node of a neighborhood network; your cable company creates a large network to service its Internet customers, with each neighborhood served by a separate network *node*. The problem with this arrangement is that your computer is now a part of a network—and on a network, all the members potentially have access to one another. That means that your computer could be visible to—and possibly accessible by—other neighbors on your node of the network.

TIP *You can get a good idea of your neighborhood network visibility by opening Windows' Network Neighborhood on your PC; chances are, if you can see other cable modem users in your neighborhood, they may be able to see you, too.*

What Do You Do Online?

Your online activities determine a large part of your security risk. The following activities are regarded as higher-risk activities, since they involve the transmittal of personal information:

- Online shopping
- Purchasing software for download
- Buying or selling at eBay or another online auction
- Online banking (paying bills, checking account balances, etc.)
- Buying or selling stocks or mutual funds at an online investment firm
- Chatting or instant messaging
- Playing online games
- Swapping MP3 and other files via Audiogalaxy, Gnutella, or some other P2P file-swapping network

On the other hand, sending and receiving e-mail and general Web site browsing (without entering personal information) are relatively safe activities, from a security standpoint. (These activities do put you at a higher risk for catching a computer virus, however.)

Do You Connect to (or Run) a Network?

The more computers funneling through your Internet gateway, the bigger target you are for crackers. Crackers like big targets, because there is more potentially valuable stuff to get at—or to damage, if that's the intent.

A multiple-computer network also has more weak points than a single computer. Every user on the network is a potential security risk, with loose passwords and sloppy practices. The more people connected, the greater the chance that *someone* will screw up and do something that will allow the cracker access. A chain, after all, is only as strong as its weakest link.

The network becomes even less secure if users are allowed remote dial-in privileges. Any access from the outside creates a hole that can potentially be exploited. If network users can get in from the outside, so can a determined attacker.

In addition, if you're connected to a network, you are at potential risk of attack from other users on the same network. While this is admittedly rare—and sure to be squelched by a savvy network administrator—internal cyberespionage and attacks are not unknown, particularly in politically volatile environments.

The bottom line is that the bigger the network, the bigger the risk of attack.

Do You Have a Web Site?

Any public exposure you create also creates a more visible and attractive target for crackers. Putting a site on the Web is like flashing a business card in a busy coffeehouse; you announce your presence, and—for crackers—your vulnerability.

This is true even if it's just a personal Web page. While experienced crackers will pass up personal pages (too small a challenge), beginning crackers might appreciate the practice they can get, at your expense. Besides, most personal Web sites have very little security; they're easy targets.

Corporate Web sites are a greater risk, of course, primarily because they're big targets. If a cracker can take down a site like Yahoo!, he really makes a name for himself. Whether the cracker is defacing the site for personal, political, or business reasons, attacking a big site can be a big challenge—and a big accomplishment.

In any case, any public exposure you have on the Web increases your risk of attack.

Formal Risk Evaluation

If you want a more formal evaluation of your risk of attack, there are several Web sites that offer free security tests. These tests typically involve sending different types of messages to your PC to see how well your system is insulated from each different type of attack.

Among the most popular security tests on the Web are:

- HackerWhacker (www.hackerwhacker.com)
- Secure-Me (www.dslreports.com/r3/dsl/secureme/)
- Shields UP! (www.grc.com)
- Symantec Security Check (security.norton.com)

Taking Precautions

Now that you have a handle on just how big your risk of attack is, it's time to take some steps to reduce that risk. While you can't stop people from trying to attack you, you can lessen the chances of an attack succeeding, and minimize any damage that might result from a successful attack.

Use Strong Passwords

The first step to security is to use passwords. Everywhere.

Start by reconfiguring Windows for password operation. You don't want your operating system to start unless the proper password is issued.

TIP *In Windows XP, you enable password protection by opening the Control Panel and selecting User Accounts; click Change An Account, select the account to change, and then click Create A Password. When the next screen appears, enter your new password (twice, as instructed) and click the Create Password button. The next time you turn on your PC, you'll be prompted to enter your password before you can enter Windows.*

Next, password-protect any and all applications that offer this feature. Or, in the case of Word and Excel, password-protect individual documents—the most sensitive ones, at any rate.

Finally, make sure you use strong passwords to access your Internet account and your network. Don't keep the default password offered to you, or enter a bunch of blanks to create an empty password field. Crackers know all the standard default passwords, and they are smart enough to try entering an empty password. You must at least put forth the effort to create a unique password.

While you're at it, try to create a *strong* password—one that's relatively complex. You'd be amazed how effective a complicated password can be; if it's too hard to crack, a cracker will give up and move to an easier target.

You see, most people choose a short password, one that's easy to remember, and then they use the same password on multiple accounts. (Who wants to remember a dozen different passwords?) This, unfortunately, creates a significant security risk—especially when it comes to logging onto your computer, or your company's computer network.

As you'll learn in Chapter 20, "Protecting Your Privacy," short passwords are easy to crack—and if you use the same password on multiple accounts, a single crack can gain the attacker multiple entrées.

For example, a three-character alphabetic password (no numbers) can be cracked in less than eight minutes. A seven-character alphanumeric password (mixing letters, numbers, and a few special characters) can take up to two years to crack, using even the most sophisticated cracking software.

NOTE *There are dozens of password-cracking programs available on the Internet, from underground Web sites and Usenet newsgroups. These programs shouldn't be confused with legitimate password recovery software and services, designed to help you recover lost or forgotten passwords.*

You should also make sure that your password isn't easy for a cracker to guess. (Good old social engineering at work, again.) Don't use passwords based on your social security number, birth date, names of family members, names of your pets, birth dates of family members, and so on. The combination of letters and numbers in your password should be as nearly random as possible—while still being somewhat easy for you to remember.

In addition, you should make sure that the password you use to log onto your computer or company network is used *only* for that single log-in. Don't use the same password for your home computer as you do your company network. Don't use the same password you use for your ATM, or to access your online banking account, or to log into your Internet service provider. Keep separate passwords for each account, and keep them separate.

Finally, you should change your passwords on a regular basis. Every time you change your password, you eliminate any risk from a previously stolen password. A stolen password is useless if the password has been changed.

All this is more work on your end (more passwords to remember), but it significantly enhances your security.

Turn Off File Sharing

Let's say an unauthorized user gains access to your system. If you're like most users, all the folders and files on your hard desk are open for anyone to access—which means the cracker will have a field day defacing and deleting your files, at will.

You can keep unauthorized users from accessing your private files and folders by disabling Windows' file- and print-sharing on your network. This will keep the contents of your system private, even to other users of your network.

To disable file sharing for a network in Windows XP, you must have administrator privileges on the network. Follow these steps:

1. Open the Control Panel and select Network Connections.

2. When the Network Connections window appears, double-click the Local Area Connection icon.

3. When the Local Area Connection Properties dialog box appears, select the General tab (shown in Figure 15.1).

4. Select File And Printer Sharing For Microsoft Networks, and then click the Uninstall button.

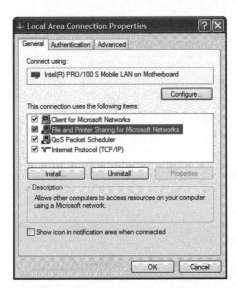

Figure 15.1 *Disabling file and printer sharing in Windows XP*

If this is too extreme a measure, you can turn off file sharing on a folder-by-folder (or file-by-file) basis. In Windows XP, follow these steps:

1. Using My Computer, navigate to the disk, folder, or file you don't want to share.

2. Right-click the icon for the disk, folder, or file, and select Sharing And Security from the pop-up menu.

3. When the Properties dialog box appears, select the Sharing tab (shown in Figure 15.2).

4. If your computer is part of a small workgroup, select the Make This Folder Private option. If this option isn't available (if you're on a larger network, for example), then make sure the Share This Folder On The Network option is *unchecked*.

5. Click OK.

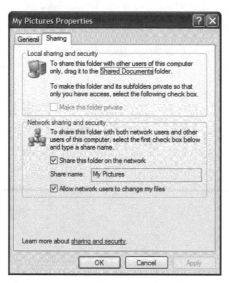

Figure 15.2 *Making sure that the contents of a folder can't be shared with other users*

TIP *To keep all your files private, it's easiest to turn off file sharing for the entire hard disk, rather than for individual folders or files.*

This process is particularly important if you're connecting to the Internet via a cable modem. Since you become part of a neighborhood network when you connect in this fashion, you want to keep your neighbors from inadvertently (or even purposely) accessing your private files.

Keep Your Software Updated

Since many computer attacks exploit bugs and security holes in specific pieces of software (and in the underlying operating system), whenever possible you should make sure that you have the latest, greatest version of all your software—the version that includes all the latest security patches. In practice, this means that you need to be aware of all available software upgrades, and then download and install all security patches, as appropriate.

For Microsoft software, monitor the Microsoft Security site (`www.microsoft.com/security/`). This is where you'll find all the latest downloadable security patches for Windows, Internet Explorer, Outlook, and other Microsoft applications. For other software and operating systems, monitor the manufacturers' Web sites.

Install a Firewall

If you have an always-on Internet connection, or if you run a small network, then it's essential that you install firewall software on your system. A firewall acts as a barrier between your computer (or network) and the Internet; attacks are stopped at the firewall, before they can reach any individual computer.

NOTE *There are many types of firewall programs available—and there's even a bare-bones firewall built into Windows XP. To learn more about choosing, installing, and using firewalls, see Chapter 18, "Choosing a Firewall."*

By the way, you should probably run your own personal firewall on your PC even if you're behind a network firewall at work. This is because the network firewall only protects you from Internet-based intrusions; it doesn't protect you from attacks by your fellow workers.

Keep Backup Copies

You've heard this advice before, and it applies again here: Always make backup copies of your essential data. Whether you're running a home PC or a small network, you need the assurance that your data won't be lost if you're the victim of a malicious attack. The only way to guarantee data permanence is to have a spare copy handy.

For home PCs, you can use Microsoft's Backup utility, included with Windows, to perform the backup. (Read more about Microsoft Backup in Chapter 11, "Preventing Virus Attacks.") If you're running a small network, you want a more robust backup solution, to back up data from across the entire network. This might be in the form of network backup software or services; in any case, you want to make frequent backups, and—in the case of small networks—always keep one backup copy offsite, in case you have some sort of physical disaster.

Use Common Sense

Finally, you can fend off a lot of attacks—especially those that use "social engineering" to obtain passwords and other private information—by using a generous amount of common sense. Don't let anyone talk you into divulging your passwords or credit card numbers. Don't reply to instant messages and e-mails asking you to supply private information, no matter how official-sounding the request. Don't accept files from anyone over IRC or instant messaging networks—or open files you receive via e-mail. Don't leave your password taped to your computer monitor, or sitting out in the open on your desk.

In other words, be careful, and be properly secretive. Don't let out any information that shouldn't be made public, and don't believe anything that strangers tell you. Keep your private information private, and be properly aware of all the dangers that exist online.

Protecting Against Physical Attack

The computer community pays a lot of attention to the types of virtual attacks that occur over the Internet. But your system could also be at risk of a *physical* attack–or, more likely, a literal computer theft.

Computer theft is a particular problem if you use a laptop computer and carry it with you when you travel. Any time your computer isn't physically at your side, it's at risk of being stolen. Untold thousands of portable PCs are stolen every year from airports alone; that number is actually on the rise, as flyers are more frequently being separated from their belongings during the increasingly rigorous security checks implemented post–September 11. You know the drill: You go one way to be patted down and wanded while your stuff goes another way, down the conveyer belt. It's quite common for your belongings to be out of sight for several minutes while you go through the security screening. Plenty of opportunity for someone to steal your laptop. Other public spaces–restaurants, subways and buses, exhibition halls–also provide opportunities for theft.

When you have your PC stolen, you not only lose a piece of expensive hardware, you also lose all the files and data you have stored on that computer. And it isn't just your Word and Excel files–it's all your passwords, and stored credit card numbers, and online banking and trading information, and on and on. A stolen laptop is every bit as bad as a stolen wallet; the thief gains access to your entire life.

Unless, of course, you had the foresight to password-protect your computer, and individual files. (And to do so with a long alphanumeric password–one that can't be easily guessed.) If your information is password-protected (or, even better, encrypted–as discussed in Chapter 25, "Employing Passwords, Encryption, and Digital Identification"), then all the thief has is a rather useless piece of computer hardware.

Continued on next page

Protecting Against Physical Attack *(Continued)*

Naturally, you should also take all reasonable precautions to avoid the theft in the first place. For laptop computers, that probably means installing some sort of locking device to "chain" your PC to an immovable object when you're out of your office, or when you leave your PC in your hotel room. When traveling, it means always keeping your laptop at your side, and never letting it out of your sight–even in airport security lines.

You can also install software that automatically dials up a central number (or sends a secret e-mail) and reports itself stolen whenever an unauthorized person attempts to use the computer. These tracking programs–such as CompuTrace (**www.computersecurity.com/computrace/**) and PC PhoneHome (**www.pcphonehome.com**)–can help you find and recover your laptop in the event that it is stolen.

Summing Up

Most individual computer users are at low risk for Internet-based attacks. However, your risk increases if your PC has multiple users (especially teenagers and younger children), if you have an always-on broadband Internet connection, if you engage in online activities that require you to transmit sensitive information, if you're connected to (or run) a network, or if you have a personal or business Web site.

You can reduce your risk of attack by always using passwords (especially longer ones, with a combination of letters, numbers, and special characters), by turning off Windows' file sharing, by updating your software and operating systems with the latest security patches, by installing firewall software, by keeping backup copies of your most essential data, and by using common sense to avoid social engineering attacks.

In the next chapter, we'll look at those security concerns unique to peer-to-peer computing—what to watch out for when you're instant messaging, swapping MP3 files, and participating in distributed computing projects.

CHAPTER 16

Protecting Your System in a P2P Environment

*P*eer-to-peer (P2P) computing is a unique subset of the online computing world. In P2P computing, two computers connect directly to one another, over the Internet, without being managed by any central server or Web site. These direct connections pose particular security problems, in that the computer you connect to might try to infiltrate your computer—or hijack it for nefarious purposes.

There's a lot of P2P computing taking place these days. Instant messaging is a form of P2P, as are MP3 file swapping and distributed computing. And any time you let others access your computer—whether to copy a file (file swapping) or to run a program (distributed computing)—you are potentially compromising the security of your system.

After all, if another user can access your computer to find and download a digital music file, what's to stop that user from downloading other files—or planting a virus on your system? If you agree to participate in a distributed computing project, what's to stop the company behind that project from taking remote control of your computer and using it for more questionable efforts? In short, what's to keep your visitors from using your computer against your will?

That's what we examine in this chapter.

TIP *Learn more about peer-to-peer computing from another book by this author,* Discovering P2P *(Sybex, 2001), available wherever computer books are sold.*

Understanding Peer-to-Peer

If you've heard at all about peer-to-peer computing, it's probably been in the context of file swapping—in particular, the swapping of MP3-format digital music files, via Napster and similar services. However, file swapping is just one P2P application.

Put simply, P2P is the direct connection of any two computers over the Internet (or any other network), without the use of another server as a "middleman" to manage the interaction. A P2P connection might be established for real-time communications (via instant messaging), swapping computer files (such as MP3 music files), sharing unused processing power for large-scale multiple-computer projects (so-called distributed computing), or collaborating on group projects.

Where P2P differs from traditional client/server computing is the elimination of the server. Figure 16.1 shows the client/server nature of a traditional Web site, while Figure 16.2 shows a typical P2P connection. No servers, no middlemen, nobody to get between you and your peers—connections are fast, direct, and unmonitored.

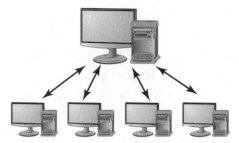

Figure 16.1 *Traditional client/server computing, in the form of a Web site and its users*

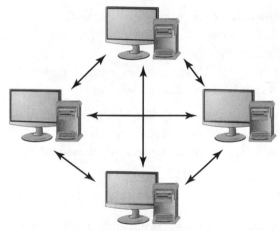

Figure 16.2 *A typical peer-to-peer network—no servers!*

P2P Instant Messaging

With more than 200 million users, instant messaging (IM) is far and away the largest current P2P application. Once users sign on to a particular IM network, they're connected directly to each other—where they can exchange text messages, audio and video messages (in some cases), and computer files.

The major IM networks include:

AOL Instant Messenger   AOL Instant Messenger (www.aim.com), also known as AIM, is the Web-based version of the "Buddy Lists" feature built into the AOL commercial online service. (AIM and AOL Buddy Lists share the same network, so that non-AOL subscribers can use AIM to converse with AOL subscribers.)

ICQ   ICQ (`web.icq.com`) was the first instant messaging program, developed by Mirabilis in 1996. ICQ was purchased by America Online in 1998, and AOL surprisingly chose to run ICQ as a separate service from its AIM/Buddy Lists network (which means that ICQ users can't converse with AIM users).

MSN Messenger   MSN Messenger (`messenger.msn.com`) is the IM client offered by Microsoft for Windows versions before XP—and is still offered to MSN subscribers. (Despite the title, MSN Messenger doesn't have to be connected to the MSN commercial service to function; anyone connected to the Web can use MSN.)

Windows Messenger   Windows Messenger (`www.microsoft.com/windowsxp/`), introduced as part of Microsoft's Windows XP operating system, supplants MSN Messenger by integrating telephony, video, and file-transfer features with the basic instant messaging functions. Windows Messenger is fully compatible with MSN Messenger and operates on the same IM network (which Microsoft has dubbed the .NET Messenger Service).

Yahoo! Messenger   Yahoo! Messenger (`messenger.yahoo.com`), like MSN Messenger and AIM, is a cross-platform IM client that operates on its own proprietary Internet-based network. Like all the other IM clients, it's available free of charge via Internet download.

P2P File Swapping

Unlike a traditional Web site, where files are stored and available for downloading to your computer, a P2P file-swapping system is actually a network of personal computers. You connect to the network via a central Web site, where you can search other users' computers for the files you want to download. When you find a match, the file is copied from that other user's computer to your PC—without any interaction with the Web site.

Internet-based P2P file swapping started with a service named Napster, which was created to help users swap MP3 audio files. A user connecting to the Napster network had immediate access to tens of thousands (later, millions) of other computers—and to all the MP3 files stored on those computers. Napster helped you find which computers had the songs you wanted; then you connected directly to those computers to download the files. Other computers, in turn, would connect to your PC to download the files you had stored on your hard disk.

NOTE *The only problem with the original Napster concept is that it enabled the illegal copying of copyrighted material. The company was brought to court by the major record labels and subsequently forced to shut down. However, other similar file-sharing services have risen in Napster's wake (and Napster itself is in the process of being reborn as a more traditional subscription service), so there are still lots of different services you can use to swap digital music files—with other users all around the world!*

When any two computers are connected to the same file-swapping network, files can be copied from one computer to another. The computer that has the file on it needs to be configured so that the particular folder can be *shared*, and then the second computer has to know which computer (and which folder on that computer) has the file. The second computer then accesses the first computer and transfers the file to its own hard disk.

Because the Internet is nothing more than a giant network, there's no reason that any two computers connected to the Internet can't share files, just as two computers on a corporate network can. That process—connecting two computers over the Internet, and then copying files between those computers—is what P2P file sharing is all about.

Let's say, for example, that you wanted to download some songs by Weezer. All you have to do is launch the client software for a particular file-swapping network, access the network, and search for "Weezer." You then see a list of users who have Weezer songs stored on their computers. You pick a computer from the list, and your computer is connected directly to the other computer. With the click of a button, the specified file is copied from that computer to your computer's hard disk.

NOTE *P2P file swapping isn't limited to MP3 files. While some file-swapping services are dedicated to swapping MP3 and other digital audio and video files, other services are broader, enabling swapping of all file types. Already the swapping of full-length movies (in DivX format) has become relatively commonplace on some services.*

Today there are dozens of P2P file-swapping networks, all of which work in a similar fashion. Here's a short list of the most popular services:

- Audiogalaxy (www.audiogalaxy.com)
- Gnutella (www.gnutelliums.com)
- KaZaA (www.kazaa.com)

- Madster (www.madster.com)

- MusicCity Morpheus (www.musiccity.com)

- Napster (www.napster.com)

P2P Distributed Computing

Distributed computing is a relatively simple concept. Where Napster and similar services are applications for file sharing, distributed computing applications are all about *cycle sharing*.

Your computer has tremendous processing power, and if you ran it full-out 24 hours a day, 7 days a week, it would be capable of tremendous computing feats. You don't use your computer 24/7, however, so a good portion of your computer's resources go unused. Distributed computing uses those resources.

When your computer is co-opted for a distributed computing project, software is installed on your machine to run various processing activities during those periods when your PC is typically unused. The results of that spare-time processing are periodically uploaded to the distributed computing network and combined with similar results from other PCs in the project. The result, if enough computers are involved, simulates the processing power of much larger mainframes and supercomputers—which is necessary for some very large and complex computing projects.

For example, genetic research requires vast amounts of computing power. Left to traditional means, it might take years to solve essential mathematical problems. By connecting together thousands (or millions) of individual PCs, project organizers apply more power to the problem, and the results are obtained that much sooner. This computing typically takes place offline, with the results uploaded once a day via the Internet.

So putting together a P2P distributed computing network is like discovering a "free" supercomputer. All that processing power is there, just waiting to be used.

A typical distributed computing project requires participants to download software from the distributed computing project's Web site. You install the software and configure it for your particular usage—when you want it to run, when you want it to connect to the Web site, and so on.

The next time your PC is idle for a few minutes—and is connected to the Internet—the distributed computing software connects to the master Web site and retrieves its task. Alternately, this connection might be programmed to take place at a certain time each day, or at night when the PC is most likely to be unused. This once-a-day configuration is preferable if you have a normal dial-up connection that isn't always connected to the Internet.

Now, whenever the PC is idle, it works on its task. (Your PC doesn't have to be online to do this work.) Some distributed computing programs kick in after the computer has been idle for a few minutes; others are always active, working in the background "between the keystrokes"—but without disturbing your foreground computer use.

When a task is completed—or at the assigned dial-up time—the distributed computing software connects to the master Web site and uploads the results of its computations. At the same time, a new task is downloaded, and the cycle begins anew.

Some of the more popular Web-based distributing projects include these:

climate*prediction*.com   This project, located at `www.climateprediction.com`, conducts a scientific study of global climate change.

distributed.net   This ongoing project, located at `www.distributed.net`, manages a variety of mathematically oriented distributed computing projects.

evolution@home   The evolution@home project (`www.evolutionary-research.org`) is using P2P technology to search for genetic causes behind the extinction of various species.

Folding@home   A distributed computing project (`folding.stanford.edu`), run by Stanford University, designed to analyze protein folding and its relationship to Alzheimer's, Mad Cow, Parkinson's, and other diseases.

SETI@home   The SETI@home project (`setiathome.ssl.berkeley.edu`) is one of the most popular public distributed computing projects; it uses the power of millions of individual PCs to search for signs of extraterrestrial life.

United Devices   United Devices (`www.ud.com`) is a company that manages both for-profit and not-for-profit distributed computing projects, including projects for genetic and cancer research.

Worldwide Lexicon   The Worldwide Lexicon project (`picto.weblogger.com`) is an initiative to create an online multilingual dictionary and translation service.

NOTE *Instant messaging, file swapping, and distributed computing are just three types of P2P computing. Other uses of P2P technology include group collaboration, distributed storage, Internet telephony, videoconferencing, and real-time interactive game play.*

Instant Messaging: Risks and Prevention

Instant messaging presents a unique platform for communications—and for computer attacks. You saw in Chapter 7, "E-mail, Chat, and Instant Messaging Viruses," that using various Trojan techniques, instant messaging can be used to spread viruses, and it can also be used to obtain private information from individual users.

As you learned back in Chapter 14, "Different Types of Attacks," one of the most common forms of Internet attack is the *social engineering attack*. This type of attack—which plagues both instant messaging and Internet Relay Chat (IRC) networks—doesn't use technology so much as it uses common trickery to con users so that they download and install malicious software (typically backdoor Trojans), and reveal passwords, credit card numbers, and other personal information.

Attackers typically use automated tools to post messages (in bulk) to unsuspecting users. These messages purport to come from some friend or authority, and they offer the opportunity for the user to download some sort of useful software—or, more often, MP3 files and pornographic pictures. If you download and install the software, the attacker has an active backdoor he can use to gain control over your computer—or enter your company's network.

One common variation on this approach is to send a message that purports to alert you to a virus infecting your computer. You're encouraged to download and install the accompanying file, which will supposedly clean the virus from your system. Instead, the file is a backdoor Trojan (like those discussed in Chapter 6, "Trojan Horses and Worms") that gives the attacker unauthorized access to your system.

Another type of social engineering attack, quite common on the AOL Instant Messenger network, sends a message from someone with an official-sounding title. This person writes that there's some sort of problem with your account, and you need to send verification of your password or credit card number. A variation on this message directs you to an official-looking Web page (for AOL users, a very good mockup of an AOL account page), where you're encouraged to enter your password, credit card number, and so forth. Once the attacker has your personal information, he can use it to hijack your account; obviously, your credit card number can be used for even greater damage.

The best protection against any social engineering attack is healthy skepticism. It's unlikely that anyone you meet online would send you files of any value whatsoever—and, besides, you should know better than to accept unrequested files from strangers. In addition, no representative from America Online or any other Internet service provider will ever use instant messaging or IRC (or even e-mail) to ask for password or credit card information. This type of information should only be given in person or over the phone, and only after someone has provided adequate identification as an authorized representative—such as a supervisor's name and verifiable phone number.

In other words, don't accept any files sent to you over instant messaging or IRC, and don't give out any personal information of any kind.

Instant Messaging and Viruses

The incidence of viruses distributed via instant messaging has significantly increased over the past few years. These viruses are typically contained within files that are sent from one user to another over the IM network, in much the same way that file attachments spread viruses via e-mail messages.

As with all file-based viruses, it's a lack of diligence (or pure user stupidity, depending on how you want to look at it) that actually activates the virus. Opening an EXE or VBS or PIF file sent from another IM user isn't the smartest thing in the world, yet it happens daily. While it's fashionable to blame the messenger for this situation, the instant messaging technology is no more responsible for spreading computer viruses than the telephone network is responsible for telemarketing scams. It's just a medium—one that can be used or abused, but it's not the cause of any single activity.

Still, as more users avail themselves of instant messaging—and as more of them do dumb things, like open strange files sent during IM sessions—it's likely that instant messaging will continue to grow as a source of virus propagation.

File Swapping: Risks and Prevention

Letting another computer user directly access your computer gives the more security conscious among us goosebumps. You don't have to be paranoid to envision some unknown user foraging through the contents of your hard disk, downloading not only the latest MP3 files, but also more sensitive data—memos, reports, even credit card information and passwords.

The good news is that most P2P file-swapping networks recognize this concern, and provide their own security measures in their client software. The bad news is—well, the bad news is, just about any security measure can be overridden.

Unwanted File Access

When you join a P2P file-swapping network, such as Audiogalaxy or KaZaA, you agree to share certain files on your hard disk with other users of the network. (You do this in return for getting access to other computers—and the files stored on their hard disks.) If you're like most users, you don't have any problem with this; you probably have a folder full of MP3 and similar files that you don't mind sharing with others who share your musical tastes.

The question, though, is whether you can effectively prevent other P2P users from accessing files beyond those you've marked as sharable.

Most file-sharing applications let you designate a single folder on your hard drive that can be shared with other users. You copy into this folder the files you want to share—and all downloads from other users are automatically stored in this folder, as well. Users go directly to your shared folder, but can't access any other folder on your system.

Of course, this system is only as good as the person running it. If you screw up and place more sensitive personal files into your shared folder, you've just opened the front door for virtually unlimited distribution of those files.

And that's not the only security problem you can run into. Any enterprising cracker capable of cracking the password you use to log onto the P2P network can probably wander out of the shared folder and start cruising through the other data on your hard disk.

Not a good thing.

Fortunately, you can reduce the risk of unauthorized hard disk cruising (and file downloading) by intelligently using the file-sharing features of your network or operating system. These features enable you (or, on a network, your network administrator) to explicitly designate who is permitted to view and download shared resources on your computer. You should be able to enable or block access at either the file or folder/directory level. On some networks, you can even enable or block individual users or IP addresses, or create more complex policies that block or permit access based on specific circumstances and behaviors.

Windows XP, for example, lets you mark selected files, folders, and even complete hard disks as shared or private. Shared items can be accessed by any user on the network, while private items can only be accessed by the machine's owner. If you want to make sure that no users can access your private files, be sure to turn *off* Windows' file-sharing feature.

NOTE *To learn how to deactivate file sharing in Windows XP, see Chapter 15, "Protecting Your System from Attack."*

In other words, you can establish more secure P2P connection by turning off any file sharing present on your system, and protecting your most sensitive data with strong passwords.

Backdoor Attacks

When you join a P2P file-swapping network, you are no longer an anonymous computer user. You have now announced your presence to the world—and become a more visible target for attackers.

Crackers who specialize in backdoor attacks—opening a hole in your system they can use to remotely control your computer—just *love* P2P networks. After all, most backdoor programs are distributed via Trojan horse files, and P2P networks specialize in distributing files. It's a simple matter to use a P2P network, originally designed to distribute MP3 files, for the distribution of backdoor Trojans.

Of course, transmitting backdoor Trojans isn't a P2P-only phenomenon, and smart computer users know not to execute strange files. But given the rate of file swapping and the way every peer is eventually related to every other peer, viruses distributed via a P2P network can spread across the entire network in mere hours.

It's that speed of infection that's scary.

It also doesn't help that virus developers are constantly thinking of new ways to infect your system, using the technology at hand. For example, P2P-oriented crackers use so-called "wrapping" tools, such as Wrapster, to hide their Trojan files. Wrapping occurs when an infected file (typically an executable or Zip file) is disguised as an innocuous file type (such as an MP3 file). You download what you think is an MP3 file, but when you go to play the file, you run the virus file, instead.

Insidious.

And by the time someone gets wise to what's going on, that wrapped file can be distributed to thousands, if not millions, of users. When you download the wrapped file to your machine, it's now available for downloading from your PC to other P2P network users. And the person who downloads it from you now has it available for download to yet more users—and on and on and on.

The best way to defend against the spread of backdoor Trojans is to employ an antivirus software program, like those discussed in Chapter 9, "Antivirus Software and Services." A good antivirus program will check the contents of the disguised file for virus code or virus-like behavior, and alert you to the presence of a Trojan infection. If you don't use an antivirus program, you could easily be tricked into executing a potentially dangerous file.

Spyware

Sometimes the security threat on a P2P network comes not from other users, but from the company running the network.

The biggest such threat comes from so-called *spyware* and *adware* programs. These are programs that hide in the background while you're connected to the Internet, occasionally popping up advertisements or (in the most insidious cases) uploading information about your surfing habits to a central database.

NOTE *Learn more about the many different types of spyware in Chapter 23, "Defeating Spyware."*

Many file-sharing services embed these spyware programs within their file-sharing software. When you install their software, you also, typically unknowingly, install the spyware.

Why does a file-sharing network sneak spyware onto your computer? Because somebody pays them to, that's why. Selling "space" for these spyware programs is a way to generate revenues from a service that their customers (you!) use for free.

For example, in 2001 it was revealed that several file-sharing programs—including Bear-Share, KaZaA, and LimeWire—came with a hidden program called "ClickTillUWin" attached. This adware program ran in the background and tracked which URLs you visited, and then sent that data to the company's host computer. Every site you visited was logged, without your knowing it.

Even worse, in spring of 2002 it was revealed that KaZaA has secretly been distributing a "sleeper" spyware program (called Altnet SecureInstall) inside its P2P client. This spyware program, created by Brilliant Digital Entertainment, is designed to be remotely activated at a preset point in time, welding each individual computer into a giant peer-to-peer network. This network of computers would then be used to host and distribute content from other companies. (The initial content is likely to be advertising, as witnessed by Brilliant's tests with DoubleClick, one of the largest Internet advertising companies.)

Brilliant claims that PCs would only be connected to their network with the owner's permission, but that claim is rather dubious. As far as Brilliant is concerned, you've granted your permission if you accept the "terms of service" you see during the installation of the KaZaA software. Since most users automatically click OK to this bit of legalese during the installation process, Brilliant has a near-100% base of users who've "agreed" to let the company use their PCs.

NOTE *Here's the relevant bit in the terms of service agreement: "You hereby grant the right to access and use the unused computing power and storage space on your computer/s and/or Internet access or bandwidth for the aggregation of content and use in distributed computing. The user acknowledges and authorizes this use without the right of compensation."*

If you use KaZaA, you—and tens of millions of others—probably already have the Altnet SecureInstall software installed on your system. It's like a giant backdoor Trojan, enabling Brilliant to use your computer for their purposes, without your knowledge.

How, then, do you avoid turning control of your computer over to one or more big companies—and how do you keep them from spying on your Internet activities?

The simple answer is to just say no—to refuse any spyware that any company wants to download to your computer. When you install a piece of P2P software, watch the installation process carefully; install *only* the P2P client, and *not* any additional programs.

The complicating factor is that some P2P networks don't give you a choice. If you want to install their client, you also have to install the spyware/adware packages that come with it. If you don't install the spyware, it won't let you install the client.

Even worse, some companies install the spyware without your knowing it. They just don't tell you that you're installing software in addition to the P2P client. It all comes down in one big lump, client, spyware, adware, and all. This type of policy makes it virtually impossible to avoid installing the spyware on your computer—without refusing the P2P client, as well.

And, just maybe, that's the best thing to do.

Uninstalling the Brilliant Digital Software

If you use the KaZaA file-swapping network, you probably have Brilliant Digital's Altnet SecureInstall software installed on your system. Uninstalling this software takes a bit of effort, but is necessary if you don't want to participate in Brilliant's P2P network.

Here's how to remove the software from your system.

1. Open the Windows Control Panel and select Add or Remove Programs.

2. When the Add or Remove Programs window appears, select b3d Projector and click Remove.

3. When the uninstallation is completed, open My Computer.

4. Locate the BDE folder, typically in the Windows folder, and delete it.

5. Locate the Temp folder (in the Windows folder), and delete it.

6. Search for the following individual files (typically in the Windows\System folder) and delete them:

   bdedata2.dll

   bdedownloader.dll

   bdefdi.dll

   bdeinsta2.dll

   bdeinstall.exe

   bdesecureinstall.cab

   bdesecureinstall.exe

   bdeverify.dll

   bdeverify.exe

Distributed Computing: Risks and Prevention

That little trick with the KaZaA software goes beyond P2P computing into the realm of distributed computing. When Brilliant Digital Entertainment uses a network of unknowing computers to perform a large computing task, they're creating a distributed computing network, just like SETI@home. And some users think that letting a third party use their computer for distributed computing processes opens an automatic backdoor into that computer—which is, on the surface, true. After all, what's to keep an unscrupulous firm from using more than just processing power on your PC—or from hijacking your computer for their own nefarious uses?

While security breaches have not yet been a real concern for the distributed computing industry, the fear of such may keep some individuals from participating in important projects. Distributed computing companies must assure their potential participants that the data generated will be secure, and that distributed computing projects will not use more of a computer's resources than originally contracted for.

You see, when you sign up for a distributed computing project, you agree to run some sort of proprietary program on your PC, during those periods when you're normally not using the machine. There is, theoretically, nothing keeping the distributed computing company from downloading some other program to your system, and running that other program in place of the distributed computing program.

Nothing, that is, except trust.

If you've signed up to a big-name distributed computing project or with an industry-leading distributed computing company, you're probably safe. Just as you trust software that comes from a major company, you can probably trust software that comes from the major players in the distributed computing space.

You only run into a problem when you download a program from a company that you're not as familiar with. That distributed computing project might turn out to be a scam to get you to download and run an infectious executable. Which means you have to do your homework, and only deal with major sites/companies/projects.

That said, the risk of running a malicious program during the course of a distributed computing project is quite low. You actually run a bigger danger any time you run a computer program with unsigned code from a remote source, or visit a Web page that contains Java applets.

Just be smart, and be vigilant. (And choose carefully who you decide to play with.)

Security Risks—On the Other End

Unlike other forms of P2P, distributed computing distributes raw data from a central source across a network of individual computers. That raw data might be fairly public data (as is the case with the SETI@home project), or it might be data proprietary to the host company.

And if you're a big company, do you really want your sensitive data spread across hundreds of thousands of relatively non-secure, virtually anonymous, personal computers?

The thought of distributing sensitive information in this manner makes many companies ill at ease. After all, what's to stop a competitor from intercepting the distributed data, reassembling it, and obtaining otherwise-carefully guarded company secrets?

For that matter, what's to stop would-be saboteurs from planting themselves in a distributed computing project with the express goal of sending false data back to the mother ship—and contaminating all the project's data?

These security concerns—which aren't your concerns, mind you—appear to be holding back some companies from taking advantage of the processing power inherent in distributed computing. The solution to these concerns will probably involve tighter security between the individual PCs and the mother ship, probably effected by strong data encryption, so that prying eyes (including yours!) can't see what's being processed or transmitted.

Summing Up

Peer-to-peer computing connects individual PCs directly, for the purposes of instant messaging, file swapping, and distributing computing. These direct connections create unique security concerns, especially when other users have direct access to the folders and files on your hard disk.

Instant messaging is often used to distribute Trojan horse software—backdoor Trojans, in particular. You can protect yourself by remaining skeptical of the typical social engineering ploys used to get you to download infected files, or to provide sensitive information to strangers.

P2P file swapping introduces the risk of strangers accessing your hard disk to download MP3 files, and instead downloading other files on your system. It's also possible for attackers to disguise virus files as MP3 files, thus planting backdoor Trojans on your system. You can protect yourself by disabling file sharing on your PC, password-protecting private folders and files, and making sure you're running an antivirus program in the background whenever you copy files from other users.

Distributed computing projects give some control of your system to people and machines running the project—and the risk exists that they could co-opt other parts of your system for disreputable purposes. However, this risk is relatively low, especially when you're dealing with reputable projects and companies.

In the next chapter we continue our look at attack prevention, focusing on how to prevent attacks on home and small business networks.

CHAPTER 17

Protecting a Network

In Chapter 15, "Protecting Your System from Attack," you learned how to protect a typical home computer from Internet-based attack. If you're responsible for a home or small business network, everything discussed in that chapter applies to your network—that is, you use many of the same methods to defend a small network as you do to defend an individual PC.

In addition, you need to augment these basic security measures with network-specific defenses. You have more at stake when you're defending a network, so it makes sense that you'd employ additional security measures. And, not surprisingly, the bigger your network, the more security you'll need.

NOTE *This chapter provides a general overview of network security concepts. Obviously, if you're running a large network, you'll want to seek out more detailed advice than I can provide here.* Active Defense: a Comprehensive Guide to Network Security, *by Chris Brenton and Cameron Hunt (Sybex, 2001), is a good starting point.*

Hardware and Software Defenses

The key to protecting a network is to create as many obstacles as possible for a potential cracker. No network can be 100% secure, but the more effort a cracker has to expend, the more likely he'll give up and try a network that's easier to break into.

This concept of multiple defenses is referred to as *Layered Security Architecture (LSA)*. As you can see in Figure 17.1, you would employ several different layers of protective software and hardware to protect your valuable network resources.

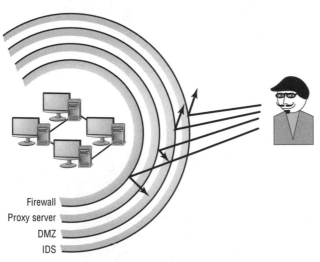

Firewall
Proxy server
DMZ
IDS

Figure 17.1 *Creating a layered security architecture*

What kinds of defenses can you employ? Here's a short list:

- Firewall software
- Firewall hardware
- Proxy server
- Demilitarized zone
- E-mail gateway
- Intrusion detection system

In addition, you need a clear and comprehensive security policy, complete with restrictions about who can log on where (and how); requirements for strong, constantly changing passwords; and frequent backups of critical data. You have to assume that somewhere, sometime, someone will try to break into your network—and you have to be prepared.

Read on to learn more about these different network security solutions.

TIP *In addition to protecting against attack, you should also protect your network against physical breakdown or power outage. That means installing an uninterruptible power supply (UPS), making frequent backups, and running various maintenance utilities on a regular basis.*

Firewalls

A *firewall* is a piece of software or hardware that acts as a barrier between your network and the Internet. As you can see in Figure 17.2, it blocks unauthorized Internet traffic from accessing your network, thus cutting off most potential attacks before they ever reach your network's users.

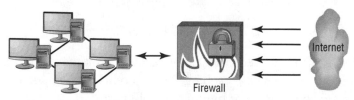

Figure 17.2 *A firewall keeps unauthorized Internet traffic out of your network.*

There are many different firewall programs on the market today, from freeware programs to corporate-sized firewalls costing $5000 or more. In addition, you can install a hardware-based firewall (actually, a router with built-in firewall protection) to provide a physical barrier between your network and the outside world.

If you only do one thing to improve your network security, installing a firewall should be it. Firewalls are so important that this book has an entire chapter devoted to the topic; turn to Chapter 18, "Choosing a Firewall," to learn more.

TIP *If you've set up a home or small business network based on the Windows XP operating system, Windows' built-in Internet Connection Firewall was enabled as part of the network installation. Read Chapter 18 to learn more about this Windows XP firewall.*

Proxy Servers

A *proxy server* is a kind of buffer between the Internet and the individual computers on your network. When you use a proxy server, the PCs on your network don't access the Internet directly; instead they access Web pages stored on the proxy server, as shown in Figure 17.3.

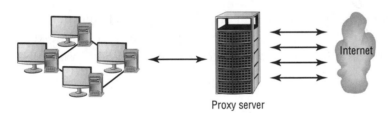

Figure 17.3 *A proxy server serves as a substitute Internet for the computers on your network.*

The way it works is that when a computer requests a Web page, that request is filtered through the proxy server. It's actually the proxy server that makes the final request; the proxy server retrieves the requested page and stores it on its hard disk. The PC that originally requested the Web page can now view that page, as it resides on the proxy server.

NOTE *The process of storing Web pages on the proxy server is called* caching.

A proxy server is like a firewall, in that it sits between your network and the Internet. But it goes beyond simple firewall protection with its Web page caching. This prevents the computers on your network from coming into direct contact with the Internet and offers an extra layer of protection. (A firewall doesn't buffer outgoing requests; a proxy server does.)

Demilitarized Zone

If there are remote users—people not part of your network—who need access to resources on your network, consider setting up a *demilitarized zone* (DMZ). In the network world, a DMZ is a part of your network that exists outside the firewall. Since it's on the other side of the barrier, any resources residing there can be accessed by computers outside your network.

You may want to create a DMZ if you're running a Web site that accepts feedback from (or serves information to) the general Web population. A DMZ is also useful if you're running an online business.

Setting up a DMZ is as easy as placing a computer between your Internet connection and your firewall, as shown in Figure 17.4. The DMZ computer remains part of your network, yet it's publicly accessible—and no one accessing the DMZ computer can gain further access to the rest of your network.

Figure 17.4 *Setting up a DMZ computer*

You might think that a DMZ is like a proxy server, and it is, in a way—but for outside users, not for network users. That is, a DMZ is kind of like a proxy server for your Web site visitors. It's different from a proxy in that it sits outside your network firewall, where the proxy is either inside the firewall or replaces the firewall. So a proxy server contains private content for your network users, and a DMZ contains public content for the world at large.

E-mail Gateways

An *e-mail gateway* is like a proxy server for your network's Internet e-mail. At its most basic, the gateway computer functions as an e-mail server, handling the typical e-mail storage and routing. In addition, the e-mail gateway manages a variety of security functions—including virus scanning, attachment stripping, content filtering, spam blocking, and attack prevention.

Figure 17.5 shows how a typical e-mail gateway works. All outgoing e-mail filters through the gateway, and all incoming messages stop at and are processed by the gateway. No e-mail comes directly from the outside world to your network's users; all messages are first processed by the gateway.

Figure 17.5 *Managing incoming messages with an e-mail gateway*

Network Intrusion Detection Systems

In Chapter 19, "Dealing with an Attack," you'll learn about the concept of intrusion detection systems. In essence, an intrusion detection system monitors various system resources and activities, looking for signs of an outside intrusion or attack. The network version of this software is called (no surprise) a *network intrusion detection system (NIDS)*, and is used to alert you to any intrusions to the network itself. When you're running a big network, or a real-time Web site with lots of traffic, installing NIDS software is a must.

Some of the most popular NIDS programs include:

- Dragon IDS (`www.intrusion-detection-system-group.co.uk`)

- eTrust Intrusion Detection (`www3.ca.com/Solutions/`)

- NFR Security (`www.nfr.com`)

- Real Secure (`www.iss.net/products_services/enterprise_protection/`)

- Snort (`www.snort.org`)

- Symantec Intruder Alert (`enterprisesecurity.symantec.com/products/`)

Big Networks, Bigger Problems

Most of the preventive measures discussed in this chapter are targeted at home or small business networks. They're also applicable to large corporate networks—although these big networks have their own unique security problems.

One of the unique statistics about large network security is that a huge number of security problems are internal. According to a survey by research firm IDC (`www.idc.com`), 81% of security breaches come from within a company—with almost half of them perpetrated by the company's own network administrators. These internal security problems have many causes: human error, slipshod password protection, and the ever-reliable malice of disgruntled employees.

Continued on next page

Big Networks, Bigger Problems *(Continued)*

Protection against internal error and attacks takes many forms. Security analysts recommend that every big company take the following preventive measures:

- Don't let any single person control your entire network—but also don't assign supervisory rights to more than a few individuals.

- Require every single employee logging into the network to use a password—and to change their passwords at least once a month.

- Back up the complete network on a weekly basis—and the key data daily.

- Establish a strict sign-in/sign-out system for backup tapes—and make sure that the person in charge of the backup is not the same person in charge of the system.

- Store one copy of your backup tapes in a remote location.

- Keep the network servers in a physically secured area.

- Be aware of and install the latest security patches for the networking, server, and operating system software.

- Install intrusion detection software to alert administrators when the system is under attack.

- Install network monitoring software to alert administrators if a person is working on a different part of the network, or at a different time, than is usual.

- Have all II personnel bonded.

- Be aware of any especially troubled or disgruntled employees, especially in the IT department, and especially if they have direct access to the network.

- For larger networks, create an information security (IS) department, separate from the information technology (IT) department, reporting to the company's chief information officer (CIO) or chief technology officer (CTO).

- Allocate at least 5% of the company's overall IT budget on information security.

- If your network administrator leaves the company, change all the passwords on the system, confirm the existence of the current backup tapes, perform a new complete-system backup, and have the new network administrator do a complete check of system security—including scanning for the presence of backdoor programs.

Wireless Network Security

Securing a wireless network is even more challenging than securing a wired network. When you're transmitting network signals via radio waves (as you are with the 802.11b WiFi protocol), anyone within range—or with a booster antenna—can receive your signals. You need to secure those signals to keep outsiders from listening or breaking in.

WiFi's built-in security revolves around use of Wired Equivalent Privacy (WEP) encryption. Believe it or not, more than half of all wireless networks don't have WEP enabled; without WEP, anyone within range can access your system with nothing more than a laptop PC with a WiFi card—and knowledge of the existence of your wireless network.

There are several widely available programs that sniff out wireless networks. These programs—such as AirSnort (`airsnort.shmoo.com`) and NetStumbler (`www.netstumbler.com`) are used by crackers on drive-by "war runs" to look for wireless networks to break into. (They can also be used to check out your own wireless system for weaknesses.)

How can you protect against unauthorized access to your wireless network? By using a little common sense, along with enabling basic security procedures, including:

- Enable WEP.

- Change the default password for your wireless access point/router.

- Change the default network name (also called a *service set identifier*, or SSID) of your wireless access point/router.

- Disable broadcast SSID (so that the SSID in each client computer must match the SSID of the access point).

- Locate your wireless access point toward the center of your building—not near the windows, where it can extend the range of your network well outside your building.

- Use NetStumbler or some similar tool to see if your network has any "rogue" access points easily accessible to outsiders.

- Use a laptop PC and booster antenna outside your building to see if your network is vulnerable to "war drives."

- Consider employing an additional level of security or authentication beyond the basic WEP protection.

Summing Up

Defending a network from attack requires a Layered Security Architecture, employing multiple security measures. These measures can include the use of firewall software or hardware, a proxy server, demilitarized zone, e-mail gateway, and network intrusion detection system. If all or part of your network is wireless, you should supplement these measures with WEP encryption and smart placement of your wireless access point.

In the next chapter you'll learn more about the most common form of attack prevention—the Internet firewall.

CHAPTER 18

Choosing a Firewall

If your computer has a persistent connection to the Internet, or if you're running a small home or business network, then you need constant protection from Internet-based attacks. The best way to protect against these attacks is with a *firewall*—a piece of software or hardware placed between your computer (or network) and the Internet. A firewall blocks unauthorized inbound traffic, thus insulating your system from any potential attack.

There are many easy-to-use PC-based firewall programs, and most are quite affordable. (Some are even free!) Even better, if you're running Windows XP, you already have a firewall installed on your system—because XP includes its own free firewall utility.

Read on to learn more about how firewalls work, what to look for when you're considering a firewall, and which firewall programs you should choose from.

How Firewalls Work

A firewall is a piece of software or hardware that acts as a barrier between your computer or network and the Internet. As you can see in Figure 18.1, it's actually more like a guard on a door—it lets good visitors in, and keeps bad visitors out. In the case of your computer system, good visitors are the normal e-mail communications and Web pages you visit; bad visitors are attackers trying to bomb or infiltrate your system.

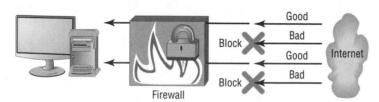

Figure 18.1 *A firewall acts as a barrier between your PC and the Internet.*

NOTE *Firewall software designed for a home or small business PC is called a personal firewall.*

If you've networked together all the computers in your house or small office, you don't need multiple firewalls. Typically, one main computer acts as the gateway to the Internet; you install the firewall software on that computer, as shown in Figure 18.2. With the firewall thus installed, all the computers on your network are protected from attack.

NOTE *If you use a DSL or cable modem to connect to the Internet, it may contain a built-in firewall. Also, many network routers contain built-in firewalls.*

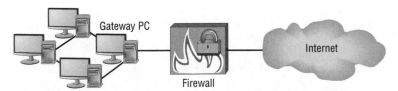

Figure 18.2 *On a network, only the gateway computer needs a firewall.*

Monitoring Traffic, by the Rules

A firewall inspects each data packet coming through your Internet connection and filters it, based on some predefined rules. The firewall passes or blocks each individual data packet, depending on whether it meets the criteria.

The rule set used by a firewall can filter traffic based on various combinations of factors. Typically, these rules look at some combination of the originating computer's IP address and the port being accessed on your computer to determine the validity of the incoming data. (A port is a specific access point into your system; different ports perform different functions.) So, as you can see in Figure 18.3, you can block access on a port-by-port basis, as well as explicitly block access from specific IP addresses and Internet domains.

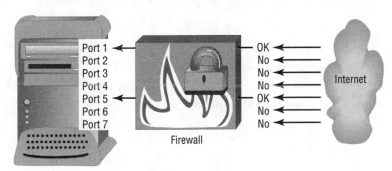

Figure 18.3 *Filtering incoming traffic on a port-by-port basis*

Matching Up Incoming and Outgoing Traffic

A more advanced filtering process uses so-called *stateful packet inspection*. As you can see in Figure 18.4, a stateful firewall works by matching incoming traffic with outgoing requests; any data not specifically requested will be automatically blocked. (The process is described as "stateful" because in order to do this matching, the firewall must keep track of each outgoing request—in computer jargon, it "maintains the state" of each request.)

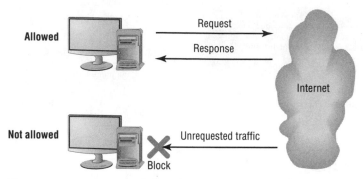

Figure 18.4 *How stateful packet inspection works*

The concept is actually simple. As a user, just about everything you do on the Internet is the result of a proactive request on your end. When you want to read your e-mail, you request that new messages be downloaded to your e-mail program. When you want to download a file, you request the download from the Web site server to your hard disk. When you want to view a Web page, you request that page to be displayed in your Web browser.

There is very little activity that isn't preceded by a request. A firewall program using stateful packet inspection will automatically block any incoming traffic that wasn't explicitly requested by you. And, since any intrusion or attack will by nature be unrequested, this is a good way to defend your system.

> **WARNING** *If you're running a Web site from your own PC, blocking unrequested incoming traffic will prevent visitors from viewing your Web pages. That's because your site visitors are doing the requesting, not you. In this instance, you'll want to configure your firewall to allow incoming HTTP requests, so your site can remain public.*

Sniffing Packet Contents

Of course, a firewall can theoretically block incoming traffic based on any criteria—including the contents of each data packet that arrives at your system's front door. As you can see in Figure 18.5, a firewall could be configured to "sniff" all incoming packets for the presence of certain words or phrases, and block access accordingly. Or a firewall could be configured to block all incoming file attachments, or attachments of a specific type. The more robust the firewall, the more filtering options possible.

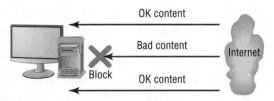

Figure 18.5 *Sniffing incoming data packets for undesirable content*

Hardware Firewalls

While we tend to think of firewalls as software programs (especially in the home and small-business areas), not all firewalls are software-based. There are also hardware firewalls that create a physical barrier to Internet-based attacks.

For small networks, you can obtain a hardware firewall protection by investing in a network router with firewall features. (See the "Choosing a Hardware Firewall" section, later in this section, for more information.) For larger corporate networks, firewall hardware is typically complex and costly (in the thousands of dollars), and it requires a working knowledge of network theory and administration to set up and keep running. For all this complexity, you get a very effective guardian; hardware firewalls are probably the best solution to thwarting attacks on corporate networks and Web sites.

Choosing Firewall Software

When you're looking for a personal firewall for your home PC or small network, there are several factors you need to consider.

Balance between ease-of-use and configurability   A firewall's no good if it's too confusing for you to use. You want a firewall program that's easy enough for you to use, but also configurable enough to meet your specific needs. If you're just a normal user with a DSL or cable modem connection, you should go with the easiest-to-use program you can find. On the other hand, if you're running a small network or a Web server, then you'll need a firewall that lets you create your own custom configuration.

Port blocking/filtering   A port is an access point into your computer system, provided by your computer's operating system. (It's not a physical input.) Every network service, such as HTTP Web transfers or SMTP e-mail, has a dedicated port, identified by number. On a default Windows installation, your computer has more than 65,000 ports available—each of which is a potential source of entry into your machine, and thus a potential source of outside attack. A good firewall will monitor attempted port access, and it will block all access that hasn't been previously approved by you.

NOTE *While a firewall can be configured to block incoming traffic to all the ports on your system, that may not always be desirable. For example, if you're using your computer to run a Web server, you need to allow remote computers to connect to your PC via port 80. Your firewall, then, can be configured to inspect every arriving packet and only permit connections to port 80; any computer trying to access your system via another port would be denied.*

Self-defined rule sets   When it comes to configuration, what you want to look for is the capability of creating your own self-defined rule sets for what gets past the firewall and what doesn't. Again, if you're just a casual home user, you probably won't need your own custom rule sets. But if you're running a network or a Web server, you'll want to be able to set your own rules and filters. Later in the chapter you'll see how to do this using Sygate Personal Firewall.

Stateful packet inspection   Stateful packet inspection works by keeping track of all communications (including Web page requests) that originate from your host computer. Incoming Internet traffic is compared against the traffic originating on your computer, and any communications that don't match are blocked. This keeps unsolicited communications—such as those in a denial-of-service attack, or backdoor remote control—from reaching your PC. It's a very effective way to stop most intrusions and attacks, and—for many users—a must-have feature.

Block unauthorized outbound traffic   The latest and greatest firewall software not only blocks unauthorized incoming traffic, but also blocks unauthorized *outbound* traffic—the kind of traffic typically resulting from a computer hijacked by a backdoor program. Outbound traffic blocking is necessary to keep your computer from being used in remote-control attacks against other systems.

When you're examining firewall software, you can also look to see if a particular program is certified by ICSA Labs. This independent organization awards its PC Firewall Certification to all products that meet the following criteria: a nonexpert user can install the product; it supports Microsoft networking capabilities; it supports concurrent dial-up and LAN connectivity; it can maintain consistent protection across multiple successive dial-up connections; it blocks common external network attacks; it restricts outgoing network communication; and it logs events in a consistent and useful manner. Among the products carrying this certification are Norton Personal Firewall, Sygate Personal Firewall, Tiny Personal Firewall, and ZoneAlarm.

TIP *Another good source of firewall information and reviews is Home PC Firewall Guide, at* www.firewallguide.com.

Popular Personal Firewall Software

Most personal firewall software is low-cost ($40 or less), easy to install, and operates in the background whenever you start your computer and connect to the Internet. The best of these programs not only block unauthorized access, but also create a log of all computers that try to attack your system— and alert you of any successful attempts.

Table 18.1 lists the most popular personal firewall programs, along with some of their key features. All of these programs are discussed in more detail following this table.

Table 18.1 *Personal Firewall Software*

PROGRAM	APPROX. PRICE	PORT BLOCKING/ FILTERING	SELF-DEFINED RULE SETS	BLOCK OUTBOUND TRAFFIC
BlackICE PC Protection	$40	Yes	Yes	Yes
eTrust EZ Firewall	$30 (one-year subscription	Yes	Yes	Yes
Kerio Personal Firewall	$40 (freeware version also available)	Yes	Yes	Yes
McAfee Personal Firewall	$30 (one-year subscription)	Yes	Yes	Yes
Norton Personal Firewall	$50	Yes	Yes	Yes
Sygate Personal Firewall	$40 (freeware version also available)	Yes	Yes	Yes
Tiny Personal Firewall	$40 (freeware version also available)	Yes	Yes	Yes
VisiNetic Firewall	$70	Yes	Yes	No
Windows XP Internet Connection Firewall	Free (included with Windows XP)	Yes	Yes	No
ZoneAlarm	$20	Yes	Yes	Yes

Of all these programs, the easiest for a nontechnical person to use are BlackICE PC Protection, eTrust EZ Firewall, ZoneAlarm, and (if you're running Windows XP) the built-in Internet

Connection Firewall. These programs are relatively simple to install and configure, often requiring no interaction on your part. The other programs here, however, typically offer more configuration and blocking options—which also makes them slightly more difficult to install and configure.

By most accounts, the most effective of the current batch of firewall programs is Sygate Personal Firewall. It's also one of the most configurable firewalls, and it isn't much more difficult to use than BlackICE and other programs of that ilk. Other firewall programs receiving high marks for effectiveness are BlackICE PC Protection, McAfee Personal Firewall, Norton Personal Firewall, and ZoneAlarm.

> **TIP** *If you're running a corporate network or commercial Web site, you'll need more robust firewall software than those presented here. To learn more about industrial-strength firewall solutions (typically costing several thousand dollars—and up), check out the Internet Computer Security Association (ICSA) Firewall Community Web site (*`www.icsalabs.com/html/communities/firewalls/`*).*

BlackICE PC Protection

BlackICE PC Protection (formerly BlackICE Defender) is one of the easiest-to-use firewalls on the market. It installs almost invisibly, and it does a good job of detecting and backtracing all manner of intrusions. It also blocks unauthorized outbound traffic, and it includes a "baselining" feature that compares the current state of your system's files with their baseline state, recorded during installation; any changes to the baseline are flagged as signs of a potential attack.

> **NOTE** *BlackICE PC Protection is available from Internet Security Systems (*`www.iss.net/solutions/home_office/`*) for approximately $40.*

eTrust EZ Firewall

EZ Firewall is an easy-to-use firewall product by eTrust, a unit of Computer Associates. The product is available electronically from the eTrust Web site, on a subscription basis only.

> **NOTE** *EZ Firewall is available from eTrust (*`www1.my-etrust.com/products/Firewall/`*) for a one-year subscription of approximately $30; the annual renewal fee is about $15.*

Kerio Personal Firewall

Kerio Personal Firewall is a very full-featured firewall product, with a host of user-customizable features. Kerio makes it easy for less-technical users by supplying three preconfigured security modes—minimum, medium, and maximum. For most users, using Kerio is as easy as choosing the minimum security mode and letting the program do its thing. Kerio Personal Firewall is available free for home use; business users should purchase the $40 commercial version.

> **NOTE** *Kerio Personal Firewall is available from Kerio Technologies, Inc. (*www.kerio.com*). This program is available in both freeware and commercial ($40) versions.*

McAfee Personal Firewall

McAfee Personal Firewall is a full-featured firewall product available on a yearly subscription basis. It blocks both ingoing and outgoing traffic, and offers all manner of rule customization.

McAfee also makes available Personal Firewall Plus, for about $10 more than the basic product, that includes an "event tracing" feature that graphically displays the source of an attack on a world map.

> **NOTE** *McAfee Personal Firewall is available from Network Associates (*www.mcafee.com*) for a one-year subscription fee of approximately $30.*

Norton Personal Firewall

Norton Personal Firewall isn't the easiest program in the world to configure, but once installed, it's very effective. It offers a host of customization options, including the ability to create your own rule sets. Fortunately for less-technical users, the program also offers several prewritten rules (great for novice users). Norton Personal Firewall is ICSA certified.

> **NOTE** *Norton Personal Firewall is available from Symantec (*www.symantec.com/sabu/nis/npf/*) for approximately $50.*

Sygate Personal Firewall

Sygate Personal Firewall is one of the most popular, and most effective, personal firewall programs available today. It's a breeze to install, and doesn't require much configuration—although there are lots of configuration options available, if you're so inclined. The program is ICSA certified, and includes protection against IP spoofing attacks.

The commercial version of this program (Personal Firewall Pro) includes more configuration options than the freeware version. Later in this chapter you'll see how to use the freeware version's basic features.

NOTE *Sygate Personal Firewall is available from Sygate* (`www.sygate.com`). *This program is available in both freeware and commercial ($40) versions.*

Tiny Personal Firewall

Tiny Personal Firewall is an effective, easy-to-use firewall program. The program is part of Tiny Software's Centrally Managed Desktop Security system, installed on about a half-million U.S. Air Force computers. Tiny Personal Firewall is ICSA certified, and it's available free of charge for home use; businesses are encouraged to purchase the commercial version.

NOTE *Tiny Personal Firewall is available from Tiny Software* (`www.tinysoftware`
`.com`). *This program is available in both freeware and commercial ($40) versions.*

VisiNetic Firewall

VisiNetic Firewall is designed for PCs on corporate networks; other VisiNetic products target large networks and Web servers. VisiNetic is an especially full-featured firewall, with extensive rule customization and importing/exporting of rules from other workstations or servers.

NOTE *VisiNetic Firewall is available from C&C Software* (`www.ccsoftware.ca/`
`visnetic/`) *for approximately $70.*

Windows XP Internet Connection Firewall

If you're using Windows XP (either Home or Professional), you may not need to purchase any additional firewall software. That's because XP comes with a built-in firewall utility, dubbed the Internet Connection Firewall (ICF).

Windows XP's ICF is a basic firewall best suited for personal or small network use. If you have fewer than a half-dozen computers connected in a home or small-business network, ICF should do an adequate job of protecting your computers from outside attack. Later in this chapter you'll see how to use its basic features.

NOTE *The Internet Connection Firewall is included free with Windows XP Home and Professional editions.*

ZoneAlarm

ZoneAlarm is a popular freeware firewall, updated to include both incoming and outgoing traffic blocking. It's ICSA certified and very easy to install and set up. Zone Labs also distributes Zone-Alarm Pro, for about $50, which includes additional features such as control over cookies and pop-up ads, "hacker tracking" (backtracing), and e-mail attachment protection.

NOTE *ZoneAlarm is available from Zone Labs (*www.zonelabs.com*) for approximately $20.*

Choosing a Hardware Firewall

A hardware firewall is a physical version of the software-based firewall. Typically included as part of a network router, it provides a physical barrier to Internet attacks.

For most home users, a hardware firewall is overkill; a low-cost software firewall provides more than adequate protection. However, if you're defending multiple PCs on a network—and have need of a router, anyway—you might as well avail yourself of a hardware-based firewall *in addition to* your firewall software.

The following companies sell routers, in the $100–$200 range, equipped with firewall features:

- Cisco (www.cisco.com)
- D-link (www.dlink.com)
- Linksys (www.linksys.com)
- Netgear (www.netgear.com)
- SMC (www.smc.com)
- Sohoware (www.sohoware.com)

Using Windows XP's Internet Connection Firewall

Anyone running Windows XP will probably want to try the built-in Internet Connection Firewall before they spend extra money on third-party firewall software. For most home and small network users, ICF will do an adequate job of protecting your system; no other software is necessary.

ICF uses stateful packet inspection to block all inbound data that doesn't match a specific outbound request. (Exceptions to this blocking rule can be configured on the Services tab in ICF's Advanced Settings dialog box, discussed shortly.)

The Internet Connection Firewall is automatically activated when you set up a shared Internet connection via Windows XP's Home Networking Wizard. You can also activate (or deactivate) the firewall manually, by following these steps:

1. From your main computer (what Windows calls the *gateway computer*), open the Windows Control Panel and click the Network Connections icon.

2. When the Network Connections utility opens, right-click the Internet connection you'll be using, and then select Properties from the pop-up menu.

3. When the Properties dialog box appears, select the Advanced tab (shown in Figure 18.6) and check the Internet Connection Firewall option. (You would uncheck this box to disable ICF—in case you want to use a third-party firewall.)

4. Click OK to activate the firewall.

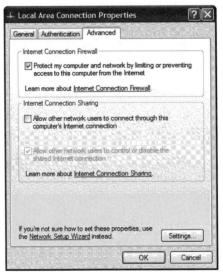

Figure 18.6 *Activating Windows XP's built-in firewall*

Once you have ICF activated, there are a number of advanced settings you can configure. Most home users shouldn't have to bother with these settings. However, if you're running your own Web site, you might want to examine these settings and configure them as appropriate.

You access ICF's settings from the Advanced tab of the Properties dialog box for your protected Internet connection. When you click the Settings button, you display the Advanced Settings dialog box, shown in Figure 18.7. There are three tabs of very technical settings:

- The Services tab enables you to select which network services outside users can access. The choices include FTP Server, Internet Mail Access Protocol version 3 (IMAP3), Internet Mail Access Protocol version 4 (IMAP4), Internet Mail Server (SMTP), Post Office Protocol version 3 (POP3), Remote Desktop, Secure Web Server (HTTPS), Telnet Server, and Web Server (HTTP). You can also add additional services by clicking the Add button and entering the service name, IP address of the host computer, and external and internal ports used by the service.

- The Security Logging tab enables you to configure the log that is kept to record attempted attacks on your system. You can select to record all dropped packets and successful connections, as well as the size and the name/location of the log file.

- The ICMP tab (for Internet Control Message Protocol) enables you to select which types of error and status information are shared with other computers on the network. You can choose to allow Incoming Echo Requests, Incoming Timestamp Requests, Incoming Mask Requests, Incoming Router Requests, Outgoing Destination Unreadable, Outgoing Search Quench, Outgoing Parameter Problem, Outgoing Time Exceeded, and Redirect messages.

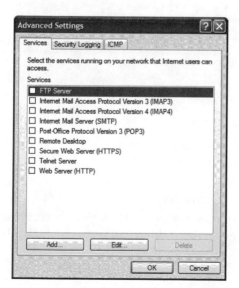

Figure 18.7 *Configuring the Internet Connection Firewall's advanced settings*

Once the ICF is up and running, it sits in the background, doing its job. The only way to tell that it's doing its job is to use Windows Notepad to read the log file, `pfirewall.log`, found in the Windows folder. (Figure 18.8 shows the contents of a typical log file; ICF has been busy!)

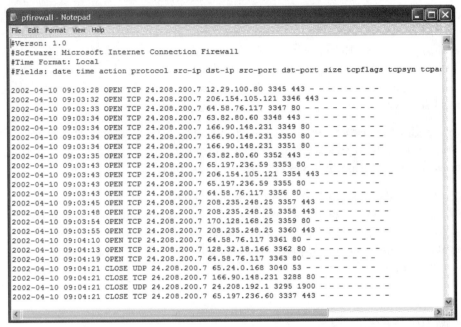

Figure 18.8 *The log file created by Windows XP's Internet Connection Firewall*

Using Sygate Personal Firewall

There isn't space in this book to go into the detailed operation of every available personal firewall; instead, we'll focus on using one of the most popular programs, Sygate Personal Firewall. Most firewalls operate in a similar fashion.

One thing that makes Sygate so popular is that it's available not only in a commercial version (for about $40), but also in a freeware version. It's the freeware version we'll look at here; if you like the free version, you might want to consider investing in the commercial version, which offers more configuration options.

Viewing Firewall Data

As you can see in Figure 18.9, the main Sygate window has three parts. At the top are graphs showing the history of recent activity and attacks; in the middle are lists of currently running applications on your PC that access the Internet (outbound traffic); and at the bottom is the message console, which alerts you to current activity.

NOTE *If the Message Console isn't displayed, click the Show Message Console button.*

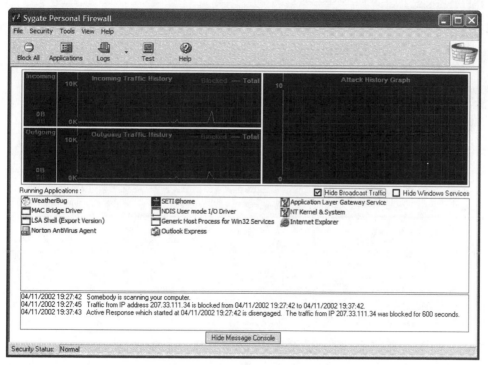

Figure 18.9 *Viewing live activity with the Sygate Personal Firewall*

It's normal for the Incoming Traffic History and Outgoing Traffic History graphs to show activity; these graphs peak upward every time one of your applications accesses the Internet. It's the Attack History Graph that you want to pay attention to, since it logs all unauthorized activity, which the program classifies as an attack.

To view more details about a particular attack, click the down arrow on the Logs button and select Security Log. This displays the Log Viewer window, shown in Figure 18.10. All recent attacks are listed here, along with the following essential information about each attack:

- Time of attack

- Type of attack (port scan, etc.)

- Severity (normal, minor, major)

- Direction (incoming or outgoing activity)

- What protocol was used for the attack

- Destination of the attack (typically your computer, unless it was an outgoing activity)

- Source IP (the address of the attacker)

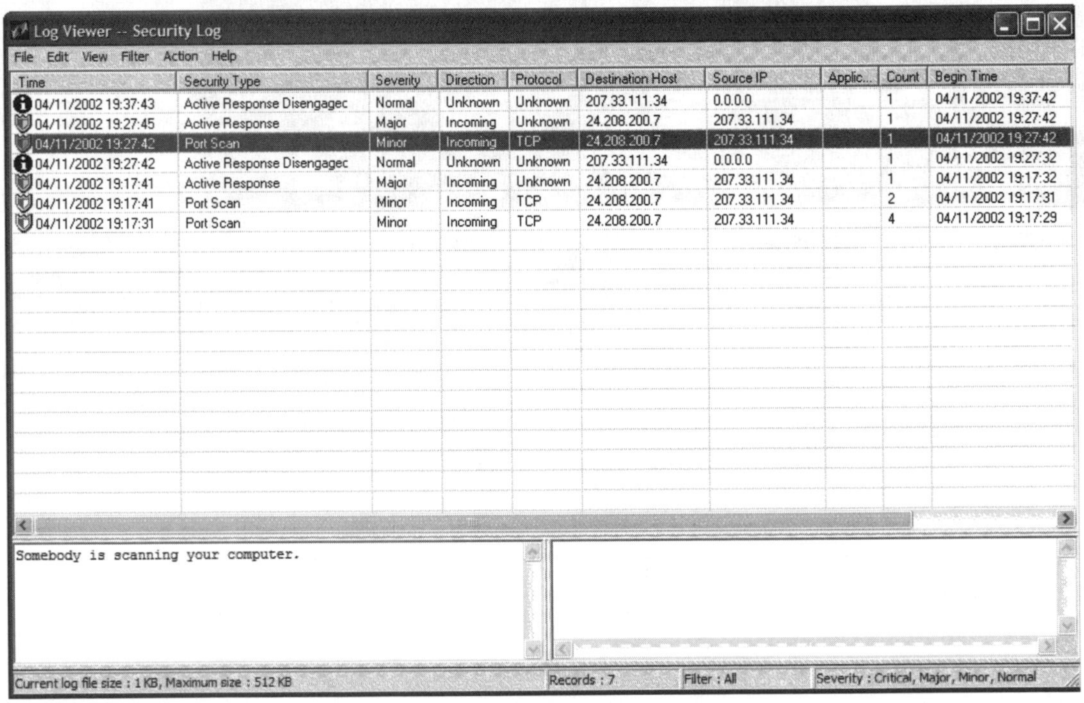

Figure 18.10 *Viewing recent attacks via Sygate's Security Log*

When you highlight an attack, a brief description of that attack is listed in the lower left pane.

You can also use the Log Viewer to display other types of logs, including the System Log (showing changes to the firewall configuration), the Traffic Log (showing all incoming and outgoing traffic—see Figure 18.11), and the Packet Log (disabled by default; if turned on, it shows every packet of data evaluated by the firewall). To view these other logs, just pull down the Log Viewer's View menu and select a specific log.

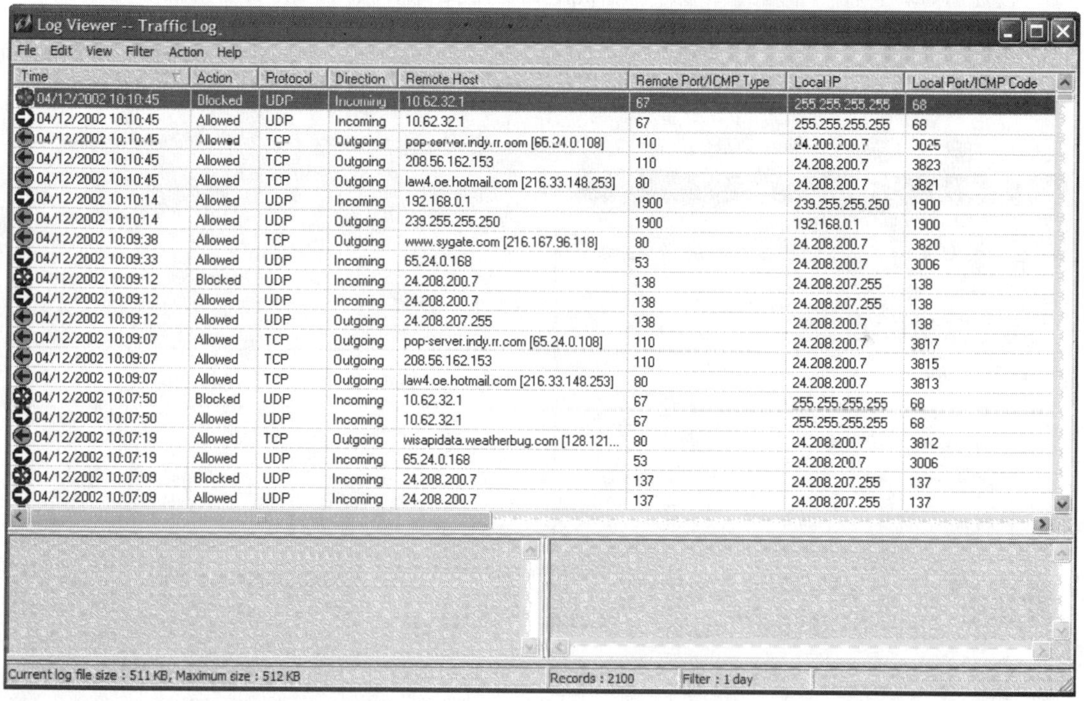

Figure 18.11 *Viewing incoming and outgoing traffic with the Traffic Log*

Dealing with an Attack

When Sygate detects unauthorized activity, it notifies you via a pop-up window. If any action is required on your part, you'll be prompted for your choice. For example, when a program on your computer attempts to connect to the Internet, Sygate prompts you and asks whether the connection should be allowed. (In most cases, the answer is yes; for example, you definitely want your e-mail program to be able to connect to the Internet to collect new messages.)

One of the interesting features of Sygate Personal Firewall is its BackTrace feature. This lets you backtrace an attack to its source. You perform a backtrace by following these steps:

1. In the Security Log window, highlight the attack.

2. Select Action ➤ BackTrace.

3. Sygate now traces the attack back through its entire route over the Internet (typically via multiple servers), and displays the results in the Back Trace Information window. Click the Whois button to display the name and address of the attack's source (shown in Figure 18.12).

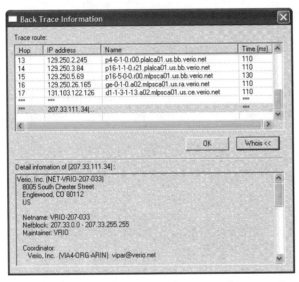

Figure 18.12 *Backtracing the source of an attack*

In most cases, the source displayed by the backtrace is not the hacker's computer, but the public router the cracker used to launch the attack. Armed with this information, you can contact the router's owner and report the attack.

WARNING *Not all router owners will have the time or the inclination to research every reported attack—so don't be disappointed if you receive no response to your report.*

Configuring the Firewall

When you first install Sygate Personal Firewall, it pretty much configures itself for your particular system. You can, however, reconfigure many of the program's settings, by following these steps:

1. Select Tools ➤ Options.

2. When the Options dialog box appears (shown in Figure 18.13), select each tab and make the appropriate selections.

3. Click OK when done.

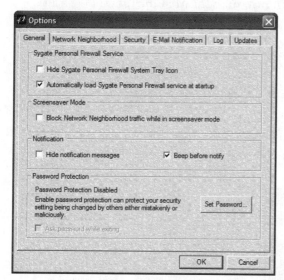

Figure 18.13 *Configuring firewall options*

Here are some of the options you can configure:

General tab   Automatically start the firewall on system service, show or hide the program icon in the Windows system tray, hide notification messages, and password-protect your security settings.

Network Neighborhood tab   Allow or disallow others to share your files and printers.

Security tab   Enable or disable various types of protection.

E-mail Notification tab   Have the program e-mail you when an attack is discovered (ideal for remote monitoring of your system).

Log tab   Configure the size and capture duration of the various log files.

Updates tab   Enable the program to automatically check for new versions.

WARNING *Not all configuration options are available in the freeware version of the program.*

Creating Your Own Rules

You can also customize the program by creating your own rules for what the firewall does and doesn't block. This can be a complex process (and you really have to know a bit about Internet security to make it work), but it goes something like this:

1. Select Tools ➤ Advanced Rules.

2. When the Advanced Rules dialog box appears, click the Add button.

3. When the Advanced Rule Settings dialog box appears, click the General tab (shown in Figure 18.14). Enter a description of the rule, select whether this rule is for blocking or allowing traffic, and then select which network interface the rule applies to.

Figure 18.14 *Creating a new rule*

4. Select the Hosts tab and enter which addresses you want to block or allow.

5. Select the Ports and Protocols tab and select which protocol you wish to invoke.

6. If you want this rule to apply only during certain times of the day (or on certain days of the month), select the Scheduling tab and enter the appropriate day and time information.

7. If you want this rule to apply to particular applications on your system (for outgoing rules, primarily), select the Applications tab and select the appropriate applications.

8. Click OK when done.

Summing Up

A firewall works by inserting itself between your computer or network and the Internet. It can either be software- or hardware-based, although most home users are well served by one of the low-cost ($40 and under) personal firewall programs currently available. These programs use a series of rules to block unauthorized inbound traffic to the host system—and, in some cases, to block unauthorized *outbound* traffic.

The most popular personal firewall programs include BlackICE PC Protection, McAfee Personal Firewall, Norton Personal Firewall, Sygate Personal Firewall, and ZoneAlarm. In addition, Windows XP includes its own built-in firewall, dubbed the Internet Connection Firewall; while not as full-featured or configurable as many freestanding programs, it's very easy to use and effective enough for most home users.

In the next chapter we'll examine what happens when an attack actually takes place—and your firewall doesn't protect you.

CHAPTER 19

Dealing with an Attack

Despite your best precautions, you can still find yourself the victim of an Internet-based attack. This attack could come in the form of a hijacked computer, a defaced Web page, or even a dreaded denial-of-service attack.

Whatever it is, it's likely to be bad.

If you find your system under attack, you need to take action—both to stop the attack and to recover from any damage inflicted. This chapter walks you through how to recognize an attack while it's still in process, how to shut down the attack, and how to get back up and running afterwards.

You can only hope you won't even need this information.

How to Tell When Your System Is Under Attack

It isn't always easy to know when your system is under attack or has suffered an intrusion. Unless the attacker has deliberately harmed your system, to the point where it doesn't run properly, you might not immediately realize that your system has been compromised.

So how can you tell if your computer is the victim of an outside attack? Here are some of the ways to discover an attack, while it's still in progress.

Watch for the Symptoms of an Attack

Perhaps the best way to tell if your system is the victim of an intrusion or attack is to examine various aspects of your computer's behavior. In particular, check the following:

Unusual amount of hard disk activity   While there are benign causes for unidentified hard disk activity (normal hard disk maintenance and cleanup, disk defragmenting, and so on), you need to be concerned if your disk light lights up for extended periods of time—especially when you're not using your PC.

Unusual amount of Internet activity   If your Internet connection shows either upstream or downstream traffic and you're not browsing the Web or receiving e-mail, *something* is causing those bits and bytes to move back and forth. That something could be an attacker coming in or zombie activity going out—or the beginnings of a potentially devastating denial-of-service attack.

Modem automatically dialing   You should be even more concerned if your computer has a life of its own, and automatically dials into your Internet service provider without your prompting. While this could be caused by some scheduled activity you previously automated, it can also occur when an intruder hijacks your system via a backdoor program.

Unusual number of e-mail messages   If you notice that your inbox is full to overflowing with unusual or junk messages, you could be the target of an e-mail bomb attack—meaning that some attacker is bombing your e-mail account.

Unusual amount of network traffic   Just as an extreme amount of Internet activity can signal the presence of an intrusion, so can an unusually high amount of traffic over your network. While there are normal causes for high traffic, the situation can also be caused by a backdoor intruder using a compromised PC to access computers across the entire network.

Unusual amount of Web site traffic   If you run a Web site, a huge influx of traffic—far above your normal traffic levels—could be the tip-off that you're on the receiving end of a denial-of-service attack.

Changed or missing pages on your Web site   If your Web site suddenly sprouts graffiti on the home page, or links that don't go where you want them to go, then you could be the victim of Web site defacement.

Missing or changed files on your hard disk   If your data has been compromised in any way, it could be the result of an Internet attack, or a virus attack.

In short, look for signs of unusual activity. Most intrusions require your system to work harder than it typically does when idle, so this type of unexpected activity is a good sign that something untoward is afoot.

Look for New and Unusual Files

When an attacker drops a backdoor program on your system, he leaves one or more new files somewhere on your hard disk. In Windows XP you can use the Search Companion utility to look for newly created files, and thus discover new backdoors and such. Follow these steps:

1. Select Start ➤ Search.
2. When the Search window opens, select All Files And Folders.
3. When the Search Companion pane appears (shown in Figure 19.1), enter *.* in the All Or Part Of The File Name blank.
4. Click the When Was It Modified button, and select Within The Last Week.
5. Click the Search button.

Figure 19.1 *Using Windows XP's Search Companion utility to look for new files on your system*

Windows will now return a list of files modified any time within the past seven days. Study this list, looking for any files that look suspicious. Keep in mind that any new files you've created or downloaded will also be listed here, and that some programs update some of their system files every time the program is opened.

TIP *If you take this approach, you should make sure that you're also searching for hidden files. The default search in Windows XP, for example, doesn't search for hidden or system files. You'll want to click the More Advanced Options button, and then select the Search Hidden Files And Folders option.*

Examine Your Log Files

Many programs create log files that capture all program activity. Many times you can discover an intrusion by examining these log files—which will typically show all sorts of unexpected activity, particularly when you haven't been using the program. Of particular interest are the log files created by your firewall program, which we'll discuss next.

Use Your Firewall

Another way to discover an attack is through the software you use to defend your system—in particular, your firewall software. Most firewall programs not only defend against attacks, but also alert you when an attack is taking place. For example, Sygate Personal Firewall displays a pop-up window (accompanied by an audio alert) on the first sign of attack. It also displays a message in the program's main window.

In addition, your firewall's log file is a terrific tool for identifying all sorts of attacks. As discussed in Chapter 18, "Choosing a Firewall," a firewall program's log file contains all sorts of useful information regarding Internet attacks; some programs even let you backtrace the attack to the originating computer or router.

Monitor for Scans and Sniffs

One surefire sign of an Internet attack is the presence of a large number of port scans. A port scan occurs when a potential intruder searches your computer for unprotected ports in which to enter your system; a successful port scan is often followed by the insertion of a backdoor file or other malicious code.

Fortunately, most firewall programs monitor port scans and alert you of unusual activity in this area. You can also install a separate port scan monitor, such as Nuke Nabber (`www.rogerdidit .com/nonuke.html`). This type of program monitors all the port activity on your system, looking for port scans from the outside. While a certain number of port scans is to be expected any time you're connected to the Internet, an undue number of scans, as well as scans of certain types, are indicative of a current or upcoming attack.

Another sign of attack is the unauthorized use of so-called sniffer (or packet sniffer) programs. Sniffers are network monitoring programs commonly used to steal account and password information. Some intruders surreptitiously install sniffer software on your system, where it works in the background recording your user activity. The intruder can then reenter your system, retrieve the sniffer's log file, and have all your keystrokes and other activity right there, in black-and-white. (For that reason, you don't just want to look for and remove sniffer software; you also want to remove any files created by the sniffer program.)

By themselves, sniffer programs are relatively invisible—until they start to send their results to the attacker. The best way to sniff out a sniffer is to use a utility such as AntiSniff (`www .securitysoftwaretech.com/antisniff/`).

TIP *Examining the sniffer log file is also a good way to see if other machines on your network are at risk.*

Use an Intrusion Detection System

An even better way to detect an attack in progress is to use an intrusion detection system (IDS)—or, in a network environment, a network intrusion detection system (NIDS). This software (or suite of software utilities) monitors a network or system for unusual or unauthorized use of network or system resources.

What does an IDS look for? Some of the activities that a good IDS monitors include IP protocol violations or anomalies, IP half scans, password attacks, and other unusual activities. Many IDS programs also use signature-based detection, which compares incoming traffic to the signatures of known intrusion techniques. (This is similar to the signature scanning technique used by most antivirus programs.)

If you run a medium-sized network, it's smart to install IDS software. It's probably the most effective—and fastest—way to become aware of intrusions and attacks, as they're happening.

NOTE *Some of the most popular IDS programs were listed in Chapter 17, "Protecting a Network."*

Shutting Down and Recovering from a Real-Time Attack

For most types of Internet attacks—including small-scale denial-of-service attacks—having your firewall up and running should fend off the attack, with no further action required on your part. (That's why you have a firewall, right?) Larger-scale attacks that get past your firewall are more problematic, however.

In general, if you discover that your system is the victim of an ongoing Internet-based attack, you want to follow these steps:

1. If you're on a network, disconnect the compromised computer from your network.

2. Disconnect your computer or network from the Internet.

3. Analyze your computer for signs of attack, or for the presence of backdoor or sniffer software; examine all your system log files. (This is also a good time to run a full-system scan with your antivirus software—virus infections and Internet-based attacks often go hand-in-hand.)

4. Examine your log files, or use backtracing software, to try to identify the source of the attack.

5. Repair any damage to the PC in question—and remove any backdoor software found. (This is also the time to restore any deleted or damaged data from your backup copies.)

WARNING *Be cautious about restoring operating system data from backups—the backup could contain the same backdoor program that enabled the attack in the first place.*

6. Examine all other PCs on your network—and any PCs that connect to your network via remote dial-up. (Once an attacker is inside your network, all machines are at risk—and they could be used to hold more backdoors for future use.)

7. Change *all* passwords used to access the network and individual PCs. (This will keep the intruder from reentering your system, if he happens to have access to a previous password.)

8. Report the attack to proper authorities, such as the National Infrastructure Protection Center (`www.nipc.gov/incident/incident.htm`) or the CERT Coordination Center (`irf.cc.cert.org`). You may also want to report the attack to your local authorities.

9. Reconnect the computer to the network and to the Internet.

10. Closely monitor all Internet traffic to determine if the attack is still ongoing; if so, you may need to go offline again for the duration.

TIP *After you've shut down an attack, you may want to try to trace the attacker— what the security industry calls* backtracing. *Most firewall products enable you to trace the attacker's route back across the Internet, from your computer back to the originating computer or router. Chapter 18 shows how to backtrace using Sygate Personal Firewall.*

Some experts recommend a more extreme response to an attack, especially an attack on a large network or Web site. They recommend that while your network is offline, you install a clean version of your operating system, and then do a program-by-program security check, downloading and installing all relevant security patches. The thinking behind this approach is that an attacker could delete or modify virtually every file on your system, and thus the only way to be absolutely sure that your system is free from sleeper and backdoor programs is to reinstall the entire operating system from scratch.

Summing Up

Realizing that an attack is in progress is more difficult than you might think, as only certain types of attacks actually shut down your system. Most attacks are of the backdoor type, and are typically discovered in retrospect.

One good sign that your system is being attacked is the presence of unusual system activity—lots of hard disk access or Internet traffic. You can also rely on your firewall software to alert you of an attack, or use one of a variety of dedicated security utilities, such as intrusion detection systems.

If your system is under attack, the first thing to do is disconnect your PC from the network (if it's so connected) or from the Internet. You can then search for backdoor programs and other damage, and change all your passwords, before you go back online.

That's all there is to say about Internet-based attacks—at least in this book. (There are lots of other resources for this topic, especially online; see the list in Chapter 13.) In the next section we look at privacy theft, starting with Chapter 20, "Protecting Your Privacy."

PART III

PRIVACY THEFT

Protecting Your Privacy

We Americans value our privacy. We don't want our neighbors to know what we do behind closed doors, and we don't like giving out our phone numbers and addresses unless we absolutely have to. We especially don't like being watched, or followed, or tracked—and that goes double for when we're online. What we do on the Internet is our personal business, and no one else's.

Right?

The problem is, the Internet is a technological environment where your every movement can be tracked. With the right tools, a person or organization can track your incoming and outgoing e-mail, newsgroup postings, chat conversations, and even the Web sites you visit and the files you download. With a little perseverance, an individual with malicious intent can even track your user IDs, passwords, credit card numbers, and other personal information—and then use that information to access your accounts and, if so inclined, steal your identity.

These threats are real—and they're pretty damn scary. If you value your privacy and the security of your personal information, this chapter is essential reading. There are ways to protect your privacy online, but only if you know what threats exist—and how to counter them.

Privacy Online

On one hand, the Internet is an environment that encourages anonymity. You can create any number of usernames and online personas, and you can pretend to be anyone you want. (You've no doubt seen the old cartoon of a canine sitting in front of a computer, connected to the Internet; on the Internet, no one knows you're a dog.)

On the other hand, the Internet is also an environment that enables extremely precise tracking. Everything you do online—every e-mail you send, every message you create, every Web site you visit—can be tracked. And, with all the personal information you leave behind in your wake, it's becoming increasingly difficult to keep your private life private, online.

How Public Is Your Private Information?

The big question on the minds of some users is: Who knows what about me, online?

This won't be very reassuring to you, but the likelihood is that your name, e-mail address, street address, and phone number are all on the Web, somewhere—just as they're all public knowledge in the real world.

That's because the online world is no different from the physical world. In the physical world, when you buy something from a direct mailer or catalog merchant, your name and contact information enters their database. Most direct merchants generate subsidiary income from selling the names in their database to other companies; that's how you end up getting all sorts of junk mail in your postal mailbox. Make one purchase, and everybody knows who you are.

The same thing happens online. When you buy something online, or enter your name and address to register for a specific Web site, your contact information goes into that company's database—which then often gets sold to other companies. These online companies are just like their bricks-and-mortar counterparts; they also generate subsidiary income by selling their databases to other companies. Enter your contact information once, and you end up getting all sorts of junk e-mail (called *spam*) in your e-mail inbox.

In this respect, online privacy is no bigger an issue than real-world privacy. Allan Carey, a senior analyst at market research firm IDC, put it this way:

"Is [using the Web] any worse than calling up a customer service person and telling them your credit card number? Because that's just the front-end part of the transaction, and the Web is just another interface for that transaction."

You provide personal information to third parties all the time. When you sign up for a bank account, you provide personal information. When you apply for a credit card, you provide personal information. When you sign up for that "90 days same as cash" program at your local retailer, you provide personal information. When you initiate service at your phone or electric or gas company, you provide personal information. When you register for your supermarket's frequent buyer card, you provide personal information.

What makes the Internet any different?

Put another way, you can't blame the Web itself for any privacy problems that you might encounter. The very nature of commerce and communication requires the exchange of personal information. The only way to ensure complete privacy is to isolate yourself from all types of transactions—and that has never been a very practical alternative.

Of course, you should practice *some* discretion in what information you make available about yourself online. If you know that every message you send online can be made public (and it can), you might think twice before hitting the Send button in your e-mail or instant-messaging program. If you know that sending personal information to a non-secure Web site poses a higher risk of theft, you might reconsider doing business with that particular site.

But there's no sense getting paranoid about it. Privacy issues online are no different from privacy issues in the real world. Take reasonable precautions, and you probably don't have too much to worry about.

Old Internet Postings Never Die—They Just Get Archived

You might not realize it, but every public posting you make—in Usenet newsgroups, online message boards, and chat rooms—becomes part of the undying fabric of the Internet. Once you put a message out there, it stays out there.

Consider the Usenet archive available at Google (`groups.google.com`). This archive stores every single newsgroup posting from the start of Usenet to today. If you posted something nasty about your boss five years ago, that posting still exists. If you mentioned an affair you had with a neighbor back in the early 90s, that posting still exists. If you asked a question about a particular illness, or proffered an opinion about a particular make of car, or let slip where you live, that information is still available to a dedicated searcher.

Which means, of course, that the biggest threat to your privacy is *you*.

It also reinforces the general warning that all veteran Internet users should know: Don't post anything in a newsgroup, message board, or chat room that you wouldn't want your future boss—or spouse—to read.

Potential Privacy Abuses

That said, what types of privacy abuses are you likely to encounter on the Internet? Start by imagining the many ways your privacy can be compromised in the real world, and apply all those situations online. Then add in a few online-specific scenarios, and you can see why some people get very concerned about the topic of online privacy.

Selling Information

Any Web site that collects information about you (name, address, whatever) is capable of selling that information to another site or company. This shouldn't shock you; it happens all the time, both online and in the real world. Many companies generate significant revenues by selling the names on their mailing lists; this is a long-standing practice that has migrated to the world of the Internet.

You can generally determine if a company intends to sell your name by examining that site's privacy policy. Most Web sites will state up front whether they're in the business of selling names, and if so, to whom. Don't be surprised, however, if you find that most Web sites will sell their customer lists to just about anyone—if the price is right.

NOTE *Read more about privacy policies in the "Understanding Web Site Privacy Policies" section, later in this chapter.*

Stolen Information

Probably the biggest fear of most consumers is that their personal information will be stolen. If you've ever had your wallet or purse stolen, you know how big a hassle this can be; bounced checks, unauthorized credit card use, and the like present a multitude of problems that you have to deal with.

Just as you can have your physical information stolen, you can also have your virtual information stolen. Your personal information can be hijacked as it flows over the Internet between your computer and its destination; it can also be stolen from the giant databases kept by Web sites and online merchants.

The good news is that the incidence of online data theft is relatively low. The bad news is that the consequences of such theft are high.

How secure is the information you provide to a Web site? It depends. While most reputable Web sites have extensive security measures in place, online robberies sometimes take place—just as they do in the real world.

For example, early in 2000 a cracker broke into the customer database at CD Universe, a large online retailer of CDs and DVDs. This cracker—let's call him a thief, at this point—then posted tens of thousands of these stolen credit card numbers on an underground Web site, free for the taking. (And, not surprisingly, many were taken—and used, without the owners' authorization.)

Can a Web site completely protect against this type of online data theft? No—no more than a bricks-and-mortar company can completely protect against physical break-ins and robberies. Crooks will be crooks, and sometimes they're successful at what they do. Fortunately, most charge card companies protect you in the event that your card (or card number) is stolen, so you'll only be out a minimal amount if the worst happens.

A bigger problem occurs if your most personal information is stolen—particularly your Social Security number. That's because your Social Security number can be used to obtain other personal information, including birth certificates and driver's licenses. This is one reason you should refrain from providing your Social Security number to third parties, especially over the Internet. But this type of identity theft does happen—albeit on a small scale—and poses particular problems for its victims.

NOTE *Read more about online data theft in the "Identity Theft" section, later in this chapter.*

Tracking Online Activities

Unique to the online world is the capability of tracking everything you do. With technology that is readily available today, a Web site can follow you as you surf from site to site, logging all the pages you visit and what you do while you're there. It's the online equivalent of someone following you through a shopping mall, snapping pictures of you as you go.

This sort of tracking is facilitated by small programs called cookies, which are automatically installed on your hard disk when you visit particular Web sites. In addition, some software programs—called packet sniffers—can log everything you do at your keyboard, every key you tap and every button you click. It's the nature of the technology; if it exists, it can be tracked.

NOTE *Learn more about cookies in Chapter 24, "Managing Cookies."*

The privacy dangers, of course, depend on what someone does with all this potential information. Is this information used to deliver personalized ads on specific Web pages? Or is it used to profile you and identify you as a potential criminal of some sort?

This information can certainly be used to identify you personally and to target you for various marketing purposes. For example, online advertising company DoubleClick announced plans to match a real-world mass mailing list with its own anonymous list of Internet users, gathered from click-through responses to its banner ads. Matching one list against the other would reveal the Web user's identities and open up all manner of potential marketing opportunities. However, faced with tremendous consumer backlash (and at least one lawsuit), DoubleClick backed off on its plans. But it's such a logical progression, someone is bound to do it—sometime.

The bottom line is that there are more companies tracking you than you think. Just because you're paranoid doesn't mean that you're *not* being followed.

User Profiling

What good is all this online tracking, anyway? Well, if you run an online business, it's in your best interest to tailor your advertising and marketing to your individual customers' likes and dislikes. Personalized marketing—sometimes called one-to-one marketing—is all the rage, and any information collected about you over the Internet can help feed these personalized appeals.

On a fairly innocuous level, consider the way Amazon.com delivers a personal welcome page every time you visit their site. Amazon stores information about your past purchases and items you've shopped for, and it uses cookie technology to know who you are and when you've returned. All this information is combined to offer "personal picks" about new products you might be interested in, served up to you in your own personalized page. Assuming that all the technology works (which it doesn't, always), you benefit from being offered merchandise closely tailored to your past purchases.

This type of activity is called user profiling. The upside of user profiling is a more personalized online experience, but the downside is that some marketers can use the information in your profile to pitch even more (and more targeted) advertising and spam in your direction, and to sell your name as part of more targeted customer lists to other companies.

User profiling can also grow to include information gathered at other Web sites or from other online activities. Imagine a company using the information contained in your posts to a Usenet newsgroup, or uttered in an online chat room, and cross-referencing this information with the data stored on a separate Web site. Even worse, imagine government authorities tracking your online behavior and assembling a profile that indicates you're at risk for terrorist activities, or for child pornography. It might sound Orwellian, but it's technically possible—and, some worry, imminently probable.

Privacy for Children

Web sites want information—even from your children. In fact, children are a great source of information; they're not as guarded as adults are, making them more prone to divulge personal details to unscrupulous Web marketers.

And some Web marketers are particularly unscrupulous. Some sites aren't above bribing children for their personal information, promising prizes and free software *just for filling in this form*. Enter this contest (which requires filling out a form with name, address, and phone number) and you might win a really big prize; tell us who you are (and where you live) and we'll let you play this really neat online game. You get the drift. Kids are easily duped, and there are plenty of folks waiting to dupe them.

> **WARNING** *If your kids have their own personal Web pages, you should check their pages to make sure that they've included no personal information that could compromise their privacy or safety.*

As a parent, you can protect against this sort of child-oriented privacy abuse by closely monitoring your children's online activities and training them never to enter personal information—no matter how tempting it might be. You should also be aware of the various laws in place to protect you and your children from this type of privacy abuse.

For example, the Children's Online Privacy Protection Act (COPPA) requires that parental permission be obtained before a Web site gathers information on children younger than 13. You can read more about COPPA at the Center for Media Education's (CME) KidsPrivacy.org Web site (**www.kidsprivacy.org**)—which also offers some fine practical advice for protecting children online.

NOTE *The Federal Trade Commission (FTC) also sponsors a Web site with information about online privacy for children. The Kidz Privacy site (*`www.ftc.gov/bcp/`*
`conline/edcams/kidzprivacy`*) offers some useful advice (ask to see the information your child has submitted to a Web site), and some fairly innocuous but ultimately useless advice (look for Web site privacy policies directed toward children). While there's nothing wrong with examining Web site privacy policies in regard to how they affect your children, you can't rely on these policy statements to protect anyone from anything. More on this in the next section, "Understanding Web Site Privacy Policies."*

You should also take the following steps to protect your children's privacy online:

- Caution your children about providing personal information to any Web site without your explicit permission.

- Make your kids ask your permission before filling in any forms online.

- Install blocking software that prevents your children from giving out their name, address, and phone number online.

- Install content filtering software that restricts the Web sites that your children can visit.

- Monitor your children's online activities; consider installing their PC in a public place (living room or den) as opposed to a private bedroom.

It's likely that if your children are online, they *will* be targeted by people and companies who want them to divulge personal information. It's up to you to train your kids to resist these queries, and preserve their anonymity online.

NOTE *Learn more about protecting your children online in Chapter 22, "Protecting Yourself from Online Predators."*

Understanding Web Site Privacy Policies

The companies that run the Internet's largest Web sites recognize the growing public concern about online privacy. They realize that users worry about Web sites keeping their private data private, and about having their names and e-mail addresses sold to the highest bidder.

In an attempt to assuage user concerns, most larger Web sites have some sort of privacy policy that they purportedly follow, as detailed by a written privacy statement, typically posted online. This statement lays out (often in legalistic detail) just what the site will and will not do with the personal information it collects.

You can typically find a site's privacy statement under the About or Help links; in some cases, there's even a link to the privacy policy somewhere on the site's home page.

TIP *If you can't find a site's privacy policy, you can search the site for the word "privacy," or just e-mail the site's Webmaster and ask.*

Does a Privacy Policy Make a Difference?

While the presence of a privacy policy might make you feel better, these policies don't necessarily do much in the way of protecting your privacy. In many cases, these privacy policies simply tell you that the Web site intends to provide your contact information to various third parties, whether you like it or not. Typically, your only recourse is not to visit or sign up for the site; only in rare instances do you have the alternative of opting out of these marketing agreements.

In addition, the privacy statements you find online aren't always legally binding—and it's not unusual for a site to change its privacy policies without notice. While some sites e-mail changes in their privacy policy to their members, others assume (incorrectly, in most cases) that you actually read the privacy policy on every visit—and will notice the changes.

While a lot of attention gets paid to these privacy statements, it's arguable just how useful they really are. It's not as if you can negotiate a privacy policy with a given site; the policy is presented in pretty much a take-it-or-leave-it fashion. You have the option of not using that site, of course, but that's about it.

Sample Privacy Policies

How useful or informative are Web site privacy policies? Take a look at a few (from some of the Web's largest sites) and make up your own mind.

Amazon.com *(www.amazon.com)*

We receive and store any information you enter on our Web site or give us in any other way... You can choose not to provide certain information, but then you might not be able to take advantage of many of our features. We use the information that you provide for such purposes as responding to your requests, customizing future shopping for you, improving our stores, and communicating with you...

Information about our customers is an important part of our business, and we are not in the business of selling it to others. We share customer information only with the subsidiaries Amazon.com, Inc., controls and as described below...

As we continue to develop our business, we might sell or buy stores or assets. In such transactions, customer information generally is one of the transferred business assets. Also, in the unlikely event that Amazon.com, Inc., or substantially all of its assets are acquired, customer information will of course be one of the transferred assets...

Google *(www.google.com)*

Google does not collect any unique information about you (such as your name, email address, etc.) except when you specifically and knowingly provide such information. Google notes and saves information such as time of day, browser type, browser language, and IP address with each query. That information is used to verify our records and to provide more relevant services to users. For example, Google may use your IP address or browser language to determine which language to use when showing search results or advertisements...

Google may share information about you with advertisers, business partners, sponsors, and other third parties. However, we only divulge aggregate information about our users and will not share personally identifying information with any third party without your express consent. For example, we may disclose how frequently the average Google visitor visits Google, or which other query words are most often used with the query word "Linux." Please be aware, however, that we will release specific personal information about you if required to do so in order to comply with any valid legal process such as a search warrant, subpoena, statute, or court order...

New York Times *(www.nytimes.com)*

During a free registration process prior to using the site, The New York Times on the Web requires that you supply a unique member ID, e-mail address, and demographic information (country, zip code, age, sex; household income, industry, job title, job function, and subscription status to The New York Times newspaper). You must agree to the terms of our Subscriber Agreement...

The New York Times on the Web shares the information it gathers, in aggregate form only, with advertisers and other partners. We will not release personal information about you as an individual to third parties, except under the circumstances described in Compliance with Legal Process below...

Yahoo! *(www.yahoo.com)*

When you register we ask for information such as your name, email address, birth date, gender, zip code, occupation, industry, and personal interests. For some financial products and services we may also ask for your address, Social Security number, and information about your assets. Once you register with Yahoo! and sign in to our services, you are not anonymous to us...

Yahoo! automatically receives and records information on our server logs from your browser, including your IP address, Yahoo! cookie information, and the page you request...

We provide the information to trusted partners who work on behalf of or with Yahoo! under confidentiality agreements. These companies may use your personal information to help Yahoo! communicate with you about offers from Yahoo! and our marketing partners. However, these companies do not have any independent right to share this information...

Yahoo! may update this policy. We will notify you about significant changes in the way we treat personal information by sending a notice to the primary email address specified in your Yahoo! account or by placing a prominent notice on our site...

NOTE *These are excerpts from longer privacy policies, current as of May 2002.*

When Privacy Policies Change

For some Web sites, privacy policies are flexible—or at least capable of being changed over time. It's not unusual to find that a site has changed its privacy policy, for one reason or another, and simply posted the new policy online, without notifying its users. Of course, there's nothing that says the site *has* to notify its users; it would be different if the privacy statement was a legally binding contract, but it obviously isn't.

So don't be surprised if your favorite Web site includes some sort of wording to the effect that "changes to this policy can be made at any time." And don't expect those changes to be in your favor.

You also have the issue of what happens when a Web site or company is acquired—whose privacy policy rules? (Hint: It's probably not that of the company being acquired.)

In most instances, the acquired company automatically adopts the privacy policy of the acquiring company, no matter what its prior privacy statement said. In many cases, users who signed onto a site with the understanding that their private information would stay private suddenly discover that the site's new owners are blissfully disseminating that formerly private information.

And these users probably aren't happy about the changes.

Take the example of Yahoo!, which changed its privacy policy in March 2002. (No acquisition involved; they just changed it.) What irked users about the change wasn't the content of the policy, but rather the default settings. When Yahoo! changed its privacy policy, it also reset all users' settings regarding marketing permissions (letting Yahoo! send ads to users via e-mail). No matter what you had selected before, your settings were now changed to the default of allowing all such marketing communications.

This was very disconcerting, especially to those users who had previously opted out of these commercial e-mailings. Of course, you could go back and reset your settings (again) to opt out of all marketing mailings, but it seemed like poor business, at best, for Yahoo! to deliberately contradict users' wishes in this fashion. (To be fair, Yahoo! did notify users of these changes in an e-mail, but the "negative option" nature of this reset upset a large number of users.)

The point is that you can't depend on a Web site to look out for your privacy. In fact, you can expect many Web sites to deliberately exploit what information they have about you. They're looking out for their business, not your privacy.

Privacy Policies Are Slipping

While most Web sites are getting better at both creating and posting their privacy policies, these policies tend to be "slipping"—offering less protection to consumers. This is verified by a series of surveys by independent researcher SimplyQuick (`www.simplyquick.com`).

A SimplyQuick survey in June 2000 found that most sites surveyed had privacy policies stating that personal information would not be supplied to third parties. A follow-up survey in November 2000 revealed that the majority of these privacy policies had been rewritten so that the firms retained the right to sell information to third parties, unless the consumer explicitly opted out of such transactions. According to this November survey, only 30% of sites said they wouldn't sell information to other companies.

Which means that if you provide your information to a Web site, it's likely that the information will be sold—and probably more than once.

How to Use Privacy Policies to Your Benefit

The best way to use a Web site's privacy policy is to alert you what to expect if you sign up for the site. In particular, you want to look for the sections that describe to whom the Web site will provide or sell your information. If there are options that prevent the site from selling your information, or sending you boatloads of advertising spam, avail yourself of those options. The last thing you want is to register for a site and then find your inbox filled with unsolicited advertising. Use the privacy policy and optional settings to your best advantage, when possible.

Assuring Privacy

An alternative to these somewhat ineffectual Web site privacy policies is to look for (and patronize) sites that have been certified as adhering to certain privacy guidelines. There are several organizations that award these "privacy seals" to Web sites that meet certain privacy provisions; sites that display these seals are typically a little more privacy-conscious than the average site. (Figure 20.1 shows what these privacy seals look like.)

Figure 20.1 *Look for these seals for better online privacy.*

These certifying organizations include:

- BBBOnline (`www.bbbonline.org`)
- CPA WebTrust (`www.cpawebtrust.org`)
- TRUSTe (`www.truste.com`)

In addition, the World Wide Web Consortium (W3C) has developed the Platform for Privacy Preferences (P3P), which will enable you to choose your own preferences regarding the kind and quality of information you want to provide on the Web. Support for this platform is included in version 6 of Microsoft's Internet Explorer browser.

NOTE *Read more about P3P at the World Wide Web Consortium's Web site, at* `www.w3.org/P3P/`.

If you're using Internet Explorer 6, you can view any Web site's P3P privacy policy (when available) by following these steps:

1. Select View ➤ Privacy Report.

2. When the Privacy Report window appears, select the main URL for the current site and click the Summary button.

3. The Privacy Policy window now appears, as shown in Figure 20.2; click the OK button when done.

WARNING *Few sites currently support the P3P standard.*

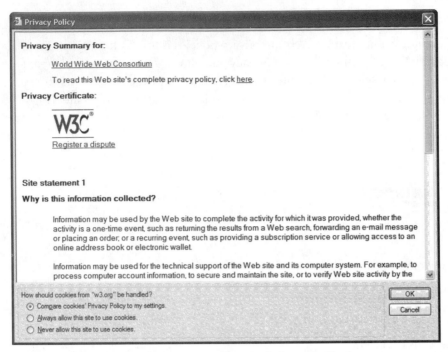

Figure 20.2 *Viewing a P3P privacy report with Internet Explorer*

When Security Cameras Are Insecure

Here's another privacy loophole you haven't thought of. It involves those wireless cameras some of you install to keep track on your house or business while you're away—"nanny cams," some call them. These cameras typically transmit their signal to a personal computer or television, which is then used to monitor ongoing activities. (In some cases, the nanny cam is fed into a live Web page and broadcast over the Internet, as a Webcam.)

The problem comes in the fact that the camera's signals are broadcast over normal radio frequency (RF) signals. In some cases, these cameras have a range of a quarter-mile or so—even more, if you have an amplified antenna to pick up the signals.

This means, of course, that the nanny cam signals can be picked up not only inside your house, but also in the surrounding neighborhood—by your neighbors, or by signal hijackers cruising the streets with a laptop computer and an outboard antenna.

And the bad news is that this type of video Peeping Tomism is legal. Current wiretapping and eavesdropping laws tend to apply only to intercepted audio, not video. So your neighbors can spy on you—using your own spy cams—without fear of legal reprisal.

Of course, you can spy on them, too—if that's any consolation.

Privacy in the Workplace

When you're at work, every move you make is subject to some sort of surveillance. Some of that surveillance comes in the form of monitoring your physical activities (via hidden video cameras and tracking of pass card usage); some comes in the form of monitoring your online activities.

If a company wants to, it can monitor virtually everything their employees do while seated at their computers. Keystroke logger software can track which keys you tap on your keyboard; e-mail sniffers can examine the contents of your incoming and outgoing e-mail; Web site sniffers can tell your boss which Web sites you visit—and what you do while you're there.

In short, there is no guarantee of privacy in the workplace.

According to a recent report by the American Management Association (`www.amanet.org`), nearly 75% of all U.S. companies use some form of surveillance to spy on their employees. That's double the number of snooping companies from just three years previous, in 1997.

And what do these curious employers find?

According to Forrester Research (`www.forrester.com`), 17% of online shoppers did their holiday shopping while at work. An eMarketer (`www.emarketer.com`) survey reveals that 70% of adults have accessed the Internet from work for personal use. And the Center for Internet Studies (`www.virtual-addiction.com`), which studies Internet addiction in the workplace, reports that 60% of companies have disciplined employees for inappropriate Internet use—and 30% have had to terminate employees for Internet abuse.

Whether these activities are permissible or not depends almost entirely on the employer. Some employers are incredibly tolerant about how their employees use their computers and Internet access; other employers view any such excursion as an inappropriate and unallowable use of company resources. In any case, these activities are almost always legal—so there's nothing to keep a company from spying on its employees but its own corporate conscience.

Keystroke Loggers

One way to track employees' computer use is to examine everything they type at their keyboards. This is accomplished via the use of keystroke logger programs. These programs intercept the electronic signals between your keyboard and your computer's operating system, and copy every keystroke into a log file. Your employer (or, in different circumstances, an external cracker) can then access the log file and see everything you entered from your keyboard—including passwords, credit card numbers, and the like.

Some of the keystroke loggers you might run into include:

- Invisible KeyKey Monitor (`www.keykey.com`)
- KeyLogger Stealth (`www.amecisco.com`)
- Spector (`www.spectorsoft.com`)

Fortunately, you can protect yourself against keystroke loggers by using a program that sniffs out their presence. These programs search your system for known spy software, alert you to their presence, and help you uninstall the problem programs.

Some of the most popular anti-spy programs include:

- Nitrous Anti-Spy (www.nitrousonline.net)

- PestPatrol (www.pestpatrol.com)

- SpyCop (www.spycop.com)

- SpyStopper (www.itcompany.com/spystop.htm)

- X-Cleaner (www.xblock.com)

TIP *See Chapter 23, "Defeating Spyware," for anti-spy software specifically targeted at spyware and adware programs.*

A company (or individual) can also log keystroke activity by using keystroke logger *hardware*. For example, KeyGhost (www.keyghost.com) is a device about the size of your thumb (virtually unnoticeable, unless you're really looking for it) that installs between your keyboard and PC. This device captures your keystrokes and stores them in its own internal memory. The device can then be removed and connected to another computer (your boss' computer, typically) and the keystrokes retrieved and analyzed.

WARNING *The tricky thing about a hardware keystroke logger is that it can't be sensed by any anti-logger or security software.*

Packet Sniffers

Another way to track an employee's computer use is to install some sort of *packet sniffer* software. This software monitors, or "sniffs," all traffic flowing over the network. The sniffer can be configured in one of two ways. An *unfiltered* configuration captures all the data packets coming over the network; a *filtered* configuration captures only those packets containing specified content.

Most employers are likely to use a filtered configuration, and set the sniffer to look for specific types of information. For example, a sniffer might be configured to look at data arriving from Web sites on a "don't visit" list, or to look for data containing particular words or phrases. Data packets meeting the specified criteria are then stored on a hard disk, for future examination.

Now comes the sneaky part. Someone has to look through all this captured data, and determine whether the communications are allowable or not. That means that someone—the network administrator, or even just some IT geek—could be reading your personal e-mail, and slogging through your Web site logs.

Log Files

Many software programs generate log files that record key events regarding the program. (Of course, keystroke logger and sniffer software generate their own specific log files.) The History list in your Web browser is a crude kind of log file; there are also specific utilities that can create log files of user activity over a network.

Any log file that resides on your work PC is the property of your employer. Your company can examine your PC and read the contents of any file on your hard drive—including all log files.

For example, your company could confiscate your computer, open your Internet Explorer History list, and look at every Web site you've visited in the past several weeks. If you happened to take a detour through some site with adult content (and your company has rules about that sort of thing), you could be handed your walking papers.

Computer Surveillance

There are other ways that your employer can monitor your computer usage. The most common is to use a desktop monitoring program, which routes the contents of one computer screen to a different computer. (The programs typically split the signal going to the original PC's video card, sending a clone of the signal to the monitoring computer.) This way, the person doing the monitoring can see everything that the person being monitored is doing on his or her PC.

This type of surveillance is labor-intensive, and it's ultimately quite disturbing. Few employees would feel comfortable about their employer standing over their virtual shoulders and watching every thing they do at their computer.

It's disconcerting that there are so many computer surveillance programs currently on the market. Some are remote monitoring programs, some alert monitoring personnel (in real time) if banned Web sites are accessed, and some alert the corporate overlords if you dare to type objectionable text.

Of course, if you're one of the corporate overlords, you can see the value of keeping your employees on the straight and narrow—and hard at work on their real jobs. Some of the most popular of these computer surveillance programs include:

- iOpus STARR (www.iopus.com/starr.htm)
- Silent Watch (www.adavi.com)
- SpyAgent (www.spytech-web.com)
- SpyBuddy (www.exploreanywhere.com)
- Stealth Activity Reporter (www.stealthactivityreporter.com)
- WinSpy (www.win-spy.com)

TIP *Many parents use computer surveillance software to keep track of their children's activities on the Internet.*

E-mail Monitoring

One last way your privacy can be compromised at work is via e-mail. It has been legally established that any correspondence you undertake on your work PC is your employer's property—not yours. Your employer has the right to monitor all incoming and outgoing e-mail messages, and to take appropriate action based on the content of these messages.

Some employers use e-mail monitoring to reduce the amount of personal correspondence taking place on company time. Other companies use it to protect themselves from sexual harassment or other similar lawsuits. Still other companies just like to spy on their staff.

There are a number of programs a company can use to monitor your e-mail communications. These programs include:

- IamBigBrother (`www.iambigbrother.com`)
- MailGuard (`www.mailguard.co.uk`)
- MailMarshal (`www.marshalsoftware.com`)
- MIMEsweeper (`www.mimesweeper.com`)
- We.C-IT (`www.dial-it.org`)

In addition, many of the computer surveillance programs mentioned earlier in this chapter also have e-mail monitoring features.

TIP *As with general computer surveillance programs, e-mail monitoring programs are useful in the home, to monitor children's e-mail messages and instant messaging activities.*

Employer vs. Employee Rights

Many people question whether an employer has the right to snoop on its employees. The answer, disconcerting to some, is an unqualified yes; an employer has every legal right to monitor its employee's activities during work hours, and while they're on company property. This might not give the employer the moral or ethical right to snoop, but ethics are decidedly situational.

The employer's rights are enhanced when they notify employees that monitoring is taking place, although this notification is hardly necessary. If you work for a large company, it's best to assume that you're being monitored, and proceed from there.

The facts bear up this assumption. According to the American Management Association, 78% of all U.S. companies conduct some sort of employee surveillance. Internet use, specifically, is monitored by 63% of employers, with 47% storing and reviewing e-mail messages and 36% intercepting and reviewing employee's computer files.

NOTE *Not all surveillance is computer-related. The AMA survey indicated that 15% of companies videotaped employees while at work, 12% recorded and reviewed employee telephone calls, and 8% reviewed voice mail recordings.*

You need to know that if a surveillance-related dispute arises, the laws are such that the courts tend to side with employers. Which means you should use caution when conducting any personal business on your work PC—and be especially careful what you put in your e-mail messages.

Identity Theft

Imagine someone stealing your life. The thief steals your name, your Social Security number, your bank accounts, your credit cards. In the eyes of many, the thief *becomes* you—and uses your personal information to commit all manner of fraud.

This type of theft, which starts with a simple theft of data, is known as *identity theft*—and can be very serious, indeed. If your identity has been stolen, you won't be able to cash checks, use credit cards, or get cash from an ATM. You'll have previously written checks bounce, creditors harass you about nonpayment on your accounts, and financial institutions refuse to issue you any new credit. You'll have your good name—and credit rating—sullied, and you'll experience all manner of problems that could take *forever* to work out.

How Identity Theft Occurs

Identity theft is not an exclusively online activity. Thieves have been appropriating personal information since the first personal information was conceived, and the vast majority of identity theft still takes place outside the online world.

How can an identity thief get his hands on your personal information? Here are just some of the ways:

- Steal your wallet or purse.
- Steal your (postal) mail—especially your bank and credit card statements, as well as all those "pre-approved" credit card offers you receive, unsolicited.

- Complete a change of address form with the U.S. Postal Service to divert your mail to another location.

- Rummage through your trash (also called *dumpster diving*).

- Fraudulently obtain your credit report by posing as a landlord or employer.

- Talk your company's human resources department into providing your personnel records.

- Buy personal information from "inside" sources, typically store or company employees.

- Use packet-sniffer software to obtain passwords and numbers while you're online.

- Purchase or otherwise obtain illegally gathered information from an underground Web site or IRC channel.

- Use social engineering techniques to con you into providing personal information via phone, e-mail, or instant messaging.

What an Identity Thief Does with Your Personal Information

Once an identity thief has obtained your personal information, what happens next? The possibilities are frightening; the thief might:

- Trade or sell that information.

- Run up long-distance phone bills in your name.

- Establish a new wireless phone account in your name.

- Use stolen credit card numbers to make unauthorized purchases.

- Open new credit card accounts in your name.

- Open a new bank account in your name—and then write bad checks on that account.

- Counterfeit checks or debit cards, and drain your bank account.

- Rent automobiles, or purchase vehicles by taking out auto loans in your name.

- Obtain a new drivers license, using the thief's picture instead of your own.

- Obtain new license plates and vehicle registrations.

- Access the Internet using your current ISP account.

- Open a new Internet account—and subscribe to various online services—in your name.

- File for bankruptcy under your name, to avoid debts they've incurred.

WARNING *An identity thief might also call your credit card companies and other financial institutions and obtain a change of mailing address. This will postpone your seeing the bills the thief is running up, at your expense.*

In short, an identity thief can do anything you can do—but without your best interests in mind.

Preventing Identity Theft

Can you prevent your personal information from being stolen?

Not completely.

But you can minimize your risk, by wisely managing your personal information both in the real world and online, and being careful about what you disclose to whom:

- Don't provide personal information to strangers.

- Never provide personal information via e-mail or instant messaging.

- Verify that you're talking to authorized personnel before you provide personal information over the phone.

- Pay close attention to your credit card billing cycles; if you haven't received an expected account statement, immediately contact your credit card company.

- Deposit all your outgoing bill payments in public post office boxes, *not* in your personal mailbox.

- Promptly remove mail as soon as it's delivered to your postal mailbox—or consider obtaining a drop box at your local U.S. Post Office.

- If you plan on being away from home for an extended period of time, have your mail put on "vacation hold" until you return.

- Don't carry every credit card you own in your wallet or purse; carry only those cards that are absolutely necessary at any given point in time.

- Shred all charge card receipts, account statements, and voided checks before you take out your trash.

- Don't give out your Social Security number to anyone, unless absolutely necessary.

- Once a year, order a copy of your credit report from each of the three major credit-reporting agencies; check this report for any unexpected, unauthorized, or incorrect activities.

Credit Bureaus

There are three major credit bureaus that keep tabs of all your credit card and loan activity. You can contact these companies to receive copies of your so-called credit record; you should also contact these companies if you are ever the victim of identity theft.

These companies are:

Equifax Credit Information Services

PO Box 740241, Atlanta, GA 30374

1-800-525-6285 (report ID theft)

1-800-685-1111 (obtain credit report)

www.equifax.com

Experian Information Solutions

PO Box 2104, Allen, TX 75013

1-888-EXPERIAN

www.experian.com

TransUnion

PO Box 2000, Chester, PA 19022

1-800-916-8800 (report ID theft)

1-800-888-4213

www.transunion.com

What to Do If You're a Victim of Identity Theft

If you find that someone has stolen your personal information—especially your Social Security and credit card numbers—take all the following steps, *immediately*:

- Contact the fraud departments of the three major credit bureaus and report that your identity has been stolen. Ask that a "fraud alert" be placed on your file and that no new credit be granted without your approval.

- For any credit card, loan, or banking accounts that have been accessed or opened without your approval, contact the security departments of the appropriate creditors or financial institutions. Close these accounts, and create new passwords on any replacement accounts you may open.

- File a report with your local police department, or with the police where you believe the identity theft took place. Get a copy of this report in case your bank, credit card company, or other institutions need proof of the crime at some later date.

- File a complaint with the FTC by calling 1-877-ID-THEFT (438-4338) or going to www.consumer.gov/idtheft/.

Playing Detective, Online

You'd be surprised what someone can find out about you online. You can see for yourself by going to Google (www.google.com) or some other search engine, and searching for your own name. (You can also search for your address, phone number, and other personal information.) While it's possible to lead a completely anonymous online life, it's more likely that you've left some personal tracks behind you on the Internet.

In addition to all the free information you can find about people online, there are also companies that specialize in digging up all sorts of even more personal information—for a fee. These firms advertise that they'll help you track down missing relatives and lost loves, or perform background checks on potential dates or employees.

For a small fee—anywhere from $20 to $100—these companies will provide you with a comprehensive report about an individual of your choice. This report is likely to include a list of past and present addresses and phone numbers; employers; spouses and children; roommates; automobile and gun licenses; credit information; and the like. Some reports will also include the individual's Social Security number, which you could then use to unearth even more information from other firms.

These companies include:

- Background Check Gateway (www.backgroundcheckgateway.com)
- Data-Trac (www.data-trac.com)
- Discreet Research (www.dresearch.com)
- PeopleFind.com (www.peoplefind.com)
- U.S. Locator (www.uslocate.com)
- USSEARCH (www.1800ussearch.com)
- YourOwnPrivateEye.com (www.yourownprivateeye.com)

Privacy and Conflicting Interests

Privacy—particularly online privacy—is a complicated issue, full of technological concerns, a high degree of misinformation, and plenty of conflicting interests. The issue pits your right to privacy against the desire of others to obtain and use your personal information for their particular purposes.

And the "others" who want to use your information run the gamut from advertisers and retailers to law enforcement agencies and the Federal government—quite a formidable list of opponents. When it comes to protecting your privacy, it certainly appears to be you against the world.

Personal Privacy vs. National Security

In an instant, the world changed.

September 11, 2001 marked the beginning of a new era for most Americans. As the horrific events of that day played out, we realized that America was not immune from the attacks of foreign terrorists. We were at war, and we needed to make important changes to help guarantee our continued safety.

The problem that quickly arose was that guaranteeing safety sometimes conflicted with guaranteeing our hard-won personal liberties. We want to track down and stop any and all potential terrorists, but how much of our personal privacy do we want to sacrifice to do so?

Let's take the issue of tracking terrorist and criminal communications. In this day and age, it's as likely for terrorists to communicate via e-mail as via traditional mail or the phone. That doesn't make e-mail a dangerous technology (it's no more dangerous than an envelope and a stamp, or a telephone handset), but it does provide a new way to hunt down the terrorists in our midst. Since virtually all Internet-based communications are traceable, why not use the technology at our disposal to find and read potential terrorist communications?

The problem is one of privacy. Does the government have the right to spy on its own citizens and if so, under what circumstances? Wiretapping has long been illegal without a court order; should "e-mail tapping" be any different?

The prevailing attitude, post–September 11, has been to grant law enforcement agencies more leeway in hunting down suspected terrorists, at the expense of personal privacy. This leeway includes more power to track suspects online—something that has traditionally been resisted by privacy advocates.

But the world changed on September 11th. Philip L. Gordon, fellow of the not-for-profit Privacy Foundation (www.privacyfoundation.org) and long-time advocate of diminished government intrusion, notes that there has been little objection to this erosion of privacy:

"Before 9-11, ISPs would generally resist efforts by government to obtain access to information about the ISP's customers. After September 11th, the ISPs were much more willing to cooperate."

After the September 11 terrorist attacks, nearly a dozen Internet-related security bills were introduced into Congress. Most of these bills sought to make more information about end-users more readily available to government and law enforcement officials.

Much of this legislation was consolidated into the omnibus USA PATRIOT Act, which was subsequently approved by Congress and signed into law by President Bush. The Internet-related provisions of the act include:

- Any Internet provider must turn over customer information—no court order required— at the FBI's request.

- Any U.S. attorney or state attorney general—without a judge's approval—can order the installation of the FBI's Carnivore surveillance system, and subsequently record the addresses of e-mail correspondents and Web pages visited.

- The current definition of terrorism is expanded to include computer hacking and many existing forms of computer crime; a new crime of "cyberterrorism" is recognized, covering attacks that cause at least $5000 in damage.

- New computer forensics labs will be created to inspect any seized or intercepted computer evidence.

The thinking behind this legislation is simple. As Senator Orrin Hatch noted, "It is essential that we give our law enforcement authorities every possible tool to search out and bring to justice those individuals who have brought such indiscriminate death into our backyard."

All of which might be useful in tracking down terrorists, but it might not necessarily be good news for the rest of us.

While you might want the government tracking the online activities of suspected terrorists, do you want them tracking *you* online, too? The increased surveillance of ordinary citizens could be one unintended side effect of these efforts. If you give the government more powers in this area, the question then becomes where you draw the line. How do you guarantee that law enforcement agencies will spy only on suspected terrorists? How do you define a suspected terrorist, anyway? And what's to stop the online cops from going after folks who have absolutely no association with terrorists—but just happen to be on someone's enemies list?

This concern might sound paranoid, but it reflects the type of behavior that the FBI and CIA engaged in during the 1950s, 1960s, and 1970s, when domestic surveillance was (covertly) commonplace. Given the technological tools available today, it's frightening to contemplate the degree of clandestine activity we could see if various agencies were let loose on an unsuspecting public.

Take, for example, the government's Carnivore software. Carnivore is part of a suite of programs (collectively titled DragonWare) designed to examine e-mail at a targeted Internet service provider. Carnivore is a packet sniffer, capable of capturing information from any and all e-mail messages flowing through that ISP. While Carnivore can supposedly only be used with a court order (as with wiretapping), and only to sniff e-mail from a specific user, it's easy to see how this powerful software could be abused—and used to sniff *all* traffic routed through a given ISP.

Do you really want the government reading your e-mail? If not, you need to get more involved in the current privacy debate. (See the list of privacy resources at the end of this chapter.)

NOTE *Read more about Carnivore in Chapter 23.*

Personal Privacy vs. Convenience

The other big privacy issue is how much information you're willing to sacrifice for the convenience of using the Internet—and for having those Internet-related services customized to your own personal preferences. In order to shop online, you have to provide your name, street address, and credit card number; in order to receive a personalized news feed, you have to provide information about what you do and don't like to read about. If you decide not to provide this information, you can't partake in these activities.

This trade-off between confidentiality and convenience isn't a new thing, nor is it exclusive to the Internet. To obtain the convenience of a monthly magazine subscription, for example, you sacrifice the confidentiality of your name and address, which ultimately gets sold by the magazine company to all manner of direct mail marketers, and you end up with a mailbox full of junk mail. To obtain the purchasing convenience of a charge card, you agree to turn over your private financial records to the issuing company—and that company then sells your information to other companies who pester you with dinnertime telemarketing calls for additional credit cards and home equity loans.

The Internet is no different from the real world. To gain access to certain Web sites, you have to provide your e-mail address; that's a sacrifice of privacy for the convenience of entrance. To take advantage of various online offers, you agree to provide your name and address and maybe even your phone number—another voluntary sacrifice of privacy. It's no different than providing your name and address and phone number to companies in the physical world, with similar privacy consequences.

That's not to say that you can't stay relatively anonymous, if that's what you really want. Just as you can lead a relatively private life in the physical world by eschewing subscriptions and charge cards and bank accounts, you can hide your identity on the Internet by never giving out your e-mail address, never signing up for any members-only Web sites, and never using your real name in any messages. You can even make the Web *more* private than the physical world, by routing all your surfing and correspondence through special "anonymizer" sites that strip out any data that could be used to trace your activities back to your ISP account or computer.

NOTE *Read more about anonymizers in Chapter 26, "How to Surf—and Communicate—Anonymously."*

The problem is, it takes an extreme amount of effort to stay completely anonymous—and you'll sacrifice much convenience in the attempt. That's why most Internet users choose some compromise between complete privacy and ultimate convenience—just as most people in the real world share some private information in order to obtain credit cards and magazine subscriptions.

Life is about compromises—and it's up to you to make the most intelligent choices possible.

How to Protect Your Privacy Online

It's possible to lead a very private online life. Unless you provide the information, no one has to know who you are—and you can even pretend to be someone you're not, if that's the kind of game you like to play.

While it's practically impossible to stay completely anonymous on the Internet, it is possible to keep your private information private, to a large degree. It takes a bit of effort on your part, but it can be done.

When you want to protect your privacy online, consider the practical advice in the following checklist:

☑ Don't reveal personal information over the Internet, period; the best way to keep your information private is to not tell it to anyone.

☑ Don't reveal personal details about yourself to anyone you "meet" online.

☑ When registering to use a Web site or service, provide the least possible amount of information—and especially avoid entering personal and contact information.

☑ Sign up for a free e-mail account at Hotmail (`www.hotmail.com`), Yahoo! Mail (`mail.yahoo.com`), or some similar service, and then use that e-mail address if you have to register to use a particular Web site; this way you can keep your main address "clean" for personal correspondence.

☑ When you post to Usenet newsgroups and Web message boards, don't add a signature that includes any personal information.

☑ Remember that anything you post in a newsgroup or message board is public, and can be read by anyone—*forever*.

☑ When you post to message boards and newsgroups, alter your return e-mail address to include a *spamblock* (literally, the word SPAMBLOCK) in the middle of your address—

for example, if your e-mail address is johnjones@web.net, you might change the address to read johnSPAMBLOCKjones@web.net; this will keep automated programs from adding your address to their spam databases. You'll learn more about spamblocking in Chapter 28, "Dealing with Spam."

☑ Never reply to spam e-mail.

☑ Configure your Web browser to not accept third-party cookies, and to ask before placing first-party cookies on your hard disk.

☑ Avoid sending personal messages via your e-mail at work.

☑ Don't keep personal information on your work PC.

☑ Examine the privacy policies of the Web sites you frequent—and, if possible, opt out of any potential "marketing offers" and select not to share your information with third parties.

☑ Patronize Web sites that display respected privacy seals.

☑ If you're sending highly confidential information via e-mail, use some form of encryption, as discussed in Chapter 25, "Employing Passwords, Encryption, and Digital Identification."

☑ If you need complete anonymity, use an anonymizer Web site to remove your IP address when you surf, and use a remailing service to send e-mail messages with all your personal information stripped out.

In the end, the only sure-fire privacy protection is your own common sense and self-discipline. All the sniffers and loggers aside, most third parties obtain personal information about you only when you explicitly give it to them—so don't give out *your* personal information, unless absolutely necessary!

Privacy Resources

Online privacy is an important issue. To learn more about the various facets of privacy over the Internet, turn to the following resources:

- American Civil Liberties Union (www.aclu.org)

- Center for Digital Democracy (www.democraticmedia.org)

- Coalition Against Unsolicited Commercial Email (www.cauce.org)

Continued on next page

Privacy Resources *(Continued)*

- EchelonWatch (www.echelonwatch.org)
- Electronic Frontier Foundation (www.eff.org)
- Electronic Privacy Information Center (www.epic.org)
- Federal Trade Commission (www.ftc.gov)
- Global Internet Liberty Campaign (www.gilc.org)
- Junkbusters (www.junkbusters.com)
- Privacy Coalition (www.privacypledge.org)
- Privacy Council (www.privacycouncil.com)
- Privacy International (www.privacyinternational.org)
- Privacy Rights Clearinghouse (www.privacyrights.org)
- Privacy.net (www.privacy.net)
- Privacy.org (www.privacy.org)

Summing Up

Any time you go online, you face the issue of privacy. How much personal information do you provide, in exchange for what kinds of services? And how do you protect against confidential information falling into the wrong hands?

The reality is that almost any communication or activity over the Internet can be tracked and traced—especially when you're at work. Any messages you leave on public newsgroups or bulletin boards are available for anyone to read, and they don't disappear with time. Many online marketing companies specialize in tracking your Web site visits, and have the technology to do so, without your knowledge or explicit consent. And on top of all that, there are any number of individuals who specialize in online data theft—and, worst of all, complete identity theft.

The best way to keep your private life private is to show restraint when online. Don't provide personal information to strangers, and avoid providing too much confidential data when you sign up for Web sites and services. Don't post anything online you don't want your future spouse or employer to read, and be especially cautious about using your work PC for personal correspondence and Web surfing.

In the next chapter we'll further examine an important aspect of online privacy—online fraud and what you can do about it.

CHAPTER 21

Dealing with Online Fraud

L ike it or not, people get ripped off all the time. And when the rip-off results in some form of financial harm, it's called fraud.

As you might expect, there's a fair amount of fraud online.

There are many ways you can be defrauded when you're on the Internet. You can be the victim of online credit card theft. You can be the victim of a deadbeat seller at an online auction. You can be the victim of an unscrupulous online retailer operating at the fringes of the Web. You can even be talked out of your life savings by an online flim-flam artist.

In short, while you're on the Internet you can be conned out of your money in many of the same ways you can be conned out of your money in the physical world.

Which means that it's not so much about technology as it is about being taken advantage of.

Online Shopping Fraud

Millions of people shop online every year. Millions more shy away from online shopping, afraid of trusting their credit card information to some unknown entity on the other end of the Internet connection. That's a shame; online shopping is every bit as safe as shopping at a bricks-and-mortar store. The fear is understandable. Once your credit card numbers are in cyberspace, what's to keep someone—anyone—from grabbing them?

There are different forms of this fear. Some users fear that their confidential information will be hijacked between their computer and the retailer's Web site. Other users fear that the Web site itself will be cracked, and the credit card numbers stolen.

Both scenarios are possible—and, fortunately, both scenarios are unlikely.

Risks

As you've learned in previous chapters, it's certainly possible for a cracker to use packet sniffers, password crackers, and other illicit programs to intercept the transmission of data packets and extract private information from the flow. However, this type of activity is extremely rare, both because it's difficult and because you're just one user out of millions. It's actually easier and more efficient for a would-be thief to steal credit card numbers by listening in on cordless phone calls via a low-cost scanner, or to go dumpster-diving for carbon copies behind a local restaurant or retailer. Sniffing and intercepting individual credit card numbers online is a lot of effort for very little return.

As for Web sites having large masses of credit card numbers stolen, it does happen—but not often. Most major online retailers are extremely secure, employing a variety of security measures to keep their customers' information private. While you can't guarantee against this form of wholesale data theft, you also shouldn't expect it to happen on a regular basis—just as you don't expect your local bank to be robbed. Yes, it can happen, but it's not a major concern.

That's not to say that all online retailers are equally safe. In general, bigger online retailers are safer than smaller ones. The biggest retailers are every bit as reputable as their big bricks-and-mortar cousins, offering safe payment, fast shipping, and responsive customer service.

Many of the smaller merchants on the Web are just as safe, although they may not have the same level of customer service as the big sites. Some smaller retailers, however, are nothing more than garage or basement operations, often not even accepting payments via credit card. When you're dealing with one of these very small retailers, you take your chances. Some of these merchants are as safe and as helpful and as friendly as the store down the street; others are no better than dealing with a stranger at a garage sale. While it's difficult to judge the size or stability of any online retailer (any size business can hide behind a fancy Web page), chances are if you use a site that is big enough to accept credit card payments, you're relatively safe.

WARNING *Accepting credit cards via PayPal, BidPay, or another bill pay service is not the same as having a dedicated merchant charge card account. While buying from a merchant that uses PayPal may be safe, it's a sign that you're dealing with a relatively small company—or even a private individual masquerading as a larger business.*

But credit card numbers do get stolen online—and from some of the biggest sites. In 2001 and 2002, intruders broke into and stole personal information from CD Universe, Creditcards.com, the gift certificate site ecount.com, Egghead.com, Playboy.com, and Western Union's Web site—just to name a few. Many sites that get cracked don't report the intrusion, fearing negative publicity. In the meantime, crackers sell the stolen information in underground online marketplaces, operated predominantly by organized criminals from the former Soviet Union.

Eventually, thieves try to use stolen credit card numbers to make fraudulent purchases. A recent survey by market research firm Celent Communications (`www.celent.com`) found that the fraud rate for MasterCard and Visa transactions on the Internet is 0.25 percent—that is, a quarter of one percent of all online credit card transactions were found to be fraudulent. This is a very low number, but not nearly as low as the offline fraud rates of 0.08 percent for Visa and 0.09 percent for MasterCard. Looking at it another way, online transactions are three times more likely to be fraudulent than offline transactions.

Fortunately, the cost of this online fraud—estimated at more than $1 billion annually—is most often covered by the issuing banks. Unfortunately, this cost is eventually passed on to you, the consumer, via higher fees and interest rates.

Using Credit Cards

The big concern about online shopping is how safe it is to provide credit card information over the Internet. The concern is that providing information online might be less safe than doing so at a bricks-and-mortar merchant. The reality is that providing your credit card information to a secure Web site is no less safe than handing your credit card to a complete stranger dressed as a waiter in a restaurant, or giving it over a cordless phone.

Besides, even if your credit card number *is* stolen, by whatever method, most credit card companies assume the brunt of any potential losses. Most credit card companies hold you liable for a small fixed amount (typically $50); any losses above this number are the credit card company's responsibility.

There are, however, steps you can take to decrease the risk or impact of a stolen card. First, never enter your credit card number for anything other than a purchase. Some sites (particularly those offering adult content) will ask for a credit card to "validate" your ID or age. This is the sure sign of a potential rip-off. *Never* provide your credit card number in this situation. The simple fact is that anyone who obtains your credit card information this way *will* use that information—and charge your card!

Second, only enter your information on sites that have secure transaction processing, discussed in the next section. Sending data to an unsecured server is much more risky than using a secure server; most major online retailers feature secure servers.

Making Shopping More Secure

When you're shopping online, you can decrease the risk of stolen credit card information by shopping only at sites that use a secure shopping server. Secure servers use Secure Sockets Layer (SSL) technology that encodes secure information sent over the Web, using a form of digital encryption. If both your browser and the Web site feature SSL security (and all modern browsers do), you know that your transaction has been encrypted and is secure.

SSL ensures a secure transaction because all information sent from the Web site to your browser (and vice versa) has been encrypted. Because of the need for security when dealing with financial transactions, most major shopping sites feature SSL-encrypted ordering and checkout. You'll know you're using a secure site when the little lock icon appears in the lower part of your Web browser:

If a site isn't encrypted, don't shop there.

> **TIP** *Learn more about safe shopping online at Safeshopping.org* (www.safeshopping.org).

How to Complain

If you've had a bad experience with an online retailer, you're not alone. While the incidence of fraud is rare, poor service is unfortunately common; many online retailers (both large and small) simply don't have the technical expertise to handle the volume of holiday sales, nor the customer-service infrastructure to adequately answer customer questions and complaints.

When you're having a dispute with an online retailer, make sure you exhaust all available means of dealing with the retailer directly. If you still aren't satisfied, there are several organizations and Web sites that you can contact to help you out. These sites include:

- Better Business Bureau (`www.bbb.org`)
- Fraud Bureau (`www.fraudbureau.com`)
- Internet Fraud Complaint Center (`www1.ifccfbi.gov`)
- National Consumers League (`www.natlconsumersleague.org`)
- National Fraud Information Center (`www.fraud.org`)

How to Shop Safely

Now that we've covered the possible risks of online shopping, I hope you're convinced that online shopping is basically safe—especially if you shop at a recognized online retailer that accepts credit cards, offers secure transaction processing, and has an 800-number customer service department manned by real live human beings. If a retailer only accepts checks or money orders, doesn't have a secure server, or offers no real-world contact information, then you're engaging in risky behavior.

So if you're ready to venture out into the virtual malls, make sure you have your credit card handy, and adhere to the following advice:

Shop only at larger, established, and familiar companies.   While it's not a given, it is likely that Amazon.com will be more secure than Aunt Mary's Little Ol' Used Book Store.

Shop only at secure sites.   Look for an indication that the site uses SSL security, and don't place an order unless you're on a secure page.

Look for the seal of approval.   Another indication of site security is the presence of the VeriSign Secure Site Seal. (See `www.verisign.com` for more information about this certification program.)

Look for contact information.   If something goes wrong with your order, you'll want to contact someone at the site to resolve the dispute. Beware of sites that don't even include an e-mail contact address, and try to choose sites that prominently list a toll-free phone number for post-sale support.

Look for a returns policy.   Find out what you have to do if you're dissatisfied with a purchase at this site. In particular, find out how easy it is to return an item, and who (you or the site) is responsible for the return shipping expense. If there is no returns or security policy to be found, skip this site.

Pay by credit card.   When you pay by credit card, you're protected by your card issuer's policy on fraudulent charges. In most cases, your liability for any bad transactions is limited to $50; the credit card company is responsible for everything above this level. You especially want to avoid paying by money order, which provides no money trail in case of a lost or misplaced payment.

Fill in only the minimum information necessary.   Many Web sites present you with large forms to fill out before you can enter or complete your purchase. In most cases, you don't have to fill out every blank on the form. Essential fields should be indicated in some fashion; you'll have to fill them out. Other fields are optional and are typically used to collect information that can be sold to marketing companies. (Be especially wary of fields that ask about your hobbies or "likelihood to purchase" items in the near future.) To keep as much information private as possible, fill in only those blanks that are required by the site.

Use a secondary e-mail account.   While we're thinking about information privacy, know that just about any online merchant is likely to take the personal information you provide— especially your e-mail address—and sell it to other companies. You can avoid future spam by providing a secondary e-mail address (from Hotmail, let's say) rather than your primary address. Your secondary account may get spammed, but your main e-mail account will stay private.

Keep a record.   Keep printed copies of all the transactions you make online. Print out the final order Web page, or the e-mail confirmation (if you receive one). You may need these records if your order is in dispute later.

Online Auction Fraud

Another potential area of online fraud comes in the form of the online auction—with the world's largest auction site, eBay (`www.ebay.com`), being particularly fertile ground for abuse simply because so many people use it.

The Internet Fraud Complaint Center reports that online auction fraud accounted for nearly 43% of all complaints it received in 2001. In addition, the FTC noted that more than 20,000 individuals lodged fraud complaints about online auctions. Most complaints involved goods that were paid for but never shipped.

This incidence of online auction fraud should be put in perspective, however. eBay claims that the percentage of auctions that end in a confirmed case of fraud account for less than 1/100 of 1 percent of all auctions on the site. That doesn't mean you can't be conned, or that you shouldn't take precautions; it only means that the vast majority of people you deal with in online auctions are honest.

Types of Auction Fraud

What makes eBay and other online auctions problematic is that the auction site itself doesn't get involved with individual transactions. The site only *hosts* the auction; it doesn't inject itself into the actual financial transaction between the seller and buyer of a piece of merchandise. Because these are one-on-one transactions between two individuals, it's easy for one individual (typically the seller) to defraud the other.

Given this structure, what types of auction fraud are you likely to encounter?

Deadbeat Bidders

Perhaps the least painful type of auction fraud is caused by a deadbeat bidder. This occurs when an individual makes the high bid in an auction, but then doesn't send payment. If you're the seller, your only inconvenience is that you have to relist the item in another auction; you aren't out any money. (That's assuming you haven't shipped the item before receiving payment, which would be a very dumb thing to do.)

TIP *You can petition eBay to refund your auction fees if the item isn't paid for.*

The key to protecting yourself as a seller is to hold onto the item until you've received payment, and until that payment has cleared the bank. If you don't get paid, you don't ship—period.

Deadbeat Sellers

A more harmful situation occurs when a buyer sends payment for an item but then never receives the item in return. If this happens to you, you're dealing with a deadbeat seller—and you have a clear case of fraud on your hands. Not receiving merchandise you've paid for is a form of theft and should be reported to the proper authorities. If the deadbeat seller can be identified and tracked down, that person can be arrested—and your payment returned, if possible.

This is the most common form of fraud on online auction sites.

Identity Theft

Of late, eBay has also been plagued with a spate of identity theft. Several users have found that someone else has hijacked their eBay IDs and then used that ID to stage fraudulent auctions. The scam artists make a quick buck, with the legitimate user (the one whose ID was stolen) left holding the bag.

This hijacking is somewhat facilitated by the fact that using eBay's secure server is optional, not mandatory. (In fact, the default sign-in doesn't use the secure server.) This absence of secure transactions makes it easier for crackers to use packet-sniffing programs to steal user IDs and passwords.

> **NOTE** *eBay blames these identify thefts on that form of password crack known as a dictionary crack. As you'll learn in Chapter 25, "Employing Passwords, Encryption, and Digital Identification," this happens when a cracker uses an automated program to take a known user ID and then match it with a list of common passwords and a dictionary of common words.*

You can help avoid identity theft by choosing eBay's secure server login. The problem is, eBay does a good job of hiding its secure server feature. You can find the secure server link on any page you use to enter your eBay user ID and password; look for the following text: `Click here to sign in using SSL`. (This typically appears in small type at the bottom of the page.) Click the appropriate link and you'll be logged in securely.

Protecting Yourself on eBay

In spite of occasional hysterical news stories to the contrary, eBay is an extremely safe environment. (Most people are honest.) Still, there are bad seeds out there, and it's possible that you'll run into a shady seller who never sends you the item you purchased, or a buyer who never sends you a check. What can you do to protect yourself against other users who aren't as honest as you are?

General Advice

eBay offers several forms of buyer protection, all of which reduce the risk of online auction fraud. Here are some general tips to help you keep your auction transactions safe:

- If you're in dispute with another user, or if you suspect someone of questionable or disallowed bidding or selling techniques, notify eBay through its SafeHarbor Customer Support Investigations service. Just click the SafeHarbor link at the bottom of eBay's home page to access this consumer-protection feature.

- eBay provides a number of discussion boards where you can converse with other eBay users on relevant topics—and, on some boards, leave real-time feedback with eBay staffers. These message boards can serve as a kind of first alert to any big-time cheats operating on eBay at the moment. The key discussion boards are the Q&A Board and the Support Q&A Board; you can access all the bulletin boards by clicking the Community button on eBay's home page.

- To determine the honesty and the quality of any users you might deal with, just look at their feedback profiles. You can generally trust users with positive overall feedback—and you probably want to avoid dealing with users who have overwhelmingly negative feedback. You can also read the individual comments left by other users by going to the user's Feedback Profile page. (Learn more about feedback in the next section.)

Finally, don't forget to communicate. If you have a question about a transaction, ask it! eBay lets any bidder send e-mails to auction sellers, and both sellers and buyers can e-mail each other after the auction ends. Make sure you exhaust all direct communication before you report another user to the eBay police!

Using Feedback

Perhaps the best way to protect yourself on eBay is by using its Feedback Forum. If you're a potential bidder, you should check the feedback rating of every seller you choose to deal with; if you're a seller, check the feedback ratings of all your high bidders. Using feedback is an excellent way to judge the quality of the other party in your eBay transactions.

A user's feedback rating is found next to the user's name (whether they're buying or selling) in an eBay item listing. What you'll see is a number and (more often than not) a colored star. These numbers and stars represent that user's feedback rating. The higher the number, the better the feedback—and the more transactions that user has participated in.

Feedback ratings are calculated by adding one point for every piece of positive feedback received, and subtracting one point for every piece of negative feedback. (Neutral feedback is worth zero.) Every user starts with zero points, and your cumulative score is calculated from all the feedback you've received.

If you build up a lot of positive feedback, you qualify for a star next to your name. Different colored stars represent different levels of positive feedback; in order, the stars go yellow, turquoise, purple, and red. The highest level—for 100,000 or more points—is the red shooting star. Obviously, heavy eBay users build up positive feedback faster than occasional users.

You should also read the individual comments left by other users by going to the user's Feedback Profile page. To access this page, just click the number next to a user's name. Look for any negative comments, even in positive reviews; they can alert you to any potential problems you might encounter with this user.

It's possible, of course, to run into a buyer or seller with little or no feedback. If you're relatively risk-averse, you may choose not to deal with these brand-new sellers until they develop a track record with other users.

Advice for Sellers

If you're selling an item on eBay, your risk is minimal—if you're smart, and don't ship your item until it's paid for. This introduces the issue of payments—specifically what kinds of payments are safest to accept. Let's take a look at your options, and the risks and benefits of each:

Cash   Cash is the safest type of payment to receive; you take it out of the envelope, and spend it immediately. However, sending cash through the mail is not a safe form of payment for the *buyer*. It's too easily stolen, and virtually untraceable. You can ask for cash payment, of course, but unless the selling price is extremely low (under $5), don't expect buyers to comply.

Personal Checks   The most common form of payment on eBay is the personal check. Buyers like paying by check because it's convenient, and because checks can be traced (or even cancelled) if problems arise with the seller. For the seller, however, checks are slightly more problematic. Just because you receive a check doesn't mean that the buyer actually has funds in his or her checking account to cover the check. For this reason, when you receive a check, you want to deposit it as soon as possible—without shipping the item. Wait until the check clears the bank (typically ten business days) before you ship the item. If, after ten days, the check hasn't bounced, then it's okay to proceed with shipment.

Money Orders and Cashier's Checks   To a seller, money orders and cashier's checks are almost as good as cash. You can cash a money order immediately, without waiting for funds to clear, and have cash in your hand. When you receive a money order or cashier's check, deposit it and then ship the auction item. There's no need to hold the item.

Credit Cards   Until very recently, if you wanted to accept credit card payment for your auction items, you had to be a real retailer, complete with merchant account and bank-supplied charge card terminal. Today, however, you can use a third-party online bill payment service—such as PayPal or Billpoint—to accept credit cards for you. These services let any auction seller easily accept credit card payments, with little or no setup hassle, and only a small transaction fee. Buyers pay *the service* by credit card, and it then sends a check or deposits funds directly into the seller's bank account. As soon as you receive the funds in your account, you can ship the item.

In short, you should feel safe accepting money orders and cashier's checks, and—if you sign up for PayPal or a similar service—credit cards. Cash is nice if you get it, but personal checks require discipline on your part to make sure they clear before you ship your items.

Advice for Bidders

As a buyer, you assume more risk than the seller does. You send your money to an individual, and hope that you receive merchandise in return—and that the item is in good condition, as described in the auction listing.

The Internet Fraud Complaint Center notes that of those individuals reporting online auction fraud, 80% used personal checks or money orders to pay for the undelivered merchandise. In other words, the buyers sent the money, and the sellers received the money and scrammed. Because the payment was in paper form, there was little that could be done to recover the payment, after the fact.

Obviously, the way you pay for an item can increase or decrease the risk of fraud; some methods of payment are safer for you than others:

Cash   The least safe method of payment for a buyer is cash. There's nothing to track, and it's very easy for someone to steal an envelope full of cash. You should avoid paying by cash, if at all possible.

Money Orders and Cashier's Checks   Also considered less safe (although better than cash) are cashier's checks and money orders. Like cash, they provide no money trail to trace if you want to track down the seller. Even though sellers like money orders, you're at the seller's mercy if the payment is in dispute—or if the merchandise never arrives.

Personal Checks   Paying by personal check is fairly safe, as you can easily trace whether the check was cashed, when, and by whom. Of course, most sellers won't ship an item immediately if you pay by check, but it's one of the least risky ways for you to pay.

Credit Cards   Perhaps the safest way to pay is by credit card. When you pay by credit card, you can always contact the credit card company and dispute your charges if the item you bought never arrived or was misrepresented. And paying by credit card provides a very good paper trail, which can come in handy should disputes occur.

When you receive the item you purchased, inspect it thoroughly and confirm that it's as described. If you feel you were misled, contact the seller immediately, explain the situation, and see what you can work out. (You'd be surprised how many sellers will go out of their way to make their customers happy.)

If the merchandise doesn't arrive in a timely fashion, contact the seller immediately. If the item appears to be lost in transit, track down the package via the shipping service. If the item never arrives, it's the seller's responsibility to file an insurance claim with the carrier, and you should receive a refund from the seller.

If a deal goes really bad, utilize eBay's SafeHarbor Insurance program. This insurance is provided free of charge to any eBay user in good standing. If you're the victim of auction fraud, you're covered up to $200, with a $25 deductible. To file a claim, you first have to register a complaint in eBay's Fraud Reporting System. (Click the SafeHarbor link on eBay's home page, and then click Fraud Protection & Prevention.) If your complaint meets the guidelines for an insurance claim, the Fraud Reporting System will provide you with an online insurance form. Fill out the form and follow the provided directions to mail it and receive your reimbursement.

Beyond eBay, you can contact other agencies if you've been defrauded in an auction deal. For example, if mail fraud is involved (which it is if any part of the transaction—either payment or shipping—was handled through the mail), you can file a complaint with your local U.S. Post Office or state attorney general's office. You might also want to contact your local police if you had a large amount of money ripped off or if your credit card numbers were stolen.

Finally, you can file a complaint with the Federal Trade Commission (FTC) by contacting the FTC Consumer Response Center via phone (202-382-4357), mail (Consumer Response Center, Federal Trade Commission, Washington, DC 20580), or the Internet (`www.ftc.gov/ftc/complaint.htm`). Although the FTC doesn't resolve individual consumer problems, it can and will act against a company if it sees a pattern of possible law violations.

The Problem with Cross-Continental Fraud

One vexing characteristic of online fraud is that the perpetrator and the victim seldom reside in the same jurisdiction. When the two parties live in different states—or different countries—it makes it difficult to track down and prosecute the crime.

Thomas Richardson, deputy assistant director of the FBI's criminal investigative division, put it this way:

"Fraud committed via the Internet makes investigation and prosecution difficult because the offender and the victim may be located thousands of miles apart. This borderless phenomena is a unique characteristic of Internet crime and is not found with many other types of traditional crime."

Which is good news for the criminals—and bad news for the rest of us.

Other Types of Online Fraud

When we're examining online fraud, we can't forget the old real-world standbys that have made their way to the online world—multilevel marketing scams, charity cons, investment fraud, and so on.

For example, during the latter half of 2001 millions of Internet users received spam copies of what has become known as the Nigerian Letter scam. In this scam, you receive an e-mail from an alleged Nigerian civil servant or businessman, containing an "urgent" business proposal. The sender has supposedly been put in charge of the proceeds from some business scheme and needs a foreign partner to help launder the money. Since this person's government prohibits him from opening foreign bank accounts, he asks you to deposit the sum (typically in the millions) into your personal account; for your assistance, you'll receive a certain percent of the total. To complete the transaction, you have to e-mail back your bank's name and address and—of course—your bank account numbers. If you do so, you end up not with a few million bucks from the Nigerian government, but with an empty bank account, thanks to your gullibility.

It's an old con, but a good one; this one scam alone accounted for more than 15% of the total complaints reported to the Internet Fraud Complaint Center (`www.ifccfbi.gov`) in 2001. (And it is an *old* con; it's been around in various forms since the early 1980s, is supposedly the third-largest industry in Nigeria, and is well documented at the 419 Coalition Website, at `home.rica.net/alphae/419coal/`.)

The Nigerian Letter is just one example of the kind of old-school con with a new life, thanks to the Internet. A quick scan of your e-mail inbox is likely to reveal any number of pyramid schemes, multi-level marketing (MLM) plans, investment scams, and other dot-cons. Don't let yourself be taken in by any of these rip-offs; if an offer sounds too good to be true, it probably is—online or otherwise!

TIP *To learn more about the latest online scams, go to the National Fraud Information Center (`www.fraud.org`), Internet ScamBusters (`www.scambusters.org`), or the FTC's Dot Cons site (`www.ftc.gov/bcp/conline/pubs/online/dotcons.htm`).*

The Nigerian Fraud Letter

The Nigerian Letter scam started out in letter form, migrated to fax machines, and then ended up being transmitted via e-mail. There have been literally hundreds of variations on the basic letter, but they all look something like this:

ATTN: President/CEO

REQUEST FOR URGENT BUSINESS RELATIONSHIP - STRICTLY CONFIDENTIAL

Firstly, I must solicit your confidentiality. This is by virtue of it's nature as being utterly "confidential" and "Top Secret". Though I know that a transaction of this magnitude will make anyone apprehensive and worried, but I am assuring you that all will be well at the end of the day. A bold step taken shall not be regretted I assure you.

I am Mr. Paulo Noy and I head a seven man tender board in charge of contract awards and payment approvals. I came to know of you in my search for a reliable and reputable person to handle a very confidential business transaction, which involves the transfer of a huge sum of money to a foreign account requiring maximum confidence. My colleagues and I are top official of Federal Government Contract Review and Award Panel.

Continued on next page

The Nigerian Fraud Letter *(Continued)*

Our duties include evaluation, Vetting, and Approval for payment of contract jobs done for the Federal Ministry of Aviation (FMA) etc. We are therefore soliciting for your assistance to enable us transfer into your account the said funds. Our country looses a lot of money everyday that is why the international community is very careful and warning their citizens to be careful but I tell you "a trial will convince you".

The source of the fund is as follow: During the last military regime here in Nigeria, this committee awarded a contract of US$400 Million to a group of five construction firms on behalf of the Federal Ministry of Aviation (FMA) for the supply and installation of landing and navigational equipment in Lagos and Port Harcourt International Airports. During this process my colleagues and I decided among us to deliberately over inflate the total contract sum of US$428 Million with the aim of sharing the remaining sum of US$28 Million. The government has since approved the sum of US$428 Million for us as the contract sum, but since the contract is only worth US$400M the remaining US$28Million is what we intend to transfer to a reliable and safe offshore account, we are prohibited to operate foreign account in our names since we are still in Government. Thus, making it impossible for us to acquire the money in our name right now, I have therefore been delegated as a matter of trust by my colleagues to look for an oversea partner into whose account we can transfer the sum of US$28Million.

My colleagues and I have decided that if you/your company can be the beneficiary of this funds on our behalf, you or your company will retain 20% of the total amount (US$28Million) while 75% will be for us (officials) and the remaining 5% will be used in offsetting all debts/expenses incurred during this transfer.

We have decided that this transaction can only proceed under the following condition:

(a) Our conviction of your transparent honesty and that you treat this transaction with utmost secrecy and confidentiality.

Continued on next page

The Nigerian Fraud Letter *(Continued)*

(b) That upon Receipt of the funds you will release the funds as instructed by us after you've removed your share of 20%.

Please acknowledge the receipt of this letter using the above e-mail address. I will bring you into the complete of this transaction when I've heard from you.

Your urgent response will be highly appreciated as we are already behind schedule for the financial quarter. Please do be informed that this business transaction is 100% legal and completely free from drug or money laundering.

Only trust can make the reality of this transaction.

Best regards,
Mr. Paulo Noy

If you respond to this e-mail, you receive a follow-up message that requests you forward to Mr. Noy your bank account number, "to enable us to follow up all pursuance for immediate approvals and transfer." Naturally, the only thing that gets transferred at that point is your money out of your account.

If you've been victimized by the Nigerian Letter scam (sometimes called the 419 Fraud, after the relevant section of the Nigerian criminal code), you can contact the U.S. Secret Service Task Force charged with handling this particular scam. The task force can be contacted via e-mail (**419.fcd@usss.treas.gov**), fax (202-406-6930), or phone (202-406-5850).

What to Do If You Think You've Been Cheated

If you think you've been the victim of online fraud, there are some definite steps you can take. These include:

- ☑ Contact your credit card company to put a halt to all unauthorized payments, and to limit your liability to the first $50.

- ☑ If you think your bank accounts have been compromised, contact your bank to put a freeze on your checking and savings accounts—and to open new accounts, if necessary.

☑ If the fraud occurred at a major online shopping or auction site, contact the site and make them aware of the problem—and take advantage of any consumer protection services they have available.

☑ Contact your local authorities—fraud *is* illegal, and it should be reported as a crime.

☑ Report the fraud to your state attorney general's office.

☑ File a complaint with the Federal Trade Commission (FTC) by contacting the FTC Consumer Response Center via phone (202-382-4357) or on the Internet (`www.ftc.gov/ftc/complaint.htm`).

☑ Contact any or all of the following consumer-oriented Web sites: Better Business Bureau (`www.bbb.org`), Fraud Bureau (`www.fraudbureau.com`), Internet Fraud Complaint Center (`www1.ifccfbi.gov`), National Consumers League (`www.natlconsumersleague.org`), or National Fraud Information Center (`www.fraud.org`).

Summing Up

Online shopping is no more risky than shopping in the real world. You should, however, take reasonable precautions to protect your personal information and keep from getting ripped off. These precautions include shopping at well-known Web sites, paying by credit card, making sure the site has a phone number for real-world contact, and always—*always*—using a secure server for purchasing.

Online auctions can also be the source of fraudulent activity. In particular, you need to protect yourself from sellers who take your money and then don't ship the item you won in their auction. The best protection in this instance is to pay via credit card, if possible; if you can't use credit, pay by check. You should also be comfortable with the seller's feedback rating, and search for any negative comments from prior transactions; you may want to avoid dealing with brand-new sellers, until they develop a track record with other users.

If you become a victim of online fraud, the first thing to do is limit your exposure by contacting your credit card company and bank. You should then contact the site where the fraud occurred and avail yourself of any protection they might offer. Finally, contact your local law enforcement authorities, file a report with the FTC, and contact any one of a number of fraud-related Web sites. It's important to alert other users to your situation, so they can learn from your mistakes and avoid being defrauded themselves.

In the next chapter you'll learn how to protect yourself—and your family—from online predators.

CHAPTER 22

Protecting Yourself from Online Predators

Y ou might think that the Internet is a safe environment. After all, when you're online you communicate with other users virtually, not physically—and you can't be hurt when you're not face-to-face.

While it's true that it's easy to remain fairly safe and anonymous online, that safety erodes when you choose to meet your online friends in the physical world. It's also possible to be harassed and stalked while you're online, no physical meeting necessary.

Read on to learn more about those unusual creatures we call online predators, and how to protect yourself from them—both online and in the real world.

Online Harassment

Harassment is defined as any deliberate action that causes you to fear for your safety. In the real world, harassment might come in the form of repeatedly following you from place to place, repeatedly sending you unwanted communications (either directly or indirectly), repeatedly watching you while at work or at home, or engaging in any threatening conduct toward you or a member of your family. Online, harassment might come from repeatedly sending you messages, threatening or otherwise, via e-mail or instant messaging or IRC.

The key word here is *repeatedly*. Someone is harassing you if they instant message you every time you log onto the Internet. Someone is harassing you if they send you unwanted e-mail messages every day. Someone is harassing you if they follow you from chat room to chat room, begging you to talk to them.

And, of course, someone is harassing you if he threatens to find out where you live and come over and beat the crud out of you.

Stalking

The most common form of online harassment is online stalking. This occurs when someone tracks you when you're online, virtually following you around and sending you unwanted messages.

Online stalking typically takes place in chat rooms and channels. You enter your favorite chat room, and you're greeted with a message from the stalker. You can try to avoid the stalker by putting him on your "ignore" list, so that his messages are automatically blocked. But if the stalker is persistent, he'll just change identities and keep stalking.

This sort of behavior typically escalates into the use of instant messaging. With instant messaging, the stalker can harass you anytime you're online, not just when you're in a chat room. Again, you can configure your instant messaging software to block messages from the stalker, but the stalker can keep on changing identities.

If you're careless with your personal information, the stalker can find out your e-mail address. Now you're in for a new level of stalking. Not only will you be deluged with instant messages, you'll now find your inbox full of unwanted messages from the stalker. And if the stalker is technologically astute, you could find yourself the victim of e-mail bombs (flooding your inbox with thousands of messages), Trojan horses, and other virus and attack activity.

And stalking can lead to worse offenses—because online stalkers don't always stay online. Consider the case of Amy Boyer, a 20 year-old woman from Nashua, New Hampshire. She was stalked by a young man named Liam Youens. After becoming obsessed with her at school, Youens targeted Amy online. He purchased her Social Security number for $45 from an online information firm, and then used it to obtain more information about his victim—including where Amy worked and where she lived. On October 15, 1999 he drove his mother's car to the office where Amy worked as a dental assistant. He parked next to Amy's car in the parking lot, and waited for her to leave the office. At 4:30 that afternoon, Amy walked to her car, and Youens shot her repeatedly with his Glock 9mm semiautomatic handgun. He then turned the gun on himself. Both Amy and her stalker were pronounced dead on the scene.

NOTE *Learn more about Amy at the Amy Boyer Memorial Web site* (www.amyboyer.org).

Fortunately, incidents like this are rare; online stalking very seldom leads to murder. But it's possible—which is why you need to take decisive action if you discover that you're being stalked.

Bullying and Flaming

It used to be that the bullies only bothered you on the playground; once you got home, you were safe from attack.

Not anymore.

Thanks to the Internet, bullies can now continue their intimidating behavior practically 24 hours a day. Bullies now send harassing messages via e-mail and instant messaging, and prey on their victims in Internet chat rooms.

A recent survey by British research firm BMRB (www.bmrb.co.uk) polled 856 children between the ages of 11 and 19. According to the survey, one in ten reported being bullied over the Internet. (One in six reported receiving bullying text messages via pager or cell phone—an extension of the online bullying phenomenon.)

And bullying isn't just for kids; even adults can get into fights online. Some individuals take on a completely different personality when they can hide behind the relative anonymity of the Internet; they get bolder and more aggressive, and less tolerant of opposing opinions.

If you ever browse through the messages on a Usenet newsgroup or Web message board, you know this is true. You've seen one individual post an opinion, and then one or more individuals "flame" the first person for being such a bonehead. When the name-calling gets hot and heavy, it can evolve into what experienced users call a *flame war*.

By itself, a flame war does no harm, outside of some aroused emotions and hurt feelings. However, flame wars *can* spill out into the real world, resulting in the possibility of real physical harm.

Flame wars also reflect poorly on the individuals and the medium involved. If a particular forum becomes more known for its flame wars than its useful information or congenial community, users will start to avoid that forum. It's a shame when the "bad element" drives out all the good users, but it happens—and the only way to avoid it is to somehow restrict the flame postings. That argues for moderated forums, where a forum administrator has the power to delete individual messages, or completely block access for troublesome users. Some may view this as a form of censorship, but it does help to keep a community on track and hospitable to the greatest number of users.

Protecting Yourself from Online Harassment

If someone wants to stalk you online, he's going to do it. You can't stop a stalker from trying, but you can limit the extent of his harassment—and protect yourself from physical harm.

Here are some tips on how to avoid being harassed online:

- Don't engage the stalker, and don't return any messages or e-mails; most stalkers eventually go away when ignored.

- If you find yourself being stalked in a particular chat room, start by ignoring the harassing messages; you can also configure the chat software to ignore or block all messages from the stalker.

- If the stalking continues, change your ID in that chat room; if the stalker figures out your new ID, consider abandoning that chat room.

- If you're being stalked via instant messaging, put the stalker on your ignore/block list.

- If you're being stalked via e-mail, configure your e-mail program to block all messages from the stalker.

- Report the stalker to your ISP, and ask the ISP to trace the identity of the stalker.

- If you still can't shake the stalker, discontinue your subscription to your ISP and resubscribe (under a different name) with a different ISP.

- If the stalker makes threatening comments or appears to know where you live or work, report the incident to your local law enforcement authorities.

- If you are physically approached by the stalker, immediately move to protect yourself; then contact your local police.

The key thing to remember is that most harassing behavior stops when ignored. Most stalkers get off on producing a response; when no response is forthcoming, the game isn't fun anymore, and they move on to their next victim. So if you receive harassing messages, just delete them; resist the temptation to reply. If the harassing behavior continues, *then* you can take action, either by changing your ID or by contacting your ISP. If the stalker can be identified, he can be kicked off the Internet by his ISP—and if his behavior becomes threatening, he can be dealt with by the proper law enforcement authorities.

Taking an Online Relationship into the Real World

Most of us have one or more relationships with people we only know via e-mail, instant messaging, or chat rooms. These online relationships can be rewarding, but they can ultimately prove risky if extended into the real world.

Of course, the biggest risk of physically meeting someone you first met online is disappointment; quite often, neither party is nearly as appealing in person as on the Internet. After exchanging a fair number of messages, it's easy to think you intimately know the other person. The reality of meeting someone in person, however, can be sobering.

It can also be dangerous. Many stalkers and attackers first identify their victims online. If you do choose to meet an online friend in the real world, you should take appropriate precautions to protect yourself, in case the meeting turns bad:

- ☑ Don't give out your address or home phone number. (Providing your cell or pager number is probably okay, as long as it can't be tied to your street address.) You don't want a bad date following you home.

- ☑ Don't meet at your house or office.

- ☑ Meet at a public place—a coffeehouse, perhaps, or a mall; someplace where there are lots of people around, in case things turn bad.

- ☑ If possible, have a friend accompany you to the meeting, even if they just sit off to the side and look bored.

- ☑ Tell a friend where you're going, and promise to check in by a certain time; if you don't check in as promised, instruct your friend to alert authorities.

Everything OK so far? Good. But don't go too fast; it takes time to get to know someone in the real world, even if you have a long-standing online correspondence.

Preying on Children

It's an unfortunate fact, but there are those in our society who prey on the weak and the ignorant—and our children. Few of these child predators attack strangers; most establish a relationship with the youngster first, and then exploit that relationship to their benefit.

Which is where the Internet comes in.

How Online Predators Work

The Internet is a terrific place to meet people. It's also a terrific place for your children to meet people they shouldn't be meeting. A predator can strike up a relationship with a child in an online chat room, or via instant messaging or e-mail; once the child feels safe with that person, the predator can lure the youngster into a real-world meeting.

Fortunately, little of this online predation is targeted at very young children. Most victims are over 13 and female (although teenaged boys can also be victims), emotionally needy kids who willingly agree to physically meet their new online "friend." Conversely, most online predators—like their real-world counterparts—are men. The situation that results isn't the prototypical one of a bad guy kidnapping an unsuspecting child; it's more often the case of a morally dubious adult taking advantage of a young teenager's bad judgment.

Some online predators stalk their victims well in advance. They hang out in teen-oriented chat rooms, pretending to be one of the gang, or just lurking and taking notes. They might even keep databases on specific targets, tracking information such as whose parents are divorced, what after-school activities a particular child engages in, who has a large group of supportive friends, and who spends most of their time alone. A predator might track a particular child for several weeks, or several months, before acting. And when they do act, it's likely to look more like a friendly gesture than an overt attack.

The predator, of course, doesn't view it as an attack. He views it more as a seduction, and himself more as a loving partner than an exploitive attacker or pedophile. But however it's viewed, this type of luring behavior is illegal, and should be guarded against.

Most online predators identify and make first contact with their victims via chat rooms and channels, with America Online chat rooms being a choice location. (That's because of the high percentage of children connecting to the Internet via AOL.) After initial contact is made, further communication is typically via instant messages and e-mail.

Is Your Child a Potential Victim?

While you shouldn't discourage your children from making online friends—that's one of the fun things about using the Internet—you should encourage your children to use caution about what information they divulge to their new friends, and to keep their online relationships online. To that end, you should be attentive as to what your children do online, and be aware of any activities that might put them at risk.

How can you tell if your child is being targeted by an online predator? Here's a list of things to look for; and remember, these are only indicators:

- Your child spends an inordinate amount of time online; most victims of online predators are heavy Internet users, especially chat rooms and instant messaging.

- Your child quickly changes the computer screen (or turns off the PC) when you come into the room; this is a sign that your child has something to hide.

- You find pornography on your child's computer; predators often use dirty pictures to seduce potential victims.

- You find suggestive pictures of your child on the computer, or stored in a digital camera; many predators convince their victims to send them pictures, as a sign of their devotion or commitment.

- Your child receives phone calls from strangers; this is a sign that the predator is moving the online relationship into the real world.

- Your child receives mail or packages from strangers; it's common for predators to send gifts to potential victims, to help grow the relationship.

Children who are most at risk are often new to the online world, and unfamiliar with Internet etiquette and the risks posed by online relationships. Also at risk are children who are especially naive or easily tricked by adults, or who are emotionally insecure, lonely, actively seeking attention and affection, and otherwise isolated from normal relationships with children their own age.

TIP *Learn more about online child predation at the Missing Kids Web site (*www .missingkids.com*), hosted by the National Center of Missing and Exploited Children (NCMEC). You can also use this site to report possible illegal activity related to child predation, child pornography, and other types of sexual exploitation. Other good sites for online child safety are ProtectKids.com (*www.protectkids.com*) and WiredPatrol (*www.wiredpatrol.org*).*

How to Protect Your Children Online

Watching over your children is hard work. There's a lot of bad stuff in the world, and it's probably impossible to completely shield them from all possible harm. Still, there's a lot you can do to protect them when they're online, including the following:

- ☑ Take an interest in your children's online pals, just as you (should) do with friends that your kids bring home to visit.

- ☑ Talk to your children about the dangers of getting together with someone they meet online.

- ☑ Provide your children with online pseudonyms, so they don't have to use their real names online.

- ☑ Forbid your children to physically meet, or speak on the phone with, anyone they meet online.

- ☑ If you do allow your children to set up a real-world meeting, accompany them to the meeting and introduce yourself to the new friend.

- ☑ Make sure your children know that people aren't always who they pretend to be online; explain that some people view online chatting as a kind of game, where they can assume different identities.

- ☑ Set reasonable rules and guidelines for your kids' computer use; consider limiting the number of minutes/hours they can spend online each day.

- ☑ Monitor your children's Internet activities; ask them to keep a log of all Web sites they visit; oversee any chat and instant messaging sessions they participate in; check out any files they download; even consider sharing an e-mail account (especially with younger children) so that you can oversee their messages.

- ☑ Instruct your children not to respond to messages that are suggestive, obscene, belligerent, or threatening, or that make them feel uncomfortable in any way; encourage your children to tell you if they receive any such messages, and then report the senders to your ISP.

- ☑ Don't let your children send pictures of themselves over the Internet; don't let them receive pictures from others.

- ☑ Caution your children about providing personal information (including passwords!) to strangers.

☑ Teach your children not to respond if they receive offensive or suggestive e-mail or instant messages.

☑ Install filtering software that prevents your children from giving out their name, address, and phone number online.

☑ Use the Internet with your children; make going online a family activity.

☑ Consider moving your children's PC into a public room (such as a living room or den), rather than a private bedroom.

☑ Use America Online as your ISP; AOL lets you set up your kids' e-mail accounts so that they can't receive files or pictures in their messages, and it also lets you block younger users from chat rooms and other risky areas.

☑ If you think that one of your children, or one of your children's friends, is in any danger, immediately contact the authorities.

Above all, teach your children that Internet access is not a right; it should be a privilege earned by your children, and kept only when their use of it matches your expectations.

TIP *If you're concerned about protecting your children online, you're probably also concerned about what content they have access to on the Web. To learn more about family-safe Web browsing, turn to Chapter 31, "Dealing with Inappropriate Content."*

Summing Up

While the Internet is a virtual environment, it's possible for individuals to track what you do online, and harass you in chat rooms, via instant messaging, and with unwanted e-mail messages. In most instances, ignoring the stalker makes him go away; in more extreme cases, you may be forced to change your online identity, or even report the stalker to your ISP or local authorities.

Online stalking can escalate into real-world stalking. For this reason, you should be especially careful about arranging physical meetings with people you first met online. If you do decide to meet an online friend in the real world, meet in a public place, ideally with a friend nearby. Make sure someone else knows where you are, and knows what to do if you don't contact them by a specific time.

Online predators also target children. Emotionally isolated teenagers are particularly vulnerable, and are typically targeted in teen-oriented chat rooms. Predators often continue their correspondence via instant messaging and e-mail, and then escalate to phone calls and real-world meetings. You can protect your children by monitoring their chat and messaging, and coaching them to keep their online relationships online.

In the next chapter you'll learn about how technology can be used to monitor your online activities—without your knowing it.

CHAPTER 23

Defeating Spyware

Imagine a piece of software installed on your machine without your knowledge. Imagine this software tracking everything you do online, from the Web sites you visit to the e-mail you send. Imagine this software sending the information it collects back to a central site, to use for its own dubious benefit.

Don't like that picture? Then you won't like reading the rest of this chapter, which takes this scenario beyond the realm of imagination into the real world—thanks to a new class of Trojan software called *spyware*.

Understanding Spyware

Spyware is a type of computer program that spies on everything you do with your computer. Some spyware monitors your Internet-related activity; other spyware tracks *all* your computer activity, down to the last keystroke. The information recorded by spyware is typically stored in a log file; that log file is then transmitted to the company behind the spyware, where it can be used in any number of ways.

How Spyware Works

Spyware is like a Trojan horse, in that it is typically installed without your consent or knowledge. As you can see in Figure 23.1, it runs in the background, hidden from view, and monitors your computer and Internet usage. That probably means it is performing some or all of the following operations:

- Recording the addresses of each Web page you visit

- Recording the recipient addresses of each e-mail you send

- Recording the sender addresses of each e-mail you receive

- Recording the contents of each e-mail you send or receive

- Recording the contents of all the instant messages you send or receive—along with the usernames and addresses of your IM partners

- Recording the entire contents of each IRC chat channel you visit—and logging the usernames and addresses of other channel members

- Recording every keystroke you type with your computer keyboard

- Recording all your Windows-related activities, including the movement and operation of your mouse

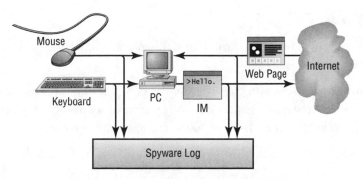

Figure 23.1 *How spyware tracks and reports your online activities.*

The information recorded by the software is saved to a log file on your machine. That log file, at a predetermined time, is transmitted (via the Internet) to a central source. That source can then aggregate your information for marketing purposes, use the information to target personalized communications or advertisements, or steal any confidential data for illegal purposes.

Popular Spyware Programs

The unfortunate fact is that there are numerous spyware programs legitimately available on today's market. Many of these programs are targeted toward the corporate market and are used to spy on a company's employees. Other programs are targeted at the home market, and are used to monitor children's Internet activities. Still other programs are designed for covert remote operation—which means they can be used by crackers and other third parties to track computer usage over the Internet.

Some of the biggest spyware programs were listed in Chapter 20, "Protecting Your Privacy." Here are some additional programs, all of which offer remote surveillance capabilities:

- iOpus STARR Pro (`www.iopus.com/starr.htm`)
- iSpyNOW (`www.ispynow.com`)
- NETObserve (`www.exploreanywhere.com`)
- Pearl Echo (`www.pearlecho.com`)
- RemoteComputer (`www.remote-computer.com`)
- SpyAnywhere (`www.spytech-web.com`)

Who Uses Spyware?

There are many different uses for the information that spyware captures—and these uses dictate who might install spyware on your PC:

- Corporations might use spyware to monitor the computer and Internet usage of their employees, as discussed in Chapter 20. (Some companies also track your Internet usage via logging functions on their firewall software, no special spyware software necessary.)

- Computer crackers and hackers might use spyware to capture confidential information from individual users.

- Parents might use spyware to monitor their family's computer and Internet usage.

- Advertising and marketing companies might use spyware to assemble marketing data— and to serve personalized ads to individual users.

The reality is that most spyware is used for unethical purposes. If you have spyware installed on your PC, you want to find it, and you want to delete it—before further harm can be done.

Spyware for Advertisers

There's a particular type of spyware that has a certain legitimacy. This spyware is used by advertisers and marketers, and is called *adware*. As you can see in Figure 23.2, adware is typically placed on your PC when you install some other legitimate software, piggybacking on the main installation. (Although, technically, you have to agree to the adware installation; the agreement is typically buried in the boilerplate terms-of-service agreement you must accept to install the main software—and most users click "OK" automatically, without reading the agreement.) Once installed, the adware works like spyware, monitoring your various activities and reporting back to the host advertiser or marketing firm. The host firm can then use the collected data for marketing purposes—totally hidden from you, of course.

Figure 23.2 *Adware piggybacks on legitimate software installations.*

For example, adware might monitor your Web surfing habits and report to the advertiser which sites you visit. The adware might pop up a window and ask for your demographic data, which it also reports back to the host. The adware might even use your personal data to generate its own targeted banner ads, which it will display on top of the normal banner ads when you visit other Web sites. (For example, the adware might generate an ad for United Airlines when you visit the American Airlines Web site.)

NOTE *Many adware programs use a technology called a browser helper object (BHO). This small program attaches itself to the Internet Explorer Web browser, and tracks Web sites visited. This information is then routed back to the adware company.*

Adware and P2P File Swapping

Adware has come to public notice primarily through its association with various P2P file-swapping services. As explained in Chapter 16, "Protecting Your System in a P2P Environment," many P2P file-swapping networks bundle spyware or adware as part of their client software. The P2P network generates revenue from the adware company; the adware company generates revenues by serving you personalized ads, or by selling the data it collects.

All you have to do is look at the numbers to realize that adware is a big problem. Six of the top P2P file-swapping sites include adware with their client software; together, these sites have more than 144 million potential users, most of whom have adware installed.

Which software is apt to include an adware component? Here are some of the biggest offenders:

- Audiogalaxy Satellite (`www.audiogalaxy.com`)

- BearShare (`www.bearshare.com`)

- Download Accelerator (`www.speedbit.com`)

- Grokster (`www.grokster.com`)

- iMesh (`www.imesh.com`)

- KaZaA (`www.kazaa.com`)

- LimeWire (`www.limewire.com`)

- MusicCity Morpheus (`www.musiccity.com`)

Adware Companies

If you use one of the major P2P file-swapping networks, chances are you already have adware installed on your PC. Many companies distributed adware in this fashion, including the following:

- Aadcom (www.aadcom.com)

- Brilliant Digital Entertainment (www.brilliantdigital.com)

- ClickTillUWin (www.clicktilluwin.com)

- Gator (www.gator.com)

- Mindset Interactive (www.mindsetinteractive.com)

- Onflow Corporation (www.onflow.com)

- VX2 Corporation (www.vx2.cc)

Of these adware programs, perhaps the most widely distributed is Gator. Gator is bundled with Audiogalaxy Satellite and other P2P clients. Its main function is to paste new pop-up ads over existing banner ads—thus hijacking ad space for their clients. To give you an idea of Gator's reach, the software sends an average of two pop-up ads per week to more than 15 million people—with most users not even knowing that it's installed on their systems.

TIP *You can uninstall the Gator software (and other subsidiary programs installed along with Gator) by using the Add or Remove Programs feature in Windows. (From the Control Panel, select Add or Remove Programs.) To find out what programs you need to uninstall, go to www.gatoradvertisinginformationnetwork.com and click the following link:* To view a list of products that are part of GAIN and installed on the computer you are currently using.

Carnivore: Your Tax Dollars at Work

There's one other big spyware program you need to be aware of. It's not available in any retail store, or over the Internet. In fact, it's not available for sale at all.

That's because it's owned by the U.S. government.

Carnivore is a spyware program developed and used exclusively by the Federal Bureau of Investigation. The FBI uses Carnivore to track down potential criminals and terrorists, by tracking their online activities.

The DragonWare Suite

Technically, Carnivore is just one part of a spyware suite. The suite itself is called DragonWare and has the following components:

- Carnivore, a packet sniffer that captures packets of information as they flow across the Internet

- Packeteer, a utility for reassembling individual packets of information into their original messages or Web pages

- Coolminer, an application for extrapolating and analyzing the data found in captured messages

The entire suite of applications works as shown in Figure 23.3. Carnivore captures the data, Packeteer reassembles it, and Coolminer analyzes it.

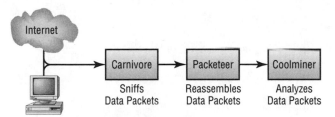

Figure 23.3 *How the FBI's DragonWare suite works*

How Carnivore Works

As you learned in Chapter 20, a packet sniffer works by examining individual packets of information as they flow across a network or the Internet. Carnivore is designed to "sniff" all the information flowing across a single Internet service provider, and to filter that data based on the user. In theory, the FBI obtains a court order to "tap" the Internet usage of a suspected criminal or terrorist, installs Carnivore at that user's ISP, and then uses the packet sniffer to record all the data sent to or from the targeted individual.

In many ways, this is like a traditional telephone wiretap. In a wiretap, the law enforcement agency listens in to all the individual's phone conversations; with Carnivore, the agency "listens in" to all of his Internet usage.

Once the FBI receives permission to tap a suspect's Internet activities, the agency contacts the individual's ISP and sets up a Carnivore-configured computer at the ISP's offices. The software on this computer is configured with the suspect's IP address, so that Carnivore knows what data to watch for. As you can see in Figure 23.4, all data packets flowing to or from the suspect's IP address are copied to some type of removable storage media. Every few days an FBI agent physically visits the Carnivore computer and retrieves the most recently stored data. That data is then returned to an FBI office for further analysis, using the Packeteer and Coolminer applications.

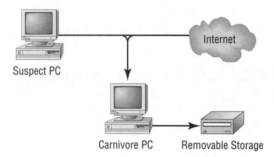

Figure 23.4 *Using Carnivore to capture data from a suspect's Internet account*

Potential Uses of Carnivore

Carnivore isn't a proposed project; it's in operation today. And, since the September 11th terrorist attacks, its use has increased significantly. The FBI is using Carnivore to track a wide variety of potential lawbreakers. The list of targeted perpetrators extends beyond terrorists to include individuals engaged in the following activities:

- Child pornography
- Espionage
- Fraud
- Information warfare

Issues

One of the biggest complaints about Carnivore is that it can suck in too much information, above and beyond what is needed for any individual surveillance operation. If the Carnivore program itself is buggy, or if law enforcement agencies go beyond what is allowed by a particular court order, it's possible for more data to be monitored than is officially authorized.

This, of course, concerns privacy advocates—especially with the expanded powers given to government agencies under the post-September 11 USA PATRIOT Act (discussed in Chapter 20). Under this act, authorities no longer need to obtain a court order to initiate online surveillance; this has no doubt contributed to the increased use of Carnivore, beginning in the later months of 2001.

Some experts are concerned that the government will apply Carnivore on a widespread basis, in an attempt to regulate the entire Internet. While this is theoretically possible, it would require the installation of Carnivore computers at every single ISP—which is such a massive buildup of infrastructure as to be practically impossible. (Such an operation could also be side-stepped by the use of foreign ISPs.)

Even if Carnivore isn't used to monitor the entire Internet, it still could be used to monitor all traffic at an ISP—not just the traffic from a specific individual. By configuring Carnivore to record all traffic that includes the words "bomb" or "terror," for example, the FBI could spread a very wide net indeed—and assume a Big Brother role that is frightening to many.

NOTE *The National Security Agency (NSA) is rumored to be working on a secret network code-named "Echelon," which would detect and capture data crossing international borders that contain certain key words, such as "bomb," "assassination," or "attack." (In fact, some claim that Echelon is already up and running.)*

How to Defeat Spyware

To defeat spyware, you first have to be aware of its presence. To that end, there are several anti-spy programs available that scan your system for known spyware, and a number of Web sites that maintain lists of all known spyware programs.

Of course, you should try to defeat spyware at the source—by not installing it in the first place. The installation of many adware programs is actually optional when you install the host program; if you look close, you're given the option *not* to install these so-called "companion programs." Check (or uncheck) the proper box on the installation screen, and you avoid installing the adware.

Other adware programs are *not* optional components; they install automatically when you install the host program. If you know that a particular program includes piggyback adware, and you don't have the option not to install the adware, you can always opt not to install the main software itself. Why deal with a company that allows other companies to secretly exploit its users?

Identifying Spyware

One way to cleanse your system of spyware and adware programs is to manually search your computer for such programs, and then use Windows' Add or Remove Programs utility to do the removal. You can find lists of known spyware programs at the following sites; scan these lists and then search your hard disk for the presence of these programs.

- Spy Chaser (`camtech2000.net/Pages/SpyChaser.html`)

- TomCat Spyware List (`www.tom-cat.com/spybase/spylist.html`)

WARNING *You might think that you could remove an adware program by removing the host program—the KaZaA client, for example. This isn't the case; simply removing the host software seldom (if ever) removes tag-along spyware and adware programs. You have to remove the spyware program separately from the host.*

Using Antispy Software

An easier way to remove spyware is to use antispy software. These programs are designed to identify any and all spyware programs lurking on your computer, and they will also uninstall the offending programs and remove their entries from the Windows Registry.

Some of the most popular of these antispy and spyware-removal programs currently include:

- Ad-aware (`www.lsfileserv.com`)

- BHO Cop (`www.pcmag.com/article/0,2997,s=1478&a=4446,00.asp`)

- OptOut (`www.grc.com/optout.htm`)

- Spybot Search & Destroy (`www.beam.to/spybotsd/`)

TIP *Another good source of information about finding and removing spyware and adware is the Counterexploitation (`www.cexx.org`) Web site. This site provides much valuable information about the topic in general, as well as specific instructions for removing various spyware and adware programs.*

Cleaning Your System with Ad-aware

Of these antispy programs, the most effective and the easiest to use is Ad-aware. As you can see in Figure 23.5, the basic Ad-aware window has big buttons for all the operations you're likely to use. To scan for and remove spyware from your system, follow these steps:

1. In the Sections to Scan pane, select those elements you want to scan; to perform a full-system scan, check the My Computer option.

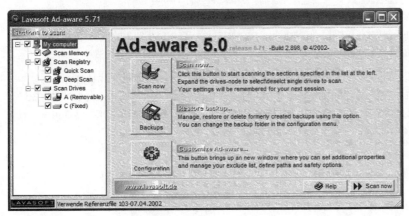

Figure 23.5 *Use Ad-aware to remove spyware and adware programs from your computer.*

2. Click the Scan Now button.

3. Ad-aware now begins the scan. The results of the scan are reported in the main window, as shown in Figure 23.6.

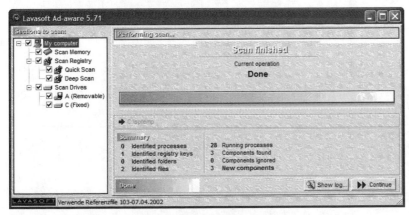

Figure 23.6 *The results of an Ad-aware scan*

4. Click the Continue button.

5. The next screen lists all the spyware programs that Ad-aware found. Check those items you want to remove, and click Continue.

6. When the confirmation box appears, click OK; the indicated files and Registry entries will be removed from your system.

Blocking Spyware Domains

Another way to stop spyware and adware from functioning is to keep it from reporting back to the host Web site. If you know the name of the server(s) that your adware contacts, you can use site blocking or filtering software to block access to the addresses of these servers, thus rendering the adware useless.

Another way to do this is to route all outbound traffic to the ad server back to your own computer. This defeats all outbound communications from the adware. To do this, you have to edit (or, if it doesn't already exist, create) a file named **Hosts** (no file extension). On Windows XP/NT/2000 systems, this file is in the `Windows\system32\drivers\etc\` folder. Open this file and add the following lines:

```
127.0.0.1       adserver1.com
127.0.0.1       adserver2.com
```

And so on. The `127.0.0.1` references the IP address of your computer; the *adserver1.com* should be the actual name of the adware server.

On Macintosh computers, the Hosts file is in the Preferences folder. The format of the file is similar, but slightly different:

```
adserver1.com       CNAME       127.0.0.1
adserver2.com       CNAME       127.0.0.1
```

Summing Up

Spyware is software that is secretly installed on your system and monitors your various computer and Internet activities. The collected data is then transmitted to a central individual or company—without your knowledge or approval—for use as that entity sees fit.

Spyware that is installed and used by an advertising or marketing firm is called adware. Many P2P file-swapping networks allow adware to piggyback on their client software, to be installed when the main software is installed. This adware typically reports marketing data back to the marketing company, and enables personalized ads to be served to your computer.

One of the biggest potential users of spyware is the United States government, through its Carnivore program. Carnivore is designed to track the Internet activities of suspected criminals and terrorists, and works as a packet sniffer installed at the suspect's ISP.

There are many utilities on the market you can use to find and remove spyware and adware programs, the most popular of which is Ad-aware. You can also protect against spyware and adware installations by not agreeing to their installation when you download and install various software programs—or by saying no to any software that includes a spyware component.

In the next chapter we'll look at another technology that can potentially compromise your privacy—Web cookies.

CHAPTER 24

Managing Cookies

Have you ever used a personalized start page, like My Yahoo! (`my.yahoo.com`), and wondered how they knew who you were? Or visited Amazon.com (`www.amazon.com`) and noticed that the site welcomed you with a list of personalized recommendations?

These personalized Web pages are possible because these sites—and many others—know who you are and track your visits to their sites. This type of activity monitoring is enabled by something called a *cookie*, which is a Web-based technology used to store and track specific data about you.

How Cookies Work

A cookie is a small file, stored on your own computer, that contains information about you and your Web activities. That information might be your username, password, age, credit card information, or just the fact that you've visited a particular Web site. As you can see in Figure 24.1, cookies are placed on your hard disk by individual Web sites and then accessed by those sites each time you visit in the future.

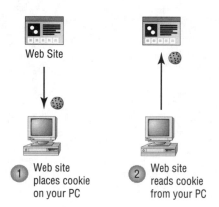

Web Site

① Web site places cookie on your PC

② Web site reads cookie from your PC

Figure 24.1 Web sites store personal information in cookies and read that information each time you visit.

The information in a cookie file is nothing more than a short text string. Each cookie stores information specific to a given Web site. The text for a cookie looks something like this:

```
name=value;expires=date;
```

The *name* field is the name of the data being stored; *value* is the value of the data. The `expires` field is the date that the cookie expires; this field is optional. In addition, other fields can be added for the path, domain, and secure status.

There are many practical uses for cookies. A site can use cookies to determine if you've previously visited the site, to store passwords and user IDs, to store any personal information obtained from user registration forms, to track what site you just came from, to track your activities while on their site, and so on. While this is great for when you want a site to remember you each time you visit, it's also scary when you think about how much of this type of information can be stored without your explicit knowledge. (For these reason, many user privacy groups decry the use of cookies to track what they feel is sensitive data.)

As an example, consider a typical visit to an online music store. When you visit the site, the online retailer might use a cookie to record the names of artists and individual CDs that you have ordered or browsed; that cookie is written to your hard disk, in the background, while you browse.

When you return to the online music site, your browser lets the site read the cookie that the site previously created. This cookie then helps the Web site create a customized start page that includes new releases from the artists that you've purchased or browsed in the past.

Cookies are also used to streamline online checkout. Without a cookie, you'd have to enter all your personal information (including credit card information) on each visit to an online retailer. Using cookies, a site can store all that information once and automatically "fill in the blanks" the next time you want to check out.

NOTE *Learn more about cookies at CookieCentral.com (*`www.cookiecentral.com`*). This site also offers a selection of third-party cookie management software.*

Cookie Management

The reason you probably don't know much about cookies is that all this cookie-related activity happens in the background. You're typically not asked to approve any cookies, nor are you even aware that any of this is taking place. While this type of behind-the-scenes operation ranks high on the convenience meter, it has serious privacy implications.

Fortunately, an individual cookie can only be viewed by the site that placed it on your hard disk; cookies cannot be shared between sites. You also have significant control over how cookies are stored on your computer, especially on newer Web browsers.

For example, Netscape Navigator 6 includes a Cookie Manager that lets you choose to accept or decline cookies based on individual sites or types of sites. In Internet Explorer 6, you can adjust the privacy level to determine which types of cookies the browser automatically accepts.

It's a good idea to familiarize yourself with the cookie management features of your particular Web browser. If you don't learn to manage your cookies, you'll find yourself either accepting all cookies or declining all cookies; the former option could compromise your security, while the latter could compromise convenience.

The best option for most users is to set your browser to accept cookies from familiar and trusted sites, since cookies enable the sites you visit frequently to provide personalized features and services without asking you to log in on each visit. However, you may want to refuse cookies from those sites that you don't know well or visit often; you probably don't need or want those cookies tracking your online behavior.

Managing Cookies in Internet Explorer

Internet Explorer 6 has six levels of cookie management, ranging from accepting all cookies to declining all cookies. These levels are detailed in Table 24.1:

Table 24.1   *Internet Explorer Privacy Levels*

LEVEL	FIRST-PARTY COOKIES	THIRD-PARTY COOKIES
Accept All Cookies	Accepts all	Accepts all
Low	Accepts all	Blocks cookies from sites that don't have privacy policies; automatically deletes cookies (when IE is closed) from sites that use personal information without your implicit consent
Medium	Automatically deletes cookies (when IE is closed) from sites that use personal information without your implicit consent	Blocks cookies from sites that don't have privacy policies or from sites that use personal information without your implicit consent
Medium High	Blocks cookies from sites that use personal information without your implicit consent	Blocks cookies from sites that don't have privacy policies or from sites that use personal information without your *explicit* consent
High	Blocks cookies from sites that don't have privacy policies or from sites that use personal information without your *explicit* consent	Blocks cookies from sites that don't have privacy policies or from sites that use personal information without your *explicit* consent
Block All Cookies	Blocks all new cookies; existing cookies can't be read (even by the sites that created them)	Blocks all new cookies; existing cookies can't be read (even by the sites that created them)

TIP *Internet Explorer differentiates between* first-party *and* third-party *cookies. A first-party cookie originates from the Web site you are currently viewing and is typically used to store your preferences regarding that site. A third-party cookie originates from a Web site different from the one you are currently viewing and is typically used for the banner ads that are fed from separate advertising sites to the current Web site. In general, third-party cookies are less desirable than first-party cookies.*

You select which level of cookie management you want by following these steps:

1. Select Tools ➤ Internet Options.

2. When the Internet Options dialog box appears, select the Privacy tab (shown in Figure 24.2).

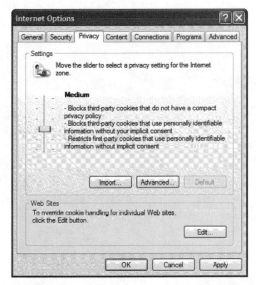

Figure 24.2 *Configuring Internet Explorer's cookie settings*

3. Adjust the slider to the level you want.

4. Click OK.

TIP *The default setting in Internet Explorer 6 is Medium, which pretty much blocks all advertising-related cookies and deletes any cookies that contain personal information when you close Internet Explorer. If you'd rather that no Web site store any personal information you haven't explicitly approved, choose the High setting.*

You can also adjust the privacy level on a site-by-site basis. Follow these steps:

1. Select Tools ➤ Internet Options.

2. When the Internet Options dialog box appears, select the Privacy tab.

3. Click the Edit button.

4. When the Per Site Privacy Actions dialog box appears (shown in Figure 24.3), enter the address of a specific Web site, then click either Block (to block all cookies from this site, regardless of your general privacy settings) or Allow (to allow all cookies from this site, regardless).

Figure 24.3 *Setting cookies for a specific Web site*

Managing Cookies in Netscape Navigator

If you're using Netscape Navigator 6, the built-in Cookie Manager lets you determine how cookies are set and modified on a site-by-site and cookie-by-cookie basis. To set your general preferences for how cookies should be handled, follow these steps:

1. Select Edit ➤ Preferences.

2. When the Preferences window appears, scroll down the Category list, find the Privacy and Security category (shown in Figure 24.4), and then choose Cookies.

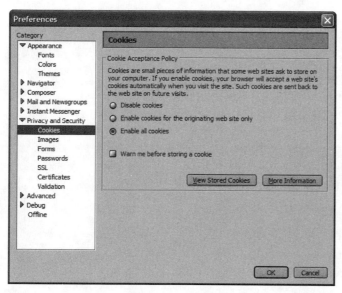

Figure 24.4 *Configuring Netscape's cookie settings*

3. To always accept cookies, select the Enable All Cookies option. To never accept cookies, select the Disable Cookies option. To have cookies work only with the site that placed the cookies (i.e., to block cookies sent via e-mail or sites that attempt to hijack other site's cookies), select the Enable Cookies for the Originating Web Site Only option.

4. If you want to be notified when a site tries to store a cookie on your PC, select the Warn Me Before Storing a Cookie option.

If you select the Warn Me Before Storing a Cookie option, the Cookie Manager will display a warning dialog box whenever a Web site tries to install a cookie. At that point you can click Yes to allow the cookie or No to not accept it. You can also select the Remember This Decision option so you won't be bothered the next time you come to this particular site.

Netscape also enables you to manage cookies on a site-by-site basis. To accept cookies from the current site, select Tasks ➤ Privacy and Security ➤ Cookie Manager ➤ Allow Cookies From This Site. To not accept cookies from the current site, select Tasks ➤ Privacy and Security ➤ Cookie Manager ➤ Block Cookies From This Site.

To remove stored cookies, follow these steps:

1. Select Tasks ➤ Privacy and Security ➤ Cookie Manager ➤ View Stored Cookies.

2. When the Cookie Manager appears, select the Stored Cookies tab, shown in Figure 24.5.

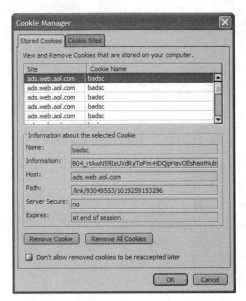

Figure 24.5 *Removing stored cookies*

3. Remove an individual cookie by selecting it from the list and clicking the Remove Cookie button or delete all the cookies on your system by clicking the Remove All Cookies button.

Cookies and E-mail

Until recently, cookies have been a Web browser issue. Of late, however, a number of e-mail spammers have been using HTML e-mail to deliver cookies to unsuspecting recipients—and then using those cookies to track your online activities.

This form of cookie abuse is possible because HTML e-mail is nothing more than a Web page delivered to your inbox. Since cookies are created via HTML code, it's relatively easy to design a nice-looking HTML e-mail message that also drops a cookie on your hard drive.

Once created, these cookies can be used in a number of ways. The spammer can use the cookie to grab your specific e-mail address, which it might not have had before, despite the fact that you received an e-mail from them. (That's because some spammers use "random address generators" to create their spam lists. More about this in Chapter 28, "Dealing with Spam.") The spammer can track which recipients actually click through to their Web site and gauge the success of particular mailings and mailing lists. The spammer can even link the information it gathers about you to other databases it may have access to and thus create a more fully formed profile of your online activities.

Continued on next page

Cookies and E-mail *(Continued)*

The best way to defend against e-mail cookies is by using the cookie-management features of your Web browser—particularly if you're using Microsoft products. That's because both Microsoft Outlook and Outlook Express use Internet Explorer to render HTML e-mail messages. If you set a high privacy level in Internet Explorer (discussed next), you'll also limit the cookie use in Outlook and Outlook Express.

Of course, this is as much a spam problem as it is a cookie problem. Learn more about spam in Chapter 28.

Summing Up

Cookies are small files created by individual Web sites and placed on your computer's hard disk to track specific information about your computer and Internet usage. Cookies are typically used to serve personal information to you on return site visits; they can also be used by Web-based marketers to track your online behavior.

You can control how cookies are stored on your system via your Web browser. Both Internet Explorer and Netscape Navigator enable you to accept all cookies, decline all cookies, or choose specific conditions under which cookies may be stored.

In the next chapter you'll learn more about how technology can affect your online privacy, by looking at passwords and encryption.

CHAPTER 25

Employing Passwords, Encryption, and Digital Identification

O ne element of ensuring your online privacy is to protect your confidential information from unauthorized viewing or use. While there are many ways to lock away your private data, two of the most common are passwords and encryption.

A password is not in and of itself a technology-based solution. However, digital technology enables the use of longer and more complex passwords, which can better protect sensitive data. (Of course, technology also enables the use of faster and more efficient password crackers, which creates the need for even longer and more complicated passwords. And so the cycle goes…)

Encryption is another way to keep private information private, and it's also made more practical through the use of computer technology. By employing ever-increasing amounts of processing power, the age-old field of cryptography can be used to encrypt messages and data so that they're unusable and unviewable by anyone who doesn't have the proper key.

A related issue is that when you're online, it's not always easy to prove that you're who you say you are. It's also not easy to prove that someone else is who they say they are—or that the file or data you supposedly received from a specific company actually came from that company.

The process of ensuring identification online is made easier by the use of digital IDs in the form of digital certificates and digital signatures. In essence, a digital ID is the electronic counterpart to a driver's license or membership card or (for a company) the certificates of authentication you might find hanging on a lobby wall. These IDs tell you—or your computer—who you're dealing with and take some of the anonymity and risk out of conducting transactions over the Internet.

Read on to learn more about these related means of protecting your data and identity online—passwords, encryption, and digital IDs.

Password Protection

The easiest way to protect your private data is to lock it away. In lieu of a physical lock and key, we use passwords to make data inaccessible. When password protection is employed, the data is accessible only to those with the proper password. If you don't know the password, the protected data remains off-limits.

However, it's a well-known fact that the weakest link in the security chain is your password. That's because too many users don't use passwords at all (which is the online equivalent of leaving the front door of your house open) or use passwords that are too easily guessed or cracked.

The problem isn't that passwords themselves are inherently insecure. The weakness with most passwords is a human weakness, not a technological one.

The fact is that many users, when prompted to create a password for this Web site or that account, come up with names or phrases that are easy for them to remember. (It's only natural—who wants a password that you can't remember?) The most common passwords, in fact, are derived from Social Security numbers, children's names, and pets' names. The conundrum is that a password that is easy to remember is also easy to guess or crack, using password-cracking software.

Password Cracking

While you could sit at a computer keyboard and keep entering different words into a password field, that's not a very efficient way to guess a password. Most crackers automate the task by using special password-cracker software. These cracker programs operate at computer speed to enter thousands of possible passwords every second. If the password is short and simple, one of these programs can crack it in a matter of seconds. If the password is long and complex, it might take days to crack—if it can be cracked at all.

Password-cracker software typically uses one of three different cracking methods. Each method has its pros and cons, and in many instances a combination of methods is necessary to crack a complex password.

Brute Force   A brute-force crack simply generates combinations of characters—and lots of them. It's kind of like monkeys pecking on typewriters; you try enough combinations, and sooner or later you crack the password. Of course, the shorter the password, the easier it is to crack via a brute-force crack; the best way to defeat a brute force crack is to use a long alphanumeric password.

Dictionary   A dictionary crack uses words from an existing dictionary as possible passwords. Most of these password dictionaries contain 100,000 words or less, and thus can be tested rather quickly; dictionary cracks typically take no more than a few seconds to see if any of the words in the dictionary match the password.

Rule-Based   The most powerful type of password crack is the rule-based attack. For this type of crack to work, the cracker has to know a little bit about the password he wants to crack. For example, some Web sites create default passwords consisting of a word and a one- or two-digit number. The cracker enters this rule into the cracking software, which helps the software generate the right types of passwords for this particular instance.

TIP *You can check out the world of password cracking for yourself at the Crack Password (*www.crackpassword.com*) and Russian Password Crackers (*www.password-crackers.com*) Web sites. These sites feature comprehensive collections of cracker software for a variety of programs and uses, as well as information about password cracking and encryption.*

Creating Stronger Passwords

With all this password-cracking software available, how do you keep your password private?

It's really quite simple. The longer and more complex your password is, the harder it will be to crack.

All you need to do is increase the length (8 characters are better than 6—and way better than 4) of the password and use a combination of letters, numbers, and special characters (!@#$%). You should also use a combination of uppercase and lowercase letters, if a particular account lets you use case-sensitive passwords.

When creating your password, you should avoid using real words you might find in a typical dictionary; any standard dictionary cracker will crack that password faster than it takes you to type it. Also, don't use easily guessed words, like your middle name or your wife's maiden name or the name of your dog or cat. Better to use nonsense words or random combinations or letters and numbers—anything that won't be found in a dictionary.

You should also make sure you don't use the same password on multiple sites. (You don't want a cracker to obtain one password and be able to break into multiple accounts.) It also helps if you change your passwords with some regularity, so that any cracked password has a short shelf life.

Most important, you should remember that your password should never be shared—with anyone. As blatantly obvious as that sounds, many people feel no compunction about providing others with their passwords, for whatever reason. This is a huge security risk; your password is yours and yours alone and should never be shared or compromised.

> **WARNING** *The practice of gaining access to passwords by gaining the trust of the user is called* social engineering. *This may take the form of a phone call or e-mail from someone purporting to be from your ISP, asking you to confirm your user ID and password. When you reply, the budding social engineers on the other end of the line now have the information they need to directly access your account. For this reason, you should never give out your password, no matter how official-sounding the request; representatives of legitimate businesses will never ask for your password.*

Of course, the big drawback to creating a stronger password is having to remember it. Most users employ simple passwords (and the same passwords on multiple accounts) because they're easier to remember. If you have to use a number of long, seemingly random passwords, they can be very difficult to remember. It's that old conundrum—increased security versus ease-of-use.

One solution is to create a password that is an acronym for a more easily remembered phrase. For example, if you're a dog lover, you might use ILMD (for "I love my dog"). Just add a random four-digit number to the end, and you have a halfway decent password that you may be able to remember.

Encryption

A password is like a virtual key to locked information. Encryption, on the other hand, is like a secret code. When data is encrypted, it's transformed into something quite different from what it was; if you try to view encrypted data, it most often looks like a bunch of seemingly random characters. The only way to view encrypted data is to decrypt it and return it to its original state.

Again, this is a lot like working with a secret code. Applying encryption is like applying the code.

You probably played around with secret codes when you were a kid. One of the most common codes was to displace every letter by a certain amount. You could, for example, displace every letter by one letter, so that A equals B, B equals C, and so on. If you apply that code to this phrase `Good morning, sunshine`, you get the following encrypted message: `Hppe npsojoh, tvotijof`. This looks like gibberish, unless you know the code and then transform it back to the original message.

Digital encryption works in a similar fashion, but with much more complex codes, called *keys*. The simple "A=B" code is just too easy to crack; when you're working with computers, you need codes that no one can crack just by guessing.

Encryption is typically used to protect confidential information sent over the Internet, typically via e-mail. You encrypt a message on your end, and the recipient decodes it when it is received. Anyone intercepting the e-mail on the way can't read the message, because it's encrypted. (Unless they've stolen or broken the key, of course.) The stronger the encryption, the harder the key is to break; stronger encryption typically comes in the form of longer keys, measured in bits.

How Encryption Works

When it comes to digital encryption, there are two main methods employed. Both require that secret *keys* be used to decrypt the coded data—and the more complex the key, the harder the code is to crack.

Symmetric-Key Encryption

Symmetric-key encryption encodes a message by using a specific key. That same key is also used to decrypt the message, as shown in Figure 25.1.

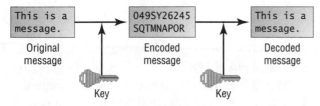

Figure 25.1 *Encrypting and decrypting a message with symmetric keys*

The main difficulty with symmetric-key encryption is that both parties—the sender and the receiver—must have the same decryption key. How, then, do you send encrypted messages to someone you don't know or avoid disclosing your decryption key to other parties?

The solution to that problem lies in the *other* encryption method: public-key encryption.

Public-Key Encryption

Public-key encryption, also called *public key cryptography* (PKC), is used for almost all the encrypted communications on the Internet. Unlike symmetric-key encryption, public-key encryption uses two separate decryption keys:

- A *public key* is published in an open directory in a place where anyone can look it up.

- A *private key* is unique to an individual. The sender doesn't know the recipient's private key, or vice versa.

The way public-key encryption works is that the sender encrypts the message with the recipient's public key. (The sender obtains this key directly from the recipient or looks it up in some public key directory.) When the message is received, the recipient uses his or her *private* key to decrypt it, as shown in Figure 25.2. Since the private key is private to that individual, no one else can decrypt the message.

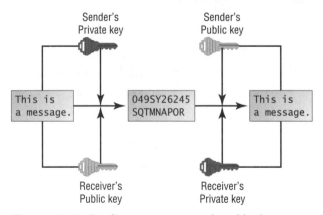

Figure 25.2 *Sending a message with public-key encryption*

This sort of encryption uses the openly published RSA cryptography algorithm to create the keys, making it virtually impossible to crack. That's because a 128-bit public key is a single prime number between 1 and 340,282,366,920,938,000,000,000,000,000,000,000,000. Mathematicians say that there are 3,835,341,275,459,350,000,000,000,000,000,000,000 such numbers;

even if you had a computer that could check a trillion numbers each second, it would take trillions of years to get through them all.

NOTE *The RSA cryptography algorithm is was designed by MIT professors Ronald L. Rivest, Adi Shamir, and Leonard M. Adleman (the R, the S, and the A) in 1977. Learn more about RSA cryptography at the RSA Security Web site (*www .rsasecurity.com*).*

Pretty Good Privacy

The most popular implementation of public-key encryption is Pretty Good Privacy (PGP), developed by Phil Zimmerman. Freeware versions of PGP are available that work with Outlook, Outlook Express, Eudora, and other major e-mail programs to encrypt outgoing messages. You can find more information about PGP—and download the software—at the International PGP Homepage (www.pgpi.org).

WARNING *The current version of PGP as this book is written—version 7.5—is not fully compatible with Windows XP and should not be installed on Windows XP systems. (However, PGP does work with previous versions of Windows, including Windows 9x and Windows 2000.) If you're running Windows XP, you will not be able to use PGP at this time.*

PGP works by creating a *session key*, which is a one-time only private key. (It's actually a random number generated by the recent movements of your mouse and keystrokes entered.) The session key then uses an encryption algorithm to encrypt the text of the message. Once the data is encrypted, the session key is encrypted to the recipient's public key and transmitted along with the encrypted message to the recipient.

When the recipient receives the encrypted message (along with the encrypted session key), he uses his copy of PGP and his private key to decrypt the session key. The PGP program then uses the now-decrypted session key to decrypt the text of the message.

NOTE *A commercial version of PGP was offered for a time by Network Associates, the company behind the McAfee antivirus and security products. However, as of March 2002, Network Associates has discontinued the personal version of PGP, while continuing to include PGP encryption in some of its enterprise products.*

Other Encryption Programs

Besides PGP, there are several other programs you can use to encrypt your e-mail messages. Most of these programs require that both the sender and the recipient have the program installed on their PCs.

The most popular of these encryption programs include:

- CryptoHeaven (`www.cryptoheaven.com`)

- Invisible Secrets (`www.neobytesolutions.com/invsecr`)

- NetMangler (`www.maidensoft.com/netmangler.html`)

- ShyFile (`www.shyfile.net`)

- Top Secret Crypto (`www.topsecretcrypto.com`)

Encryption in Outlook Express

If you're using Microsoft Outlook or Outlook Express, you can purchase a digital certificate—a kind of electronic identity certificate—that will enable you to automatically send encrypted messages from within your e-mail program. These certificates are available from VeriSign (`www.verisign.com/products/class1`) for $14.95 per year.

NOTE *Learn more about digital certificates in the "Digital Identification" section, later in this chapter.*

Configuring Outlook Express for Encrypted E-mail

Before you can send encrypted e-mail, you first have to configure your e-mail program for the digital certificate you've just purchased. (This is assuming you've purchased a VeriSign certificate, of course.) Follow these steps:

1. Select Tools ➤ Accounts.

2. When the Internet Accounts dialog box appears, select the Mail tab.

3. Select your e-mail account, then click the Properties button.

4. When the Properties dialog box appears (shown in Figure 25.3), click the Select button in the Encrypting Preferences section.

Figure 25.3 *Configuring Outlook Express for your new digital ID*

5. When the Select Default Account Digital ID dialog box appears, select your new certificate, then click OK.

6. Click OK to close the Properties dialog box.

NOTE *You follow a similar procedure if you're using Microsoft Outlook.*

Obtaining a Recipient's Digital ID

Once you have your digital ID installed, you only have half the encryption equation. The recipient of your encrypted message must have a similar digital ID installed on his or her computer—and you have to know the number of that certificate.

Fortunately, Outlook Express automatically adds digital IDs to your Address Book when you receive digitally signed mail from other users. You can also add digital IDs to your Address Book manually, by following these steps:

1. Open your Address Book and either create a new contact entry or open an existing contact.

2. In the contact Properties dialog box, select the Digital IDs tab (shown in Figure 25.4).

Figure 25.4 *Adding a digital ID to an Address Book contact*

3. Click the Import button.

4. When the Select Digital ID File to Import dialog box appears, locate the digital ID file, then click Open.

Sending an Encrypted Message

Once you have your digital ID and the digital ID of your intended recipient, you can send an encrypted message to that person. In Outlook Express, this is as easy as sending a regular e-mail, with one extra button click. Just follow these steps:

1. Open a new message, fill in the To and Subject fields, and enter the message text.

2. Click the Encrypt Message button, or select Tools ➢ Encrypt.

3. Click the Send button to send the message.

Reading an Encrypted Message

When you receive an encrypted message in Outlook Express, that message is identified by a "lock" icon in the message list. When you open the message, you see a message from the certification authority telling you that you've received an encrypted message, as shown in Figure 25.5. Click the Continue button to read the unencrypted message text.

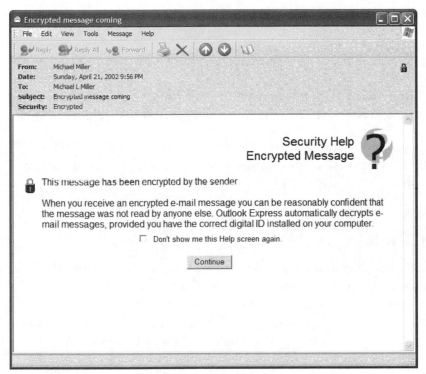

Figure 25.5 *Reading an encrypted e-mail message*

Encryption in Windows XP

If you're running Windows XP Professional, and are using XP's optional Encrypting File System (EFS), you have the option of encrypting the files and folders as they reside on your hard disk.

With EFS, each file you choose to encrypt has its own encryption key, which is also used to decrypt the file's data. The file encryption key is itself encrypted, using your public key.

To encrypt a file or folder, follow these steps:

1. From within My Computer or My Documents, right-click the file or folder that you want to encrypt, and then select Properties from the pop-up menu.

2. When the Properties dialog box appears, select the General tab.

3. Click the Advanced button.

4. When the Advanced dialog box appears, select the Encrypt Contents to Secure Data option.

5. Click OK.

WARNING *If there is no Advanced button on the General tab, your computer is not using the Encrypting File System, and you cannot encrypt files and folders in this manner.*

Decrypting a file folder is as simple as following these steps and then clearing the Encrypt Contents to Secure Data option.

Digital Identification

Authenticating identity online is difficult, because you're not meeting face-to-face with the other party. In a way, you have to take that person's word that they're who they say they are—and we know how risky it is, in this day and age, to take anyone's word for anything.

Fortunately, we can use digital technology to securely identify people and companies online. In particular, public-key encryption is used to create a virtual certificate that verifies an entity's identity.

This digital certificate is nothing more than a computer file issued by a separate certification authority. The certificate typically contains the following information:

- Certificate owner's name

- Owner's public key (along with the expiration date of the key)

- Name and digital signature of the certification authority

- Serial number of the digital ID

When you receive a verified message or file from another party, that data is signed with the certificate authority's private key. Your computer then compares this signature with the one on the previously issued digital certificate and confirms that the data came from the identified source.

Figure 25.6 shows a real-world example of the use of digital certificates. When you use your Web browser to connect to your bank's Web server, your browser must authenticate the server before a safe transaction can be conducted.

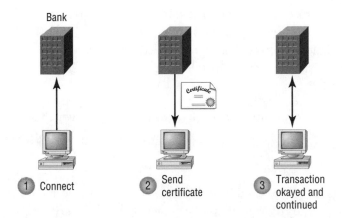

Bank

1 Connect

2 Send certificate

3 Transaction okayed and continued

Figure 25.6 *Using a digital certificate to verify communications with your bank's Web server*

The process begins when you access the bank's secure server, using SSL authentication. The secure icon appears in the lower-right corner of your browser, indicating that you've established a secure connection, and then the bank's Web server automatically sends a digital certificate to your Web browser.

Your Web browser now accesses the certificate store on your computer's hard disk. (This is a list of trusted certification authorities and is created when you first install your Web browser.) If the certificate authority that sent the certificate is found in the certificate store, that means the certificate came from a *trusted authority*, and the transaction can proceed.

The balance of the transaction will now continue, in an encrypted fashion. (So no one can intercept the confidential data.) Your Web browser creates a decryption key that is unique to this session (called a *session key*). The session key is then encrypted with the public key in the bank's Web server certificate so that only the bank's server can read the messages sent by your browser and vice versa.

Types of Digital IDs

There are actually three distinct types of digital IDs. They all function in much the same manner, even though they're designed for widely varying uses.

There are three types of digital certificates:

Server IDs   Server IDs enable Web servers to operate in secure mode. The ID identifies and authenticates the secure server and encrypts any data sent between the server and your Web browser.

Developer IDs   Developer IDs use Microsoft's Authenticode software validation technology to verify the identity of software developers when you're downloading software and components from the Internet. So-called "signed" software has been verified safe, so you know the code has not been tampered with and it can be safely installed on your computer; you install unsigned software at your own risk.

NOTE *During software installation, you're prompted to give your okay that you trust the software's manufacturer; if you're dealing with a major developer like Microsoft, you can probably trust them.*

Personal Digital IDs   Personal Digital IDs are used by individuals to enter and verify personal data when registering with Web sites or exchanging messages with other verified individuals.

Using Personal Digital IDs

Digital certificates are used to authenticate various identities online, including the identities of secure servers. Most of this authentication takes place automatically, without your involvement or awareness.

You can also use digital certificates to authenticate *your* identity—and ease the process of entering information at various Web sites. For this, you use a Personal Digital ID.

You're well aware that some Web sites require you to enter your user ID and password every time you visit in order to confirm your identity and enter the site. This constant entering of passwords can become tedious, and it's often difficult to remember which username and password you used with which site. This is where the Personal Digital ID comes in.

You can use your Personal Digital ID to ease the juggling of IDs and passwords. The certificate, stored in your Web browser, can automatically send your registration information to participating sites. In essence, the certificate manages your various user IDs and passwords so that you don't have to both remember the information and enter it manually on each visit.

You can also use your Personal Digital ID to digitally sign e-mail messages. Your digital signature is used by the recipient to verify that the message actually came from you and wasn't altered in transit.

Personal Digital IDs for e-mail can be obtained from VeriSign (`www.verisign.com/products/class1`). Certificates cost $14.95 per year.

Signing E-mail

To demonstrate how these digital certificates work, let's examine how you can use your Personal Digital ID to send an e-mail message with Outlook Express. (These steps assume that you've already purchased and installed a Personal Digital ID from VeriSign and that you're using Outlook Express 6.)

Configuring Outlook Express for Digital Certificates

Before you can send signed e-mail, you first have to configure your e-mail program for your digital ID. In Outlook Express, this is very similar to the way you configure the program for encryption. Follow these steps:

1. Select Tools ➤ Accounts.

2. When the Internet Accounts dialog box appears, select the Mail tab.

3. Select your e-mail account, then click the Properties button.

4. When the Properties dialog box appears, click the Select button next to the Signing box.

5. When the Select Default Account Digital ID dialog box appears, select your new certificate, then click OK.

6. Click OK to close the Properties dialog box.

NOTE *You follow a similar procedure if you're using Microsoft Outlook.*

Sending and Receiving Signed Messages

To send a digitally signed e-mail message in Outlook Express, follow these steps:

1. Open and create a new message.

2. Click the Digitally Sign Message button or select Tools ➤ Digitally Sign.

3. Click the Send button.

When your message is received, the recipient first sees an HTML screen like that in Figure 25.7. This informs the recipient that the message has been digitally signed and is authentic. (The digitally signed message also displays a VeriSign seal in the top-right corner and a Security line under the normal Subject line; these elements also appear in the Outlook Express preview pane.) When the recipient clicks the Continue button, your original message appears.

The recipient can view your digital certificate by clicking the VeriSign seal (which is actually a button); this displays a Properties dialog box for that message with the Security tab displayed. Click the View Certificates button to display the View Certificates dialog box, then click the Signing Certificate button. Outlook Express now displays the Signing Digital ID Properties dialog box, shown in Figure 25.8.

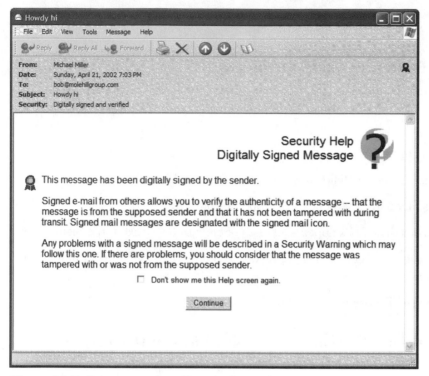

Figure 25.7 *Receiving a digitally signed e-mail*

Figure 25.8 *Viewing the sender's digital ID certificate*

The Next Generation of Authentication: Biometrics

Numeric encryption and digital certification are both very powerful ways to authenticate confidential data. The next generation of authentication, however, will go beyond numeric keys—which can still be cracked—to incorporate biometric technology. Biometric authentication uses unique biological signatures to confirm identity and, thus allow access to confidential data. (Biometric identification is also being evaluated for other security purposes, including ID cards and as a way to guard access to secure areas.)

Some possible forms of biometric identification include:

- Voice ID
- Fingerprint scans
- Retina scans
- Face scans
- DNA matching
- Breath analysis

The key thing about biometric identification is that it is less easily duplicated. Your fingerprint pattern, for example, is unique; there's no easy way to duplicate it. The same with voice patterns, retina patterns, and the like. By utilizing biometrics, the crime of identity theft may become a thing of the past.

Summing Up

Passwords are used to restrict access to sensitive data or private services. When an item is password-protected, it can be accessed only by entering the correct password. Since passwords can be guessed or cracked (using special cracker software), it's important to use a long password, composed of a combination of letters, numbers, and special characters. You should also avoid passwords that are easily guessed, and never use the same password for more than one account.

Another way to protect sensitive data is by encrypting that data. The data is then decrypted using a special password-like code, called a key. The most common form of encryption on the Internet uses both public and private keys and, with current technology, is virtually uncrackable. One of the most popular public-key encryption program is PGP, which can be used to encrypt e-mail messages in Microsoft Outlook, Outlook Express, and other e-mail programs. You can also purchase a digital certificate from VeriSign and use it to send encrypted messages from within Outlook Express or Outlook.

Neither passwords nor encryption actually authenticate the identity of the person sending data over the Internet. To confirm the identity of people, Web servers, and software manufacturers, you use digital certificates. You can register for your own personal digital ID to digitally sign your e-mail messages at the VeriSign Web site.

In the next chapter you'll learn how *not* to authenticate your identity online—by surfing and communicating anonymously.

CHAPTER 26

How to Surf—
and Communicate—
Anonymously

One component of privacy is anonymity, when desired. Not only do you want to keep your private information private, there are also occasions when you want to keep your identity secret.

Maybe you're browsing Web sites that your coworkers or family members might not approve of. Maybe you're leaking confidential information to a competitor—or to the press. Maybe you just want to lurk online without fear of anyone discovering who you really are.

Whatever the case, there is sometimes a need to hide your true identity online. Unfortunately, most normal online activities carry threads of your identity; a smart person (or company) with the right tools can easily suss out who you are, even if you think you've left no visible evidence behind. (Remember the backtracing tools in most firewall programs? They're able to trace the identity of an attacker with just the click of a button.)

How, then, can you stay anonymous on the Internet? Read on to find out.

Anonymous Web Surfing

You'd think that Web surfing would be a fairly anonymous activity. But then you remember all those Web forms you fill out, leaving behind your e-mail address and who knows what other personal information, as part of many sites' registration process. And then there are all those cookies that various Web sites place on your hard disk, creating a permanent record of your Web surfing activities.

Of course, you don't have to fill in any of those Web forms. And, as you learned in Chapter 24, "Managing Cookies," it's possible to configure your Web browser not to accept cookies. So then you'd be surfing anonymously, right?

Unfortunately, the answer is still no.

That's because wherever you visit on the Web, your IP address travels with you. When you enter a page's URL into your browser, you send out a request to view that page. That request is enclosed in a small data packet sent from your PC to the host site, and every data packet sent from your machine includes your IP address as part of its header code.

Any Web site, then, can use special software to pull your IP address from the header information. The same software can also track what browser you're using, what pages you visit at the site, and what Web site you last visited.

So much for surfing anonymously.

There *is* a way to surf anonymously, however. All you have to do is funnel all your Web browsing through an *anonymizer* Web site. The anonymizer Web site strips your IP address off all the data packets that pass through the site, so there's no way for any other site to trace your activity back to your individual computer or ISP.

How Anonymizers Work

Figure 26.1 shows how an anonymizer site works. You essentially surf the Web through the anonymizer site, going to that site first and then routing all your pages from there. When you send a page request through the anonymizer, it acts like a super-proxy server, stripping off the header of each data packet, thus making your request anonymous. The requested page is then fed through the anonymizer back to your Web browser.

Figure 26.1 *Making Web page requests anonymous*

When you enter a URL at an anonymizer site, the page you request is appended to the anonymizer's URL, like this: `http://anon.free.anonymizer.com/http://www.whitehouse.gov`.

Once you've accessed a particular site through an anonymizer, all the subsequent links you click are accessed in the same indirect fashion.

TIP *You can even anonymize bookmarks and favorites in your Web browser. Just append the anonymizer's URL in front of the bookmark's normal URL.*

Using an Anonymizer as a Proxy Server

Another way to use an anonymizer is to use it as a permanent proxy server in your Web browser. As you learned in Chapter 17, "Protecting a Network," a proxy server functions as a kind of super firewall to your system, hiding your computer from the rest of the Internet. When an anonymizer site is used as a proxy, your IP address will never be revealed to any of the sites you browse—and you won't have to directly access the anonymizer site.

Configuring Internet Explorer for an Anonymous Proxy Server

To set up an anonymizer as a proxy server in Internet Explorer, follow these steps:

1. Select Tools ➤ Internet Options.

2. When the Internet Options dialog box appears, select the Connections tab.

3. Click the LAN Settings button.

4. When the Local Area Network (LAN) Settings dialog box appears (shown in Figure 26.2), check the Use a Proxy Server for Your LAN option.

Figure 26.2 *Configuring Internet Explorer for an anonymous proxy server*

5. Enter the anonymizer's Web address in the Address field, then enter 8080 in the Port box.

6. Click OK.

Configuring Netscape Navigator for an Anonymous Proxy Server

In Netscape Navigator, you make the configuration for an anonymous proxy server like this:

1. Select Edit ➤ Preferences.

2. In the Category list, select Advanced ➤ Proxies.

3. Select the Manual Proxy Configuration option (shown in Figure 26.3).

4. Enter the anonymizer's Web address in the HTTP Proxy field, then enter 8080 in the Port box.

5. Click OK.

WARNING *There are some limitations to the effectiveness of an anonymizer. In particular, certified ActiveX controls can still access your system and reveal personal information. In addition, some anonymizers may disable or not work with certain technologies, including SSL servers, Java applications, and JavaScript applets.*

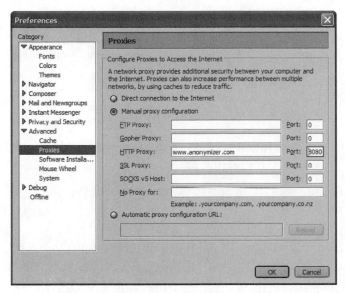

Figure 26.3 *Configuring Netscape Navigator for an anonymous proxy server*

Popular Anonymizer Sites

There are several anonymizer sites on the Web. All work in pretty much the same fashion; some of these sites are free, while others require registration or subscription.

The most popular anonymizers include:

- @nonymouse.com (`@nonymouse.com`)

- Anonymize.net (`www.anonymize.net`)

- Anonymizer.com (`www.anonymizer.com`)

- Anonymizers.com (`www.nymproxy.com/anonymiser`)

- IDzap (`www.idzap.com`)

- iPrive.com (`www.iprive.com`)

- Rewebber (`www.rewebber.de`)

- Somebody (`www.somebody.net`)

- Stealther (`www.photono-software.de/Stealther`)

- Surfola.com (`www.surfola.com`)

- Ultimate Anonymity (`www.ultimate-anonymity.com`)

Some of these services, such as Anonymize.net, go the extra step and create a completely new online identity for you. When you register, you are assigned a new IP address through a virtual private network (VPN); whenever you connect through their service, you're identified by the new, anonymous address—not your old address.

Using Anonymizer.com

Probably the most popular anonymizer is located at Anonymizer.com. (It's easy to remember, anyway.) To use Anonymizer.com to browse other Web sites, follow these steps:

1. Enter the page you want to access into the URL blank at the top left of the page, as shown in Figure 26.4.

2. Click Go.

Figure 26.4 *Anonymous Web surfing via the Anonymizer*

Anonymizer.com now sends your anonymous page request to the URL you indicated and then displays the requested page in your Web browser.

Anonymous E-mailing

E-mailing is a particularly non-anonymous activity. Not only do you provide visible proof of your identity (in the From field of your message), the hidden code behind the message—called the e-mail header—contains your e-mail address, the address of your ISP's outgoing e-mail server, and other similar information. This data is sent automatically whenever you send an e-mail, and is easily read by anyone on the receiving end.

> **NOTE** *To view header information for messages in Outlook Express, select a message in your inbox, then select File > Properties; when the Properties dialog box appears, select the Details tab. To view header information in Microsoft Outlook, right-click a message in your inbox and select Options; the header information is displayed in the Internet Headers area of the Message Options dialog box.*

For your e-mail to be anonymous, all this information needs to be stripped from your message header. The easiest way to do this is to use a Web-based service called a *remailer*.

How Remailers Work

A remailer functions as a middleman in the e-mail operation. As you can see in Figure 26.5, you send your e-mail to the remailer, which strips out your header information and then remails the messages to the intended recipients. Since your original header information is no longer present, the e-mail you send can't be traced back to you.

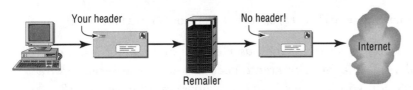

Figure 26.5 *Remailing anonymous e-mail*

Some remailers operate with any standard POP e-mail program, such as Microsoft Outlook and Outlook Express; you use your e-mail program to compose and send the message (to the remailer), then the remailer does the rest. Other remailers are entirely Web-based, requiring you to compose your messages on their site.

All remailers are fairly effective at what they do—and some even take an extra step and add encryption to all outgoing messages. As with anonymizers, some remailers are free and some are subscription-based.

TIP *For maximum security, you can send your e-mail through multiple remailers.*

Popular Remailers

The most popular anonymous e-mail services include:

- Anonymize.net (`www.anonymize.net`)
- Anonymous.To (`www.anonymous.to`)
- HavenCo Anonymous Remailer (`remailer.havenco.com`)
- HushMail.com (`www.hushmail.com`)
- iPrive.com (`www.iprive.com`)
- POP3Now (`www.pop3now.com`)
- PrivacyX (`www.privacyx.com`)
- SecureNym (`www.securenym.net`)
- Send Fake Mail (`www.sendfakemail.com`)
- Somebody (`www.somebody.net`)
- Ultimate Anonymity (`www.ultimate-anonymity.com`)
- W3 Anonymous Remailer (`www.gilc.org/speech/anonymous/remailer.html`)

WARNING *Traditional Webmail services, such as Hotmail and Yahoo! Mail, are not anonymous remailers. While you can create accounts on these services with "dummy" IDs, messages can still be traced back to your computer via the IP address included in each message header.*

Using the W3 Anonymous Remailer

Figure 26.6 shows the W3 Anonymous Remailer. To use this free remailer, follow these steps:

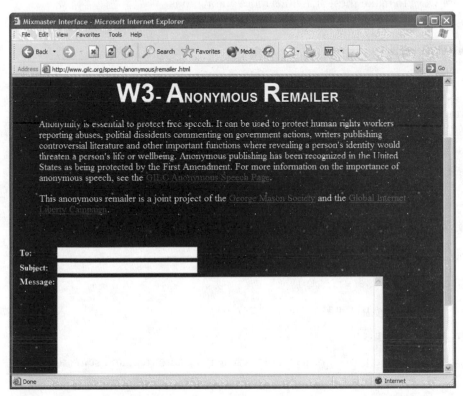

Figure 26.6 *Using the W3 Anonymous Remailer to send anonymous e-mail*

1. From the W3 Anonymous Remailer page, enter the recipient's e-mail address in the To field.

2. Enter the subject of the message in the Subject field.

3. Enter the text of the message in the Message field.

4. Click the Send Mail button.

The remailer now sends your message to the recipient—anonymously.

WARNING *It may take longer than usual—much longer than usual, in some cases— for the anonymous message to reach its recipient. (Secure remailing takes time…)*

Other Anonymous Communications

Now it's time to consider other popular online activities, including instant messaging and Usenet newsgroups. Are there ways to make these activities more anonymous?

Anonymous Newsgroups

Postings on Usenet newsgroups are typically identified by the poster's e-mail address. Unfortunately, using a fake address isn't enough to create an anonymous posting; when you post to most Usenet servers, your posting is automatically logged—accompanied by your ever-present IP address.

Anonymous Usenet access is facilitated by the use of anonymous Usenet servers. These servers don't keep public postings and download logs, so your IP address never finds its way to all the other servers on the Usenet network. The most popular of these anonymous Usenet servers can be found at the following:

- Anonymous Newsfeed (`www.anonymousnewsfeed.com`)

- My-Newsgroups.com (`www.my-newsgroups.com`)

- News Service (`www.news-service.to`)

- Ultimate Anonymity (`www.ultimate-anonymity.com`)

- Usenet.com (`www.usenet.com`)

As with Web anonymizers and remailers, some of these services are free, and some require a subscription.

Anonymous Instant Messaging

Instant messaging programs are surprisingly insecure. It's relatively easy for a dedicated entity to intercept your messages and deduce your true identity; for that reason, you probably shouldn't use IM to transmit confidential information or conduct conversations that you don't want tracked back to you.

Unfortunately, there aren't a lot of "anonymizer"-type solutions for instant messaging. Those few solutions that do exist tend to be designed for a specific IM network. The few available IM anonymizers include the following:

- Anonymize.net (`www.anonymize.net`), a proxy service for ICQ

- Somebody (`www.somebody.net`), a proxy service for ICQ

- SpyShield (`www.commandcode.com/spyshield.html`), for MSN Messenger and Windows Messenger
- Top Secret Messenger (`www.encrsoft.com/products/tsm.html`), an encryption-based solution for ICQ; also encrypts Outlook Express e-mail messages

Anonymous IRC

Internet Relay Chat is also a relatively insecure environment; your IP address is readily available to other chatters. The workaround to this problem is to use a proxy server, between your computer and the IRC network. You log onto the proxy server, then your communications to the IRC network use the proxy server's IP address; your own IP address stays hidden.

The most popular of the IRC anonymizers include:

- Anonymize.net (`www.anonymize.net`)
- Somebody (`www.somebody.net`)
- Ultimate Anonymity (`www.ultimate-anonymity.com`)

Anonymous Communities

In addition to all the "anonymizer" applications talked about in this chapter, there are also entire communities devoted to the totally anonymous exchange of ideas—free speech communities, if you will. These free speech communities utilize peer-to-peer technology to ensure that no personal data is stored on any central server.

Anonymous Communication with Freenet

The biggest of these anonymous communities is called Freenet. Freenet is an ambitious project that promises nothing less than the ability to communicate and share files online without being tapped, traced, or monitored in any way, shape, or form.

What makes Freenet unique from other online communities is that it's entirely peer-to-peer in nature; content on the Freenet network is constantly being moved from one computer to another, in total anonymity. A file might reside on one computer today and a totally different computer tomorrow. The file moving takes place without the knowledge of either computer; in fact, there's no way for anyone (even the owner of a host computer) to know which files are where, physically. This inability to physically locate any given file is what makes Freenet totally anonymous and censorship proof.

Information is stored on the Freenet network on personal Web sites called *Freesites*. Unlike traditional Web sites, the pages on a Freesite do not reside on any fixed server. Instead, the pages bounce around from computer to computer (in true P2P fashion), so no one really knows where they're hosted at any given point in time.

As a further means of ensuring anonymity, all communications between Freesites are encrypted. No site can tell where a request originated, which makes it almost impossible to determine which user issued any particular request.

Unfortunately, Freenet today is very much a work in process. Its use is recommended only for technically confident users; more casual users will find the necessary manual configuration of the Freenet software somewhat daunting.

If you're interested in learning more about Freenet, go to the official Freenet Web site (`www.freenetproject.org`).

Other Anonymous Communities

Beyond Freenet, there are several other communities that offer relatively anonymous communications between members.

For example, Cryptobox (`cryptobox.sourceforge.net`) is a project designed to keep private information and communications out of the hands of large corporations. The project's focus is on preventing large commercial Web sites from obtaining, using, and sharing private information about their users.

Another interesting attempt at ensuring information privacy is the by-product of a development effort at AT&T Labs. Publius (`publius.cdt.org`) enables users to post information online that can't be altered without the permission of the author—thus thwarting any attempts at censorship.

NOTE *The name Publius comes from the pseudonym used by Alexander Hamilton, John Jay, and James Madison, the authors of the Federalist Papers, a series of historic newspaper articles that influenced voters to ratify the proposed United States Constitution in 1788.*

Publius encrypts a document and divides it into fragments that then reside on multiple servers. The servers are selected randomly and belong to volunteers who don't know what information they're hosting. This random distribution of document fragments has the same impact as hiding the individual pieces of a jigsaw puzzle; even if someone were to obtain a piece or two, there is no way that the complete document can be reconstructed.

Summing Up

All normal activities and communications on the Internet contain information about the originating computer. In order to ensure complete anonymity, this information needs to be stripped from Web page requests and e-mail headers.

Anonymous Web surfing is enabled by the use of anonymizer Web sites. These sites strip the header information out of the data packets sent as part of each Web page request. You browse through the anonymizer site, and the sites you visit can't trace your visits back to your computer.

Anonymous e-mail is accomplished by the use of remailers. A remailer accepts your e-mail message, strips out the personal information in the message header, and then remails the message to its intended recipient.

There are also anonymizer services for most other Internet-based activities, including Usenet newsgroups, instant messaging, and Internet relay chat. There are even anonymous online communities, such as Freenet, that specialize in providing secure and anonymous access to a variety of messages and documents.

This ends our discussion of online privacy theft. In the next part we turn to the very annoying issue of online junk mail—or what we commonly call *spam*.

PART IV

E-MAIL SPAM

CHAPTER 27

Understanding Spam

Yesterday was a normal day. The temperature was seasonal, the sky was partly cloudy, and my coffeehouse had a hot cup of spiced Chai waiting for me when I walked in the door. Back at home, I had a total of 63 messages in my e-mail inbox. Thirty of these were messages from friends, family, and colleagues, or messages containing news and other information that I subscribe to on a regular basis. Two messages carried viruses (!), and the other 31 messages were junk messages, the kind of unsolicited advertisements and come-ons that are more commonly referred to as *spam*.

Like I said, yesterday was a normal day. The fact that almost half of my e-mail messages were unwanted annoyances isn't unusual. In fact, many users report an even higher percentage of junk mail cluttering up their inboxes. Spam, like junk mail from the post office and telemarketing phone calls at dinnertime, is a part of our daily lives, whether you like it or not.

And, if you're like most users, you don't like it.

Understanding Spam

If you have an e-mail account, you know what spam is—it's those unsolicited, unauthorized, and unwanted marketing messages that show up on a daily basis in your e-mail inbox. These messages are sent en masse to millions of users across the Web, hawking adult Web sites, mortgage refinancing, and Viagra without a prescription.

In short, e-mail spam is like the junk mail you receive in your postal mailbox. It's a major-league bother but easy enough to throw away—until there's so much of it that it interferes with your regular mail.

Spam, Spam, Spam, Spam

You might think that the name "spam" comes from Hormel's canned meat product of the same name, but you'd be wrong. Hormel claims—and Internet history backs it up—that the adoption of the name "spam" to stand for unsolicited e-mail actually came from the classic Monty Python comedy sketch.

You probably remember the Python's "Spam" sketch. It's set in a restaurant that offers dozens of different Spam-infested dishes, including "Spam, sausage, Spam, Spam, bacon, Spam, tomato, and Spam." At periodic intervals, a group of Vikings (!) starts singing "Spam, Spam, Spam, Spam," over and over again, and somewhere in there the sketch ends, or mutates into something else.

If you're really into Spam (of the non-computer type), visit Dan Garcia's wonderfully goofy Spam Homepage (`www.cs.berkeley.edu/~ddgarcia/spam.html`). Among the page's many odes to Spam is the complete text of the Monty Python sketch—still hilarious after all these years.

Examples of Spam

You know spam when you see it—and it can take many forms. Just to give you a few examples, here are some of the headers and content of the different spam messages currently taking up space in my personal inbox:

- $50 Savings Bond with Your .US Domain (new domain names)
- %^% How to Get Hundreds of Fresh Leads!!!! (25 million e-mail addresses for only $150)
- 90 XXX Sites (adult Web sites)
- ADV: It Will Be Too Late Soon… (mortgage refinancing)
- ADV: Wall Street Bulletin (stock recommendations)
- Attention Home Owners (mortgage refinancing)
- Confirming Your FREE Welcome Gift (ad for magazine subscription)
- EASILY Lose Weight * Build Muscle (human growth hormone)
- FREE Money Making Magazine (magazine subscription)
- Free Mortgage Loan Analysis (mortgage refinancing)
- Funny Cartoons (human growth hormone and herbal Viagra)
- Get a Low Interest Loan or Mortgage! (mortgage refinancing)
- Great Gifts for Mom & FREE SHIPPING! (ad from online retailer)
- Interest Rates Have Never Been Lower (mortgage refinancing)
- Interest Rates Won't Remain Low Forever (mortgage refinancing)
- Joke-of-the-Day! (human growth hormone and herbal Viagra)
- Keep Your Resolution, Get Ready for a Great Surprise (human growth hormone)
- Over 40…The Sooner, The Better (human growth hormone)
- Processing Judicial Judgements (training course in "How to Collect Money Judgments")
- Recess for Grownups (online gambling)
- Retire with Money in the Bank (multilevel marketing)
- SEND This FREE Crystal Set to Your MOTHER for Her DAY (enticement to fill in market research form)
- Service is Free for Borrowers (mortgage refinancing)

- Special Prices on Viagra, Phentermine, and Other Drugs (Viagra, etc.)

- TRIPLE YOUR SALES, ACCEPT CREDIT CARDS! (merchant credit card accounts)

What can we learn from this list of spam—other than maybe I should be refinancing my home mortgage and taking human growth hormone? It's that spam typically advertises the kind of goods and services that don't quite fit within mainstream retailing. When you peruse spam messages, you find a lot of shady come-ons and get-rich-quick schemes, promoting goods and services that are often dealt with under the counter instead of over it.

The spam messages you receive also can vary tremendously in sophistication. Some of the spam you receive is fairly simple—a plain text message, perhaps with a link to a related Web site, like that shown in Figure 27.1. Other spam is much more elaborate, like that in Figure 27.2, with graphically intense HTML messages, complete with buttons and links and all sorts of things to click. Of course, when you click—or reply to the message via e-mail—you're hooked. Be prepared for a hard sell about this particular offer, lots of pop-up windows (if you clicked through to a Web site), and lots more spam in your inbox. (That's because the spammer can now add your specific e-mail address to their database, so you can be targeted for numerous future mailings.)

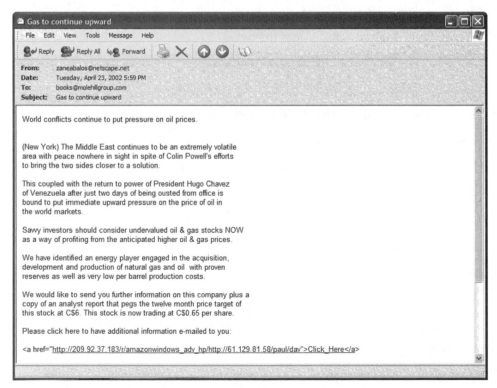

Figure 27.1 *A plain-text spam message*

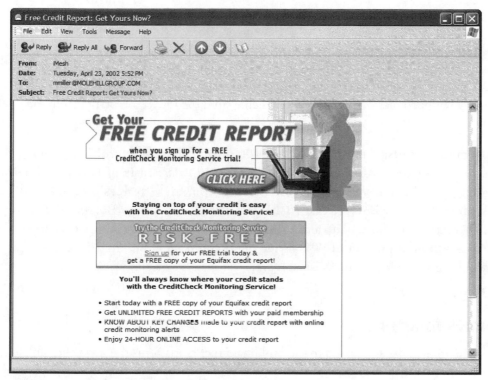

Figure 27.2 *A fancy HTML spam message—like an annoying Web page in your inbox*

How Spam Works

The process of spamming is actually fairly easy to understand. As you can see in Figure 27.3, the spammer creates his message, gathers a list of e-mail addresses, and then bulk e-mails his message to all the names on his list. The spam message then travels across the Internet to your ISP's e-mail server and eventually to your e-mail inbox.

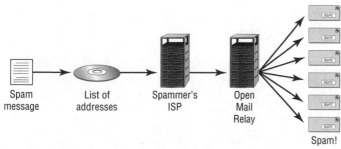

Spam   List of   Spammer's   Open
message   addresses   ISP   Mail
                                                Relay   Spam!

Figure 27.3 *A typical spam mailing*

The spammer's bulk mailing typically is routed through the e-mail server on an open mail relay (OMR). This is a separate server (*not* the e-mail server offered by the spammer's ISP) that forwards—without restriction—e-mail aimed at third parties. (It's similar in many ways to a remailer, as discussed in Chapter 26, "How to Surf—and Communicate—Anonymously.") Spammers bounce their e-mail off unsuspecting OMRs to mask the true origin of the spam; when you receive a bounced message, it looks like it came from the OMR server, not from the spammer.

NOTE *By some accounts, there are close to 100,000 of these vulnerable servers worldwide, many located in China and other Asian countries. Lists of OMRs (called blackhole lists) can be used to block e-mail coming from these servers and are kept at the Distributed Sender Boycott List (*dsbl.org*), MAPS Realtime Blackhole List (*mail-abuse.org/rbl*), and Open Relay Database (*www.ordb.org*) Web sites. Anti-spam activists estimate that up to 90% of all spam could be eliminated by closing down or blocking messages from these servers.*

Finding Names to Spam

One of the overwhelming appeals of spam to the budding direct marketer is the low cost. Unlike postal mail, where you have to put a stamp on every envelope or catalog, e-mail messages are essentially sent for free—assuming, that is, that you have the e-mail addresses to send to.

Spammers accumulate e-mail addresses through a variety of methods. Some use high-tech methods to harvest e-mail address from Web pages and Usenet newsgroup postings. Others use the tried-and-true approach of buying names from list brokers. In any case, the cost of name acquisition is kept to a minimum, so that millions of addresses are available for a fraction of a penny apiece.

NOTE *Learn more about how spammers get your e-mail address in Chapter 28, "Dealing with Spam."*

Forging Headers and Spoofing Addresses

One problem with spam, from the spammer's standpoint, is that it's becoming more and more difficult to get users to click on your particular spam message. For that reason, many spam messages try to trick you into not deleting them.

One trick is to spoof the address of a trusted institution, such as the Bank of America or eBay. (Both have been victims of this type of spoofing.) When you see an e-mail in your inbox from one of these companies, you're apt to at least look at it—and thus read the spammer's message.

How does a spammer spoof a specific address or domain? It's all in the software. There are spoofing programs available today that make it relatively easy to insert any address or domain name into the spam message's header. Some software even works interactively, inserting the recipient's address (that's you) into the sender's address field, so it looks as if the e-mail you receive is actually coming from you.

The problems posed by these types of header spoofs are obvious. By spoofing a trusted address or domain, a spam message is less likely to be filtered by spam-blocking software and services. In addition, you're more likely to open a message if it looks as if it's coming from some person or organization you know.

TIP *When a spammer spoofs the sender's e-mail address, it's called* spamouflage.

Tricking You Into Looking

Spammers are getting more and more clever. They know you're apt to hit the Delete key if you see a subject line like ADVERTISEMENT: BUY SOME OF THIS or REALLY DIRTY PICTURES INSIDE. But what if the subject line says Your mailbox is over its size limit, and appears to come from your ISP or corporate network administrator? Or how about a subject line that says Returned mail: User unknown—you'd open that up to see what message you sent got bounced, wouldn't you?

This is a step beyond the generic message lines spammers adopted for a brief while—the ones that read Here's the information you requested, or HI! REMEMBER ME? The reality is that spammers are becoming more clever in their marketing, tricking you into thinking that the spam message is actually something more important or urgent. It's their way of standing out from the flood of spam that clutters the inboxes of users today. This sort of misleading subject heading isn't illegal, although it does strain some ethical boundaries.

And, unfortunately, it often works.

Learn More About Spam

There are many organizations and Web sites dedicated to fighting the rising tide of spam e-mail. Check out the following Web sites to learn more:

- Coalition Against Unsolicited Commercial Email (`www.cauce.org`)
- EmailAbuse.org (`www.emailabuse.org`)
- Junkbusters (`www.junkbusters.com`)
- Mail Abuse Prevention System (`www.mail-abuse.org`)
- National Spam Mail Abuse Association (`www.natsma.com`)
- Network Abuse Clearinghouse (`www.abuse.net`)
- Spam.abuse.net (`spam.abuse.net`)
- ScamBusters.org (`www.scambusters.org`)
- Spam Recycling Center (`www.spamrecycle.com`)
- SpamCon Foundation (`www.spamcon.org`)
- SpamCop (`spamcop.net`)
- Spamhaus (`www.spamhaus.org`)

Why Spam Is a Problem

If you're a typical Internet user, you hate spam. A recent study by Pew Internet and American Life Project (`www.pewinternet.org`) revealed that spam led the list of Internet users' complaints; 44% of respondents said that spam was a problem, and more than half had received e-mail containing pornographic content.

Indeed, when it comes to spam, the numbers are staggering.

Research firm eMarketer (`www.emarketer.com`) estimates that the average U.S. Internet user receives twice as many e-mails as he or she sends. AT&T WorldNet, one of the largest ISPs, says that about 20% of their incoming messages are junk e-mail, nearly double the number from the previous year. The Gartner Group (`www.gartner.com`), a leading research firm, estimates that the amount of spam increased at least fivefold in 2001 alone.

According to Internet researcher Jupiter Media Metrix (`www.jmm.com`), by 2006, the amount of junk e-mail received by the average Internet user will increase to 1400 pieces each year. That's up from 700 pieces, on average, this year—and comes to a total of 206 billion individual messages.

A recent study by the European Union estimated the global cost of spam at $8.6 billion annually. According to a 1998 study from the Washington State Commercial Electronic Messages Select Task Force (what a name!), at that time, between $2 and $3 of your monthly Internet bill went to processing spam. That number is no doubt higher today; ISPs spend a lot of money processing—and fighting—spam, and those costs are passed on to you.

And here's another sign of the true cost of spam. On February 18 and 19, 2001, AT&T World-Net's e-mail system was virtually shut down, thanks to an overload of spam. The service eventually got back up and running (and all delayed e-mail was eventually sent on its way), but the damage was done.

To you as an individual, the cost of spam can't be measured in dollars and cents. Instead, it's measured in minutes and hours, the time you spend dealing with all the spam in your inbox. It's an inconvenience, and one that also threatens the viability of e-mail as a communications medium. When half the e-mail you receive is spam, how eager are you to check your inbox? How many legitimate messages do you block or delete in your quest to eliminate spam from your inbox? And when do you decide that the signal-to-noise ratio is too low, and cease using e-mail at all?

When Is Spam Not Spam?

To most users, spam is easy enough to define—it's any e-mail advertisement that shows up, unrequested, in your inbox. However, some online marketers are more selective in what they call spam.

For example, many marketers refuse to define as spam any correspondence from any company you have previously purchased from. As Jerry Cerasale, senior vice president of government affairs at the Direct Marketing Association (`www.the-dma.org`), put it:

> "It wouldn't be spam if the sender has had a prior business relationship with the consumer or he has joined a list."

So all those e-mails you get from L.L. Bean and the Sharper Image? They're not spam—at least in the eyes of the DMA. (By the DMA's definition, all those catalogs and mailers in your postal mailbox must not be junk mail, either.)

Why Companies Spam

It's a simple dynamic. Companies employ spam because it works. If it didn't work, if it didn't result in some profit above and beyond the cost, there'd be no point in using it. The very fact that spam exists tells you that someone, somewhere, is clicking through a link embedded in a spam message and entering his or her credit card number for some advertised product or service. Since the costs of sending spam are so low, all it takes to make a spam campaign worthwhile is for some small percentage of spamees to respond.

Which, unfortunately, they do.

But where did spam come from? Who first discovered the power of unsolicited commercial e-mail? Read on to learn about the history of spam—and why so many direct marketers have turned into unrelenting spammers.

The History of Spam

By most accounts, the first e-mail spam hit way back in 1978, when what was to become the Internet was then known as ARPANET. The spam was sent by DEC, one of that era's largest computer companies, to announce the release of a new computer, called the DEC-20. DEC sent e-mail to all ARPANET addresses on the west coast, which broke with existing protocol *not* to use the Net for such commercial announcements.

Over the next decade ARPANET morphed into the Internet, and the number of users increased by a staggering degree. It also created a much larger base of potential customers, if you had something to sell. Fortunately for users in the 1980s, commercial advertisements were very much frowned upon in this new communications medium.

That didn't mean that individuals couldn't use the Internet for their own personal gain, however—which is what happened on May 24, 1988. On that date, a college student named Rob Noha posted individual messages on a large number of Usenet newsgroups. His messages—with the subject HELP ME!—pleaded with other users to send money for his college fund, as he was running out of cash. There's no indication whether his pleas were heeded.

> **NOTE** *In the early days of the Internet, Usenet newsgroups were one of the primary forums for communicating with other users—and were much more integral to the Internet then than they are today.*

In 1991, the age-old concept of the chain letter first reared its annoying head on the Internet. Using a series of e-mail messages, forwarded from one user to another, the "dying kid" hoax took form. This was a chain letter about a sick boy named Craig Shergold who wanted to amass enough business cards to set a world record. The chain mailing was almost immediately identified as a hoax, but a lot of business cards got sent to a small hospital in England—and the chain letter, incredibly, still circulates to this day.

> **NOTE** *Learn more about Craig Shergold, chain letters, and Internet hoaxes in Chapter 29, "Dealing with Other Unwanted E-mails."*

In 1993, a chain letter with the subject MAKE MONEY FAST made the rounds of various Usenet newsgroups and e-mail mailing lists. This was a classic "send $5 to make $50,000" pyramid scheme, initially attributed to a user named Dave Rhodes. (Subsequent versions of this chain letter came from a variety of different sources.) Untold numbers of users sent five-dollar bills to the names on the list; few, if any, received any money in return.

The first mass e-mailing to be called spam was actually a mistake. Early in 1993, a user named Richard Depew suggested some changes to the structure of Usenet—in particular, he had developed software that would moderate the content of Usenet newsgroups. On March 31, he tested this software, and accidentally posted 200 messages in a row to the news.admin.policy group. This proliferation of similar messages reminded some of the "Spam, Spam, Spam, Spam" of the Monty Python skit, and so the phenomenon got a name.

The first all-newsgroup spam happened on January 18, 1994, when an unidentified student fired off a posting to all Usenet newsgroups, with the subject Global Alert for All: Jesus is Coming Soon. While this wasn't an ad, it was the first time that the same message had been posted to all Usenet newsgroups, simultaneously. No matter which group you visited, you saw the same message. It started a trend.

While these small-scale spams were the first true spams, the first large commercial spam came on April 12, 1994. That was when Laurence Canter and Martha Siegel, two technology-savvy immigration lawyers from Scottsdale, Arizona, flooded all 6000 Usenet newsgroups with a spam known as the "Green Card Lottery." This spam message advertised the services of their law firm for obtaining green cards for immigrants; Canter and Siegel purportedly generated close to $200,000 from the mailing.

Canter's scheme might seem like small potatoes today, but back then it was a major deal. Believe it or not, advertising was not tolerated on Usenet newsgroups, nor was the type of cross-posting that let a single message appear on multiple groups.

The reaction to the "Green Card Lottery" was extreme. Loyal Internet users of the time didn't want their playground sullied by this type of crass commercialism and responded with tens of thousands of flame e-mails, along with a few mail bombs lobbed in Canter and Siegel's general direction. That resulted in Canter and Siegel's e-mail server crashing more than 15 times over the following few weeks, which led to their ISP terminating their account.

Usenetters didn't like it, but the "Green Card Lottery" was the start of a very disturbing trend. Other marketers took Canter and Siegel's lead and began to think of the Internet as the new frontier in direct marketing.

NOTE *The "Green Card Lottery" spam led to further profit for Canter and Siegel, who wrote a book titled* How to Make a Fortune on the Information Superhighway: Everyone's Guerrilla Guide to Marketing on the Internet and Other Online Services. *(It's no longer in print, sorry.)*

By 1995, spam had pretty much migrated from Usenet to the realm of e-mail. (Not that Usenet became devoid of spam; today, many newsgroups are so overrun with junk messages as to be virtually unusable.) Spammers started sending out millions of e-mails at a time, thanks to newly developed spam software and the availability of millions of e-mail addresses on CD-ROM. The number of spam messages began to increase faster than the number of new Internet users, with the rate of increase speeding up over time. Today, spam is a fact of everyday Internet life, to the degree that some states have enacted anti-spam legislation—and the Federal government is considering ways to block the onslaught of junk messages.

And still it comes.

The Costs of Spam Marketing

Spam is popular among direct marketers because it's cheap. In an age where a first-class letter costs 37 cents to mail, the incremental cost of sending a spam e-mail message is close to zero. The only costs to the spammer are those fixed costs of setting up the campaign; it doesn't matter whether he sends five or five million messages. (In fact, the spammer is encouraged to send out more messages to more quickly recover his fixed costs.)

What are those fixed costs?

First, the spammer has to obtain a list of names. While the more sophisticated spammers employ spambots and other high-tech methods of trolling for and generating e-mail addresses, the old low-tech method of buying addresses is still used by many. It's also a cheap way to get started; you can buy a CD containing more than 20 million e-mail addresses for under $200.

Then the spammer has to find an e-mail server.

As stated previously, many spammers siphon bandwidth from insecure e-mail servers or open mail relays, typically overseas. (Asia is a big problem region, relaying—by some accounts— up to 90% of all spam received in the U.S.) Since these servers are insecure, the spammer uses the server at no cost—and relatively anonymously. This helps to keep the costs of a spam campaign low, making even a minimally successful campaign profitable.

How to Block Spam

If you have an inbox full of spam, you'd probably like to block some of those junk e-mail messages. While it can be done, spam blocking is less than 100% effective—and comes with its own set of problems.

NOTE *Learn more about blocking spam in Chapter 28.*

How Spam Blocking Works

To keep spam from hitting your inbox, you have to somehow identify spam messages and then block them. To that end, there are two different types of spam blocking: content filtering and block lists.

Content Filtering

Content filtering blocks e-mail based on specific words and phrases in the message text. Each message is searched for a list of specific words and phrases—"incredible offer," "buy today," and so on. Any messages containing the verboten phrases are blocked.

Block Lists

Block lists block mail from specific addresses and domains. You can create your own block lists from the addresses of the spam you personally receive, or you can use block lists assembled from third parties. For example, the Mail Abuse Prevention System (MAPS) and Spamhaus both create block lists that list IP addresses known for sending spam.

Block lists can block individual addresses or complete domains. For example, if you think that you're getting too much spam from the spamyou.com domain, you can block all e-mail from any address originating from spamyou.com. You can even block all messages coming from a specific country; you could block, for example, all British e-mail by blocking the complete .uk domain.

The block list method is the most-used method of spam blocking today.

Issues and Challenges

There are two main problems with trying to block all spam from arriving in your inbox—you can't catch all of it, and you might block some good e-mail with the bad.

It Isn't Effective Enough

No matter what type of anti-spam software or service you use, the spammers somehow manage to stay one step ahead—and keep from getting blocked. It's almost as if there's a technological "arms race" between the spam filters and the spammers. As soon as one company figures out a way to block a certain type of spam, the spammers figure out how to get around the block.

For example, content filters might be employed to block all messages containing the word "sex." Spammers can get around this prohibition by using the words "s e x" (note the spaces), "s-e-x" (note the hyphens), or "ssexx" (note the intentional misspelling).

The reality is that no spam blocker can block 100% of your incoming spam messages. (The makers of SpamKiller, for example, admit that their software is designed to catch 97% of mass e-mails—*not* 100%.) So no matter how good the blocker, some spam will get through.

It Blocks Legitimate Messages

A bigger problem is that spam blockers are often overzealous, blocking good messages along with the bad. This is especially the case with block lists, that block out all the messages coming from a particular domain. This blocks the spammer's e-mail, but it also blocks any e-mail coming from that domain that isn't spam. It's like throwing the baby out with the bathwater; to block the spam, you risk missing legitimate messages coming from the same domain.

For this reason, many individuals and companies refuse to use spam blockers. The cost of accidentally blocking one important message is higher than the cost of dealing with thousands of spam messages. Better safe than sorry, the logic goes—and many users agree.

Overzealous Spam Blocking: A Personal Example

I'll provide a personal example of overzealous spam blocking, one I promised my editor I'd include in this book. It illustrates how crude today's anti-spam technology really is—and it's pretty funny.

One Monday morning I sent an e-mail to my editor at Sybex, the publisher of this book. The e-mail was about this book, which, as you know, is a book about viruses, security, and spam.

The e-mail came back, undelivered. It was accompanied by a message indicating that the Sybex e-mail server doesn't receive messages from servers listed on the MAPS Realtime Blackhole List. My e-mail was being blocked.

I tried again and got the message back again. Then I picked up the phone, called my editor, and told her I'd been having trouble sending e-mail to her. She mentioned that her inbox had been surprisingly empty that morning, and suggested I talk to the company's chief IT person.

When I talked to the IT guy, I told him my problem and asked if Sybex had recently employed a spam blocking service. Yes, he said, they activated it over the weekend.

Aha, I replied. Apparently the spam-blocking service is blocking my legitimate e-mail.

We spent the next few minutes exchanging IP numbers and other technical information, then the IT person discovered the problem. It appeared that the service I used to host my e-mail account was reported as having 85% or so of the messages sent from its servers classified as spam. (That doesn't mean that 85% of its *users* were spammers, of course; all that spam could have come from one heavy spammer, with all the other users being legitimate.) Since this service had such a high percentage of spam messages, it was placed on a spam block list, and all messages from all of its users were blocked.

I have no doubt that this cut down on the amount of spam received by my publisher. However, as I informed the IT person, it also blocked my legitimate non-spam messages. And how, I asked, was the publisher going to publish my book (a book about spam, to add to the irony) if they blocked all my e-mails?

Continued on next page

Overzealous Spam Blocking: A Personal Example *(Continued)*

It took the better part of a day, but the IT person finally arrived at the solution of editing the spam block list to allow my particular domain. (Or maybe he just removed my e-mail hosting service from the list—I'm still not quite sure.) In any case, Sybex no longer blocks my e-mails, and they've been receiving the manuscript of this book just fine.

And now you know how a spam-blocking service almost caused a book about spam not to be published!

Summing Up

Spam—unsolicited commercial e-mail—is a major problem. The average Internet user receives at least two spam messages a day, and that number is rapidly growing.

The more spam clogs your inbox, the harder it is to manually deal with. You can employ spam-blocking software to filter out unwanted messages, but this software is not 100% effective—and it can also accidentally block legitimate e-mail.

Spammers spam because it's a relatively low-cost way to reach millions of people with an advertising message. Spammers can buy millions of names and e-mail addresses for a few hundred dollars and then use "leaky" mail servers to send their messages across the Internet for next to nothing. Even a few users replying to a spam campaign can make that campaign worthwhile.

In the next chapter you'll learn more about how spammers obtain names and e-mail addresses, the steps you can take to keep your contact information out of the hands of spammers, and steps you can take to minimize the amount of spam in your personal inbox.

CHAPTER 28

Dealing with Spam

S pam sucks. It's a major annoyance, and it interferes with your ability to manage and read your normal e-mail messages.

So how do you deal with it?

It's probably impossible to completely eliminate spam from your inbox. You can, however, minimize the amount of spam you receive, without completely disrupting your daily e-mail routine. Read on to learn how to manage your spam and reclaim your inbox as your own.

Where Spammers Get Your Address

To keep your e-mail address out of the hands of spammers, you need to know how spammers assemble their lists of potential victims. Armed with this knowledge, you can more easily avoid being captured in their nets.

When it comes to capturing names and e-mail addresses, spammers are incredibly creative. Here are a few of the ways they assemble their lists.

NOTE *Spam addresses can come from anywhere. For example, I know I receive some amount of spam through the e-mail addresses I publish in all my books. One of my previous books for Sybex (Discovering Bluetooth) was recently translated into Japanese, with a unique e-mail address listed in the introduction. Just days after the publication of the Japanese edition, I started to receive Japanese-language spam to that book's unique e-mail address—proof positive that spammers at least can read!*

Buy the Names

Probably the easiest way to obtain e-mail addresses for a spam mailing is to buy them. Spammers can purchase commercial CD-ROMs containing tens of millions of names and addresses for just a few hundred dollars, then use these names for their mailings. (Many spam mailings are in fact advertising these "spam name" CD-ROMs.)

In addition, many legitimate Web sites sell lists of their members' names and addresses to third parties—just as real-world magazines and catalogs sell their mailing lists to other companies. While this type of activity is prohibited by some sites' privacy policies, other sites have no qualms about selling to the highest bidder any and all information you provide.

The bottom line is that whenever you provide your name and e-mail address to a Web site— whether you're buying something or just registering to use the site—you're increasing your chances of ending up on a spam mailing list.

NOTE *Companies in the business of buying and selling mailing lists are called* list merchants.

Harvest Names from the Internet

More sophisticated spammers use automated software—called *spambots*—to scour the Internet for publicly available e-mail addresses. These e-mail addresses can come from a variety of sources, including:

- Web pages (most Web pages—even personal pages—include some sort of contact address)

- Public directories of usernames and addresses, like those found on Yahoo! (Yahoo! Profiles) and those sites that host personal Web pages

- Web-based public message boards

- Usenet newsgroup postings

- IRC and Web-based chat rooms

Probably the most popular approach uses spambots to scour the major Web search sites (Google, Yahoo!, and so on) for e-mail addresses. If your e-mail address is on a Web page that is listed at the search site, it's available to the spambot via a quick search of the search engine.

NOTE *By the way, just because you receive sex-related spam doesn't mean you've actually visited an adult Web site. The source of the spam address seldom has any relationship to the content of the spam message.*

Trick You Into Providing Your Own Name

Some spammers are tricky. They'll try to con you into providing them with your e-mail address, which they can then use for future e-mailings.

For example, many spammers send out "blind" spams to all the possible addresses in a given domain (see "Make Up the Name," next), asking you to reply to the message. When you reply, the spammer scrapes your address off the reply e-mail and adds it to their database of valid addresses. (A similar method retrieves all the addresses from messages sent to the "unsubscribe" link in many spam messages.)

Even trickier are those spammers that lure you to a bogus Web site that asks for your e-mail address and other information, purportedly to register for the site or obtain some free gift. When you fill in the form—sometimes disguised as a survey—you provide your e-mail address for future spam mailings.

Make Up the Name

One of the most-used means of generating e-mail addresses today is the *dictionary spam*. This type of spam occurs when the spammer uses special software to guess every possible name in a given domain. For example, the spammer might start sending e-mail to `aaa@thisdomain.com` and end with a message to `zzz@thisdomian.com`. More sophisticated dictionary spammers make sure to include all known given names (and possible first- and last-name combinations) so if you have a common name at a major ISP—for example, `mike@aol.com` or `jimbrown@att.com`—you're likely to get hit with an inordinate amount of spam.

Use Spyware

Finally, spammers conceivably can retrieve your e-mail address by installing packet-sniffing or keyboard logger spyware on your computer. This software captures the information you send or the keystrokes you enter—either of which could contain your e-mail address—and then feeds that information back to a central source.

Fortunately, this method is little used; there are easier ways to harvest e-mail addresses.

NOTE *Learn more about spyware in Chapter 23, "Defeating Spyware."*

Easy Measures

You don't have to take crazy steps to get rid of spam. In fact, the easiest and most effective way to deal with spam is to simply ignore it.

Let's look, then, at some of the easiest things you can do to minimize the amount of spam you receive.

Don't Respond

Many spammers get your address when you give it to them. When you receive a spam message in your inbox, don't respond to it—period. Don't click through to the spammer's Web site. Don't buy anything advertised in spam e-mail. Don't mess with the message at all. Just delete it. It's when you reply that they harvest your e-mail address; don't reply, and they're left empty-handed. If no user anywhere in the world responded to spam, it would eventually cease to exist. The best thing to do is automatically delete any spam you receive—and gain your satisfaction from hitting that Delete key.

By the way—and this should go without saying—many of the offers sent via spam are bogus. Don't be surprised if you purchase something via a spam ad and then never receive the item. Not that *all* spammers are also crooks, but a lot of them are. Spam is a precursor to online fraud, which is another good reason never to respond to a spam message.

Don't Unsubscribe

You should also resist the temptation to click the link found on some spam that promises to remove you from the spammer's mailing list. In almost all cases, clicking this link will *not* remove your name—it will, in fact, *add* your name to their list. Remember, many spam addresses are generated automatically, which means that the spammer actually doesn't have your real address on file. Until, that is, you do the spammer the favor of delivering your address on a platter by clicking that "please remove" link.

> **NOTE** *A recent experiment by the FTC had staffers reply to "unsubscribe" links in 215 e-mail messages. Two-thirds of the "unsubscribe" messages actually went nowhere, routed to either nonexistent or already shutdown e-mail addresses.*

Don't Give Out Your E-mail Address—Any More Than You Have To

To cut down on spam, make sure as few people as possible know your e-mail address. The more you expose your e-mail address, the more likely it is that a spammer will find it—and use it. If the spammers don't know where you are, they can't bother you much. What you want is the online equivalent of an unlisted phone number. While it might be impossible to have a totally anonymous e-mail address, there are ways to minimize your exposure to spammers, and thus decrease the amount of spam that you receive.

Here's a list of big no-nos when it comes to keeping your e-mail address private:

- *Don't* fill out Web-based registration forms.
- *Don't* fill out online surveys.
- *Don't* include your e-mail address when you post on Usenet newsgroups and public message board.
- *Don't* put your e-mail address on your Web site or your company's Web site.
- *Don't* add your name and e-mail address to any user directory at your ISP or elsewhere.
- *Don't* include your e-mail address in any signatures you attach to IRC or chat room.

TIP *You may need to alter the account settings in your newsgroup reader so that your real e-mail address isn't automatically included with Usenet newsgroup postings.*

In short, don't post your e-mail address in any public environment.

It also pays to minimize the amount of e-mail you send to public companies. If you need to contact a company, instead of sending an e-mail, look for a Web-based comments form on the company's Web site instead. These forms enable you to leave your comments or request without sending e-mail—and thus providing your e-mail address for future spam-related purposes.

Don't Use Common Names in Your Address

Dictionary spam adds common names to popular Internet domains to "guess" at valid e-mail addresses. For this reason, the address bob@myisp.com will receive more spam than b2qb475@myisp.com. So learn from the dictionary spammers and create an e-mail address that looks as random as possible; it'll be harder to guess.

Moderate Measures

The previous measures were easy to implement; in fact, most of them involved *not* doing something.

If you want to block even more spam from your inbox, there are an additional set of measures you can employ. These measures require a bit more work on your part, but they shouldn't inconvenience you—too much.

Use Your ISP's Spam-Blocking Features

Many Internet service providers provide their own spam-blocking services. Some ISPs activate their spam blocking automatically, in the background; others provide a set of tools you can choose to use on the e-mail you personally receive. To cut down on the spam you receive, you should avail yourself of your ISP's spam blocking.

For example, if you're an America Online subscriber, you can use AOL's Mail Controls to block e-mail from all non-AOL addresses or from all addresses save those you've specified. Just follow these steps:

1. Select Mail ➤ Mail Controls.

2. When the Mail Controls window appears, select the Customize Mail Controls for This Screen Name option, then click Next.

3. When the People and Places screen appears (shown in Figure 28.1), select one of the following options:

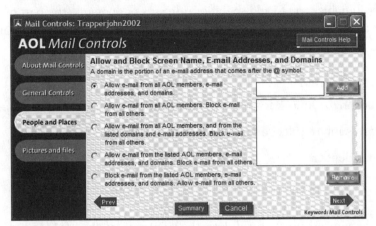

Figure 28.1 *Spam blocking with AOL*

- Allow E-mail from All AOL Members, E-mail Addresses, and Domains (lets all e-mail through; no blocking)

- Allow E-mail from All AOL Members. Block E-mail from All Others (only lets messages from AOL members through; blocks all non-AOL member e-mail)

- Allow E-mail from All AOL Members, and From the Listed Domains and E-mail Addresses. Block E-mail from All Others (lets messages from all AOL members through, and lets you select specific non-AOL addresses and domains *not* to block)

- Allow E-mail from the Listed AOL Members, E-mail Addresses, and Domains. Block E-mail from All Others (blocks all e-mail except for those addresses and domains you specify)

- Block E-mail from the Listed AOL Members, E-mail Addresses, and Domains. Allow E-mail from All Others (lets you specify which addresses and domains you want to block)

4. Click Summary.

5. Click Save.

Other ISPs have similar features, although they're not often well publicized. If in doubt, check with your ISP's technical support department to find out what spam-blocking services they offer.

Use Your E-mail Program's Spam Filter

Many e-mail programs include their own spam-blocking features. For example, Outlook Express includes a crude spam filter that enables you to add specific addresses or domains (the part of the address after the @) to a Blocked Senders List; any further e-mail from that person or domain is routed directly to Outlook Express' Delete folder.

Blocking Senders in Outlook Express

To add a sender or a sender's domain to Outlook Express' Blocked Senders List, follow these steps:

1. From the Outlook Express inbox, select a message from a sender you want to block.

2. Select Message ➤ Block Sender.

WARNING *Outlook Express doesn't actually block any e-mail messages; the messages are still received by your computer, but are sent immediately to the Delete folder—where they can be viewed until you delete the contents of that folder.*

You can also manually add names and domains to the Blocked Senders List. Follow these steps:

1. Select Tools ➤ Message Rules ➤ Blocked Senders List.

2. When the Message Rules dialog box appears, make sure the Blocked Senders tab is selected (shown in Figure 28.2), then click the Add button.

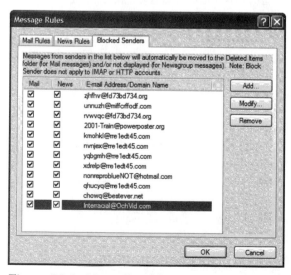

Figure 28.2 *Manually adding names to the Blocked Senders List*

3. When the Add Sender dialog box appears, enter the full address or domain name that you want to block, then select the Mail Messages option.

4. Click OK.

Removing Blocked Senders in Outlook Express

You can also edit the Blocked Senders List to resume receiving messages from a blocked sender. Follow these steps:

1. Select Tools ➤ Message Rules ➤ Blocked Senders List.

2. When the Message Rules dialog box appears, make sure the Blocked Senders tab is selected.

3. Uncheck the name or domain you want to remove.

4. Click OK.

Use a Spamblock in Your E-mail Address

If you do have to leave your e-mail address in a public forum, you can leave it in a way that will trick most spambot software. All you have to do is insert a *spamblock* into your address—a foreign word or phrase that will cause spambots to add a bogus address to their database. For example, if your e-mail address is `johnjones@myisp.com`, you might change the address to read `johnSPAMBLOCKjones@myisp.com`. The benefit of using a spamblock is not only that it foils spambots, but also that real human beings—people you *want* to contact you—can typically figure out your real e-mail address (by removing the spamblock) and still send you personal e-mail if they like.

Create Two Separate E-mail Addresses

As you have probably personally experienced, the longer you keep the same e-mail address, the more spam you receive. That's because your address gets known to more and more spammers, and you enter your address at more and more Web sites and on more and more message boards. And once your name has been compromised, it's out there—there's no way to remove your name from a spammer's list.

If you're resigned to the fact that you're going to get spam, there is still hope. If you establish two separate e-mail accounts, you can direct all your spam messages to the first account and keep the second account clear for private messages.

The way to do this is to create a Web-based e-mail account (typically at Hotmail or Yahoo! Mail), and use it for all your public postings and Web site registrations; use your other address only for private e-mail correspondence. Your public e-mail account will be a magnet for all potential spam, while your private account will stay private and relatively spam free.

Use Anti-Spam Software

When you're really overwhelmed by spam, it's time to take more drastic measures—in the form of anti-spam software. Most anti-spam software uses some combination of spam blocking or content filtering to keep spam messages from ever reaching your inbox; their effectiveness varies, but they will decrease the amount of spam you receive, to some degree.

The most popular anti-spam software includes the following:

ANT 4 MailChecking (ant4.com)   Combination of spam e-mail filter and notification.

E-mail Chomper (www.sarum.com/echomp.html)   Lets you delete unwanted mail without downloading it to your PC.

MailWasher (www.mailwasher.net)   Lets you view, delete, and bounce unwanted e-mail messages.

RoadBlock (www.roadblock.net)   Enables you to view waiting e-mail before downloading to your e-mail client and delete spam before it hits your PC.

Spam Buster (members.aol.com/contplus4/spambuster)   Freeware spam-blocking program.

Spambam (www.epage.com.au/spambam)   Sits between your e-mail client and your e-mail server to filter and block spam messages.

SpamEater Pro (www.hms.com/spameater.asp)   Goes online to your ISP's e-mail server and checks all messages found there—before you download them to your regular e-mail program.

SpamKiller (www.spamkiller.com)   Lets you block messages by sender's address, message subject, or message text. (SpamKiller was recently acquired by McAfee.com.)

SpamScan (www.webster-image.com/SpamScan97)   Lets you filter messages containing advertising text, adult subjects, and other junk.

SpamKiller, shown in Figure 28.3, is one of the most popular anti-spam programs. You configure the program to connect directly to your ISP, where it checks messages before they're downloaded to your e-mail program. When you view a message in SpamKiller, you can choose to add the sender to your Friends list (which isn't blocked) or to your list of filtered addresses. You can also click the Complain button to trace the message and send an automatic complaint letter to the sender's ISP.

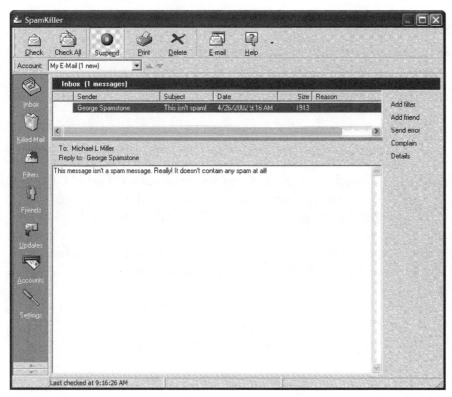

Figure 28.3 *Filtering spam with SpamKiller software*

Use a Spam Filtering Service

If anti-spam software isn't powerful enough for you, you can subscribe to one of the several online services that interactively block spam, using a variety of filtering and blocking techniques. Many of these services are also available for small business and large corporate networks; most are priced on a per-month subscription basis.

Here are some of the more popular spam-filtering services:

- Brightmail (`www.brightmail.com`)

- Emailias (`www.emailias.com`)

- Mailshell (`www.mailshell.com`)

- SpamCop (`spamcop.net`)

- SpamMotel (`www.spammotel.com`)

Extreme Measures

If you're really obsessive about eliminating the spam menace, there are more aggressive steps you can take. The following measures will not only decrease your personal spam problem, they'll also turn you into an anti-spam activist, working to wipe spam from the face of the Earth.

Change Your Identity

This is a fairly extreme step—but sometimes necessary. If your e-mail address is so polluted with spam as to be unusable, it's time to kill that address and start over from scratch. Cancel the problem e-mail account, and start over with a new, clean account. Follow the advice mentioned previously in this chapter about choosing a name that isn't prone to dictionary spam, and then keep this new account completely private.

At the same time, create a second, public account (also discussed previously) to use for all your public correspondence and registration. Use this account as your public persona, and treat your other e-mail account as a kind of secret identity.

And, if you're really paranoid, use a remailer (discussed in Chapter 26, "How to Surf—and Communicate—Anonymously") for all your outgoing mail.

If you do it right, no one will ever discover your new identity. (Or guess that Batman is secretly Bruce Wayne!)

Trace and Report

If you're aggressively anti-spam, you can take the battle to its source—by tracing the spam's sender and complaining to the spammer's Internet provider.

However, this takes some work.

You might think that you have the spammer's e-mail address—it's listed in the From field of the spam message, right? Wrong. The From address is easily spoofed and, more often than not, totally bogus. To find out the spammer's *real* address, you have to display the message header, which your e-mail program typically hides.

> **TIP** *To display header information in Outlook Express, open the message and select File ➤ Properties. When the Properties dialog box appears, select the Details tab.*

Figure 28.4 shows a typical e-mail header. The information you want is the ISP address in the Received field. (Note that many messages have multiple Received fields; use all the addresses in all the fields.)

Figure 28.4 *Displaying the header for a spam message*

You'll need this header information if you want to complain to the spammer's ISP. In fact, the best way to respond is to forward the spam message, with the header information copied into the body of the message, to each of the domains listed in From field of the header. Send the message to the following addresses, which are typically used for handling spam complaints: abuse@*domain.name* and postmaster@*domain.name*.

If there's a Web page address in the spam message, you can trace down who owns the page (and how to contact them) by performing a WHOIS lookup at the openrbl.org site (openrbl .org/trace.htm). Just enter the URL or IP address into the Whois Lookup box, then click the Lookup button. The resulting page will list who owns the domain, which service hosts the domain, and how to contact the owners. You can then contact the spammer directly with your complaint.

TIP *When you enter a URL, don't enter the* www.*, just enter the main name and domain. So, for example, if the spammer's URL is* www.imaspammer.com, *just enter* imaspammer.com.

Anti-Spam Action at the ISP Level

AOL has called junk e-mail "public enemy number one," and employs various spam-reduction utilities on its service. Other ISPs—including MSN, EarthLink, and AT&T WorldNet—have adopted various spam-filtering software for their users, as well. (BrightMail is a big favorite here.) In fact, about a third of all U.S. ISPs use block lists to refuse spam at their mail servers, before it hits subscriber inboxes.

Even better, ISPs actively guard against their services being used to send spam messages. When they receive complaints about spam coming from their domain, most ISPs act quickly to suspend or shut down the offending e-mail account. So it's worth tracing and reporting the spam you receive; the more complaints an ISP receives, the more likely it is that they'll kick the spammer off the service.

Legal Remedies

U.S. law 47 USC 227, the so-called "junk fax law," makes it a federal offense to send unsolicited advertising via fax machine. This law has dramatically reduced the problem of spam faxes, to the point where junk faxes have almost ceased to exist. Unfortunately, there is no similar federal law for junk e-mail—although that doesn't mean that there *won't* be.

There are several anti-spam proposals currently before Congress. These include the Anti-Spamming Act, which requires spammers to send accurate identifiers (non-spoofed domain, originating e-mail address, and so on) in all their messages; the CAN SPAM Act, which prohibits deceptive headers and return addresses; and the Wireless Telephone Spam Protection Act, which would ban the spamming of wireless phones via their built-in messaging systems.

Even without federal action, some individual states (California and Washington among them) have adopted their own anti-spam laws. These laws typically allow consumers to opt out of receiving spam, and—in some cases—require spammers to add the word **ADV** to the subject line of any commercial e-mail they send. Consumers can then set their spam filters to catch the **ADV** and thus block all advertising-oriented messages.

> **NOTE** *Of course, spammers can always find ways to get around the* ADV *requirement—by using* Ad V *or* A D V *instead of* ADV, *for example.*

On the national level, the FTC has been the traditional watchdog for all online scams and frauds. If you've been taken in by anyone over the Internet, the FTC is one of the first entities you should contact.

For example, the FTC just completed a two-year effort, code-named "International Net-force," which resulted in 63 cases filed against alleged cyberscammers. One of the most prominent charges was filed against a man named David L. Walker, who used an Internet site to sell products that he claimed cured cancer; he charged customers up to $5,200 for his anti-cancer program. Other cases involved fraudulent retailers, illegal chain letter schemes, and online auction fraud.

TIP *Let the government know you've been spammed! The FTC encourages users to forward their spam to the agency's junk e-mail database, at* uce@ftc.gov. *The agency has received more than 10 million forwarded spam messages since 1998.*

Naturally, spammers object to any attempts to further regulate their activities.

The Direct Marketing Association (www.the-dma.org), for example, recently notified Congress of its objection to any new legislation regarding mass e-mails. The DMA couched their objection in terms of First Amendment freedoms; the organization even opposes the forced application of ADV labels. Jerry Cerasale of the DMA said, "If the U.S. creates a regulation that says you can't send out information because it's information that I may not necessarily want to receive, that's a green light to the rest of the world that you can do that not just on commercial stuff, but on anything. That's something we have to be careful about."

Makes it sound like anyone opposing spam must be anti-American, doesn't it?

Certainly, one can see where overaggressive anti-spam legislation could conceivably interfere with the civil rights of legitimate advertisers. In this battle, there is a fine line between the privacy of the individual and the rights of the advertiser, although if you're on the receiving end, you're likely to have little sympathy for the spammers' right to clog your inbox with their "freely spoken" advertisements.

NOTE *As the author of this book, I should make known my personal opinions on this topic. While I'm an outspoken advocate of free speech and First Amendment rights, I am equally opposed to unsolicited advertisements via e-mail, fax, and telephone. I personally view such efforts as intrusions into my private space, have little sympathy for the companies doing the spamming, and support most efforts to curb these abuses.*

The Least You Need to Do

Now that you know all the steps you can take to reduce spam, which steps are absolutely necessary to take—without becoming obsessive about it?

Consider the following items a checklist for common-sense spam reduction:

- ☑ Don't reply to any spam messages you receive—and don't click the "unsubscribe" link, either.

- ☑ Don't include your e-mail address on any posting you make to a public message board or Usenet newsgroup.

- ☑ Don't include your e-mail address on your personal or company Web page.

- ☑ Create a second, "public," e-mail address to use when you have to enter your e-mail address on the Web; reserve your main e-mail address for private communication.

- ☑ Use any spam-blocking features offered by your ISP.

The bottom line is that it's very difficult, if not impossible, to stop all junk e-mails, just as it's difficult to stop postal junk mail. The best thing to do is limit the exposure of your e-mail address and learn to ignore the spam.

Summing Up

The biggest impact you can have in reducing spam is to limit the number of places you publicly post your e-mail address. That means not including your address on your Web page or in any public postings you make. You should also resist the temptation to reply to spam; responding will only increase the amount of spam you get in the future.

Further spam prevention is provided by the anti-spam services provided by many ISPs. You can also purchase spam-blocking software and subscribe to more robust spam-filtering services.

More extreme anti-spam activists can trace the source of the spam and send complaining e-mails to the spammer's ISP. Most ISPs will respond to complaints and ban suspected spammers from their systems.

Now that you know how to manage spam, how do you deal with all the other annoying e-mail messages you receive? Turn the page to learn all about e-mail hoaxes, chain letters, and urban legends—and what to do about them.

CHAPTER 29

Dealing with Other Unwanted E-mails

Not all unwanted e-mail messages come from spammers. Some of the junk that clutters your inbox comes from friends and family, who do a great job of perpetuating chain letters and other hoaxes spread via the medium of e-mail.

You know the messages I'm talking about. They typically start with the words "send this to everyone you know" and contain get-rich-quick schemes, warnings about deadly computer viruses or government plots, misinformation of various sorts, or urgent pleas to help some sick child. You're typically just one of hundreds of recipients, each of whom is urged to forward the message to dozens more users, and on and on, creating a huge amount of useless e-mail traffic across the entire Internet.

These messages, of course, are all false. They're the products of hoaxters, pranksters, or naïve Internet users falling for an old chain letter or urban legend. All they do is clog up your inbox; no one ever got rich by replying to a chain letter—and no one ever died by breaking the chain.

But in an age where too many Internet users forward every useless message to everyone in their address book, how do you deal with this onslaught of annoying e-mails—from people you know, who basically mean well? That is the focus of this chapter…and of a lot of users' attention.

Understanding Chain Letters

Annoying rumors and chain letters are nothing new. Hoaxes, urban legends, and chain letters have been around in one form or another since the invention of spoken language. (And some hoaxes have had monumental impact—remember Orson Welles' classic *War of the Worlds* radio broadcast?) Certainly all of these annoyances are still around in letter form, disseminated via the postal service.

The sole purpose of many of these letters appears to be distribution; they almost always encourage the recipient to send the letter along to additional friends and family. (In fact, you can typically recognize one of these annoyances by the enticement to "send this message to everyone you know" or something similar.) They offer good luck or a monetary reward if you send the message on to additional recipients. They prey on your fear of bad luck—or your greed—to get you to pass them on. And their content is invariably untrue.

While there are many variations, there are typically three parts to a classic chain letter: the *hook*, the *threat*, and the *request*.

The hook is dangled in front of you to get your interest and entice you to read the rest of the message. In e-mail chain letters, the hook is typically in the message subject line or in the first few lines of the message itself. Think of the hook as the headline on an advertisement—"Make Money Fast" or "Satisfy Your Lover" or some other such enticement.

Once you're hooked, it's time for the threat. The classic chain letter threat warns you of the terrible things that will happen if you break the chain. Other, less typical, threats play on your sympathy or greed to keep the message moving.

Finally, we get to the request. Some of the more aggressive messages (such as the pyramid scheme chain letter, described in more detail in the "Scams" section, later in this chapter) request that you send a dollar to all the names listed in the letter. More typical chain letters simply request that you forward the message to five or ten or some other number of people. The whole goal is to spread the scam; no money changes hands.

Types of Chain Letters

There are many different types of chain letters that are disseminated via e-mail. Almost all of these types have real-world counterparts; in fact, many online chain letters and hoaxes had their start in postal or fax or even word-of-mouth versions.

The following sections, then, examine the three predominant types of e-mail chain letters: the classic chain, the hoax, and the urban legend.

The Classic Chain

The classic chain letter is very simple. A message is forwarded to you. The message can contain just about any type of text—a short story, a prayer, or a wish for good health. You're encouraged to forward the message to X number of people. If you *don't* forward the message, and therefore break the chain, something bad will happen to you. (Some messages even provide examples of bad luck happening to chain breakers.) If, on the other hand, you do forward the message, you'll receive all sorts of good luck. (Again, examples are often provided.) Since you don't want bad luck, you forward the message.

Here are some examples of the classic chain letter:

Good Luck!   This is a very typical classic chain letter. It's a plain text message, claiming that it's been sent to you for good luck. The message has (purportedly) been around the world nine times (or so), and the luck has now been sent to you. You'll receive good luck within four days (or so) after you receive the message—provided that you pass it on within 96 hours (or so). The message then typically goes on to list the good things that have happened to people who passed on the letter—as well as the bad things that happened to people who didn't.

The Chain Letter Protection Pact   This is a different kind of chain letter that purports to protect you against future chain letters. You're supposed to pass on this chain letter to other people, with the promise that you won't send them any more chain letters. (Whoever sent it to you also makes this promise.) The natural illogic of a chain letter to end chain letters apparently escapes the people who perpetuate this particular chain.

Hoaxes

A hoax is a type of chain letter that contains deliberately falsified or fabricated information. Like the classic chain, the point of a hoax is to disseminate it as widely as possible—with the side benefit of convincing large numbers of people of the misleading information that is part of the hoax.

We talked about a specific type of hoax, the virus hoax, in Chapter 8, "Virus Hoaxes." Here are some examples of other types of hoaxes, from the false information hoax to the interesting category of hoax warnings.

False Information

Put this type of hoax in the "spreading rumors" category. These messages purport to disseminate some important piece of news or information—except that the information is either partly or totally false. Here are some examples of false information hoaxes:

9/11 Contributions   According to this bit of misinformation, American automakers have contributed beaucoup dollars to various post-9/11 charities, while their foreign competitors have contributed nada. (This is all in an effort to encourage users to buy American.) The facts, however, state that both domestic and foreign carmakers have made large contributions to a number of 9/11 funds; there's no nationalistic insensitivity here.

Hanoi Jane   This old chestnut started recirculating in the wake of the 9/11 terrorist attacks and the resultant upsurge in patriotic fervor. The message purports to detail Jane Fonda's anti-American activities during the Vietnam War, but plays fast and loose with the facts. While Ms. Fonda did visit North Vietnam in 1972, she did not (as the hoax claims) turn over POW messages to their captors or have a POW beaten for spitting at her.

Nostradamus and the Terrorist Attacks   This hoax comes with a list of unsettling quatrains, supposedly from the 17th century seer Nostradamus, that appear to predict the 9/11 terrorist attacks on the World Trade Center. The only problem is, these predictions didn't come from Nostradamus; they're totally made up, after the fact.

TWA Flight 800   Remember the crash of TWA Flight 800 on July 17, 1996? The jet crashed shortly after takeoff, off the coast of Long Island. This hoax purports to tell the "true" story of the crash, that "TWA Flight 800 was SHOT DOWN by a U.S. NAVY AEGIS MISSILE fired from a guided missile ship." The truth is being covered up by the FBI, the message alleges; you can help spread the true story by forwarding the message. Of course, the National Transportation Safety Board (NTSB) discredits this theory and says the crash was caused by an explosion in one of the plane's fuel tanks.

The Vonnegut Speech   This hoax purports to detail a speech that author Kurt Vonnegut supposedly gave to the graduating class of MIT. The speech, as reprinted in the e-mail message, sounds a lot like Vonnegut; it has the same wry humor and weary cynicism. The problem is, Vonnegut never gave a commencement address at MIT. The supposed speech is actually a newspaper column by Mary Schmich, of the *Chicago Tribune*. And so it goes.

WTC Tourist   This is a particularly fascinating hoax. The misinformation comes in the form of a photograph that purports to show a tourist standing on the top of one of the World Trade Centers just seconds before one of the hijacked planes slammed into the building. It's all a hoax, however; it's just something that someone put together in Adobe Photoshop. (Interestingly, a whole cult has sprung up around the "WTC Tourist"—also known as "Waldo." Check out Waldo's official site at www.waldoconspiracy.com for more faked pictures; my personal favorite shows Waldo with a certain Nazi dictator...)

Giveaways

This type of hoax promises some sort of valuable giveaway by a large company. If you forward the message, you're informed, the big company will send you money, merchandise, a free vacation, or something similar. Exactly how the company knows if you forward the e-mail (e-mail tracking isn't that advanced!) is never stated.

Here are some examples of giveaway hoaxes:

Applebee's Gift Certificates   This hoax promises you a $50 gift certificate from Applebee's if you forward the e-mail to nine other people. Sorry, folks—no free food is forthcoming.

Disney and Gates   This hoax relates an "exciting experiment" that Bill Gates (of Microsoft fame) and Walt Disney Jr. (of... well, you figure it out) will give you money to test. If 13,000 people help test Gates' new "Beta Email Tracking Application" (BETA, for short), the first 1300 respondents will receive $5000 each, and the balance will receive free trips to Disney World. All you have to do is send the message to everyone you know; the "BETA" will do the rest. Naturally, there is no such beast, and neither Gates nor Disney are that generous with their money.

Neiman Marcus Cookie Recipe   This hoax comes in the form of a recipe for chocolate-chip cookies. The message is purportedly from a customer of the Neiman Marcus department store chain. The person supposedly asked for and received a recipe for Neiman Marcus' delicious cookies. However, the company billed her $250 for the recipe, and now the lady wants revenge. So she's sending the recipe to as many people as possible, in an effort to make Neiman Marcus' recipe worthless. The only problem, of course, is that Neiman Marcus didn't (at the time) sell chocolate-chip cookies. (They've since added cookies to their product mix, in honor of the hoax.)

Kids

There are lots of hoaxes involving kids—enough to warrant their own subcategory. The typical kid-related hoax involves a sick or dying child, and preys on your sympathy to work. Other kid-related hoaxes turn on alleged class projects; again, the hoaxter assumes that you'll be sympathetic to any request coming from a youngster.

Some of the more popular of these kid-related hoaxes include:

The Class Project   This e-mail purports to come from a teacher or a class of students at some grade school or middle school. The class is participating in a project to see how far around the world their e-mail will carry. You're encouraged to e-mail back with your location and forward the message "to everyone you know;" the class will then map all their responses. Naturally, there is no such project or class or school; it's just another hoax.

The Dying Kid   This letter supposedly comes from a seven-year-old British boy named Craig Shergold, who is dying from cancer. Craig is trying to collect as many business cards as possible before he dies and asks you to send your business card to a specific address. There's a bit of truth behind this hoax; there really was a Craig Shergold, and he really did have cancer, and he really did collect cards (get-well cards, actually)—back in 1989. He collected so many that he was recognized by the *Guinness Book of World Records*. He's not collecting anymore, however; he survived his bout with cancer and is now a healthy 20-year-old. (This scam keeps on scamming; newer versions replace Craig Shergold with other terminally ill children—and sometimes ask for cash donations instead of business cards.)

Make-a-Wish   This hoax is similar to the dying kid hoax, only this time it's the Make-a-Wish Foundation of Phoenix that's collecting cards for a dying child. While the Make-a-Wish Foundation exists, the dying child doesn't—and the Foundation doesn't want any more of your cards, thanks.

Warnings

There are a lot of hoax warnings floating around the Internet. These are messages that warn about either inconsequential or nonexistent problems. (Virus hoaxes fit in this category.) Many of these hoax warnings play on age-old urban legends; others perpetuate themselves to a degree that they eventually become urban legends.

Examples of hoax warnings include:

Gel Candles Explode   This is a scary one. The message relates an incident that happened to someone the sender purportedly knows; that person had a gel candle burning in her bathroom, which exploded and burned down her house. While any candle can be a potential fire threat, there is no validity to this particular warning. It's just a hoax.

Internet Tax   This is one of the oldest online hoaxes around; it's been floating around for at least a decade, in one form or another. The hoax message describes a bill before Congress that would impose a tax on dial-up Internet access. (Or, in some variations, a tax on e-mail messages.) There's no such bill, of course—so don't bother writing your Congressman.

Terrorists Stealing Trucks   According to this hoax warning, authorities have been put on alert following a rash of thefts of Ryder, U-Haul, and Verizon trucks. Naturally, no such thefts occurred, so no terrorist attacks are imminent.

Urban Legends

You gotta love urban legends. These are the seemingly self-perpetuating stories you hear—"true" stories that happened to a friend of a friend of a friend, really—that purport to relate some sordid or hard-to-believe incident. These stories get repeated so often that they attain the appearance of truth; some are so widespread as to seemingly come from somewhere deep in our collective subconscious.

And now, thanks to the Internet and e-mail, these urban legends can be disseminated much faster and farther than previously possible. Whether in the form of a chain letter or a hoax, urban legends now prowl the Internet, taking up valuable bandwidth and convincing a new generation of their seeming validity.

What kinds of urban legends are you likely to find clogging your inbox? Here are a few of the more popular examples:

Child Abducted from Sam's Club   According to this legend, a child was abducted in your local Sam's Club. The abductor tried to disguise the child by wearing a wig and changing her clothes. Variations on this urban legend have the abduction taking place at Disney World or at your local mall.

Deadly Toilet Spiders   This urban legend tells of killer spiders that nest under toilet seats; supposedly, these deadly spiders have killed three people in Chicago.

Gang Initiations   There are all sorts of urban legends surrounding supposed gang initiations. There's the one where a gang member slips into the rear seat of a car while a woman is filling it up with gas—and then rapes her. Another one says that gang members throw gasoline-filled balloons into passing cars, in a game called "Spunkball." Yet another warns of gang members driving at night with their lights out and shooting at unsuspecting motorists. All false, of course.

KFC Mutant Chickens   This one claims that the food you get at Kentucky Fried Chicken doesn't come from real chickens, but rather from genetically-altered organisms of some sort. No need to change your eating habits; the Colonel uses real chickens that it buys from a number of traditional poultry producers.

P&G Satanism   This urban legend claims that the president of Procter & Gamble appeared on the Sally Jesse Raphael show and admitted that the company's profits go to support the Church of Satan. No such appearance occurred, of course—even though other rumors of P&G's satanic ties have been circulating since the early 1980s. (It has to do with the P&G logo, which some people apparently find satanic.)

Stealing Kidneys   The story goes like this. Some guy is in some bar, in some city, and meets this really attractive woman. They go back to her hotel room, then she spikes his drink and the next thing he knows, it's the next morning and he's lying naked in a bathtub full of ice, with a note on his chest: "Call 911 or you will die." He does and the emergency medical technicians discover that he's just had a kidney removed—another victim of the phantom kidney-stealing ring. Aaaah!

Scams

You receive a spam message in your inbox, typically titled something like "Make Money Fast." The message describes a way to get rich without doing any work, which has its appeal. All you have to do is send money (maybe a dollar, maybe five dollars, maybe ten) to a list of people, then pass the e-mail along to ten of your friends or colleagues, who also send money along to the list—to which your name has now been added.

This is a classic pyramid scheme—and it's blatantly illegal.

Anytime that money changes hands for fraudulent purposes, the law is being broken. The perpetrator of this type of scheme—if he or she can be identified—is responsible for all the funds that flow from the innocent (?) victims. It's fraud, pure and simple, and if you're a victim of such fraud (and can identify the perpetrators), you can take legal action.

NOTE *Learn more about these money-making scams in Chapter 21, "Dealing with Online Fraud."*

The pyramid scheme is a classic, but it's not the only online scam you may encounter. Here are some more examples of scams via chain e-mail:

Free Videogames   This scam, shut down by the FTC in April 2002, involved an e-mail message that informed users they had won a free Sony PlayStation2 videogame console. To claim their prize, users had to click a link embedded in the e-mail message. This link took them to a fake Yahoo! page that showed them how to download the program they needed to install to claim the prize. What was actually downloaded was a background dialing program that automatically dialed into a pornographic service that secretly charged them $3.99 per minute.

Multilevel Marketing Scams   Multilevel marketing (MLM) works like a pyramid scheme, but in a business setting. You join up to be a distributor of some product or service, but you really don't sell a thing. What you sell are more franchises or distributorships, and these folks sign up more folks, and so on. Every new member who signs up pays a fee to join; the person who signed him up gets a cut of the fee, with the bulk of the fee going to the parent company. The parent, of course, makes money whether any products are sold or not. There are numerous MLM schemes drifting around the Internet, and they make up a significant portion of spam mailings.

Nigerian Letter Scam   Probably the most prevalent online scam is the decades-old Nigerian Letter Scam. As discussed in Chapter 21, this scam asks for your bank account number so you can help a Nigerian official launder a large amount of money that he scammed from some U.S. corporations; if you go along with the scam, you end up losing all the money in your bank account.

How to Deal with Chain Letters and Other Annoying E-mails

If you're expecting a pages-long checklist of things you can do to minimize the effect of online chain letters and hoaxes, you're likely to be disappointed. That's because the only tried-and-true method to deal with these online annoyances is to *ignore them*. That's right, if you receive a message that says it should be shared with *lots* of people or starts with "send this to everyone you know," the best thing to do is to ignore the plea and delete the message. Whatever you do, do *not* perpetuate the gag and send the message to anyone else.

And you won't incur any bad luck by breaking the chain. Trust me.

Learn More About Internet Chain Letters and Hoaxes
For more information on Web-based hoaxes and the like, check out the following Web sites:

- Break the Chain (`www.breakthechain.org`)
- Don't Spread That Hoax (`www.nonprofit.net/hoax`)
- Hoaxbusters Internet Hoax Information (`hoaxbusters.ciac.org`)
- Hoaxkill (`www.hoaxkill.com`)
- ScamBusters (`www.scambusters.org`)
- Snopes.com Urban Legends Reference Pages (`www.snopes2.com`)
- Urban Legends Archive (`www.urbanlegends.com`)

Summing Up

Many annoying messages in your e-mail inbox aren't commercial spam. Instead, these messages are chain letters, hoaxes, and urban legends, perpetuated by naïve friends and family. These annoying e-mails are the online equivalent of their real-world counterparts; formerly passed on by word of mouth or the U.S. Postal Service, these myths and fabrications are now disseminated at Internet speed, preying on the gullibility, sympathy, and greed of online users around the world.

As annoying as these chain letters are, there's not much you can do about them except delete them. There's little point in informing the sender as to the falsity of the message; save your breath and hit the delete key, instead.

This ends our discussion of spam and other annoying e-mails. In the last section of this book we look at some of the most annoying aspects of the World Wide Web—starting with pop-up advertisements.

PART V

WEB-BASED INTRUSIONS

CHAPTER 30

Dealing with Unwanted Ads and Pop-Ups

You enter a Web site's URL into your Web browser. The page begins to load, then you notice a new browser window open on your desktop. Or maybe the new window appears when you leave a Web site. Or maybe several of these windows open, one after another—pop! pop! pop!

Congratulations. You've just experienced one of the most annoying advertising vehicles on the Internet—the pop-up ad.

The pop-up ad is just the newest type of advertisement to be shoved in front of your face as you surf the Web. Old-fashioned banner ads have been around almost as long as the Web itself, cluttering up Web pages and tempting you to click through to learn more about some or another product or service. Some sites feature so many banners and pop-ups that it's hard to identify the site's actual content. It's all you can do to avoid the banners and close the pop-ups, before you're overwhelmed.

While it's probably impossible to avoid all Web advertising—just as it's impossible to avoid newspaper ads and television commercials—there are things you can do to minimize the number of these intrusions you have to deal with. Read on to learn more.

Blocking Pop-Up Windows

Pop-up windows came into their own late in 2000, thanks to the brilliant marketing minds behind the X-10 camera. (And if you've never heard of the X-10, you're doing a pretty good job of blocking pop-up ads yourself—mentally, that is.) For a while it seemed that every other Web page you visited was accompanied by a smaller, pop-up window advertising this ubiquitous little camera. In fact, during the first few months of X-10 pop-up advertising, the X-10 Web site received so much traffic (whether purposeful or accidental was hard to tell) that it was ranked among the top five trafficked sites on the Web.

The success, as it was, of the X-10 campaign led to a lemming-like rush to pop-up advertising. These annoying little intrusions were apparently more effective than traditional banner ads in encouraging customer click-throughs and quickly became the ad format of choice for many Internet advertisers.

And when it comes to pop-up ads, some sites just can't contain themselves. There are numerous examples of sites where one pop-up is launched when you first access the site, and another pop-up is launched when you leave. You can even launch pop-ups by clicking a link on the page or by just hovering over a link. And, particularly on adult Web sites, it's not uncommon for more than one pop-up to launch at a time—or for a new pop-up to launch whenever you close an existing pop-up.

It's pop-up hell—you can't get rid of them!

NOTE *Ad agencies sometimes refer to pop-up ads as interstitials.*

Different Types of Pop-Ups

Interestingly, pop-up ads are nothing more than browser windows, typically without the menus and navigational features you find in a normal browser window. (Technically, they're *daughter windows* of your Web browser.) While pop-up windows can contain useful information (product data, privacy data, and other specific information subsidiary to the content of the main Web page), they're more often used to serve advertisements. So when a pop-up pops up, what you're seeing is a new instance of your Web browser, without the navigational elements, pointed to an advertising page.

That said, there are several different types of pop-ups you may encounter:

Standard Pop-Up   The standard pop-up, shown in Figure 30.1, is a normal browser with the menus and navigational elements (scroll bars, close button, etc.) turned off. The window is typically sized smaller than a normal browser window, so that it looks more like an ad than a typical Web page. In addition, the standard pop-up normally is stacked on top of other windows already on your desktop.

Figure 30.1 *A standard pop-up window; like a regular browser window, but without menus or controls*

Frameless Pop-Up   A popular variation of the standard pop-up is the frameless pop-up, shown in Figure 30.2. As the name implies, this window has no frame—so the ad page appears to float on top of the other windows on your desktop. The most annoying thing about a frameless pop-up is that there are no buttons to click to close it (unless the ad designer was nice enough to include a "click here to close" link); you have to close the window from the keyboard (press Ctrl+W) or by right-clicking the browser button on the Windows task bar, then selecting Close from the pop-up menu.

Figure 30.2 *A frameless pop-up window; no frame and no close button*

Pop-Under   Where a standard pop-up appears on top of all other windows, the pop-under window appears beneath the other windows on your desktop. In fact, it often appears to be hiding, so that you don't see it and reflexively try to close it.

TIP *If a pop-under window is hiding beneath your normal browser window, you can note its presence by observing the new browser button on the Windows taskbar.*

Peeker Pop-Up   A peeker pop-up is typically a frameless pop-up that slowly slides up from the bottom (or in from the side or down from the top) of the screen. As with any frameless pop-up, the absence of a close button is probably the most annoying thing about it.

Fake Message Window Pop-Up   Some ad designers like to use pop-up windows to mimic typical Windows system message boxes. These fake message pop-ups, like the one shown in Figure 30.3, trick you into clicking a button in response to what you think is a real system message.

Figure 30.3 *A pop-up window designed to look like a Windows system message*

Whatever type of pop-up is used, they're all fairly intrusive—especially when several appear at once. In fact, when you have pop-ups launching pop-ups, it's easy for your desktop to become so cluttered as to become unusable.

Making Your Own Pop-Ups

Pop-up windows are typically created with JavaScript, one of the most popular and easiest-to-use scripting languages. The JavaScript code is inserted into the normal HTML code for a Web page, to be activated either when a visitor opens the original Web page or when the visitor leaves that page.

The surprising thing about creating pop-up windows is how easy it is. The pop-up window is created with a single JavaScript command, `window.open`. If you know how to use HTML, you can very easily add a pop-up window to your Web site.

While there are many different types of pop-ups you can create, the basic pop-up window is just a frame that contains whatever Web page you desire with no navigational controls or other browser elements. To create such a pop-up, all you have to do is insert the following JavaScript code into the head of your original Web page:

```
<script language="JavaScript">
<!--
function genericPopup(popupAddress)
{new_window =
window.open(popupAddress,'AnnoyingWindow','width=300,height=200')}
// -->
</script>
```

(You can change the width and height numbers to create bigger or smaller pop-ups; these dimensions are measured in pixels.)

You then have to add another snippet of code to the **<body>** tag in your original Web page, to instruct the user's browser to open the new window. To open the pop-up when the initial page is opened, add this code:

```
<body onLoad="genericPopup('popup-url')">
```

To open the pop-up when the user leaves the initial page, add this code:

```
<body onUnload="genericPopup('popup-url')">
```

In either case, you'll need to replace *popup-url* with the URL of the Web page you want to display inside your pop-up window.

That's all there is to it. Is there any doubt that the proliferation of pop-up windows is due at least in part to how easy it is to create them?

Closing Pop-Ups Manually

When you're presented with an unwanted pop-up window, you want to close it. With a standard pop-up, you can close it as you would any window, by clicking the Close button (the big X) in the top right corner of the windows. If there is no close button on the pop-up window (and there often isn't), you can still close the window, by using one of the following methods:

- Right-click the pop-up window's button on the Windows taskbar, then select Close from the pop-up window.

- With the pop-up selected as the active window, press Ctrl+W on your keyboard. (Alternately, press Alt+F4.)

- Press Ctrl+Alt+Del to open the Windows Task Manager, select the Applications tab, select the pop-up window in the Task list, then click the End Task button.

TIP *When faced with an overwhelming number of pop-up windows, I've found the Ctrl+W method to be the most efficient.*

Pop-Up Killer Software

When the number of pop-up windows you face becomes totally unmanageable, it's time to call in the cavalry—in the form of pop-up killer software. These programs work to either close pop-ups immediately on opening or keep them from opening in the first place.

Most of these programs work in the background by counteracting the JavaScript code typically used to create pop-up windows. Other programs also block access to known advertising sites, thus rendering the pop-up ads useless. All deal with all the different types of pop-ups, including pop-unders and peekers.

TIP *As a bonus, many of these pop-up stoppers also block banner advertisements— which are discussed next.*

The most popular of these pop-up killer programs include:

- AdsGone (`www.adsgone.com`)
- AdSubtract (`www.adsubtract.com`)
- Advertising Killer (`www.buypin.com`)
- AntiPopUp (`www.webknacks.com/antipopup.htm`)
- Exit Killer (`www.exitkiller.com`)

- KillAd (`wwwwin.wplus.net/pp/fsc`)

- PopNot (`www.hdsoft.com/popnot`)

- Popup Ad Filter (`www.meaya.com`)

- PopUpCop (`www.popupcop.com`)

- Popup Eliminator (`www.popupeliminator.com`)

- Pop-Up Stopper (`www.popupstopper.net`)

- Pop OFF (`www.8848soft.com/products.htm`)

- SMASHER (`www.popupstop.com`)

- Surf In Peace (`www.iconlabs.net`)

- Web Window Killer (`www.anarelion.com/aalku/WebWindowKiller`)

- WebWasher (`www.webwasher.com`)

- WindowSmasher (`members.rogers.com/windowsmasher`)

- Zero Popup (`tooto.plastiqueweb.com`)

WARNING *Some pop-up killers will also keep some legitimate pop-ups from appearing—including those used by some sites to display additional product or security information. If you run into problems displaying this type of informative pop-up, you may need to disable the pop-up killer software when visiting that particular site.*

Other Pop-Up Stopping Options

While using pop-up killer software is the easiest way to keep pop-up windows off your desktop, there are other, more technically complex solutions you can employ.

Disable Scripting

Since most pop-up windows are generated via JavaScript code, you can keep most pop-ups from appearing by disabling scripting in your Web browser. Of course, this will affect lots of other Web page special effects—buttons, counters, and the like—but it will stop pop-ups.

WARNING *Disabling scripting is an extreme solution to the pop-up problem, and it is not recommended for most users.*

To disable scripting in Internet Explorer 6, follow these steps:

1. Select Tools ➤ Options.

2. When the Internet Options dialog box appears, select the Security tab.

3. Click the Custom Level button to display the Security Settings dialog box.

4. Scroll down to the Scripting section, then to the Active Scripting option (shown in Figure 30.4). Select Disable.

5. Click OK.

Figure 30.4 *Disabling scripting in Internet Explorer*

Switch Browsers

Another option is to switch browsers—in particular, switch from Internet Explorer or Netscape to the Opera browser. Opera (`www.opera.com`) offers the option of clicking a button to either accept pop-ups, send them into the background, or stop them from popping up completely.

> **WARNING** *The freeware version of Opera displays annoying banner ads—you're trading off pop-ups for banners. If you'd rather have a clean browser without banners, Opera's premium version (about $40) does away with the ads.*

Removing Banners and Other Web Page Ads

The profusion of pop-ups makes one long for the days of the simple, relatively less intrusive, banner advertisement. Banner ads are a fixture on most commercial Web sites today, in various shapes and sizes, and most users have become rather adept at ignoring them. (Of course, it's the fact that most users do ignore ads that led to the switch to pop-up ads.)

Still, even though it's easy enough to mentally block out all those banner ads, wouldn't it be nicer to eliminate the ads completely? Believe it or not, it's relatively easy to scrub the banner ads from a page—and leave your browser virtually ad-free.

Types of Banner Ads

In the "old days," there was only one type of banner ad: the standard 486×60 pixel ad placed across the top of a Web page. As the online ad market dried up in the year 2000—and as research indicated that most banner ads had an unacceptably low click-through rate—advertisers demanded more versatility in ad placement. This resulted in the creation of a veritable plethora of banner sizes, both vertical and horizontal in orientation. Figure 30.5 shows some of the banner ads specified by the Internet Advertising Bureau (`www.iab.net`).

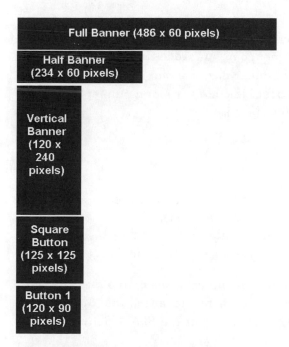

Figure 30.5 *Different types of banner ads*

What lies within the confines of a banner is determined by the advertiser, of course. Some ads are just plain JPG or GIF files, others are animated GIFs, still others have so-called "rich media" content—Shockwave or Flash animation. Almost all banner ads are linked to the advertiser's Web site, so clicking the ad banner (which the ad industry calls a *click-through*) takes you to another Web page.

How Banner Ads Work

The banner ad that you see in your Web browser is typically not technically a part of the underlying Web page. The URL for the banner ad is referenced within the Web page's HTML code, just like any other graphic element. (The graphics on a Web page are actually separate files, inserted into the page by an HTML **<href>** tag.)

If you've ever gone to a Web page twice and seen two different banner ads, that's because the ads are being served up, somewhat randomly, by an ad agency's ad server. The Web page simply references a URL on the agency's server; different ads are in place of a generic filename, as part of an overall rotation.

Advertisers pay sites for the placement of their banner ads, typically based on some combination of impressions (page views) and click-through. The more users see an ad, and the more users click an ad, the more the advertiser pays.

TIP *If you want to create your own banner ads for your Web site, check out ABC Banners (*www.abcbanners.com*) or AdDesigner.com (*www.addesigner.com*). If you want to be paid for displaying commercial banner ads, you can contact a big banner network such as DoubleClick (*www.doubleclick.com*) or join a banner-exchange program such as BannerSwap (*www.bannerswap.com*).*

How to Block Banner Ads

Because banner ads are just graphic files referenced in a Web page's HTML code, it's actually fairly easy to strip out that code and keep the banner ad from displaying.

One way to do this is to turn off the display of graphics in your Web browser. If your browser is configured to not display graphics, it also won't display any banner ads. Simple as that.

TIP *To turn off the graphics display in Internet Explorer 6, select Tools ➤ Options; when the Internet Options dialog box appears, select the Advanced tab. Scroll down the Settings list to the Multimedia section, and then clear the Show Pictures option.*

Of course, you probably don't want to hide all the graphics on all the Web pages you visit. To more selectively hide banner ads, you need a more sophisticated solution, which is provided by a type of software called a banner-ad blocker.

Figure 30.6 shows how banner-ad blockers work. Your browser requests a Web page, as normal. But when the Web page is delivered, it's filtered through the banner-ad blocker. The blocker software looks for embedded URLs on the Web page that point to known banner-ad servers. Those URLs are stripped from the served Web page (and sometimes replaced with transparent or otherwise innocuous graphics), which is then delivered to your browser. You see the page you requested, sans ads.

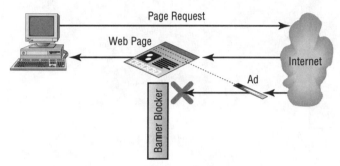

Figure 30.6 *How to block banner ads*

The most popular of the banner-blocking programs include:

- Ad Extinguisher (`adext.magenet.net`)
- Ad Muncher (`www.admuncher.com`)
- AdDelete (`www.addelete.com`)
- ADfilter (`www.adscience.co.uk`)
- AdsGone (`www.adsgone.com`)
- AdSubtract (`www.adsubtract.com`)
- Advertising Killer (`www.buypin.com`)
- Banner Zapper (`www.bannerzapper.net`)
- Guidescope (`www.guidescope.com`)
- Internet Junkbuster Proxy (`internet.junkbuster.com`)
- Internet Watcher 2000 (`www.internetwatcher.com`)
- WebWasher (`www.webwasher.com`)

Figure 30.7 shows AdDelete, one of the more popular banner-ad blockers. AdDelete works in the background, blocking any ads that try to display on your current Web page. All blocked ads are displayed on the program's History tab.

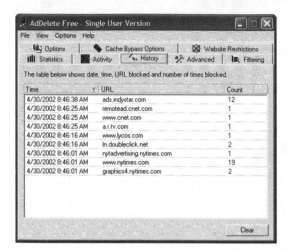

Figure 30.7 *Using AdDelete to block banner advertising*

Blocking Banner Ads with the *Hosts* File

You can also block banner ads manually by adding the IP addresses of known advertising sites to your Windows Hosts file. This file—with no extension, just the name Hosts—is typically found in the Windows\system32\drivers\etc folder and helps speed access to particular Web sites by "hard coding" an IP address to a Web site name. (On Windows 9x/Me systems, the Hosts file is typically found in the Windows folder.)

You use the Hosts file to block banner ads by referencing the banner ad's home site back to your computer—not to the ad site itself. You do this by adding the following lines to the Host file:

        127.0.0.1   *adserver1.com*

        127.0.0.1   *adserver2.com*

The 127.0.0.1 is the IP address for your computer; the *adserver1.com* is the URL of the ad site. When a Web page tries to load a banner ad from the ad site, it redirects the request back to your computer, instead, which leaves the ad space blank.

Of course, for this technique to work, you need to know the names of all the Web sites that serve up banner ads. You can find a list of these servers at the Hosts File Information site (www.smartin-designs.com); just add each of these sites as a separate line in your Hosts file, and you'll have created your own banner-ad blocker.

Exterminating Web Bugs

Not only are pop-up and banner ads annoying, they're also used by some companies to gather information about consumers. Ad response is monitored when the ad is clicked or, in the case of ads sent via HTML e-mail, when the e-mail advertisement is opened.

NOTE *The kind of information typically captured by banner ads and Web bugs— and stored in cookie files on your hard disk—include the IP address of your computer, your e-mail address, the date and time the ad was viewed, the type of browser you're using, and so on.*

Sometimes you open e-mail ads without knowing it, because the ads themselves are so small as to be virtually unnoticeable. These so-called *Web bugs* (or *Web beacons*) are small graphics files, typically 1 × 1 pixel, all but invisible unless you're looking for them. (In fact, Web bugs are sometimes referred to as *clear GIFs*.)

The bug isn't actually attached to the e-mail message; it's a separate file on a separate Web site that is referenced in the message's HTML code. You activate the bug when you open the HTML e-mail message, and your e-mail program accesses the Web to find and load the referenced file. When the bug's site is accessed, your browsing is tracked, and a cookie is placed on your hard disk.

WARNING *Web bugs aren't limited to e-mail messages; they can also be placed on normal Web pages.*

It's tough to avoid Web bugs in your e-mail. Of course, if you turn off the HTML viewing function of your e-mail program, you also prevent Web bugs from loading. But since so much e-mail today is HTML e-mail, it's almost impossible to limit your inbox to just plain text messages.

A better solution is to use a banner-ad blocker program, such as Ad Extinguisher, that also blocks Web bugs. You can also minimize the impact of Web bugs by setting a rather restrictive cookie level in your Web browser (which is used to render HTML messages in your e-mail program). This process is described in Chapter 24, "Managing Cookies."

Evading Unwanted Downloads

A new annoyance has recently hit the Web. This new intrusion—the download pop-up—tries to download one or more files (typically spyware programs) when you access a Web site.

Fortunately, the download pop-up requires your assistance to work. When the Web site tries to download a file, you're notified of the action and asked if you want to complete the download. If you answer no, no harm is done. (If you answer yes, who knows what you're downloading!)

Download pop-ups become really intrusive in quantity. If you're overwhelmed by multiple pop-up windows when you access a site, it's easy to become confused and accidentally click the Yes instead of the No button in the download pop-up window.

It's also easy to be confused by the wording in some download pop-up windows. If the site is particularly sneaky, you might think you have to download some new plug-in in order to view the content on the site. You might even think that you're downloading a system update from Microsoft when it's really a Trojan backdoor or spyware program!

The key is to remain calm and aware, and never—never!—download any program that is forced upon you in this manner.

Taking Control of Your Browser

There are many other intrusions that Web sites try to foist upon you when you honor them with your presence. Most of these intrusions are more annoying than harmful, which is good, since there's little you can do to avoid them.

Take, for example, the *forced frame*. This highly annoying intrusion is used by many sites as a branding mechanism. When you're visiting a site and click a link to jump to another page, the old site seems to follow you wherever you go. That's because, instead of jumping cleanly to the new page, the new page opens in a frame in your browser window—with some logo or other branding information about the previous site appearing in the surrounding frame. (This effect is shown in Figure 30.8.)

You can see forced frames in action at About.com. Every site you link to from this site is forced into an About.com frame; no matter how many clicks you make, you can't get away.

Forced framing is irritating for a number of reasons. First, you don't get a full-window view of the other sites, because the branded frame takes up part of the available real estate. Second, you never get to see the URL of the linked-to pages, because the URL in the address bar reflects the complete frame document that contains both pages. Third, you're forced to look at the branding frame, wherever you go.

As a user, there are two things to do to break out of a forced frame—one practical, one not. The practical thing to do, assuming that you're using Internet Explorer as your browser, is to right-click on the new page within the frame and select Open Frame in New Window. This displays a new browser window containing the new page, no frames.

NOTE *If you're a Web page developer, you can insert specific JavaScript code into your HTML page to block forced framing from other sites.*

Figure 30.8 *A forced frame around a new page*

The less practical solution recognizes that the force-frame effect is created with JavaScript code in the original Web page. If you disable scripting in your browser, the JavaScript won't run, and you won't be subject to forced framing.

Of course, forced frames aren't the only annoyances you'll run into. Some sites hijack your cursor and replace it with another image. This is most often done with the Comet Cursor (www .cometzone.com), a Web-based service that supplies JavaScript code to replace visitors' normal cursors with hundreds of alternate cursors. As a user, you probably don't have much recourse to this hijacking. If you're asked if you want to install a particular Comet Cursor, you can decline. But not all Comet Cursors ask you first; in this instance, the only solution (impractical as it is) is to disable scripting in your Web browser.

Another JavaScript trick causes all the elements of your browser window (menus, scroll bars, and so on) to change color. As long as you have scripting enabled, you're a potential victim of this intrusive practice.

Other Web intrusions automatically play a sound file when you visit a page or force you to watch a Flash animation before you can enter a site. There's not much you can do about these annoyances, save stop visiting the offending sites.

Summing Up

Pop-up ads are advertisements that are displayed in small browser windows; these pop-up windows are typically launched when you enter or leave a Web site. While these pop-up windows can be avoided by disabling the scripting function in your Web browser, the better solution is to install a pop-up killer program, that intercepts the offending JavaScript code and prevents the new window from launching.

Banner ads are those graphic advertisements that appear anywhere on a Web page. Banner ads can also be removed, by using ad-blocking software that either blocks or redirects access to the Web site that serves the ads.

Some ad-blocking software also blocks Web bugs, which are near-invisible "beacons" placed in HTML e-mail messages. Web bugs are actually loaded from an advertiser's Web page and drop cookies on your hard disk to track certain online activity. Blocking access to the advertiser's site disables the bug.

In the next (and final) chapter we'll look at another Web-related issue: the challenge of avoiding inappropriate content.

CHAPTER 31

Dealing with
Inappropriate Content

You've done it. You click one link too many, and end up at a site offering very adult content and photographs. Or maybe you enter a phrase into your favorite search site and find that the results include links to several adult Web sites. Or maybe you receive an adult-oriented spam message in your e-mail, encouraging you to click for even more explicit content.

The problem is, if you can stumble across this type of inappropriate content, so can your kids. And you want to protect them not only from online predators, but also from the type of content that should be labeled "for adults only."

What, then, can you do? How do you isolate your family from dirty pictures and bad language when they're online?

How Content Filtering Works

To protect your family from inappropriate content requires the ability to filter that content from all the good stuff on the Internet. There are many software programs and organizations offering different types of content filtering, all designed to protect younger users from the worst of the Web.

Most of these content-filtering programs use one (or more) of three distinct approaches: software-based analysis, human analysis, and site rating. Each approach has its pluses and minuses, although none are 100% accurate in the sites that they block.

Software-Based Analysis

This approach to content filtering requires the software to examine the content of a Web site and then pass judgment based on the presence of absence of key words and phrases. In other words, if a site contains inappropriate language or images, it gets blocked.

The problem with software-based analysis is that it can't make human judgments. For example, some content-filtering software will block sites that include the word "breast." While this will block out a lot of adult-oriented sites, it will also block sites about breast cancer—hardly an objectionable topic.

For this reason, many experts recommend against using software-based analysis alone; it's too restrictive.

Human Analysis

A more objective approach is to have a reviewer (or multiple reviewers) visit a site and then pass judgment. Those sites that are judged objectionable for younger users are added to a list of inappropriate sites, which are then blocked by the content-filtering software.

This approach enables sites to be analyzed in terms of actual content and approach, not just which words are used on the page. A human analysis also provides for full-length reviews in addition to the basic ratings; a detailed review will tell you more about what to expect than just a pass/fail type of rating.

Content Rating

The big problem with human analysis is that it's extremely time and labor intensive. Another, less resource-intensive approach is to let somebody else review the sites.

To this end, there are several organizations that review and rate Web site content. This rating typically labels sites for different types of content, including drugs, alcohol, adult situations, and so on. If a site is rated as including these elements, then the content-filtering software blocks access.

One problem with site rating is that not all sites are rated, and some content-filtering software allows access to non-rated sites. (Other software blocks access to all non-rated sites, which is equally problematic.) Another problem is that many organizations require sites to review themselves; this sort of voluntary rating might be efficient, but it isn't always effective—particularly if a site is less than honest about its content.

Labeling Content

When you're examining Web site content, you can look for the following labels of approval. These labels indicate that a site has content approved for users of all ages.

- Internet Content Rating Association (www.icra.org)
- Platform for Internet Content Selection (www.w3.org/PICS)
- SafeSurf (www.safesurf.com)

Content Filtering Software

Several companies produce the sort of content-filtering software we've been discussing. Most of these programs guard against either a preselected list of inappropriate sites or a preselected list of topics, and then block access to Web sites that meet the selected criteria.

NOTE *This chapter deals with content filtering for Web content. When it comes to filtering the content of e-mail messages, you need an e-mail content filter, as discussed in Chapter 28, "Dealing with Spam."*

The most popular filtering programs include:

BrowseSafe   BrowseSafe (`www.browsesafe.com`) is a Christian-oriented content filter approved by the Trinity Broadcast Network.

CyberPatrol   CyberPatrol (`www.surfcontrol.com/home/products`) is a utility that blocks access to a preselected list of Web sites, and also detects sites with questionable words or images.

Cyber Snoop   Cyber Snoop (`www.cyber-snoop.com`) not only blocks access to preselected Web sites, but also logs users' Web browsing, instant messaging, Internet chats, e-mail, and file transfers.

CYBERsitter   CYBERsitter (`www.cybersitter.com`) blocks access to a preselected list of Web sites, FTP sites, and Usenet newsgroups; it also detects offensive words and phrases.

FamilyConnect   FamilyConnect (`www.familyconnect.com`) is a filtered ISP service you use to connect to the Internet. The block list resides on FamilyConnect's servers, so that when you connect via FamilyConnect, you have automatic content filtering.

Net Nanny   This popular program (`www.netnanny.com`) blocks access to a preselected list of Web sites, Usenet newsgroups, and chat rooms.

Norton Internet Security   Norton Internet Security (`www.symantec.com`) is a suite of utilities that includes Norton AntiVirus and Norton Personal Firewall, along with the Norton Parental Control content filter.

TIP *If you're an America Online subscriber, check out AOL's built-in (and very effective) Parental Controls feature. (Select Settings ➤ Parental Controls; when the AOL Parental Controls window opens, select Set Parental Controls.) You can select different filtering options for different AOL screen names and choose from four age-rated categories—Kids Only (12 and under), Young Teen (13–15), Mature Teen (16–17), and General Access (18+).*

Figure 31.1 shows the control panel for CYBERsitter, perhaps the most-used content filtering program on the market today. You can choose what types of content to filter by selecting the Filters tab and checking the various options—Adult/Sexually Oriented, Gambling Sites, and so on.

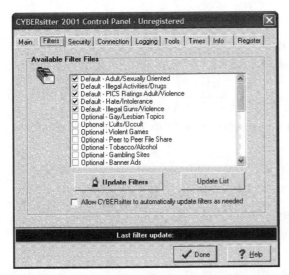

Figure 31.1 *Use CYBERsitter to block access to selected sites, based on multiple criteria.*

As useful as these programs are, the reality is that most parents don't use them. According to a survey by online research firm Jupiter Media Metrix (`www.jmm.com`), only 6% of parents use stand-alone content-filtering software. Most parents (seven out of ten) prefer to manually "filter" their children's browsing by being present while their kids are online.

There is also the issue of how effective these content-filtering programs actually are. Many users complain that even the best content-filtering software still allows access to *some* inappropriate content; a few sites always slip through the cracks. In addition, many filters tend to filter out some degree of legitimate content; it seems that many programs err on the side of overzealousness.

Finally, even if you do use these programs, if your kids are tech-savvy, they can figure out how to defeat the blocking mechanisms. Popular "hacking" magazines, such as *2600*, have printed numerous articles on how to disable these content and site filters, which is why physically monitoring your children's online behavior is still the best approach.

Content-Filtering Browsers

If you have young children in the house (and on the computer), you may want to consider using a kid-safe Web browser that offers built-in content filtering. These browsers work just like Internet Explorer or Netscape Navigator, but are specially designed for younger users; some even feature simplified kid-friendly interfaces and fun additional features.

The following are some of the most popular kid-safe browsers:

Bounce   Bounce (`www.bouncefilterware.com`) is an easy-to-use browser with simplified controls, combined with user-configurable Internet filtering. Includes kid-changeable "skins" for a fully personalized look and feel.

Internet Safari   The Internet Safari browser (`www.heartsoft.com`) is specifically designed for children's cognitive thinking skills and includes integrated security features and "Teacher Features" for classroom use.

kROWSER   kROWSER (`www.krowser.com`) is a browser for pre-teens that screens out offensive sites through a combination of content recognition and a human-edited database.

SurfMonkey   SurfMonkey (`www.surfmonkey.com`) is a fun-looking browser with built-in links to all the best kids' sites, as well as an integrated safety service to block access to inappropriate content.

Figure 31.2 shows the Bounce kids-safe browser. Parents can create separate accounts for each family member, with specific levels of content filtering. Filtering is based on a list of inappropriate words/phrases, as well as approved and disapproved Web sites.

Figure 31.2 *Kids-safe browsing with the Bounce Web browser*

Content Filtering in Internet Explorer

If you use Internet Explorer, you don't have to switch browsers to get built-in content filtering. Newer versions of IE include the Content Advisor feature, which is used to block access to Web sites that meet specified criteria. Content Advisor enables you to set your own tolerance levels for various types of potentially offensive content, and then blocks access to sites that don't pass muster.

WARNING *Turning on Content Advisor (especially at the highest levels) is likely to block access to a lot of sites you're used to visiting on a normal basis. (News sites, in particular, include stories about sex and violence and hatred that can activate the Content Advisor filter.) If you find that Content Advisor is blocking too many sites, try moving the slider more to the left or add your favorite sites to the approved sites list.*

Here's how to activate and configure Content Advisor in Internet Explorer 6:

1. Select Tools ➤ Internet Options.

2. When the Internet Options dialog box appears, select the Content tab.

3. To enable the Content Advisor, click the Enable button; when prompted for your Supervisor Password, enter your Windows password and click OK and proceed to Step 5.

4. If you've already enabled Content Advisor, click the Settings button.

5. When the Content Advisor dialog box appears, select the Ratings tab (shown in Figure 31.3).

Figure 31.3 *Configuring Internet Explorer to filter various types of content*

6. Select a category; a Rating slider appears. Adjust the slider to the right to increase the tolerance for this type of content; leaving the slider all the way to the left is the least tolerant level. Click OK when done.

TIP *To disable Content Advisor, return to the Internet Options dialog box, select the Content tab, and click the Disable button.*

You can also configure Internet Explorer to always block specific sites or always allow access to specific sites, regardless of your content settings. To configure IE on a site-by-site basis, follow these steps:

1. Select Tools ➤ Internet Options.

2. When the Internet Options dialog box appears, select the Content tab.

3. Click the Settings button. (Or, if you haven't yet activated Content Advisor, click the Enable button.)

4. When the Content Advisor dialog box appears, select the Approved Sites tab (shown in Figure 31.4).

Figure 31.4 *Configuring IE to always or never allow access to specific pages*

5. Enter the URL for a specific Web page into the Allow This Web Site box, and then click the Always button (to always view the site, regardless of its rating) or the Never button (to completely block access to the site).

6. Click OK.

Filtered Search Sites

While content-filtering software will block access to inappropriate Web sites, they typically don't filter the results of searches you make at Google and other sites. Since these searches often produce at least a few misleading and inappropriate results, you may want to consider using a search site that incorporates its own built-in results filtering.

Here are the most popular kid-safe search sites on the Web today:

AltaVista—AV Family Filter   The AV Family Filter (`www.altavista.com`; click the Family Filter link) is a filtered version of the popular AltaVista search engine; adult and other inappropriate sites are deleted from normal search results.

Apple Learning Interchange   This site (`ali.apple.com/ali/resources.shtml`), from Apple Computer, contains a list of more than seven million teacher-reviewed, kid-safe Web pages, categorized by subject and grade level.

Ask Jeeves for Kids   Ask Jeeves for Kids (`www.ajkids.com`) is a unique service where you enter queries with a plain-English question; Ask Jeeves provides the answer via a short list of highly qualified and filtered Web sites.

Fact Monster   The Fact Monster (`www.factmonster.com`) is one of the largest information-oriented sites on the Web for kids, from Information Please and the Learning Network.

Google SafeSearch   Google, the most popular search site on the Web, offers two levels of filtering. (Go to `www.google.com`, select the Preferences link, then choose a SafeSearch Filtering option.) Moderate filters images only, while strict filters both text and images.

OneKey   OneKey (`www.onekey.com`) is a kid-safe search engine (using the Google SafeSearch engine) and directory of kid-safe sites, organized into more than 500 different categories. Each site in this directory has been personally reviewed.

Yahooligans!   This site (`www.yahooligans.com`) is the Yahoo! Web guide, for kids (7–12 years old). Sites in this directory are hand-picked for appropriateness.

TIP *These kid-safe search sites are good to use as the start page for your children's browser, because they're launching pads to guaranteed safe content.*

Issues with Content Filtering

Like most things Internet-related, content filtering is not without its issues. One big issue concerns the effectiveness of content-filtering software; some users complain that the filters don't catch all the inappropriate sites, while others complain that these programs sometimes block sites that aren't inappropriate at all.

This debate points out that technology alone is seldom a solution. In the case of guarding against inappropriate content, no content filter is as good as parental supervision; you will always make more appropriate judgments than any software program.

A bigger question is when content filtering violates First Amendment rights. This is a particularly potent issue within the library community, where some local governments want to block access to inappropriate content within the public library environment—and most librarians view such blocking as censorship. (And librarians really don't like censorship!) This is also an issue in K–12 schools, where parents want inappropriate content blocked, and school librarians want free and open access to all content. To most librarians, blocking access to a Web site is tantamount to ripping pages out of an encyclopedia; it just isn't done.

This issue extends outside schools and libraries into the general public, where civil libertarians oppose attempts to censor all types of content—including Internet-based content. These individuals view content-filtering programs as *censorware* and believe them to be an ineffective solution to the problem of protecting children from inappropriate content.

NOTE *The Supreme Court has already struck down one content-filtering law, the Communications Decency Act, on First Amendment grounds. Congress responded by passing the Children's Internet Protection Act, requiring schools and libraries that want Federal funding to filter objectionable online content. This law was subsequently struck down as being unconstitutional by a Federal judicial panel, setting up a further review by the Supreme Court.*

You can read more about these content-filtering issues at the following Web sites:

- American Civil Liberties Union Cyber-Liberties
  (`www.aclu.org/issues/cyber/hmcl.html`)

- American Library Association Office of Intellectual Freedom
  (`www.ala.org/alaorg/oif`)

- Censorware Project (`censorware.net`)

- Computer Professionals for Social Responsibility (`www.cpsr.org`)

- Electronic Frontier Foundation: Internet Blocking & Censorware (`www.eff.org/Censorship/Censorware`)
- Electronic Privacy Information Center (`www.epic.org`)
- Peacefire (`www.peacefire.org`)

Summing Up

The problem of protecting children from inappropriate Internet content is most often addressed by content-filtering software. Some content-filtering programs work by blocking access to sites that contain verboten words and phrases; others work by blocking access to a preselected list of inappropriate sites. There are also organizations that provide reviews and ratings of site content to assist the content-filtering process.

There are also content-filtering features built into Internet Explorer. IE's Content Advisor enables you to configure settings for various types of content and adjust what is allowable and what isn't.

Finally, many civil libertarians take issue with content filtering, particularly in the library and school environments. What one user sees as protection for younger users, another sees as censorship; the issue continues to be debated.

And that ends this book. If you've read it straight through, you've learned how to protect yourself from destructive computer viruses and Internet-based computer attacks, how to preserve your privacy and identity online, how to avoid being inundated with spam and unwanted chain e-mails, and how to avoid other Web-based intrusions, including pop-up advertisements and inappropriate content. I hope you've found this book useful and that it leads to safer—and more enjoyable—Internet use.

Feel free to visit my Web site (`www.molehillgroup.com`) for more information about my latest projects or to contact me via e-mail (`security@molehillgroup.com`) with any questions or comments. I can't guarantee I'll answer every message, but I definitely enjoying hearing from readers!

Now it's time to close the book, grab your mouse, and get back online. Just remember: surf smart and surf safe. You'll be glad you did!

GLOSSARY

adware
Stealth software that tracks your online activity and sends that data to a marketing or advertising company; some adware also uses that data to serve up replacement ads on specific Web sites.

algorithm
A mathematical process or formula used to create a number.

anonymizer
A Web site or service that enables anonymous Web browsing or e-mail communications.

antivirus program
A software program that scans for and cleans viruses from computer systems.

authentication
The process of determining whether someone or something is, in fact, who or what it is purporting to be.

auto-execute macro
A macro that automatically launches when a document is opened.

backdoor
Undocumented (and typically unauthorized) entry point into a system.

backdoor Trojan
Trojan horse file that opens a backdoor on your system for potential unauthorized remote access.

backtracing software
Software used to trace an attacker's identity and host ISP.

banner ad
A graphic advertisement placed on a Web page.

batch file
An executable file containing separate lines of commands—actually, "batches" of commands.

biometrics
The science of measuring and analyzing biological identifiers, such as fingerprints, retinas, voice patterns, facial patterns, and so on.

blackhole list
A list of open mail relay servers, created for the purpose of blocking all messages from those servers.

block list
A list of specific addresses and domains known to send spam.

boot sector virus
A virus that infects the boot sectors of floppy disks and the Master Boot Record of hard disks.

boot sector
The area located on the first track of a floppy or hard disk.

browser helper object (BHO)

A small software program that attaches itself to your Web browser.

buffer overflow

A bug in some programs that enable the program's data buffer to be overloaded with data, forcing the original program code out so the buffer can be rewritten with malicious code.

Carnivore

The packet sniffer software used by the FBI to spy on suspected criminals and terrorists; part of the DragonWare suite.

censorware

Another word for content-filtering software.

certificate authority

The company that issues a digital certificate.

certificate store

The repository of digital certificates stored on your hard disk and accessed by your Web browser.

chain letter

A letter or e-mail directing the recipient to forward multiple copies of the message to other people.

chat channel

A public chat on an IRC network, typically organized by topic.

clear GIF

A small, transparent graphics file used to create a Web bug.

click-through

A measurement of advertising effectiveness; a click-through occurs whenever a user clicks a banner ad or link.

code signature

A sequence of binary code unique to a computer virus; used to identify each virus.

companion virus

A file infector virus that creates a clone of the host file, which is then run instead of the original file.

computer virus

A computer program or piece of malicious code that attaches itself to other files and then replicates itself.

content filter

Software that analyzes Web page content and blocks access to inappropriate content.

cookie

A small file created by a Web site and stored on your computer's hard disk, used to track specific user information.

Coolminer

An application used by the FBI to extrapolate and analyze the data found in captured messages; part of the DragonWare suite.

cracker

An individual who maliciously breaks into another computer system.

cryptography

The science of information security; the process of hiding or coding information either in storage or in transit.

data diddling

The process of surreptitiously altering (but not deleting) the data on another computer system.

data-driven attack

A virus or Trojan attack on a computer system; the attack is launched when a file is downloaded and opened.

daughter window

Another name for a pop-up window.

decryption

The process of decoding encrypted data.

demilitarized zone

A server that sits outside a company's firewall and enables public access to specified content.

denial of service attack

An attack that floods a computer or network with data or messages that overwhelm and ultimately shut down the system.

desktop monitoring program

A spyware program that monitors and logs the operations of another personal computer.

dictionary spam

A means of generating e-mail addresses by matching common names with known domain names.

digital certificate

An electronic credential that confirms the identity of a person, server, or software manufacturer.

digital signature

A form of digital certificate used to authenticate the identity of the sender of a message or the signer of a document.

distributed computing

A form of P2P computing where multiple computers are connected together to harness their total processing power; typically used for large projects that would otherwise require use of a supercomputer.

DNS spoofing

An attack resulting from the hijacking of a computer's DNS name by an attacker; the DNS name is redirected to the attacker's IP address.

download pop-up

A pop-up window that tries to download software to your hard disk.

DragonWare

A suite of spyware programs used by the FBI; includes the Carnivore, Coolminer, and Packeteer components.

dynamic system monitoring

The real-time scanning mode of a virus scanning program.

e-mail bomb

The sending of a large number of e-mail messages to a single address, with the intent of flooding that person's inbox.

e-mail gateway

A proxy server for e-mail.

encryption

The process of coding data into a format that can't be read.

entry-point obscuring virus

A file infector virus that doesn't insert its own code into the host file, but rather inserts code that launches a separate virus program.

executable file

A program that you run on your computer system.

exploit

An attack that takes advantage of a bug or hole in a piece of hardware or operating system.

file infector virus

A virus that infects the code of executable program files.

firewall

Software or hardware that insulates a computer or network from the Internet.

forced frame

A technique for forcing a new Web page into a framed page from another site.

frameless pop-up

A pop-up window without a traditional window frame.

freeware

Computer software distributed at no charge.

FTP bouncing

A form of session hijacking, where an unwitting FTP server is used to send e-mail to other computers.

gateway computer

That computer on a network that hosts the connection to the Internet.

hacker

An individual who enjoys exploring the details of computer systems and programming code, typically by "hacking" into those systems and programs—but without causing any intentional damage. (Not to be confused with a *cracker*, who engages in intentionally malicious behavior.)

header

That part of a data packet or e-mail message, normally hidden, that contains the sender's IP address and other technical information.

Heuristic scanning

A method of scanning for computer viruses by looking for general virus-like behavior.

hoax

False information about a purported virus attack.

HTML e-mail

E-mail messages that incorporate HTML code, just like Web pages.

HTML

Hypertext markup language; the script language used to create Web pages.

hybrid virus

A virus that combines the capabilities of multiple types of viruses. (For example, a virus that can contain both boot sector virus components and file infector virus components is a hybrid virus.)

ICMP bombing

An attack that knocks a computer off the Internet by bombing it with bogus ICMP messages.

ICMP

The Internet Control Message Protocol, used by Internet routers to notify a host computer when a specified destination is unreachable.

identity theft

The theft of personal ID and financial information, enabling the thief to assume the identity of the victim.

impersonation attack

A computer attack that occurs when an attacker steals the access rights of an authorized user and then configures his computer to impersonate the other, authorized computer.

in the wild

A virus is referred to as being "in the wild" when a verified infection has been noted outside a laboratory situation.

infection

The process of a computer virus inserting itself into a computer file.

instant messaging

An Internet-based network for conducting one-on-one text messaging.

integrity checking

The process of checking the size of a file against a previously identified size; changes in file size are indicative of virus infection.

Internet Relay Chat (IRC)

An Internet-based network of chat servers and channels that facilitates real-time public text messaging (called chats) and file exchanges.

interstitial

Another name for a pop-up advertisement.

intrusion detection system

Software or hardware that monitors a computer network or system for signs of an attack.

IP half scan

A type of pre-attack probe on a computer system.

IRC

See *Internet Relay Chat*.

junk e-mail

Another name for *spam*.

key

A code—actually, a really big number—that works with a cryptographic algorithm to produce a specific encrypted result.

keylogger

Software or hardware that records the individual keystrokes entered by a user.

keystroke logger

A software program that tracks and logs the keystrokes typed on a personal computer.

LIB virus

A file infector virus that spreads via a modification of a program's compiler libraries.

link virus
A file infector virus that modifies the first cluster of the host file to point to a different cluster that contains the virus code.

list merchant
A company that buys and sells mailing lists.

log file
A computer file that contains a record of specific user or program activity.

macro
A series of instructions, using a simple coding language, used to automate procedures in a computer application; macros are typically attached to individual documents or templates.

macro virus
A macro that contains malicious code.

malware
Short for "malicious software," a generic term for viruses, worms, and other malicious code.

Master Boot Record
A software routine placed at the very beginning of a hard disk which analyzes the Disk Partition Table, loads the hard disk's boot sector into system memory, and then passes control to the boot sector.

MIME
Multipurpose Internet Mail Extensions, a protocol that specifies how binary files are encoded, so that any e-mail program can correctly interpret the file type.

multi-level marketing (MLM)
A business organized so that people at each level make money by signing up more employees/distributors/franchisees at the next lower level.

multipartite virus
A virus that combines file infection and boot sector infection.

newsgroup
See *Usenet*.

OBJ virus
A file infector virus that spreads via a modification of a program's object modules.

open mail relay (OMR)
An unprotected server that can be used to initiate mass e-mailings.

overwriting virus
A file infector virus that overwrites a program's original code with its own code.

P2P
Peer-to-peer computing, where two or more computers work together as equals, without benefit of a central server.

packet sniffer
A software program that examines the contents of data packets flowing over a network or the Internet.

Packeteer
A utility used by the FBI to reassemble individual packets of information into their original messages; part of the DragonWare suite.

parasitic virus
A file infector virus that changes the contents of an infected file but still enables that file to remain completely or partly usable.

password cracker
Software that can decrypt passwords or otherwise disable or bypass password protection.

password
A sequence of characters used to protect access to specific information or services.

payload
The deliverable aspect of a computer virus; the noticeable effects of a virus attack.

peeker pop-up
A pop-up window (typically frameless) that slides up, down, or in from the side of the screen.

peer-to-peer
A type of computing where similar computers are connected directly, without benefit of a master server; abbreviated P2P.

peer-to-peer file-swapping
The act of exchanging files between similar computers over a peer-to-peer network.

personal firewall
Firewall software designed for a home or small business PC.

phreaker
An individual who cracks into telecommunications systems.

plain-text e-mail
E-mail messages that incorporate text only, without any HTML code.

polymorphic virus
A file infector virus that is capable of changing itself as it travels from one system to another.

pop-under window
A pop-up window that hides itself behind other open windows on your desktop.

pop-up window
A small browser window, typically without menus or other navigational elements, that opens seemingly of its own accord when you visit or leave another Web site.

port scanner
Software that looks for open ports on other computers.

port
An access point into your computer, as provided by your computer's operating system.

Pretty Good Privacy (PGP)
One of the most popular tools for public-key encryption.

private key
A secret key that can be used, either by itself or (in public-key encryption) in conjunction with a public key, to decrypt encrypted messages.

proof of concept
A virus created solely to test the viability of a concept or technology.

proxy server
A server that buffers all incoming and outgoing communications between a network and the Internet.

public key cryptography (PKC)
See *public-key encryption*.

public key
A key, provided by some authority, that, when combined with a private key, can be used to decrypt encrypted messages.

public-key encryption
A means of encrypting data and messages using a combination of public and private keys.

pyramid scheme
Similar to multilevel marketing, a scheme where new members of the pyramid are encouraged to send money to those higher up in the hierarchy.

racing authentication
An intrusion that occurs when an attacker fills in the last digit of the user's password before the user does, thus logging in as that user.

real-time scanning
The constant monitoring of a computer system for new viruses.

remailer
A service used to send anonymous e-mail; the remailer strips out the header from the original message, then remails the now-anonymous message to its intended recipient.

remote access trapdoor (RAT)
See *backdoor Trojan*.

remote access Trojan (RAT)
See *backdoor Trojan*.

sandboxing
The process of running a program within an isolated (or virtual) environment, thus protecting the computer system from any ill effects of virus infection during the test.

scanner
See *sniffer*.

scavenger bot
See *spambot*.

script kiddie
A would-be cracker who isn't a technically adept programmer.

script language
An easy-to-use pseudo-programming language that enables the creation of executable scripts composed of individual commands.

script virus
A computer virus written in ActiveX, Java, JavaScript, or another computer script language.

secure server
A Web server that uses encryption to secure consumer transactions.

Secure Sockets Layer (SSL)
A form of encryption used in secure servers.

session hijacking
An attack where the attacker commandeers use of a computer, typically via some sort of backdoor Trojan, in order to use that computer to attack another computer or network.

session key

A temporary key used to encrypt/decrypt a specific message.

shareware

Computer software distributed for free but requiring a paid registration for full operation.

signature scanning

A method of scanning for computer viruses by matching known sequences of binary code.

sleeper

A virus or worm that resides, hidden, on a system, waiting to deliver its payload at some later date.

sniffer

Software used to determine a computer's online availability.

social engineering attack

An intrusion resulting from the attacker conning another person into revealing usernames and passwords.

source code virus

A file infector virus that spreads via a modification of a program's source code.

spam

Unsolicited e-mail.

spamblock

A string of letters or numbers inserted into an e-mail address; used to thwart the automatic harvesting of e-mail addresses by spambots.

spambot

An automated software program that trolls the Web, Usenet newsgroups, and public message boards, looking for e-mail addresses that is later used in spam mailings. (The name is short for "spam robot.")

spamouflage

When a spammer spoofs the sender's e-mail address in a spam message.

spyware

Software used to surreptitiously monitor computer use (i.e., spy on other users).

stateful packet inspection

A method of firewall protection that matches incoming traffic with outgoing requests.

static virus

A file infector virus that doesn't change as it travels from one system to another.

stealth virus

A virus that, when running, hides itself to avoid detection.

symmetric-key encryption

A means of encrypting data where both parties (sender and recipient) have access to the same private key.

system file

A key file used by the computer's operating system.

TCP sequence guessing
An attack resulting from intercepting data flowing into the target computer and then guessing the next possible data sequence.

TCP splicing
An attack resulting from the attacker splicing into a legitimate connection between two computers.

tracking program
Software used to locate stolen laptop PCs; they typically work by automatically dialing into a central number and disclosing their location.

transitive trust attack
An attack that exploits the inherent trust in a host-to-host or network-to-network relationship.

Trojan horse
A malicious program that pretends to be another, harmless program or file.

urban legend
A popular story, told as being true or having happened to a friend of a friend, that has no basis in fact.

Usenet
An Internet-based network used to exchange messages between users, utilizing topic-oriented newsgroups.

virus scanner
A computer utility, typically part of an antivirus program, that searches for suspicious program code.

war driving
The act of driving around a business district with specific electronic equipment, looking for insecure wireless networks.

warez
Illegally distributed software, from which normal copy protection has been cracked or removed. (Pronounced "wheres.")

Web beacon
See *Web bug*.

Web bug
A small, typically transparent graphics file (typically 1 × 1 pixel) hidden in an HTML e-mail message, that is loaded from an advertising site and drops cookies on your hard disk.

WEP
Wireless Equivalent Privacy, the encryption and security protocol for WiFi networks.

WHOIS
An Internet lookup service used to trace the owner of a specific Web page or domain.

WiFi
The 802.11b wireless networking standard; short for "wireless fidelity."

worm
A parasitic computer program that replicates but does not infect other files.

zombie
A computer that has been hijacked by another computer, typically with malicious intent.

INDEX

Note to the Reader: Throughout this index **boldfaced** page numbers indicate primary discussions of a topic. *Italicized* page numbers indicate illustrations.

B

Uncover XP!

D o you find Windows® XP frustrating? You're not alone. Best-selling author Dan Gookin lays bare the best (and worst) of Windows XP in this book for users who want to work faster, easier, and smarter. If you want real help dealing with Windows XP's imperfections, take a deep breath and let Dan be your guide. Using easy-to-follow instructions, Dan reveals alternative (and better) ways of completing particular tasks, shows you how to use powerful productivity-increasing commands, and teaches you how to configure Windows to suit your needs. You'll also learn how Windows works so that you can always remain one step ahead of it. *Dan Gookin's Naked Windows XP* transforms you into a more expert, dynamic, and headache-free user.

Dan Gookin's Naked Windows® XP
by Dan Gookin • 0-7821-4076-9 • $29.99

Expert Advice That Will Change Life As You Know It (For the Better)

- Why the System Configuration utility is a buried treasure…and what it can do for you
- Whipping Internet Explorer into shape
- Dinking with and wrangling the Taskbar
- Sending the Quick Launch bar to obedience school
- Fixing, pruning, and grafting menus
- Making the Desktop your own
- Protecting files from death, destruction, or mere accidental erasure

- Teaching the Notification Area to obey your whim
- Secrets and solutions for working with images and graphics
- How MediaPlayer's playlists can make your life easier
- Curing those Internet connection blues
- How to say "No!" to spam
- Disk management chores you really need to do
- And much more!

SYBEX®
www.sybex.com

TELL US WHAT YOU THINK!

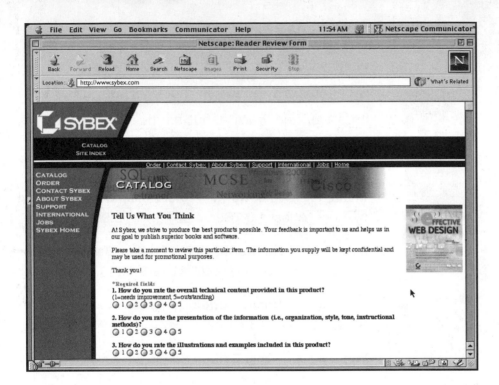

Your feedback is critical to our efforts to provide you with the best books and software on the market. Tell us what you think about the products you've purchased. It's simple:

1. Visit the Sybex website
2. Go to the product page
3. Click on **Submit a Review**
4. Fill out the questionnaire and comments
5. Click **Submit**

With your feedback, we can continue to publish the highest quality computer books and software products that today's busy IT professionals deserve.

www.sybex.com

SYBEX Inc. • 1151 Marina Village Parkway, Alameda, CA 94501 • 510-523-8233